D1436205

Take Charge Of Your Medical Practice

...Before Someone Else Does It For You

Practical Practice Management
for the
Managed Care Market

Neil Baum, MD
New Orleans, Louisiana

with
Elaine Zablocki
Corona Communications
Arlington, Virginia

AN ASPEN PUBLICATION®
Aspen Publishers, Inc.
Gaithersburg, Maryland
1996

Library of Congress Cataloging-in-Publication Data

Baum, Neil, 1943–
Take charge of your medical practice . . . before someone else does
it for you : practical practice management for the managed care
market / Neil Baum, with Elaine Zablocki.
p.   cm.
Includes bibliographical references and index.
ISBN 0-8342-0799-0 (hardcover)
1. Medicine—Practice—United States. 2. Managed care plans
(Medical care)—United States. I. Zablocki, Elaine. II. Title.
R728.B364   1996
610'.68—dc20   96-6738
CIP

Copyright © 1996 by Aspen Publishers, Inc.
All rights reserved.

Aspen Publishers, Inc., grants permission for photocopying for limited
personal or internal use. This consent does not extend to other kinds of
copying, such as copying for general distribution, for advertising or
promotional purposes, for creating new collective works, or for resale.
For information, address Aspen Publishers, Inc., Permissions Department, 200 Orchard Ridge Drive, Suite 200, Gaithersburg, MD 20878.

Editorial Services: Donald L. Delauter
Library of Congress Catalog Card Number: 96-6738
ISBN: 0-8342-0799-0

Printed in the United States of America

1 2 3 4 5

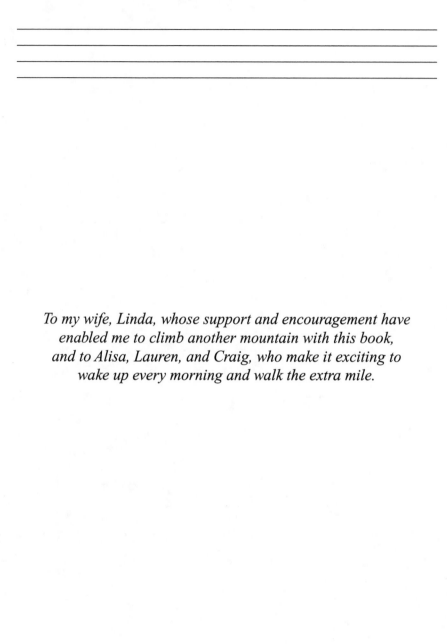

*To my wife, Linda, whose support and encouragement have
enabled me to climb another mountain with this book,
and to Alisa, Lauren, and Craig, who make it exciting to
wake up every morning and walk the extra mile.*

Contents

Acknowledgments

The following people have my heartfelt gratitude:

Elaine Zablocki, my coauthor, who has listened to my ideas and put them into readable prose.

Jackie Aucoin and Sibyl Berkel, my nurse and receptionist, who have always gone the extra mile for our patients.

Sandra Aytona, my office manager, who not only manages my office but provides invaluable help on other, nonclinical projects.

Sara Baum, my dear mother, who has been my source of creativity and has put the magic in my life.

Roger Bonds, the nation's foremost recruiting expert, who has been a valuable resource for many aspects of the book.

Jack Bruggeman, our editor, who has been behind this book from the very beginning and has been available whenever we needed him.

Dr. Christian Chaussy and Tina Chaussy, my friends from Munich, who have kept an unguided missile on course.

Joan Chromicz and Monica Craven of Computype, Arlington, Virginia, who skillfully transcribed many of the interviews.

Dip Ganguly, my hardware and software expert, who has attended to all my computer needs and thereby made it possible for me to write this book.

Shannie Goldstein, my friend and colleague, who has demonstrated compassion and concern for all our patients and provides so much fun and excitement in our practice.

Charlotte Gottesman, my mother-in-law, who has set the example by always going the extra mile, and then some, for me and my family.

Dr. Jim Gottesman, a urologist and computer wizard, who has provided me with the opportunity to become more knowledgeable about computers and their role in contemporary medicine.

Bob Katz, my accountant and colleague, who has offered assistance on several chapters of this book and has also been responsible for keeping my practice financially sound.

Howard Larkin, my editor at *American Medical News*, who has encouraged me to continue to write a monthly column and allowed me to use the material in this book.

Dr. Michael LeBoeuf, a good friend, who has been a major source of inspiration for my writing and speaking career.

Stan Levenson, for all his assistance and support on this book and other marketing projects.

Drs. Richard Levine, Ron Swartz, Jerry Rosenberg, and Alfred Colfry, my urologic associates and colleagues, who have always been available to help and assist with my practice so that I could write this book.

Wendy Lund and Trina Aytona, my assistants, who make it possible to pay attention to the little details.

Dr. Sam McNeely, emeritus professor of English at Tulane University, who has always been helpful in editing my material.

Dr. David Mobley, a fellow urologist and dear friend, who has given me many practical ideas on marketing to managed care plans.

Dr. Steve Newman, Medical Director at Touro Infirmary, who has provided me with resources and advice that made this book possible.

Introduction—
Why I Wrote This Book

For the past several years I've met often with physicians, their office staffs, and other health care professionals. It seems that almost everyone complains about contemporary medicine and reminisces about the good old days. Indeed, when making a presentation to an audience, I often begin by asking this question: "How many of you have children under age 20?" I then say, "Hold up your hands and keep them up. If you have children, would you advise them to enter the health care profession tomorrow?" When I ask the second question, almost every hand goes down.

Many physicians today obviously feel that there is no future in health care. In reality, there are great opportunities for providing care and treatment, but few of us will be able to continue practicing the same way we did 20, 10, or even 5 years ago. This book is intended to identify the opportunities and describe what all of us in the health care profession can do to make our practices successful and enjoyable.

Most of us embrace changes in techniques and technologies. We welcome new drugs that can cure diseases that in the past required surgery or were simply untreatable. We learn new techniques that allow us to enhance our diagnostic and therapeutic effectiveness. If we refused to accept changes in clinical practice, we would eventually cease to be effective health care providers. Yet when it comes to obtaining patients and maintaining our relationships with them, we balk at making the necessary alterations in our strategies.

There are reasons for the changes we see in health care today. First, costs have been rising so rapidly that health care is called on to make the best possible use of limited resources. Second, patients have become accustomed to judging physicians on the basis of the outcomes of the care they receive. In consequence, there is a growing emphasis on health promotion strategies to prevent disease and increased preventive testing to detect disease in the early, curable stage.

Physicians who avoid acknowledging the changes that are inevitably coming in health care will see their practices shrink and possibly wither away. On the other hand, those who proactively seek ways to adapt to the current flood of changes are likely to prosper and thrive.

This book provides methods and techniques for offering high-quality, cost-effective services, developing satisfying relationships with fee-for-service patients, and at the same time attracting managed care contracts. By reading this book and implementing some of the ideas, you will be way ahead of those who continue practicing in exactly the same way that they did just a few years ago.

When changes occur in the tax laws, accountants and tax attorneys just love that, because the changes create new business for them. I wonder if entrepreneurial physicians shouldn't try to learn a lesson from the accountants and attorneys and start to look at changes as opportunities instead of obstacles.

TWO MYTHS TO IGNORE

Two myths are currently running rampant. The first is that the solo practitioner is an anachronism—a relic from the past. The second is that once physicians have managed care patients and are paid on a capitated basis, they are guaranteed a certain number of patients and don't have to market their practices.

Both of these ideas are absolutely and unequivocally false. This book describes ways to continue as a solo practitioner who can be an attractive partner for managed care plans and also win patients in the fee-for-service sector. In addition, I will show you ways to market your practice today—and why this is so important as you enter the managed care marketplace.

A PLACE FOR THE SOLO PRACTITIONER

Let's start by considering the myth that solo practitioners will eventually go the way of the dinosaur. Some people argue that managed care plans prefer to contract with a multispecialty group and write one contract instead of working with individual doctors and writing multiple contracts.

My response is that I've never heard of a managed care plan saying to a doctor, "We won't talk to you because you don't belong to a group." After all, writing a contract is the least difficult part of a managed care plan's relationship with physicians. As a matter of fact, managed care plans may find that working with several solo doctors or several small group practices is easier than working with a large group practice. Individual doctors tend to be less sophisticated and easier to negotiate with than a larger practice with an office manager and a set of attorneys.

Managed care is becoming ever more prevalent, so it's important for physicians to know how to work with managed care plans. However, I am sure there will always be a place for excellent fee-for-service care. Even in countries like Canada or Great Britain, which have a more regulated system than we are ever likely to have, about 10 percent–15 percent of the population still receive care through a private sector that offers amenities the public system cannot provide. Won't this also be true in the United States? Of course it will. Many people in this country buy luxury cars, stay at fine hotels, and shop only at boutiques or other stores noted for their excellent service and pricey goods and services. Won't these people continue to demand a similar standard of excellence and be willing to pay the cost for outstanding, patient-friendly services? Of course they will.

There will always be patients who want physicians who can see them when they need to be seen, who make house calls, who offer appointments before or after normal working hours or on the weekend, and who return calls quickly. These patients are going to say, "Wait a minute, I'd much rather have a physician I can call and speak to without going through intermediaries and gatekeepers. I want a physician who offers absolutely first-class care, and I am able and willing to pay the added price."

Many young physicians with a large educational debt are unnerved by the expense of starting a practice and prefer working on salary for a staff or group model HMO. They like coming to work at nine in the morning and leaving at five in the afternoon. They like having an advice nurse to triage patients who call with questions or problems in the evening or on weekends. They like having regular and predictable hours, little or no paperwork, and no business hassles—benefits they are willing to pay for by the reduction in income that goes with this type of practice style. But some physicians are more entrepreneurial and want more control over their working lives. They want a more direct, personal relationship with their patients and recognize that some patients want a higher level of communication with their physicians and are willing to pay a premium for outstanding services.

In order to continue to attract fee-for-service patients, entrepreneurial physicians must change the way they provide services. For example, they will need to call patients at home, get to the office early in the morning, meet patients at the emergency room, squeeze patients in who require immediate attention, and offer care that is high touch as well as high tech. But if they are willing to make the necessary effort, they will discover people eager to knock on their door and receive the high-quality, personal care that they offer.

WORKING UNDER MANAGED CARE CONTRACTS

Managed care is so widespread today that physicians need to serve managed care as well as fee-for-service patients. Some physicians think that once they get a managed care contract they can cruise on automatic pilot. Nothing could be further from the truth. Managed care plans measure patient satisfaction and track key measures of quality and use the findings to decide which physicians will be part of their panels.

Once on a panel, a physician still must offer high-quality services to attract enrollees. The physician must be affable and efficient and keep overhead expenses at a minimum. The physician, in addition, must promote his or her practice.

Marketing is particularly important for specialists, since one of the ways a managed care plan cuts costs is by sending patients to primary care physicians first and limiting the number of specialists who are part of the plan. In the past, a large pool of specialists competed for lots of patients. In the future, relatively few specialists will be competing for relatively few patients, so the competition will probably be at least as keen as it has been.

After publishing my first book, *Marketing Your Clinical Practice: Ethically, Effectively, Economically*, I received so much positive feedback from colleagues and friends that I wanted to try to do it again—only this time do it even better. Therefore I sought the advice of experts in managed care, communications, training, motivation, and finance. I have also asked leaders in other fields, such as Disney and Federal Express, how physicians might apply their principles to the health care field.

I also wrote this book for another reason. During the past few years, I've had the opportunity to interact with hundreds of physicians and office staffs throughout the country. Many of them have shared ideas and described methods that have worked in their practices. I have incorporated many of the suggested methods into my own practice and discuss them when I have an opportunity to make a presentation. I hope this book makes clear the value of sharing creative ideas in meeting the demands of our changing health care environment.

This book contains many ideas that could make an important difference in the way you practice medicine. These ideas are offered in the hope that you'll implement some of them in your practice, perhaps after adapting them or finding ways to improve them.

Some of you may read this book and feel the ideas presented are good but claim you lack the time or energy to try them. My advice is to select one or two areas of your practice that you believe need improving and use the table of contents and index to find relevant chapters or sections. Take just one or two ideas from the book and incorporate them into your practice. Then measure the results. I am convinced that when you see the significant positive response that you get from your patients, your staff, and the managed care plans you contract with, you will be so delighted that you will be eager to explore additional ways to improve your practice by managing care, time, and the bottom line.

HOW DID WE GET IN THIS MESS AND HOW DO WE GET OUT OF IT?

Many of us are wondering how the current health care crisis developed and how we can extricate ourselves from it. Of course, there are no easy answers and certainly no painless solutions, but those who are willing to accept that changes are occurring in the health care system and are willing to modify the way they practice medicine will have successful and profitable practices. The Chinese symbol for crisis is also the symbol for opportunity. The reality is that the health care crisis affecting all Americans also offers great opportunities for service providers.

A major concern for everyone is the rapidly rising price of care. Costs have risen rapidly in part because consumers have not been sensitive to costs. In the old days, a patient would contact a physician, who would provide a service in return for a reasonable payment from the patient. Next came insurance companies and other third-party payers. For most people, insurance companies pay for a large portion of health care expenses and "someone else" (employers, Medicare, or Medicaid) pays for the insurance. Consequently, people who receive services in our health care system usually do not directly pay for them.

When purchasing goods and services, a consumer is typically aware of price and partially bases purchase decisions on price. Since in our country the bulk of health care costs are paid by someone else, price does not act as a restraint and demand for health care services tends to grow. As demand grows, providers such as physicians, hospitals, pharmaceutical companies, and medical supply companies tend to raise their prices. The transfer of financial responsibility from patients to insurance companies has caused greater demand and higher prices for health care services than would have occurred if the natural laws of supply and demand had taken place.

Although individual patients may not be aware of the rapid increase in health care costs, employers who either self-insure or purchase group health insurance policies are very mindful of the increase and are determined to slow the rate of growth. In 1965, corporate spending on health care equaled 9 percent of pretax corporate profits, whereas in 1987 it equaled 50 to 70 percent of pretax profits.

During the same period, hospital and physician expenditures as a percentage of gross national product (GNP) rose from 3.3 percent to the current level of 14 percent. Since providing health care benefits has a significant impact on corporate profits, employers are looking for ways of controlling spiraling health care costs.[1]

It is very difficult for American companies to compete with companies in countries that have lower health care costs. High health care costs can decrease the net profits or earnings of a company substantially. Since earnings drive the stock price, the value of the company's stock will be lower, which increases the cost of raising capital and adds to the price of the products, thereby making the products less competitive in the global market. In addition, as the cost of capital increases, it becomes more expensive for the company to invest in new research and development, purchase new technology, and expand existing facilities. If American companies are to remain competitive in the global market, they need to lower their costs. Decreasing health care costs is one way to accomplish this goal.

Companies are responding to the growing burden of paying for health care by negotiating with managed care plans to obtain less expensive care for their employees. Some set price differentials to make managed care more attractive to employees and many now require employees to pay a larger share of health care premiums. It is also becoming more common for companies to institute workplace health promotion programs designed to get employees to quit smoking, exercise more, and eat a healthy diet.

What does this mean for doctors? If we continue to lower our fees and accept lower capitation rates, our profit margins and the quality of our services will certainly decline—and lower quality of care is unattractive to patients. All of us need to carefully examine proposed fee schedules and capitation rates offered by payers to avoid taking on an abundance of patients for meager remuneration. Remember, a full office and no profit is no better than an empty office.

Surveys indicate that people are concerned about the quality of their health care and are willing to pay more for superior quality. Our challenge as physicians is to provide people with a way to assess quality of care. We must not allow insurance companies to convince the public that outcomes and cost are the only indicators of quality. We need to measure quality and explain to our patients what quality in health care really is. For example, one important component of quality is access. A doctor who is never available when needed can hardly be said to be providing high-quality services.

Sometimes the solutions are very simple. Michael Naslund, a physician and a professor at the University of Maryland, suggests using basic marketing principles to increase the demand for our services. One principle is to consciously set out to provide the type of health care services that the public wants.

In the past, the only relationship that mattered was that between the patient and the physician. Now physicians have to think about their relationships with insurance companies and employers as well. Employers want low prices and employees who are satisfied with their health care services. Insurance companies want low prices and a broad range of services. Patients want high-quality care and personal attention.

Physicians need to balance the various wants and demands. We will always have an ethical duty to care for our patients. But we will also have to be sensitive to the desires of insurance companies and employers since they now control a large percentage of patients.

By offering high-quality services that are acceptable to patients and managed care plans, we will be able to continue to gain satisfaction and profit from our practice of medicine. This will require us to change with the times. Abraham Lincoln said it perfectly more than 100 years ago: "Things may come to those who wait but only those things left behind by those who hustle." If we sit back and wait or put our head in the sand and pretend changes aren't occurring, then we will get what is left over by those who proactively modify their practices to meet current needs.

WHO SHOULD READ THIS BOOK?

As I wrote this book, I was of course thinking of physicians and their special needs. In addition, I wanted to offer valuable suggestions to office managers, office staff, nurses, physician extenders, and anyone else who interacts with patients and contributes to the success of a medical practice.

If you are concerned about the penetration of managed care into your market area, you will find Chapter 32 the best place to start your reading. If you are being confronted with capitation and need to determine the break-even capitation rate to make your practice profitable, then I suggest you begin with Chapter 29. If staff turnover is causing low morale, high expenses, and loss of efficiency, then perhaps Chapters 12 and 15 on staff motivation and training should be read first.

The general layout of the book is as follows. In Part I, I describe ways to understand the essential core of your practice—your patients and their needs. In Part II, I look at ways to make your office more efficient. In Part III, I examine proactive steps you can take that will make your practice managed care–friendly, and in Part IV, I present innovative ways to market your medical practice in this era of managed care. In Part V, I look at ways to win favorable attention from the media. Finally, in Part VI, I focus on how to balance personal and professional activities and responsibilities and continue to lead a satisfying life while adapting to our changing health care system.

In short, there is something for everyone in this book—something that can help in the achievement of success in the new health care world of the 1990s.

NOTE

1. D. Hess, "History of Managed Care," *Journal of the American Association of Clinical Urologists* 7 (July 1995): 3–8.

Your Patients

1

Walking in the Shoes of Your Patients

*T*he Doctor, a movie starring William Hurt, shows what it feels like when the shoe is on the other foot. The protagonist is a swashbuckling, cavalier heart surgeon who develops throat cancer. He has to undergo a biopsy, await results, and then receive daily radiation therapy. He learns first-hand what it's really like to be a patient. In the end, as a result of walking in the shoes of his patients, he becomes a more sensitive and understanding physician.

Most physicians won't be initiated into the world of patients in such a drastic way, but all of us can develop an understanding of what patients experience when they interact with medical professionals. This chapter discusses the mindset of patients and makes suggestions about ways to make their health care experience a positive one.

WHAT DO PATIENTS WANT TODAY?

In order to have a successful medical practice, there are several fundamental questions you need to ask: What do patients want today? And why do physicians have to think about this, anyway? If you know you possess high-quality medical skills, why do you need to worry about what your patients are thinking?

When you know the answers to these vital questions, then you'll have a practice where patients feel they've received value for the money they spend. Tom Peters, the well-known business management and consulting guru, said, "Find out what your customer wants and give him/her more of it; find out what he or she doesn't want and avoid it; and you will be filthy rich." According to Tom Peters, it's just that easy.

Times have changed. The level of patient loyalty we depended on in the past has been eroded. We can no longer count on patients to return over and over again to see the same physician solely because of a long history of medical care. For a few dollars' difference in the copayment, members of managed care plans will gladly switch doctors. Further, if you ask patients what bothers them most about appointments with health care providers, they say waiting too long to be seen. Years ago patients would wait an hour or two and not complain. When I first entered practice, people signed in at nine in the morning or one in the afternoon and were seen in whatever order they arrived. When a person went to see the doctor, he or she took half a day off from work. That was how it was and everyone accepted it.

Today patients feel that their time is just as valuable as the physician's time. Even patients who are currently unemployed or retired still have buses to catch, appointments to keep, and errands to run. Excessive delays in the doctor's office unbalance the rest of their schedules—and they don't appreciate it! They are likely to ask for their records and switch to another practice.

Alvin Toffler, in his book *Future Shock*,[1] writes that two generations ago people moved once or twice in a lifetime. Our parents probably moved 5 or 6 times, but people of the current generation may move 20 or 25 times. With each move, people adjust to a new environment, make new friends, and become more dependent on others for specialized services and products. Because they have more exposure to professionals in different geographic areas, they can make comparisons. People expect the same level of service from all the professionals they see. If dentists, accountants, lawyers, and veterinarians can see people promptly, is there any reason why physicians can't do the same thing?

Another factor is the way our sense of time has changed in daily life. Fax machines and Federal Express make us more efficient, but they also increase moment-by-moment demands. People find themselves trying to save a minute here and shave a minute there. We have become a nation obsessed with time and efficiency, so a long delay in the doctor's office or waiting by the phone for a return call is inconsistent with the mindset of modern patients. They expect a physician to be able to answer all their questions and/or provide educational materials about their medical problems promptly and efficiently. They expect the medical profession to offer the same efficiency that they find in other areas of their lives, where services and products are offered in a timely fashion. (Chapter 23 describes a way to schedule patients so they never have to wait more than a few minutes.)

Here's a story I heard recently from a pharmaceutical representative. A patient who belongs to a managed care plan had an appointment with his primary doctor, who was delayed in seeing him. He knocked on the window, and the nurse said the doctor was running late. The patient opened his briefcase, went through the list of plan physicians, and called one on his cellular phone. "I have an appointment this afternoon and cannot be seen. Can you take me this afternoon? Can you see me right away?"

He walked out the door, and three other patients who were members of the same plan walked out with him. The worst part of this story is that the pharmaceutical rep who was sitting there waiting for the doctor noticed it all but the doctor probably still doesn't have a clue why four patients left his practice. The incident probably cost the doctor more than $60,000, since one patient in a primary care practice is valued at $15,000 over the lifetime of that patient.

THE ERA OF MANAGED CARE

We are now practicing medicine in an era of managed care. That means employers and health plans will be looking very closely at several practice issues when considering whether to contract with a physician: Is the physician cost efficient and cost sensitive? How do the outcomes of the care provided compare with those achieved by colleagues? Does the physician spend enough time with patients? Does the physician try to educate patients about health and the essentials of a healthy life style? How long do patients wait in the waiting room? How long does it take to get urgent or routine appointments? Is the phone answered promptly? Are staff members friendly? Do they answer patient questions?

Studies of consumer attitudes toward health plans show that good service may be the single most important factor in creating satisfied patients. The quality of service will play just as large a role as costs and outcomes when employers and health plans choose the providers they will partner with in future years.

LEARNING TO ACCEPT CHANGE

Many physicians today spend a lot of time talking about the good old days (Figure 1-1). They say medicine isn't as much fun as it used to be. There are so many changes and so much time is spent on boring paperwork.

Actually, their attitude is easy to understand: Uncertainty produces anxiety, and uncertainty is what physicians are experiencing today. We all wish we knew what's about to happen to the health care system. If we did know, we could relax, adjust to the developments, and get on to the business of taking care of patients.

Change produces uncertainty but it also produces something else: opportunity. Perhaps physicians would be more inclined to accept change in health care if they

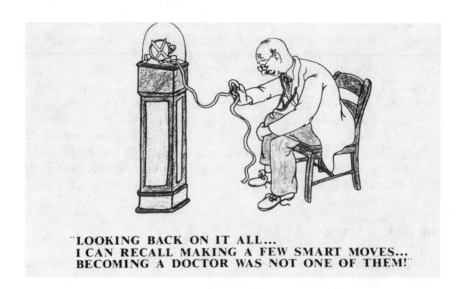

Figure 1-1 Physicians sometimes muse about the way things used to be.

recognized that it brings with it the potential for growth, development, and ultimate success.

For example, the public today is interested in being healthy and staying well. Any physician who embraces wellness instead of illness stands to attract hundreds of patients to his or her practice.

When you go to an ice cream store you see fat-free, cholesterol-free, sugar-free ice cream. When you go to McDonald's today, you see a salad bar and chicken and fish. Every community has at least one health and fitness center. Americans are spending millions of dollars on home exercise equipment. Many businesses now provide fitness centers for employees to use before work, at lunch, or at the end of the day. Others offer employees fitness center memberships instead of country club memberships.

Americans are also smoking less and drinking less alcohol. Insurance companies offer discounts for members who don't smoke and maintain a healthy weight. They know that smoking and extra weight are likely to result in higher medical expenses, and they are willing to discount premiums for employees with a healthy life style.

By all indications, Americans today are genuinely interested in fitness and wellness. Physicians who recognize and embrace the trend toward wellness will be those who have successful practices.

For example, anyone planning to enter an exercise program should get a preliminary checkup from a physician. I think industry should make it possible for employees to have blood pressure exams and cholesterol screening tests at regular intervals—at work, during the lunch hour. Cholesterol testing is very important, and the public understands the significance of total cholesterol and high-density lipoprotein levels. Women need to learn about breast self-examination, and men similarly need to learn about testicular self-examination.

Today, any practice can easily do a series of wellness promotions. As a urologist, I urge all men over the age of 50 to get an annual rectal exam and a prostate-specific antigen (PSA) test, which is an American Cancer Association–approved screening test for prostate cancer. I encourage all men to do regular testicular self-exams, which are just as important for men as breast exams are for women and yet receive very little attention in the media. I have a waterproofed card on how to do a testicular self-exam (Figure 1-2) that I give to all men so they can post it in the shower. In fact, I give it to women too, hoping they'll share it with their husbands or significant others.

If I were a gynecologist, I would try to increase understanding of premenstrual syndrome. If I were a neurologist and saw people with headaches, I would talk to them about stress reduction. If I were an orthopedist, I would show patients how to prevent running injuries. If I were in primary care, I would focus on ideal weight, stress reduction, and dietary changes to decrease the risk of high blood pressure and heart disease. In every field, there are numerous wellness promotion opportunities ready at hand.

Wellness education is a way to attract new patients and meet the needs of current patients. It also can give you an edge in the marketplace. However, focusing on wellness doesn't mean your practice will be limited to wellness services. You must ensure patients who are attracted to you because of your forward-looking wellness services will stay with you if they do become ill and need additional services.

In addition to wellness, patients are much more interested in illness than they used to be. Information about various diseases, current research, and possible treatments is now much more widely available. The media covers treatment issues as news. For example, an article in the *New England Journal of Medicine* or the *Journal of the American Medical Association* is often discussed on CNN before it appears on a physician's desk. Computer-literate patients have access to all sorts of medical information through computer bulletin boards and on-line services. I have had patients with increased PSA levels arrive with 200 on-line summaries and even personal responses from the chairpersons of urology departments.

In the past, a patient would come to a doctor who would write out a prescription, pat the patient on the back, and ask the patient to return in two weeks—

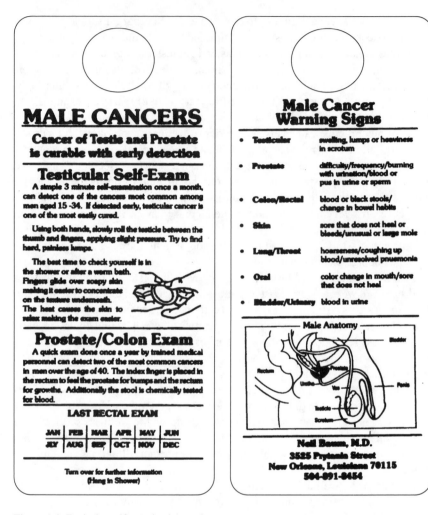

Figure 1-2 Testicular self-examination card.

without any explanation of the medical problem or diagnosis. Today patients typically want to know about possible drug interactions and alternative courses of treatment they've read about. This desire for information represents a big change, but it also represents an opportunity for physicians willing to respond to the demand.

*   *   *

In the next chapter, I will discuss the enormous value of your existing patients, and ways you can use excellent service to keep existing patients as well as to attract new ones.

NOTE

1. A. Toffler, *Future Shock* (New York: Random House, 1970).

2

The Pot of Gold at the End of the Rainbow Is As Close As Your Patients

Each of your patients is someone to be cherished. First, each is a human being who is turning to you and your staff in an hour of need. You also have to recognize, however, that each patient plays a role in maintaining the financial health of the practice.

It costs much more to attract a new patient than to keep a current patient. This is a basic business principle that applies to any product or service. One estimate is that it takes five or six times more effort and money to attract a new patient than to keep a patient.[1]

Consider the example of magazines. Every magazine reader gets a flood of special offers in the mail promoting new magazines. Publishers may send brochures to a hundred people for each new subscriber, which means that no money is made on the first year's subscription. So why keep on looking for subscribers? Publishers know that if they publish good magazines, readers will remain faithful and for years. The profits are made on the subscribers who renew.

The same principle applies in the fast-food industry, in consumer goods, and in retail products and services such as health care. Why do you think McDonald's spends such a large part of its total budget on promotional activities? Why do you think AT&T spends $750 million a year promoting their telephone service, and Proctor & Gamble spends $1 billion promoting its consumer products? They are trying to build brand loyalty. They want customers to remain committed to their products and services for a long time.

Physicians of course want new patients, and Chapter 3 contains many ideas on how to find them. But the first thing to recognize is that promoting a practice, just like promoting a product, is expensive in terms of time and money. If you decide to publicize your practice by giving a noontime talk, you will have to leave half an hour early and return an hour late to your practice—it takes roughly two hours to do a 45- or 60-minute presentation, and that does not include the time necessary for research and preparation. An ad in the Yellow Pages may cost hundreds of dollars a month. An ad in the paper, even a very small ad, can cost several thousand dollars, especially in a big city.

Because of the expense of attracting new patients, it is imperative to take good care of the patients you already have. Treat them well and make sure they have a positive experience each time they interact with you and your practice. If you do this, they will stay with you and even act as goodwill ambassadors.

THE POWER OF WORD OF MOUTH

According to Mike Cafferky,* author of the best-selling book *Patients Build Your Practice*[2] and Executive Director of Managed Care for Walla Walla General Hospital, Walla Walla, Washington, current patients are essential for promoting a practice through word of mouth. Nearly 90 percent of new patients enter a practice because of what someone else said about it. Nearly 70 percent rely on information from a family member or friend or another doctor when choosing a health care provider.

People frequently rely on just a single information source when deciding whom to go to for health care. Can you imagine the marketing that will result if all your patients have a positive experience at each appointment?

For years, plastic surgeons have used to advantage publicity generated through operating on movie stars and other famous people. When a plastic surgeon does a face lift on a well-known person and the result is satisfactory, instant and abundant word-of-mouth marketing occurs. The same holds true for orthopedic surgeons who operate on famous athletes. Remember the accolades that Dr. Frank Jobe garnered when he successfully operated on Joe Montana's back?

Let's look at a few statistics. According to Cafferky, every patient who knows you also knows 200, 300, or even 400 other people. Each of those other people knows a few hundred more people. The potential total is enormous. Perhaps more to the point, every patient probably knows three or four dozen people well enough for them to discuss their health with him or her. Then think about the dozens of other people who might overhear your patients talking to their friends about the care they have received from you.

---

*Executive Director of Managed Care, Walla Walla General Hospital, P.O. Box 1398, Walla Walla, WA 99362, 509-525-0480.

THE VALUE OF CURRENT PATIENTS

The value of a current patient, in dollar terms, will vary from practice to practice. For example, the value of each patient to a urology practice is about $300 to $1,000. I'd estimate that in pediatrics or primary care, a patient could easily be worth $15,000 to $20,000 over his or her lifetime. After all, a baby comes in every few months for immunizations and well-child exams, an adult comes in every year or two for a checkup, and both children and adults require health care services whenever they are sick. Over a lifetime, that means major dollars, even in this era of health care reform.

Patients tend to come to see a specialist for one problem, then go back to their primary care physician after it is solved. Specialists often receive a larger payment for a specific service but don't necessarily form a lifelong relationship with patients. This implies that relationships with current patients are particularly important for primary care doctors.

When I ask doctors about the strengths of their practice, they always say, "Outstanding service." When I ask them how they know, there's always a lengthy pause. They don't know, they just *believe* that they're giving outstanding service. But this issue is too important to be left a matter of belief. Physicians must find ways to give extraordinary service to their patients and to objectively measure patients' responses. Their report cards from patients will ultimately determine their success. Chapters 8 and 35 discuss techniques for surveying patients and gathering objective data useful in assessing service quality.

HOW TO KEEP PATIENTS

How do you keep your current patients? By giving them outstanding service—service that exceeds their expectations. By asking them, "What can we do to be of better assistance to you?"

I remember when I first went into practice. The people who advised me often talked about the three A's: availability, affability, and affordability. The three A's still apply but now they are taken for granted. You'd better be available, you'd better be likable and affable, and your prices better be comparable to those of the doctor down the street—but that is not enough these days. You must make an effort to give value for the money paid for your services.

I'm suggesting that patients need to be *rewarded* for coming into the practice. They want to get solid value for their precious health care dollars. Ask any group of patients if they feel that they received good value for time and money spent and most will say no. Excessive waiting, an unfriendly staff, and a doctor who is in a hurry add up to a negative experience. On the other hand, patients seen in a timely fashion by an enthusiastic staff and by a doctor who demonstrates caring and compassion have a positive experience. If the physician takes time to answer all their questions, offers explanations about their medical problems, provides practical suggestions for life-style changes, and tells them about ways to avoid needing medical treatment in the future, patients feel they are getting their money's worth.

Achieving quality service is simple: Find out what patients want and give it to them; find out what they don't want and avoid it. If you do that, you'll be very, very successful. Unfortunately, very few practices take the time to find out and fewer still devote the time and energy necessary to act upon the information they receive. How do you obtain this information? You must ask. You can't just assume that you are doing a great job—you have to ask.

I think it's important that physicians make an effort to copy stellar companies such as Disney, Federal Express, and Nordstrom's. For example, Nordstrom's has developed a national reputation for high-quality customer service because their staff is trained to exceed customer expectations. Their motto is "no problem." There are thousands of stories of Nordstrom's employees going the extra mile not just to satisfy but to delight customers with outstanding service. You never hear Nordstrom's employees say to customers, "I don't know." They always tell customers, "Wait here, I'll go down the street and get it for you from our branch store" or "I'll send it to you FedEx."

Here's one typical customer service story from Nordstrom's. A couple wanted to return a set of tires for a refund. The store manager knew the tires were not purchased at Nordstrom's—because the stores don't sell tires! Nevertheless, the customer service representative asked the couple how much the tires cost and then gave them the refund. That service representative understood that the customer is always right. It was far more important to keep the couple happy (and accept the cost of two tires) than to risk losing their business. Health care wouldn't be experiencing its current crisis if providers adopted the same philosophy as Nordstrom's.

When a patient undergoing pain and discomfort calls for an appointment, it is unacceptable to tell the patient no appointments are available for three weeks. When a patient calls for a lab report that is currently unavailable, it is unacceptable to say, "Call back tomorrow." The physician's response should be that he or she will call the lab and get the report and contact the patient by the end of the day. If the lab doesn't yet have the results, the physician should call the patient back, apologize for the delay, and state when the results will be available.

When customers go into a store like Nordstrom's, they expect quality merchandise and quality service and are willing to pay extra if that is what they receive. People are generally willing to pay extra for superior service, in health care as much as in any other business or industry. Note that *superior* service means attention to all the details. For example, patients will judge you by your restrooms!

I walked into one of my restrooms one day at four o'clock in the afternoon and found that the wastebasket had overflowed, a urine sample had spilled on the sink, there was no toilet paper, and the soap dispenser was empty.

I gathered all my staff and asked them, "Would any of you use this restroom?" They all said no. "Well," I said, "our patients wouldn't feel comfortable about using this restroom either. Let's make a note to talk about this at our next staff meeting." Can you imagine the first impression that a new patient will receive or what a current patient will feel about the cleanliness and hygiene of our practice if we have filthy restrooms?

When we discussed it at the next staff meeting, we realized that someone had to be responsible for checking the reception area and restrooms every couple of hours. We agreed that a patient who enters the reception area or the restrooms at four o'clock is entitled to the same level of cleanliness as a patient using the facilities at one o'clock, and we resolved that the receptionist and/or the patient coordinator would be responsible for ensuring these areas were clean and user friendly at all times of the day.

Carl Sewell said, "Nobody ever bought a car from us just because we had clean restrooms. But it's like finding coffee stains on the pull-down tray when you're on an airplane. If that's how they take care of the inside of the plane, you may get to wondering how much maintenance the engines get."[3] Likewise, no one ever selected a medical practice because of the clean restrooms, but why give patients even the smallest opportunity to feel dissatisfied with their visit?

Any patient visit includes as many as 25 different interactions between the patient and the physician and staff. All of these moments of truth need to be managed because each one affects the final impression the patient will have. If you manage all of them, the patient will think well of you and your practice. But you have to manage *all* the interactions, not just most. You can see the patient on time, make an accurate diagnosis, and be sensitive to the patient's feelings, but a messy restroom will negatively affect the patient's perception of your practice. Getting all the details right is a challenge, but if you meet the challenge you will likely have a prosperous and enjoyable practice.

Look at the way Disney deals with the same circumstances. Every guest in a Disney amusement park has approximately 80 interactions with Disney cast members every day. The way the staff manages each interaction determines what the visitor feels about the Disney experience, whether he or she will tell others about the experience, and whether he or she will return.

We need to do something similar in health care. We have to think in terms of managing every interaction the patient has with our practice: the first phone call, the reception area, the exam room, the restroom, paying the bill, making the next appointment—everything until he or she walks out the door. Each step along the way should be managed. If every interaction is a positive one, then patients will feel that their health care dollar has been well spent. If we just get most of them right, that's not enough. Just as one weak link destroys the strength of the chain, one unmanaged interaction can make the patient's total experience a negative one. Outstanding practices are able to manage all the moments; they are attentive to the little details because they realize that they make a very big difference.

It is not enough to just make the right diagnosis and prescribe the right pill or treatment. Nearly all your colleagues can do that. Now it is necessary to make a visit to the doctor a positive experience. This is a challenge to each and every one of us. Those who can meet this challenge will have a prosperous and enjoyable practice. To ignore the needs and wants of the patient while yearning for the good old days will certainly result in a practice that has a net loss of patients, deterioration in the morale of the staff, and ultimately a loss of income.

WHY PATIENTS LEAVE

Today, patients have lots of choices. Unless you perform an operation nobody else does, your patients can easily choose to go elsewhere.

Why do people leave a practice? In many cases, it is because they are moving to a different community or have joined a health care plan that does not include the practice as a possible or preferred provider. Some patients, however, may leave because they don't think that they are being treated appropriately. They may feel that the physician and staff are not friendly, not compassionate, and not listening to or meeting their health care needs.

When a patient leaves out of discontent, the negative ripple effect can be devastating. The patient may complain to dozens of people, and those who hear bad things about you may tell additional people, some of whom might be current patients who also decide to leave. Others might be potential patients who will now never be a part of your practice. You can see that just one patient who has a bad experience and a big mouth can create havoc.

It is a well-known phenomenon that people tend to report negative experiences to more friends and acquaintances than positive experiences. One reason is that when something negative happens, people want to talk about it just to blow off steam. Compounding the problem, most people view a visit to the doctor as a negative experience even when everything goes well. That makes it even more important to ensure no little glitches create a bad impression.

A TRUE STORY

I'm going to tell a story from my own practice to demonstrate why some patients leave. A patient who needed to purchase catheters for herself called the office to ask if they would be ready when she came to pick them up. We told her we'd be happy to have someone bring them down to her car so she wouldn't have to park and come up to the office. We mentioned the cost of the catheters because our usual policy requires patients to pay for products or medications themselves, with cash, a check, or a credit card.

For some reason, the patient didn't bring any money with her, and the staff member who went down to the car refused to give her the catheters. The patient drove off and never came back. She asked for her records and went to another doctor.

I wrote her a note of apology, saying this shouldn't have happened. "I am so sorry. Here are your records. Please let us know if there is anything we can do for you in the future." But she was angry and upset, and she spread the story throughout the community. She told so many people that the story got back to my wife, who felt embarrassed as a result. The story was framed in a way that made me appear to be more interested in monetary compensation than in giving medical service.

The purpose of my sharing this unfortunate incident is to make clear that everyone in a medical practice must focus on doing whatever is right and in the best interests of the patients. Often it's the little things that can cause problems. If the staff member had handed over the catheters to the woman, the worst that could have happened would be a loss of about $50. Continuing to have her as a patient would have been worth many times that amount. Preventing the damage she did to my reputation in the community would have been worth a hundred times the cost of the catheters.

There is a grocery store that sells more groceries per square foot of retail space than any other grocery store in America. In front of this store, there is a rock. Carved on that rock is the store policy:

Rule 1: The customer is always right!
Rule 2: If the customer is ever wrong, reread Rule 1.

In our office we've adopted the same basic policy: Do whatever is in the best interest of the patient; all other policies are null and void.

LET ALL YOUR PATIENTS KNOW ABOUT YOUR SERVICES

You can have finely honed clinical skills and the latest technology in your office, but if your patients aren't aware of the services you offer, you won't get to use them.

Many years ago I operated on a woman for kidney stones. When I saw her later for a recurrent kidney stone, I noticed she had a midline scar in her lower abdomen. I asked her about it, and she told me that she had had surgery for urinary incontinence. She had gone to a new physician, a gynecologist, for the operation.

When I casually asked why she had sought out a new physician, she said in surprise, "I didn't know you treated patients for incontinence."

That experience taught me how important it is for all my current patients to know about all the services I offer.

One way to inform patients of services is to send them a quarterly newsletter, either by itself or included with the monthly statement. Another tactic is to have educational materials available in the reception room. I have a rack with pamphlets and brochures on nearly all the areas of urology for which I provide treatment (Figure 2-1).

I also design special bill stuffers to include with bills. I have used bill stuffers to inform patients about Prostate Cancer Awareness Month and the need for an

Figure 2-1 Rack containing brochures on urological problems.

annual PSA test and a digital rectal exam for all men over 50 years of age. If you use a computer for billing, you may have a program that allows you to add customized messages on the bill. For example, when I began to offer collagen injections for treatment of urinary incontinence, I mentioned it on the computer-generated bill (Figure 2-2). You'll find that bill stuffers and messages on com-

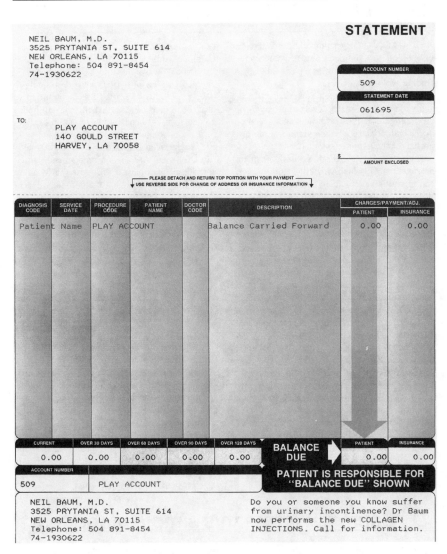

Figure 2-2 Computer-generated bill with a message about a new service.

A-6   WEDNESDAY, AUGUST 25, 1993   THE TIMES PICAYUNE   2

NATIONAL NEWS

Blood test finds prostate cancer better than exam

By BRENDA C. COLEMAN
AP medical writer

CHICAGO—A new study of the effectiveness of a blood test for detecting prostate cancer found it twice as effective as a physical exam at finding early malignancies.

More than 10,000 men participated in the study of a test measuring levels of prostate-specific antigen, or PSA, a protein that seeps out of the walnut-sized prostate gland if a tumor is present or the gland is enlarged.

High PSA levels are a possible indicator of prostate cancer, which will kill 35,000 American men this year, said researchers led by Dr. William Catalona of the Washington University School of Medicine.

Their study, supported by the company that makes the PSA test and by the federal government, was published in today's issue of *The Journal of the American Medical Association*.

Before PSA screening was available, nearly 70 percent of cancers detected with the traditional rectal exam were in an advanced stage, Catalona said from St. Louis.

"PSA flip-flops that. Now, with the blood test, 70 percent of prostate tumors are localized when they are diagnosed," increasing patients' chances for a cure, he said.

Also, the PSA test overwhelmingly detected serious cancers, as opposed to small, insignificant tumors that seem to pose little problem and require no treatment, Catalona said.

The $30 to $50 test has been endorsed as a routine cancer-screening aid by the American Cancer Society and the American Urological Association but has not been approved by the Food and Drug Administration for screening. Nor has the National Cancer Institute made a recommendation on PSA for that purpose, Catalona said.

"I think the whole thing is very politically charged, in view of the fact that we're going to have to decide whether PSA is included in health-care packages and whether it will be included in basic benefits under health-care reform," Catalona said.

The American Cancer Society and the American Urological Association recommend that, at age 50, all men have a PSA test yearly, along with a finger rectal exam. Catalona supports that recommendation. A recent cost-effectiveness study of screening methods also supports the combination screening approach.

Dr. Peter Littrup, lead author of the cost-effectiveness study and an assistant professor at Wayne State University, said the latest study is important but should "be taken with a grain of salt."

"PSA is one of the most important screening blood tests that we've ever had," Littrup said. He ranked the test with Pap smears and mammograms.

Still, he cautioned, "But we've got to reduce the false positives."

Catalona said that PSA suggests a lot of cancers that aren't there. But he said the notion of "false-positive" results is misleading, because PSA tests don't give yes-or-no answers, like pregnancy tests.

The study, conducted from 1989 to 1992 in St. Louis, compared 10,251 healthy men older than 50 who underwent PSA screening with 266 comparable men who did not but had been referred because of abnormal rectal exams.

Dr. Baum performs this simple blood test.

Figure 2-3 Sample bill stuffer alerting patients to test for prostate cancer. Reprinted with permission from B.C. Coleman, Blood Test Finds Prostate Cancer Better Than Exam, A-6, August 25, 1993, © 1993, *The Times Picayune.*

puter-generated bills do encourage current patients to call for information and use services they haven't used before (Figure 2-3).

I also take current materials in the field of urology to a copy store and have them laminated, then hang them in the reception area or in the exam rooms. These materials include articles I've written as well as articles taken from popular publications. For example, in August 1994 there was a front-page article in *USA Today* on the use of a blood test to diagnose prostate cancer. I put laminated copies of the article in all the exam rooms. In addition, I included copies in bills sent to 250 patients, along with a note telling them about the importance of the PSA test.

You'll find that patients will read laminated articles in the reception area and exam rooms and often ask for copies. Having the articles laminated extends their usefulness—they are unlikely to get soiled, damaged, or destroyed.

They provide just one more way for physicians to educate and inform current patients about the services and procedures they offer. Of course, it is nice to attract new patients, but we all need to be sure the ones we have don't leave our practice for another.

*   *   *

In the next chapter, I will explore a variety of ways to attract new patients and help them feel at home in your practice.

NOTES

1. M. LeBoeuf, *How To Win Customers and Keep Them for Life* (New York: Putnam, 1987), 13.
2. M. Cafferky, *Patients Build Your Practice* (New York: McGraw-Hill, 1994).
3. C. Sewell and P.B. Brown, *Customers for Life* (New York: Pocket Books, 1990).

3

Coming Attractions: Encouraging New Patients to Your Practice

The best way to attract new patients is to provide quality service and thereby increase the likelihood of getting referrals from current patients and other physicians. A satisfied patient will tell friends, "I saw Dr. Jones, who understood my case. The staff was helpful and friendly, and my problem was solved." This is a very persuasive type of endorsement. Patients who have heard about you from friends arrive in your office with positive expectations. They know someone who had a good experience with you, so they feel relaxed and comfortable and expect to have the same kind of experience. Similarly, patients referred to you by a physician they respect will arrive in your office already convinced you know how to help them.

Referrals and recommendations still generate a large percentage of new patients, but the times call for additional methods. Some patients have limited funds for health care; some belong to plans that limit their choice of providers. As a consequence, it is essential to let the community know who you are, what you do, what your areas of expertise are, and how to get in touch with you. You will have to reach out to many different groups by mailing out brochures, giving public talks, writing informative newspaper articles, or implementing any number of innovative ideas.

For example, Dr. Steve Wilson, a colleague from Fort Smith, Arkansas, encouraged a local bank to include in each bank statement information on prostate screening during Prostate Cancer Awareness Month (Exhibit 3-1). Patients learned about the importance of screening and where to go for a free test. Dr. Wilson provided the mailer, the hospital where Dr. Wilson admits his patients helped pay postage,

Exhibit 3-1 Flyer Designed for Inclusion in Monthly Bank Statement

FREE

**PROSTATE CANCER
SCREENING**

Free. Well, not exactly.

It doesn't cost you any *money* to participate in the Prostate Cancer Screening sponsored by Wilson Urology and Crawford Memorial Hospital.

But it does cost you a little time. A few important minutes to have a rectal exam and a PSA blood test that can indicate the presence of cancer. That's all it costs.

What does it save? Lives. Maybe yours.

Prostate Cancer is the most common male cancer, and the second leading cause of cancer death among men.

A prostate exam can also rule out the possibility of BPH, a non-cancerous enlargement of the prostate which affects most men, middle-aged and older.

Treatments ranging from medication to surgery can relieve the slow urine stream, increased urination frequency, and the painful, burning sensation associated with BPH.

If you're a male over 50, or care about someone who is, don't miss this Prostate Cancer Screening.

After all, it only costs a few minutes.

Free Prostate Cancer Screening:

**Friday, September 15   1-4 pm &
Saturday, September 16   9 am-noon
Crawford Memorial Hospital,
Van Buren**

**Appointments recommended.
Call 1-800-521-4463 or 501-783-1225**

FREE

**PROSTATE CANCER
SCREENING**

Friday, September 15   1-4 pm &
Saturday, September 16   9 am-noon

Crawford Memorial Hospital,
Van Buren, Arkansas

Appointments recommended.
Call 1-800-521-4463 or
501-783-1225

See Other Side For More
Information!

Source: Steve Wilson, M.D., Van Buren, Arkansas.

and the bank was delighted to provide this community service. It was truly a win-win-win situation. Of course, the same method can be used to publicize other health care techniques and services, such as mammograms and well-baby immunizations.

Below are some other tried and true methods for attracting new patients.

HEALTH CARE SCREENING

Employers and other organizations often set up screening sessions to provide a large number of people with easy access to several simple but important tests. When you go to a screening, spend some time talking with people. Answer their questions and have something to give them—a copy of your newsletter or an informative brochure.

In addition, ask for a list of the names and addresses of all the people who participated in the screening. You can then mail them appropriate information soon afterward. Of course, all your materials should include your name, address, and phone number.

Screening sessions constitute a valuable form of community service, and when I do one I generally get new patients, especially when I follow up with a letter or a newsletter.

HOSPITAL AUXILIARY

Another good idea is to participate in the local hospital auxiliary—volunteer to give a talk or to contribute in any appropriate way. A hospital auxiliary consists of people who are interested in health care and who devote many hours of volunteer service to help the hospital. It's nice for a doctor to speak to the group as a way of showing appreciation for all its work.

Again, get a list of all those attending any talk you give and send them a letter with a copy of your newsletter. You may want to include a short note saying, "It was a pleasure for me to talk to the auxiliary last week," so they remember where they met you. I typically get new patients when I speak to my local auxiliary.

WELCOME WAGON

Visit with the people from the Welcome Wagon and give them informative brochures they can hand out to people who have just moved to the area. You may want to offer a free "get acquainted" visit, since everyone who moves to town will be looking for new health care providers.

PUBLIC SPEAKING

Many community groups will enjoy hearing you speak. You would do best to target your efforts toward the people who will be most interested in your field. Ob/Gyns will want to address women's groups, such as the National Association of Women Business Owners. Pediatricians would profit from speaking to school groups and PTAs, while ophthalmologists and urologists should target audiences with a large percentage of members over age 50. Pediatric ophthalmologists might want to talk to schoolchildren as well as teachers interested in the causes of learning disorders. Dermatologists might want to speak to a meeting of the Ostomy Society, since people who have an ostomy need information about skin care and diseases related to ostomies. Every physician has areas of expertise he or she can promote.

The point is, don't assume referrals and recommendations will automatically supply you with a sufficient number of patients. You might have to stir things up. Consider where to target your efforts and then go out and communicate what you have to offer. You will need to motivate your audience to take action, which you can do by stressing the benefits they will obtain by making an appointment with you.

One important caveat is necessary: you can't go out and give a talk and expect that as soon as you arrive back in the office the phone will ring off the hook with new patients requesting an appointment. Over the long run you will certainly see results, but you need to be prepared for deferred gratification. Most physicians want to get to the promised land without trekking through the wilderness. Remember that nothing worthwhile is ever achieved without patience and hard work.

SERVICE CLUBS

When you speak to a service club, you have to make your talk short (20–30 minutes) because your audience is made up of business persons who have tight schedules. Such talks are worthwhile, despite their brevity, because most of the audience is likely to spread word of your services to a large circle of friends and acquaintances. Again, you want to distribute an informative handout that contains your name, address, and phone number. Send a follow-up letter containing additional information to everyone who attended the meeting.

The Junior League might be another valuable group to address. Usually these members are the movers and shakers in the community and have a strong interest in health care. Thus they can influence many other people.

GETTING ACCUSTOMED TO PUBLIC SPEAKING

If possible, find out a bit about the organization you're addressing and try to refer to it during your talk. When I spoke to the Shriners, I praised the wonderful work they do to help the medical community. That was a good way to segue into my topic—the unique health care problems that affect men. When I spoke to a union of merchant seamen, I talked about their travels into other countries. This was a natural lead to discussing how to prevent sexually transmitted diseases and how to identify the symptoms of the most common sexually transmitted diseases.

Some physicians aren't used to public speaking and may be reluctant to volunteer to give a talk. Speaking is a skill, like golf or surgery, and as with any other skill, grace and ease only come with practice. A certain amount of discomfort at first is natural. There's an old saying: "The human brain starts working the moment you're born and stops the moment you stand up to give a speech."

For those who can tolerate some anxiety and are willing to live through the inevitable stress of the learning period, there are many ways to master the art of public speaking. Groups such as Toastmasters International* and the National Speaker's Association† are designed to teach the basics. They offer a safe environment for practice as well as valuable techniques to improve your ability to speak.

MAKING USE OF THE WRITTEN WORD

If you feel unable to do public speaking or want to pursue additional ways of reaching out to potential patients, you should consider writing brief articles on health care subjects of interest to the general public. You will certainly have no trouble finding a local publication glad to publish your work, and once you have a file of clippings, you may be able to gain access to larger audiences by publishing in regional or even national magazines.

For example, I write a monthly column called "Man to Man" for a local magazine, *Health and Fitness*. That column generates 5 to 10 new patients a month. In addition, readers often contact me seeking medical advice. They assume the written word makes me an authority and they ask me to recommend local physicians for their medical problems. That gives me an opportunity to send new patients to my colleagues.

A few years ago, Rodale Press published a book called *The Doctor's Book of Home Remedies*,[1] for which I contributed a chapter on impotence. When the book

---

*23182 Arroyo Vista, Rancho Santa Margarita, CA 92688, 714-858-8255.
†3877 North Seventh Street, Suite 350, Phoenix, AZ 85014, 602-265-1001, fax 602-265-7403.

first came out, I received hundreds of calls from all over the United States, Latin America, and Canada. I still get two or three calls or letters a month because of that one chapter. Naturally I can't see many of these people myself, but I refer them to colleagues in their communities, colleagues who might reciprocate when any of their patients move to New Orleans.

REACH OUT AND TOUCH SOMEONE NEW

When physicians open an office, they traditionally put an announcement in the newspaper, send out announcements to other physicians in the community, list the office number in the phone book, then wait for patients to arrive . . . and sometimes wait and wait and wait. I think there are ethical ways to get patients through referrals from other types of professionals. I'll start by discussing the three I think are at the top, then describe how to motivate your own staff to bring in new business.

Referrals from Nurses

Every nurse is asked, "Who should I go to for this problem?" because patients naturally expect that nurses are likely to know who the best doctors are.

Here's how I stumbled onto the importance of telling nurses about the services I provide. Years ago I did an incisionless bladder suspension operation. At the end of the operation, I demonstrated the improvement in the patient's ability to retain urine. An operating room nurse who was watching said, "That was so impressive. I'm having this problem myself. Can I come and see you?" Not only did she come for an appointment but she also sent her mother and two friends.

Since then, whenever I introduce a new procedure at the hospital, I make a point of speaking about it to the hospital nurses. When I started using radioactive implants for prostate cancer treatment, many nurses were afraid to be in the room. Once I explained that the radiation only extended one inch from the implant and there was no danger of exposure, they were more comfortable. In general, nursing education should be given a high priority. If you are a surgeon, educating your OR staff will make new operative procedures go much more smoothly.

Referrals from Pharmaceutical Representatives

Now think about pharmaceutical representatives. They see all sorts of doctors; they sit in reception areas and hear what patients say; they visit with the staff; they really see each practice from the inside. All their acquaintances know they have this exposure and call for advice when they're looking for a doctor.

This means pharmaceutical representatives can be a big help in building your practice, and it makes sense to treat them well. Oddly, doctors typically treat pharmaceutical reps as if their time isn't valuable. They frequently make them wait and then spend just a few minutes with them. This behavior is not the way to win the respect of a pharmaceutical representative.

When I started practicing years ago, I could spend 15 to 20 minutes with a pharmaceutical representative. Today, when everything is more hurried, I can usually afford less than five minutes. But I still try to make each visit beneficial and productive. One tactic I use is to ask the pharmaceutical representative to send an agenda ahead of time (Exhibit 3-2). After reviewing the agenda (Exhibit 3-3), I can tell the representative which topics I'm interested in discussing and how much time I'll be able to spend discussing them. I then schedule a suitable amount of time. During the meeting, my goal is to focus on the designated topics, not chat about my family or my tennis game. I am prompt in starting and ending the

---

Exhibit 3-2 Letter Requesting an Agenda for a Meeting with a Pharmaceutical Representative

Dear Mr. Miller:

There have been many changes that have occurred in health care recently that have impacted my practice. As a physician, I am seeing patients that are more medically educated and are demanding more of my time. Consequently, I have less time to spend with medical manufacturing and pharmaceutical representatives.

I want to continue to have a relationship with you and your company but I want to make an effort to keep our visits short and focused.

I would appreciate an agenda for each of our meetings. Would you please include in the agenda what you want to talk about, what you want to know from me, and how long you anticipate the visit will take. I will approve the agenda and have my secretary make the appointment for you.

I will make every effort to see you on time and to end at the appropriate time.

Thank you very much for accommodating me. I believe it will help both you and me to be more efficient.

Sincerely,

Neil Baum

Exhibit 3-3 Pharmaceutical Representative Meeting Agenda

MERCK

DATE: JUNE 15, 1993

TO: NEIL BAUM

FROM: ROB GAUDIN

RE: AGENDA FOR CALL SCHEDULED JULY 7, 1993

CC: Charles Leach

Dr. Baum, enclosed you will find a detailed agenda for our meeting next month.

1. Will discuss ideas for a primary care physician speaker program on prostate disease.
2. Literature search and review of dihydrotestosterone and its role in the pathogenesis of BPH requested.
3. I will deliver the prostate model requested.

Dr. Baum, I anticipate that our meeting will take approximately 15 minutes. Look forward to meeting you and the staff next month.

Sincerely,

Rob Gaudin

Source: Rob Gaudin, Merck Inc., Lafayette, Louisiana.

---

meeting so the pharmaceutical representative feels I value his or her time as well as my own.

My request for an agenda letter also implies a commitment on my part—a commitment to see the representative in a timely fashion. I have been informed that the cost to a pharmaceutical company for a single visit to a physician ranges from $125 to $150. It is obviously not fair to allow representatives to wait a long time in the reception area. I have never found a representative who failed to complete the agenda letter, and they all appreciate the fact that I see them promptly.

Developing good relationships with your pharmaceutical representatives will demonstrate your respect for them and will endear you to them—especially if you use their products! I always feel complimented when a representative either comes to me as a patient or sends a friend or family member. After all, representatives see lots of practices and talk to lots of patients in reception areas. Their decision to select my practice must mean that they approve of my skills, clinical judgment, and practice style.

Referrals from Pharmacists

Pharmacists are another group that can be very helpful in generating new patients for your practice. They have an opportunity to know a great deal about physicians and they're often asked for recommendations. If you're interested in attracting new patients, you should develop good relationships with local pharmacists.

How do you do that? To start with, make your handwriting easy to read. When pharmacists call you, call them back promptly and treat them as professional colleagues. Years ago, physicians might occasionally treat pharmacists abruptly, even rudely, because they were so busy. That sort of behavior has no place in today's world.

If you publish a newsletter about your practice, put local pharmacists on your mailing list. Speak at meetings of the local pharmacy society and educate pharmacists about issues of current interest.

I'll never forget one time when I wrote a prescription for imipramine. This drug is usually prescribed as an antidepressant, but in low doses it is also used to treat certain forms of urinary incontinence. The pharmacist asked the patient, "Why are you taking this? This is for depression." Naturally the patient called me back and asked me to explain why I was treating him with this medication. I think some physicians in this type of situation might allow themselves to be irritated at the pharmacist. I prefer to look for a win-win response. First I explained the reasons for the use of imipramine to my patient, then I called the pharmacist and explained the reasons to him (treating him like a professional colleague). I also sent him a journal article that describes imipramine's urologic application. That pharmacist sent me two patients: his wife and his mother!

Another time I gave a local pharmacy group a talk on impotence and the drugs that commonly cause impotence as a side effect. Then I wrote a short book on the subject and sold it at publisher's cost to 150 drugstores in the community. Many have it on the counter where the patients pick up their prescriptions. I estimate I receive three to five patients a month because of this form of almost free publicity.

Referrals from Your Staff

Don't forget that your own staff can be the source of new patients. At our practice, all staff members have business cards with their name and title and the name of the practice, so they can easily give our name and address to potential patients.

I think it makes sense to reward staff members financially when they bring in new patients. We estimate that the value of a new patient in our practice is $700 to $1,000, so staff receive 10 percent of that amount as an incentive to refer friends and acquaintances.

Referrals from Nontraditional Health Care Providers

In the continuous search for new patients, I think it is very important to reach out to what I call nontraditional health care providers: chiropractors, nutritionists, reflexologists, and acupuncturists. These practitioners are seeing many people. They are treating people you should be seeing. And if they know when to refer, if they know a physician who will see their patients and offer them appropriate professional recognition, they'll be happy to send that physician their patients.

I'm reminded of an orthopedist who was treating a patient with back pain. When he asked the patient about his previous treatment, the patient said, "I went to a chiropractor." The orthopedist said, "What did that fool tell you?" The patient's response: "Why, he sent me to you!"

An article in the *New England Journal of Medicine* reported that in 1990 Americans made 425 million visits to providers of nontraditional therapy and only 388 million visits to primary care physicians.[2] Americans spent about $23.5 billion for all physician services and $11.7 billion on the services of providers of nontraditional therapy. In fact, about three-quarters of the money spent on nontraditional medicine was not reimbursed by insurance. Obviously, many patients have a strong commitment to nontraditional medicine, and it is reasonable and appropriate for physicians to develop a rapport with the providers.

For example, I gave a talk to the local chiropractic association on the relationship between back pain, urinary problems, and impotence. I exchanged newsletters and articles with them, sent them referral letters, and made sure their patients returned to them. This type of communication, plus a promise to return their patients, usually results in several chiropractic referrals a month. Most nonmedical doctors are looking for physicians to refer patients to. Most are only asking for appropriate respect, for a referral letter, and for the physician not to belittle their form of treatment in front of patients.

The most successful ophthalmologists have optometrists working in their practices screening people. Ophthalmologists develop a rapport with optometrists and say, "You take care of prescriptions and contact lenses, I'll take care of the cataracts and other surgical problems, and we'll both prosper."

Referrals from Non-Health-Care Professions

I know an orthopedist who was getting referrals from manicurists. He specialized in hand surgery, so he talked to manicurists about arthritis and joint replacement. Many manicurists have warm relationships with their regular clients. When they noticed someone with swollen joints or when someone mentioned a problem opening jars, it was easy for them to discuss some of the new orthopedic treatments that can improve hand function.

I once gave a talk to a group of barbers. It's very interesting—just as women often confide in their hairdressers and manicurists, men often confide in their barbers. I talked to the group about impotence, and it was amazing how many barbers came to see me afterward. In addition, many of them mentioned my name to their clients, and I saw many new patients because of that one talk.

Referrals from the Clergy

If I were a psychiatrist, I would make a point of meeting every minister, rabbi, and priest in the community, because every one of them sees people regularly for marital problems, alcoholism, depression, and other emotional problems. A significant number of those people have problems that require a psychiatrist. They may be able to benefit from medication or psychiatric therapy. Clerics need a referral option. A psychiatrist who is willing to work with the clergy and teach them the signals they need to recognize in order to refer appropriately will be performing a useful community service as well as gaining new patients.

Although it is possible to generate some referrals from a minister, rabbi, or priest by simply attending the appropriate church or synagogue, using the tactic effectively requires a more active role on the part of the psychiatrist. I suggest contacting church- or synagogue-based organizations. They often have breakfast meetings and welcome outside speakers. Give a talk on recognizing depression and differentiating it from situational blahs or gloom. Suggest an article for their newsletter and mail attendees a follow-up letter containing an article on the topic you discussed. If you communicate on a regular basis with the clergy, in a very short time you will find yourself getting referrals from them.

*   *   *

In the next chapter, I will look at a very special group of patients—the "champions" who can promote your practice.

NOTES

1. W. Gottlieb, ed., *The Doctor's Book of Home Remedies* (Emmaus, Pa.: Rodale Press, 1990).

2. D. Eisenberg, et al., Unconventional Medicine in the United States: Prevalence, Costs, and Patterns of Use, *New England Journal of Medicine* 328 (1993): 246–252.

4

The Care and Feeding of Champions

Mike Cafferky suggests that certain patients, whom he calls "champions," provide a great opportunity for positive word-of-mouth promotion of your practice.[1] This chapter discusses how to identify and utilize your champions.

Who are your champions? Cafferky believes they are easy to recognize. A champion is a patient who has had a positive experience with you and your practice and lauds you and your practice to other people.

Some people tend to be talkers, others tend to be listeners, and of course some fall in the midrange. Talkers have lots of friends and lots of social interaction—they belong to many clubs and other social organizations. Champions are usually found among the talkers. They are believable and sincere and radiate enthusiasm.

Your champions are able to speak with knowledge and authority about your practice. If a champion can point to a recent positive experience he or she had with you and your practice, listeners are more likely to believe the champion's assessment of you and of the services you offer.

Champions demonstrate their interest in your practice by asking questions and making positive comments. When a patient shows gratitude for your services by talking to you in person, calling you, or writing a thank-you note, you should realize that that patient is a potential champion. So are the patients who offer comments on how to improve your practice. In our practice, we check the suggestion box in the reception area at the end of every day and thank each patient who has offered a suggestion or recommendation. We believe that if a patient has taken the time to offer an unsolicited critique of the practice, then he or she is likely to talk to others about the practice—so they are potential champions.

Many champions are patients of long standing. But champions may also be new patients. What you're hunting for are patients who are talkers and leaders, the sort of people whom others look to for guidance.

Cafferky suggests making photocopies of articles on health topics and placing them in the exam room and reception areas with a sign encouraging patients to take copies. Those who pick up this material are usually interested in their health care and are likely to talk to others. If your staff notices the patients who take the material, add their names to your list of potential champions.

HOW TO INCREASE THE EFFECTIVENESS OF YOUR CHAMPIONS

How can you enlist your champions in a word-of-mouth marketing campaign? Start by identifying the patients who are responsible for your current reputation. For example, start by tracking the patients who have referred others to your practice. If they thought enough of you to recommend one new patient, then they probably would be willing to send others.

Provide these champions with ample information about your practice and staff. Every time a champion interacts with the office, make certain he or she hears the latest news. This ensures champions will always have interesting information to share with their friends and acquaintances. For example, if you or a staff member presented a paper at a national meeting, were mentioned in the local paper, received an honor, or had an article published, offer champion patients written information about the event. Also, your résumé and continuing medical education certificates should be available to all your patients, particularly your champions. They can be kept in a notebook in your reception area, along with articles about your participation in civic activities.

Provide your champions with plenty of educational materials, including newsletters and pamphlets about your practice and your specialty. Let your champions know that you are on the cutting edge of your specialty and that you are continuing to refine your skills and broaden your knowledge.

Make educational videos available to all of your patients, especially your champions, and encourage them to watch the videos with someone else. This will provide an opportunity for a conversation between a champion and a potential patient.

You can also enlist the assistance of champions in reducing the negative impact of misinformation or weakly supported views that appear in the media. For example, recently an article was published in *JAMA* connecting vasectomies and prostate cancer. The American Urologic Association (AUA) prepared a position paper on this subject that refuted or at least neutralized the information in the article. I made copies of the AUA position paper and had copies sent to all of my champions, hoping they would be interested in this subject and help share the information with others. Champions enjoy having "inside" information and being a source of information for others. They appreciate it if you add to their knowledge and help them gain attention and status within their peer group.

MAINTAIN CONTACT WITH CHAMPIONS

Contact your champions often—and when they least expect it. Call a few each week to ask about their health, thank them for a referral, or congratulate them on some recent accomplishment by a family member. Let the champions know that they are special to you and your practice. Sometimes I've sent my champions postcards while on vacation. Sending postcards is such a simple way of letting patients know that you continue to care about them even when you are away, but this inexpensive gesture truly makes them feel special.

INCLUDE YOUR STAFF

Make a list of your champions and share it with your staff. Our practice has a "Wall of Champions" poster in the employee lounge (Figure 4-1). This poster contains the names of all of our champions written on stars. Occasionally I or a staff member will take a patient who we consider a champion into the lounge and show him or her the poster. I have never seen a patient who didn't smile and glow when seeing his or her name on the wall.

During staff meetings, ask staff for additional suggestions on who might be a potential champion. Remember, you can't find and encourage champions on your own; you'll need help from everyone on your staff to identify and nurture your practice's champions. Everyone should keep the names of the champions in mind. When champions have appointments, let all the staff know that they are coming so they can be overwhelmed with outstanding service. In my practice we have a one-minute marketing meeting at the end of every day. We briefly (and I do mean briefly) identify the problems that occurred during the day and mention the champions who will be visiting the practice the next day.

When I first discussed the concept of champions with my staff, they did not embrace the idea and even commented that all our patients should be treated like champions. I agree that ideally all patients deserve extraordinary attention. Every patient is a potential champion. Some people are not naturally gregarious, but when someone asks them about their doctor, they still have a chance to be a champion and talk about their positive experience with the doctor and his or her practice.

Figure 4-1 The "Wall of Champions" poster that hangs in the employee lounge in my practice.

Since we don't live in an ideal or perfect world, Cafferky advises physicians to identify their champions and be sure they get the best medical care possible and knock-your-socks-off service. They will provide a wealth of word-of-mouth referrals for you and your practice.

NOTE

1. M. Cafferky, *Patients Build Your Practice* (New York: McGraw-Hill, 1994).

5

All's Fair at the Fair

Never before have health care providers had the kind of opportunity to educate and inform the public about their areas of interest and expertise that is provided by community health fairs. The public is more health conscious than ever before and is thirsty for information on health and wellness. This chapter presents techniques that can make your participation in community health fairs successful and also attract new patients to your practice.

Why are health fairs important to the promotion of your practice? Participating in a health fair allows you to offer a friendly smile to people who are not current patients but who may become patients. They are viewing you as an individual with information who may later become their physician or at least an important member of their health care team. They are able to interact with you in a different way than if you were standing across from them with their chart and they were sitting on the examination table clad in a paper gown. At a health fair, the intimidation factor is gone. You have a unique opportunity to begin a relationship on a positive note.

The simple fact that you are present at a health fair sends a message to a prospective patient, whether consciously or subconsciously, that you have a genuine interest in helping people deal with their medical problems. You have taken time to attend. They know you could be on the golf course or fishing instead.

Some physicians find many forms of advertising and promotion unappealing. A health fair is an ideal way to let people know you exist without resorting to an expensive Yellow Pages ad or advertising in the local newspaper. You don't have to reach very deep into your pocket to participate in a community health fair.

How do you learn when and where health fairs will be put on? The hospital you are affiliated with will probably know about local health fairs, including those given by organizations such as American Association of Retired Persons (AARP), Community Chest, and the United Way. Check with the marketing department of your hospital for information on these matters. Health fairs are frequently held in shopping malls. If you are visiting a mall on a Saturday or a Sunday and a health fair is in progress, ask to meet the coordinator. If the coordinator is there, ask for his or her card and offer to participate in the next health care fair that he or she organizes.

Most people attending a health fair are there for knowledge. Offer them information about yourself and your practice, any medical problem for which you provide expert treatment, and additional resources for getting information on their ailments and illnesses.

Information on additional resources is particularly important because you never want to leave people with the impression that you are their only source of information. Encourage them to be participants in their own health care. Introduce them to resources such as the American Cancer Association, the American Foundation for Urologic Diseases, the National Cancer Institute, and the American Diabetes Association.

DESIGNING YOUR EXHIBIT

You will need an attractive, attention-getting display. You can't simply send a staff member with a few brochures and expect people to stop at your table. Request a booth near the entrance of the mall or display booth area so people will see you and visit your exhibit early on. As people walk by your booth, you have about 15 seconds to catch their attention and provide them with useful information—not much more time than a billboard has to attract your attention as you drive by at 65 mph.

Allow four to six weeks to prepare for your first health fair. This is the amount of time necessary to gather together educational materials and design an attractive exhibit. Make a concerted effort to make your presentation neat and tidy because for many people who stop by this will be their first impression of you and your practice.

For the table covering, a clean linen tablecloth is preferable. Plastic coverings seem "temporary" and "tacky." Vivid colors such as blue, green, and yellow serve as memory aids. Several items can be used to add color: Balloons, flowers, brightly covered boxes, or posters mounted on cardboard are great attention getters.

Remember that you are in the health care profession. Never allow the people representing your practice at a health fair to dress in an inappropriate manner, eat while at the table, place drink containers on the table, smoke, chew gum, or carry on lengthy personal conversations. They cannot greet people if they are engaged in conversation with a friend or the exhibitor at the next booth. Being attentive while working a booth is critical. Those staffing the booth must focus on the individual walking past. You want to create a positive first impression, and a friendly smile goes a long way toward getting the process started.

FOLLOW-UP

Follow-up is critical. You are only one exhibitor among many. Do not fool yourself into believing that you will stand out in the memory of health fair participants, even if you give your services away. Follow-up can be facilitated by asking people who stop by your exhibit for their name, address, and telephone number. The list you compile will be the most valuable result of your participation. It is important to send a letter to the individuals on the list immediately after the health fair thanking them for stopping by your exhibit. Include a practice brochure and your newsletter. Be sure to mention special features of your practice, such as early morning, evening, or weekend office hours.

GIVEAWAYS AND FREE PREVENTIVE SCREENING

If you use giveaways, they should be functional. In fact, the more useful they are, the more chance they will remind people about you and your practice, especially if your name, address, and telephone number are printed on them. Suggested giveaways include wallet-size cards containing specific health information, such as commonly consumed foods and their caloric, fat, and carbohydrate contents; ink pens with your name engraved; small, flat rubber disks used to open jars (particularly useful for the elderly or patients with arthritis); refrigerator magnets; and stickers that attach to the telephone and display emergency numbers (police, fire, and poison control), along with your name and number, of course. Companies that offer these types of products can be found under "specialty advertising" in the phone directory.

My favorite giveaway is a testicular self-exam card modeling on a breast self-examination card. It is made of plastic and can be hung in the shower or closet as a reminder to men to regularly examine their testes and have an annual digital rectal exam to detect prostate and rectal cancer. An ophthalmologist might give out a reading card that says, "If you can't read this, it's time to go see your ophthalmologist."

In addition to eye-catching free gifts, you can offer free preventive screening at a health fair. The possibilities include blood pressure tests, cholesterol screening, glucose screening for diabetes, eye exams, pulmonary function tests, and screening for glaucoma. You can also hand out tests to take home, such as a fecal occult blood test used as a screening for colon and rectal cancer.

It's best if the doctor is at the health fair, but most physicians don't have the time to attend. At our last health fair we showed a video of our practice. I spoke on the video, so it was almost as if I were there.

MEASURING EFFECTIVENESS

Participation in a health fair, like any marketing activity, should be measured and quantified. You always want to know the return on any marketing investment. I add up the cost of my participation in the fair, including the entrance fee, the cost of paying my staff to attend the booth, and the cost of the educational materials and other giveaways. I then track how many new patients I received as a result of the health fair and the fees that they generated four to six months after the fair ended. I believe you can count on a two- to three-dollar return for each dollar invested.

I'll never forget a health fair I did at one of the local malls. We gave out waterproof cards for men to hang in their closet or shower showing how to do a testicular self-exam, something most men should do but don't. The card had my name and address on it as well as information on the importance of testicular self-examination (see Figure 1-2). We offered this card to both men and women, asked for their names and addresses, and mailed them copies of our quarterly newsletter. We collected about 125 names, and from those names we generated eight new patients in the first six months after the fair. It was certainly worth the time and expense.

Health fairs are an excellent way to not only generate new patients for your practice, but also create a positive public image. They are ethical and effective, and economically they "make cents!" If you haven't participated in a health fair, I suggest you are missing out on a good way to market and promote your practice.

*   *   *

In the next chapter I will discuss how to give each patient a stellar, positive experience with you and your practice.

6

Positive Experiences Mean Plenty of Patients

Welcome, willkommen, bienvenu, shalom, bemvindo, benvenuto, croesawiad. All these words mean the same thing: enter and let us show you our hospitality.

When patients arrive at a doctor's office, they are often worried about their health and irritated because they have to take time off from work. We need to do everything we can to help them feel welcome, provide a comfortable environment, see them quickly, and meet their health care needs. This chapter looks at ways to welcome patients into the medical office and treat them with due consideration.

Patients want to be processed quickly. They don't want to go into an exam room, put on a short crepe paper robe, and just sit there. In other words, patients want to be seen on time and leave on time. They want the entire health care process to be systematic and efficient.

ORIENTING NEW PATIENTS PRIOR TO THEIR FIRST VISIT

Each practice must take the time to think about steps that will make patient visits run more smoothly. Sometimes, simple things can prevent a logjam. For example, when a patient comes to our practice, we generally need to look at a urine sample. A significant number of first-time patients, because of anxiety or nervousness, urinate just before coming. We then have to ask them to drink more fluids and wait in the reception area, which delays the process by half an hour or more.

To avoid such delays, we send new patients a packet with a letter that welcomes them to the practice and tells them about the services we offer. The letter also mentions that on their first visit they will be asked to give a urine specimen and instructs them to drink fluids before they arrive. Consequently, everybody who comes to our office is educated prior to their first visit. We can manage patients better because we invest a few minutes, with minimal expense, to explain our expectations in advance.

Similarly, primary care physicians may want to write a letter asking patients to bring all their current medications with them when they come for their first visit. An endocrinologist may want to remind patients they need to fast before their blood tests. An orthopedist will want to see previous X-rays and studies, and any physician who is asked for a second opinion will naturally want to see all the relevant studies and copies of the previous medical records. Avoid delays by informing patients ahead of time about the information they will need to bring with them to the office.

In our welcome letter we also discuss our payment policies so there are no surprises and patients have the chance to think about the method of payment they will use. Members of managed care plans who have a copayment are informed in the welcome letter that they are expected to pay this fee at the time of their first visit.

We ask all patients to fill out an insurance information form at home and bring the form with them. We also ask them to fill out a questionnaire (Exhibit 6-1) on allergies, medications, past surgeries, and other pertinent medical history. We try to identify what a patient's medical problem is before the first appointment so we can mail out appropriate educational materials before the visit. If the patient has a problem with urinary incontinence, we send information on possible causes, how we evaluate the problem, and possible treatments. If the patient calls for a prostate checkup, we send information about prostate problems. I have found that patients appreciate receiving pertinent information, and, more important, it makes their first visit easier and more efficient. They have few anxieties or uncertainties because nearly everything has been explained to them in the welcome letter.

Some physicians hesitate to send out information on sensitive health subjects. However, in our practice we deal with impotence, incontinence, and infertility—and what could be more sensitive than those subjects? We find that our patients appreciate receiving educational material before their visit. We ask them whether they want to receive the material and which address to use. We mark the material "personal and confidential."

Physicians, regardless of specialty or type of practice, can send out preliminary educational materials before a patient's first visit. A gynecologist might send information on infertility and how to take the basal body temperature. An ophthalmologist who sees patients for cataracts could send information on recovery following a cataract operation—in large print. A pediatrician might send infor-

Exhibit 6-1 Patient Questionnaire

NAME _____ AGE _____

Please describe the reason you have made an appointment:

_____

_____

_____

List all of your allergies to medication: _____

_____

What medications are you taking on a regular basis? Please include over-the-counter drugs such as aspirin, Motrin, and vitamins:

_____

_____

Are you presently being treated for any medical problems? ☐ yes ☐ no
If *yes*, what are they?

_____

What previous surgical procedures have you had? _____

_____

Do you smoke? ☐ yes ☐ no   If *yes*, how many packs per day? _____

Do you drink alcoholic beverages? ☐ yes ☐ no   If *yes*, how many drinks per day or week? _____ per ☐ day ☐ week

Do you presently have any of the following problems? *(circle)*

Severe headaches	Cough	Hemorrhoids	Arthritis
Fainting	Nausea	Abdominal pain	Constipation
Dizziness	Diarrhea	Swelling	Nervousness
Chest pains			

Please list below any questions that you would like to have answered during your visit to my office.

_____

_____

_____

_____

mation about the well-child exam and immunization schedule. A primary care doctor might want patients to know about the screening procedures that will be part of their first visit, such as the cholesterol exam, ECG, chest X-ray, and stool examination.

Mailing them information will educate and orient your patients before they walk in the door. It will help them to have confidence in you and your practice and will significantly improve the efficiency of your practice.

MAKING NEW PATIENTS FEEL WELCOME

Every new patient who comes to our practice receives a two- to three-minute tour of the practice so they feel comfortable and at home—and so they know where the exam rooms or restrooms are. Even though the tour is very brief, it serves to familiarize patients with our practice. The nurse introduces herself by name and says, "We'd like to introduce you to our practice. Please leave your specimen here in the restroom and we will then show you our office. After you have seen our office, the doctor will be with you shortly. After you're finished in the exam room, I'll be back to answer any additional questions you may have. When you're finished there, we'll escort you to the business office where you'll take care of your bill."

In the reception area we periodically show an introductory video that includes a tour of the practice. I introduce myself and explain what urologists do and where I was trained. Then our patient coordinator introduces herself and describes her role in the office. Finally the office manager describes her function. We all talk about our families and hobbies and how long we've been with the practice. The video was made by a friend. It's not a professional job but it does let people know who the doctor and the staff are before they've had a chance to meet them. After all, new patients are anxious about their first visit to an office, and our video helps our new patients relax and feel more comfortable.

SHOW PATIENTS PROPER CONSIDERATION

One way to let your patients know you care about them is to send them a birthday card. Our computer gives us a list of all the people with birthdays each month, and we circulate each card so all staff members can sign it. We use different colored pens so our patients see that real people, not a machine, signed the card. If a staff member has a close relationship with a particular patient, he or she will add a special note.

Sit down when you talk to patients. It's such a simple thing, but it creates the perception that you are relaxed and have all the time in the world. Two minutes sitting down eyeball to eyeball with a patient is worth much more than an eternity when your hand is on the door.

After examining a patient, ask him or her to sit up. Talk with the patient as an equal, sitting face to face. Also, avoid talking to a patient who is undressed, male or female. After examining the patient, step out of the room and let the patient get dressed, then come back and talk. The patient is now more likely to retain what you say. If you are going to discuss something with the patient, you want his or her full attention, which he or she won't be able to give if worried about modesty.

Whenever possible, avoid physical barriers between you and the patient. Some physicians sit at their desk and put the patient on the other side. When you're both on the same side of the desk or exam table, there's no physical barrier between the two of you, communication flows more easily, and the patient feels more relaxed.

Avoid referring to patients by their diagnosis or room number. I hear doctors talk this way all the time. They'll say, "Schedule the gallbladder in room 3 on Monday" or "Put the prostate in room 2." Patients don't like this because it's so impersonal—it treats them as "problems," not human beings. Once patients hear you talking like that, even if you're referring to other patients, they begin to feel degraded. I may be more aware of this issue than most because as a urologist I deal with particularly sensitive problems. But even primary care patients don't want to be referred to as "the ulcer" or "the back sprain."

If I want to order a test on someone, I always refer to the person by name. Sometimes just the fact that you're ordering a test can be very sensitive. An AIDS test would be a prime example. Therefore, I don't speak to the nurse about tests in the hallway; I pull the nurse into the room, close the door, and then say, "Would you also include an HIV on Mr. Smith." It's very important to reassure patients that you respect their privacy—they really notice this.

Another privacy issue relates to curtains or shades on the windows. My office suite is on the 6th floor, and all the windows are one-way: we can see out but nobody can see in. We often find that when we examine a woman, she wants the curtains closed regardless of who can see in or out. I think it's important to respect feelings of discomfort so we always explain that we have one-way windows and nobody can see in but also state that we're still happy to close the curtains if that would please the patient.

Never discuss financial arrangements in earshot of another patient. These days people are naturally concerned about costs, so you often do need to discuss financial issues. Some patients may need to set up a payment plan, or you may want to determine the exact amount they need to pay after their insurance company pays you. Most people just don't like to talk about anything financial in front of someone else. Make sure all financial discussions occur in private. Set up a business area for these discussions. You can also ask your nurse or office manager to go to the exam room to discuss payment arrangements with patients.

CALL YOUR SPECIAL PATIENTS

Just a few years ago, physicians admitted patients to the hospital the night before surgery, took a history, did a physical exam, and answered all questions. Now we are all required to admit patients the day of surgery. As a result, patients' questions are often left unanswered.

One thing you can do to make your current patients feel more comfortable and show them you're concerned is call them at home. Just say, "I know you're having surgery tomorrow, can I answer any questions?" Almost every patient will have a question or two.

When you take the time to answer patient questions over the telephone, there are several benefits. First, you get fewer calls from patients at odd hours or in the middle of the night. Second, you can warn patients of dos and don'ts (for example, not to eat or drink after 12 on the night before surgery). In fact, since procedures are often set up weeks or months in advance, your call sometimes will remind a patient that he or she is scheduled for surgery.

Most of all, patients are grateful for the gesture. When you call a patient, you can almost hear the phone drop—the patient just can't believe that his or her doctor has called without being asked. Sometimes I'm introduced as "the doctor who calls his patients at home." That's not a bad reputation to have.

In fact, I will never forget a story told by Stanley Marcus of Neiman Marcus. He said he took a dog to the veterinarian and the veterinarian called him at home to check on the dog. Marcus asked, "Don't you think physicians should care about their patients just as much as veterinarians care about theirs?" In other words, if veterinarians can find time in their schedules to call their customers, certainly doctors can find the time to call theirs.

In addition to calling people who are coming in for surgery, it also makes sense to call someone with a negative diagnostic test, someone who needs special reassurance, or anyone with special needs. For example, if you send a patient for a CT scan to differentiate a cyst from a tumor and the finding is a benign cyst, do you think the patient wants to wait 10–14 days to get the results? Of course not. Phone that patient at home and you will be amazed how much your call is appreciated.

When my nurse can't answer a question herself, she tells the patient, "Doctor Baum will call you this evening." At the end of the day I ask her who should be called. Usually it's two or three people, rarely more, and sometimes there's no one. On average, calling patients takes me 10 minutes a night.

And patients really are tremendously grateful. Once a group of ophthalmologists surveyed their patients and asked what they would rather have after surgery:

a limousine ride to and from the hospital, a dozen roses when they got home, or a call from their physician? One hundred percent said that what they wanted most was a call from their physician. There's nothing wrong with limos and flowers but a call from you or your staff will be even more deeply appreciated.

I remember the story of one mother who worked at a local hospital. When her baby had pneumonia, her pediatrician called her at home to check on how the child was doing. This mother was so impressed that when her friends asked her to recommend a pediatrician she referred five new mothers and their families to the pediatrician. All he did was take five minutes to call the woman at home and check on her sick child. That one phone call resulted in nearly $100,000 of new income for the practice. That's not a bad return on a five-minute phone call.

I think if you ask doctors who call their patients, they'll tell you it's such a positive thing for them and their practice. I would encourage anybody who isn't calling key patients to give it a try.

RETURN PATIENTS' CALLS PROMPTLY

In addition to initiating calls to patients, always return their calls promptly. If a patient calls with a question, my staff will give a reasonable estimate of when I'll be able to call back. Some companies schedule a service call or a delivery for a certain day but give no specific time frame, which can leave the person hanging around home from nine o'clock to five o'clock. To avoid that, we tell patients approximately when I'll be able to return their call and encourage them to be home and leave the phone free. That way they don't have to wait anxiously by the phone all day.

DON'T TAKE CALLS WHEN YOU'RE SEEING A PATIENT

Once I was in the exam room with a patient and I took one call from a physician, and then another call made me leave the room a second time. When I walked back into the room, the patient said, "I don't think you have your mind on my medical problem, and I feel I would be better off seeing someone else!" He was curt but polite. I immediately apologized, but he got up and left. I assume he found another urologist who gave him undivided attention and remained in the exam room during the entire patient visit.

Don't take calls when you're with a patient. Give that patient your focused attention. Physicians and gatekeepers of course do call with questions and they need answers in a timely fashion. Suppose a primary care doctor has a patient in his or her office and wants to discuss the case with me before making a referral decision. The doctor needs a quick response. My receptionist will word her reply very carefully: "Doctor Baum is with a patient right now. If it is an emergency I can interrupt him. If not, he can call you back in five to seven minutes."

I think it's nice to offer the doctor the possibility of an interruption, but most physicians will understand the situation if I'm with a patient. We try to use the wording "he's with a patient" first, and say "he can call you back" as the last part of the reply. Nearly every primary care physician or other caller accepts this explanation.

We do take calls in special circumstances—when a patient is in the emergency room or recovery room or when a patient is clearly anxious. But those are the exceptions.

We also supply special fax referral forms (Exhibit 6-2) that physicians can use to refer patients to our office. These forms allow physicians to refer without needing

---

Exhibit 6-2 Fax Referral Form

Referral from: _____

Referring doctor's telephone number: _____ Fax: _____

Referral to: _____

Patient's name: _____

Home phone: _____

Work phone: _____

Insurance info: _____

ID#: _____

Reason for referral: _____

_____

_____

Needs to be seen: ____ Immediately   ____ Within 1 week
                      ____ Within 2 days   ____ At patient's convenience

Please report findings to me by:
                      ____ mail   ____ telephone
                      ____ fax

to speak to me. They can check the appropriate request, insert one or two re-marks, and fax the form to our office. I've found that physicians really like this form; they will often ask for additional copies or modify the form to fit their practice style.

We need to roll out the red carpet for all of our patients. Making patients feel welcome is vital in this era of managed care. We are going to be getting report cards, and how patients are treated in our practices will influence the grades we receive. All of us will need to pay attention to the little details and manage all the moments of truth. It is not only the time the patient is with the physician that counts but also all the interactions that occur before and after. The successful practice will not only have above-average clinical outcomes, have short lengths of stay, and be cost-effective, but it will also pay attention to the little details and go the extra mile to ensure patients feel comfortable and welcome from the moment they call for an appointment until they leave the office after visiting with the physician.

*   *   *

In the next chapter, I will take a careful look at the importance of exceeding patients' expectations.

7

Exceed Patient Expectations

It is no longer enough to just satisfy patients. Now we have to make every effort to delight patients and exceed their expectations.

With rare exceptions, nobody looks forward to going to the doctor or dentist. There is always an element of the unknown—people are afraid they may discover they have a serious illness or need to make a significant life-style change. They fear a visit to the doctor may be painful or at least uncomfortable. The encounter will cost money, often a great deal of money. And patients frequently spend substantial time in the waiting room, sitting and thinking about these unpleasant possibilities while the other things they need to get done must be set aside. For all these reasons, people tend to have negative preconceptions about a doctor's appointment.

In our practice, we try to make it enjoyable and even fun to see the doctor. We try to interject a modicum of humor into health care so that patients enjoy the experience and look forward to their next visit.

The first moment of truth typically occurs when a patient enters the reception area. The area should be clean and cheerful and contain interesting things to occupy patients' attention while they are waiting to be seen by the doctor. The goal is to stimulate all the senses by providing attractive things to see and pleasant things to smell and hear and, if possible, touch. The more senses are stimulated in a positive way, the more relaxed and distracted your patients will be. By surrounding patients with a positive environment, you can often prevent anxiety and other negative feelings that are common in the health care environment from occurring.

In our reception area, we have joke books as well as books about old movies and the history of baseball. Another option is to provide hot herbal tea, bottled water or soda, and some healthy snacks, such as raisins, on a counter. I know one dentist who targets his practice to baby boomers; he has "I Love Lucy" reruns available on the VCR in his reception room. The specific details will depend on the personality and tastes of each practitioner and the people he or she wants to attract to the practice. But all physicians should make an effort to have an attractive, welcoming reception area. This is your chance to make a good first impression on your patients (and there are no second chances to make a good first impression).

Another thing you can do to allay patients' fears is to publicize the positive experiences previous patients have had. When you receive glowing letters from patients, as nearly every doctor does, make copies of those letters (with the patients' permission, of course) and put them in a notebook in your reception area. Patients will be able to open up the notebook and learn about times when you came in to see a patient on your day off, donated services for a community benefit, or solved some very puzzling case. They will then start to think of you in a very favorable way. Instead of being anxious about visiting your practice, they may even look forward to the patient-doctor interaction. (Figures 7-1 to 7-3 present samples of the letters I keep in the notebook in our reception area.)

In all my exam rooms, when patients lie down to be examined, just when their anxiety is at its peak, they see a big sign on the ceiling that says, "Smile, you're on Candid Camera." The typical response is a smile or even a giggle, which can be helpful in getting a patient to relax. I've never met a patient who can't be examined if he or she is smiling. I've been asked how this sign might strike older or very conservative women. I have surveyed older women and even nuns, and they all indicated they liked the sign and found it fun and not at all inappropriate.

We make a point of having fun in the office. On Halloween we wear costumes. On Christmas, we wear red aprons and Santa Claus hats. For Mardi Gras, we wear costumes again. When patients walk in, they see a sign: "In order to avoid delays, please have your symptoms ready."

If you want patients to enjoy their health care experience, you need to have a positive attitude and let your sense of fun and humor have free play. That's because your attitude, whatever it may be, will be passed on to both patients and staff. You can't expect your staff to be cheerful and enthusiastic if your outlook is one of doom and gloom. You're the person who sets the tone and creates the ambience.

Staff are affected by their physical environment. Even the weather can influence their behavior. A sunny day may make them radiate goodwill; an overcast day may make them lethargic and dispirited. When the doctor treats them well, they feel good and will pass that good feeling along to the patients. When the doctor treats them with indifference or is inattentive, they become protective or defensive. They spend their emotional energy healing their own psychic wounds instead of helping with the healing and nurturing of the patients. On the other

Dr. Neil Baum   11-11-94

Dear Neil,

Just a note to thank you + your very efficient staff for having made my visit so atraumatic.

What a contrast to last Halloween afternoon when my son-in-law fell from the roof (1 floor) decorating the house ē his 3 boys. I brought him to TME's ER for an X-Ray — + had arranged for an orthopedist to see him. The lady at their desk asked "Don't you want him triaged?" Regardless of my negative reply, their nurse had to see him + he had to complete 4 pages of information for their computer. He didn't remember my daughter's SS-number!

It was a pleasure in your smooth office. Thanks to all.

Figure 7-1 Sample letter from a patient, which I keep in a notebook in the reception area.

---

hand, when a practice is led by an enthusiastic physician and office manager, the staff can tune out external factors that might affect their attitude and will give the same high-quality service day after day.

PRACTICE MAKES PERFECT

Train your staff. They determine what each patient's first impression of you and your practice will be.

Although everyone realizes the importance of making a good impression during an employment interview, many staff members fail to maintain a polished

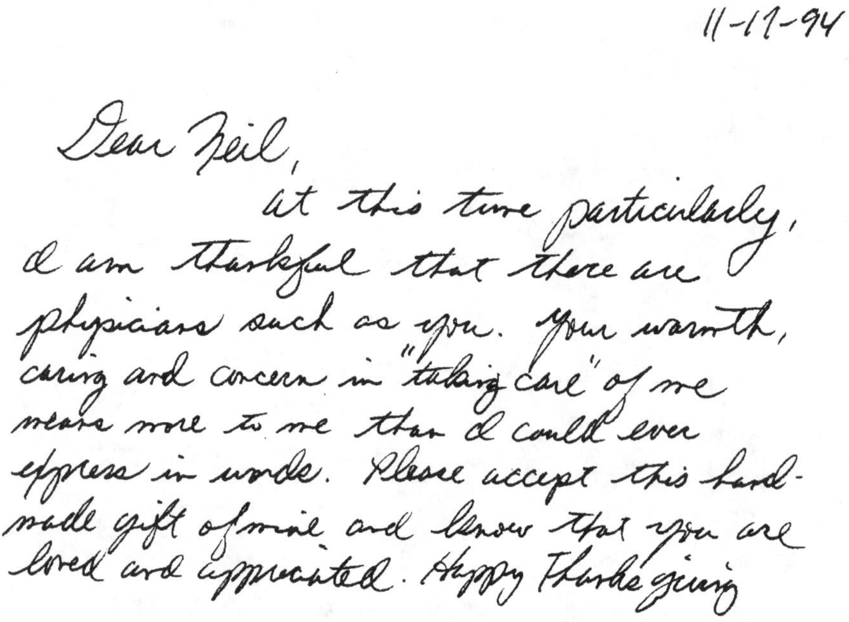

11-11-94

Dear Neil,

At this time particularly, I am thankful that there are physicians such as you. Your warmth, caring and concern in "taking care" of me means more to me than I could ever express in words. Please accept this hand-made gift of mine and know that you are loved and appreciated. Happy Thanksgiving

Figure 7-2 Sample letter from a patient, which I keep in a notebook in the reception area.

image after they're hired. Staff who are careless about business etiquette, office neatness, personal appearance, and language create negative vibes that may cost you patients and even a managed care contract. One of the questions that managed care organizations will ask their plan members is, "Was the doctor's office staff friendly and courteous?" If the answer is repeatedly no, then no matter what your skills and the outcomes you achieve, you will not have any patients to treat.

Make sure your staff are trained to present themselves in an appropriate manner. You can't expect every new staff member to know how to handle patients on the first day of employment. The best way to train staff is to role-play the sort of service you expect them to provide from the time the patient calls on the telephone until he or she pays the bill and leaves the office. For example, coach receptionists in the way you want them to greet patients on the phone and in person. Instead of saying, "Doctor's Office, please hold," they should learn to say, "Good morning, Dr. Smith's office. This is Sibyl. How may I help you?" Don't assume that staff members know what you expect. You must be specific, since office personnel can't read minds.

Neil Baum M.D.   11/4/94
"Warm & Fuzzy Dept."

Dr. Baum,

Again, I thank you and your staff
for helping me with my condition. I
had my trust in you, when you said the
antibiotics, along with your instructions,
would keep me from (going under the
knife). As I was leaving your
office with your instructions, one of
your receptionist said — "I'll say
some prayers for you Mr. _ _ _ _ _ _,
that you would not have to have
the surgery." That was comforting.

Well — Everything turned out
just the way you said it would!
Again, thanks for your professional help.
"It was like magic!"

Your Friend,

Figure 7-3 Sample letter from a patient, which I keep in a notebook in the reception area.

If you have many patients who are elderly and you want the staff to communicate appropriately with their families or caregivers, you need to explain and demonstrate what you consider appropriate communication. If you have methods in mind for managing an upset patient on the phone (a situation that occurs in every practice), you need to role-play the responses you want the staff to use. Without training and knowledge of your expectations, your staff will fail to manage such crises the majority of the time. Dr. Michael LeBoeuf, in his book *How To Win Customers and Keep Them for Life*,[1] points out that when a practice deals with a patient's complaint successfully and in a timely fashion, the patient does indeed become a patient of that practice for life.

You need to give staff opportunities to act out the scenarios they will face in real life, and then critique in a supportive way their methods for handling the situations. For example, you might use staff meetings to practice handling the upset patient. You could pretend to be an upset patient calling about your bill. The receptionist could practice taking the call and asking the nurse or patient coordinator to handle the call. The call could be given to the insurance clerk to see if he or she could resolve the problem, and finally the office manager could give it a try. Then the whole group could critique how each of the staff members managed his or her interaction with the patient. Only with practice will the staff learn the skills that are necessary to deal with a real patient who calls with a real problem.

HIGH TECH CAN STILL MEAN HIGH TOUCH

We have a sign posted where patients leave the office that says, "If you are feeling less than B+, let us know and we'll give you a hug." We got the idea from Bernie S. Siegal's book *How To Live between Office Visits*.[2]

I had a patient with lower back pain and problems with urination. One day when I asked him how he was feeling, he said, "I'm feeling so bad, I got a gun out the other day. I was really thinking of putting a bullet in it and cashing in."

I said, "Wait a second." I told my staff, "Come on out here. Mr. G. is feeling less than B+, so let's give him a hug." We all gathered around and gave him a hug and he smiled. During the next few days each of us wrote him a note and told him that we were looking forward to his next visit. I learned that this patient had a psychiatrist and I discussed the situation with him—he was already familiar with the problem.

Later, this patient said to us, "I've been under psychotherapy for two years. I take four different antidepressants and tranquilizers. Your hugs and notes meant more to me and gave me more of a reason for living than all the psychotherapy and all the drugs I'm receiving."

Let's not forget the value of touching our patients. Physicians are given permission to reach out and touch someone, and we shouldn't pass up this wonderful method of healing. Just a few years ago, before the introduction of antibiotics and high-tech diagnostic studies, the art of medicine included the "laying on of the hands"—and it worked wonders then. We should make sure that it is included among the methods of treatment we use today.

OFFERING MEDICATION SAMPLES

Most people, when they leave the doctor, have already spent an hour, sometimes more, in the doctor's office. So most of them, when given a prescription, don't get it filled right away. They've already devoted half a day to health care; the last thing they want to do is to go spend another half hour waiting in line. What we like to do is give them two to three days of sample medication just so they can get started with the medication right away. We also look up the number of their preferred pharmacy and call in the prescription so it is ready when they go to pick it up. It takes us a minute to save a patient half an hour. If the patient is a senior citizen and unable to pay for the medication, we contact the Program to Help Older Americans,* which provides free medication for indigent senior citizens. This is another example of thinking of the patient first.

It is important to be sure patients have the information they need about the medications they are taking. I recommend a book called *The Pill Book*.[3] I find the 10 or 20 drugs used most often and photocopy information about those drugs and hand it to patients so they understand the dos and don'ts about drug interactions and the side effects of the drugs. If you see 30 patients in an afternoon, and each one gets two or three prescriptions, often you don't have time to tell them about each medication in detail (and anyway they won't remember the information if they only hear it once). So I give each patient the photocopied information and record that fact in the chart. Patients appreciate getting the information and many have asked me for similar information on other medications prescribed by someone else. And of course we're happy to give them that information because our philosophy is to be of service to the patients.

We also give patients information about the costs of the drugs at various pharmacies in the community. They may choose to go to the pharmacy in my building, which is convenient but expensive, or they may choose to go to a discount pharmacy where they can save 20 percent to 40 percent. You can ask your pharmaceutical representatives to obtain this information for you, and I suggest that you update it every six months.

---

*For a directory of pharmaceutical manufacturers that participate in the indigent patient drug program, contact your local office of the Council on Aging.

EMPOWERING THE STAFF

Many times when a problem arises, somebody has to solve it right away. Suppose a patient is concerned about the cost of the bill or is upset because the doctor was late and feels he or she shouldn't have to pay. Well, the staff should be allowed the freedom to respond immediately to handle the situation.

Once, while standing in line to pay a bill at Kinko's Copying, I overheard an employee at the counter make a $300 adjustment on a customer's bill without consulting anyone. I was so impressed that she was able to do this, I wanted to learn more about it, so I asked to speak to the manager. He said Kinko's policy, throughout the entire organization, is to allow front-line employees to handle customer problems without any authorization, up to a $500 limit.

I thought this policy really expressed profound trust in Kinko's front-line employees. In fact, I was concerned that Kinko's might be vulnerable to abuse of the policy by employees. However, the manager told me the policy wasn't used as often as it should be.

We have adopted that philosophy in our practice. Whenever there is a problem with a patient and the amount of money is less than $200, each employee in my office is authorized to make an adjustment without checking with me or the office manager. For example, if a patient is upset about a delay, the receptionist can make the visit a "no charge." Isn't our reputation worth more than the $35 fee for an office visit? Of course it is. It is far better to write off the fee and have the patient leave feeling good about the practice than to collect $35 and lose the patient—and experience all the negative word of mouth that can occur if the patient tells others about his or her experience.

Suppose a blood test is lost. I'd expect my staff to explain the situation, apologize, and go to the patient's home or business to draw the blood. I don't think a patient should be asked to take time off from work, pay for parking, and go to our office a second time because of a mistake made by my office or the lab. In that situation, we would write off the lab fee altogether. We feel that if we made the mistake, we have to correct it. How often does this happen? Maybe once every three or four months. But it sends a clear message to my staff and to our patients. If we make a mistake (and we occasionally do, of course), we will stand behind our work and do whatever is necessary to make sure the work is done right.

What if a patient comes by the office to pick up a piece of equipment for home monitoring and finds out at home it's not working? Why should the patient have to come back to our office? We were lax in not testing the equipment, so we'll deliver the replacement to the patient's home. It has been our experience that patients really appreciate this level of service and will tell others about our "go the extra mile" philosophy.

One of our patients had a problem with an indwelling catheter and had no one to drive her to the emergency room. An employee, on her own, went to the patient's house and changed the catheter. The patient later donated $1,000 to the hospital in honor of the extraordinary service of Dr. Neil Baum and his staff. This was wonderful for us—it was like a public statement to the community about the value of the service we provide.

We would like to provide that quality of service to all our patients, so we relish the times we succeed in going the extra mile and cringe when we make a mistake. Of course, everyone makes mistakes. Exceptional patient service means that when you make a mistake, you apologize and explain how you will correct it. We think patients will forgive an occasional mistake if they see that staff immediately take action to correct it.

When a patient calls and asks for an appointment right away, my staff are empowered to make an appointment for that day—if it really is an emergency. However, I train staff to recognize the difference between an emergency and a problem that, while important, can wait for a few days. We have a sign in front of the receptionist's phone that clearly indicates which medical problems merit immediate attention (Exhibit 7-1). We also design our schedule so we can accommodate a true emergency without making other patients wait past their scheduled times.

When a patient demands to be seen today even though he or she doesn't meet the criteria for an emergency appointment, the receptionist tactfully explains our emergency policy and offers the patient the next available appointment. If this is not satisfactory, the receptionist offers to make an appointment with a colleague who is able to see the patient the same day.

If the patient doesn't accept these alternatives, the receptionist tells the patient that I'll call him or her back shortly. Usually a call from me reassuring the patient there would be no danger in waiting a few days (the problem might already have existed for days or weeks) will allay the patient's anxiety and he or she will accept a later appointment.

Occasionally the phone call from me doesn't work and the patient still demands a same-day appointment. I then allow the patient to come in at the end of the day. This situation occurs less than once a month.

Exhibit 7-1 Medical Problems Meriting Immediate Attention

1. Urinary retention
2. Hematuria
3. Fever, chills, or flank pain
4. Back pain that moves to groin or testicle
5. Testicle pain
6. Burning on urination, frequency and urgency
7. Persistent, painful erection

If you do as I have done and empower your staff, they occasionally will make an error in judgment, but that should be treated as an opportunity to learn from mistakes. The more empowered your staff is, the more likely they are to meet the needs and wants of your patients in a timely fashion. In addition, empowering your employees reduces the number of nonmedical decisions you have to worry about and frees up your time and energy for the more important medical decisions that you enjoy and are trained to make.

*   *   *

Surveys are an important tool to use in meeting and exceeding patients' expectations. In the next chapter, I will discuss easy and effective ways to survey patients and find out what they really want.

NOTES

1. M. LeBoeuf, *How To Win Customers and Keep Them for Life* (New York: Putnam, 1987), 14.

2. B.S. Siegal, *How To Live between Office Visits* (New York: HarperCollins, 1994).

3. *The Pill Book: The Illustrated Guide to the Most Commonly Prescribed Drugs in the United States*, L.D. Chilnick, ed. (New York: Bantam, 1992).

8

Survey Your Patients

 f you don't ask, you don't really know. If it doesn't get measured, it doesn't get done.

Many practices think they know that their patients are happy—and then discover only when it's too late that there are problems or that they really didn't understand the needs and wants of their patients.

If you ask physicians how they demonstrate their practices are of a high quality, they tend to throw their hands up in the air and say, "I can just tell that my patients are satisfied and they like me and my practice." Yet in many cases, unbeknownst to the doctors, patients are complaining to the staff and getting angry about long waits. When they become truly dissatisfied, patients are not averse to asking for their records and leaving to seek health care elsewhere.

The reason doctors are the last to know is that the office staff shield them from many of the consequences of their way of practicing medicine. Until now they haven't had to measure the quality of their services, but in the near future this will become a necessity. All practices are going to receive report cards that will objectively grade them with regard to access, outcomes, length of stay, and the user-friendliness of physicians and staff. Of course, cost-effectiveness will be a prerequisite for obtaining and maintaining a managed care contract. These other issues, however, will also be important, especially when there is parity in the cost of providing health care services.

Meanwhile, all physicians believe they provide excellent care and quality service. "Patients love us. We don't have any patients leaving. We don't have any office employee turnover." These things are commonly said, but perhaps only

1 practice in 20 conducts a patient survey and only 1 in 50 actually takes action based on survey results.

A survey offers a quick, efficient, standardized way to discover more about what your patients really need and want. Many hospitals survey their patients, but very few practices take the time and energy to find out what their patients are thinking. Finding out is well worth the effort.

For this chapter, I called on the expertise of David Kettlewell, president and founder of MEDI Medical Marketing Services, a division of Kettlewell and Associates.* Kettlewell sets the following goals for patient satisfaction tracking systems:

- Patients should leave with a warm and caring feeling for your practice. They should receive the impression that you care deeply and personally about how they feel, and you are concerned about their honest reactions to services received.

- We want to accurately identify problem areas in ways that do not threaten physicians or office staff.

- We want to encourage as high a response as possible, so the surveys must be easy to fill out and return.

- We want the program to be inexpensive.

- We want the surveys to be rigorously used by the practice as part of an ongoing search for excellence where the surveys become part of a system resulting in consistent, quality care for patients. A positive mental attitude alone does not create constant results; it requires systems. Your system should include training on how you want your staff to answer the phone, greet patients, handle busy periods, etc.

Kettlewell observes, "Patient satisfaction tracking is a simple research tool of very limited scope which answers a very narrow question: what are major areas of satisfaction and dissatisfaction your patients are experiencing related to the service your practice provides? Note that we are not tracking clinical treatment efficacy, we are tracking the way the patients are treated and how they feel about your practice."

For those who want in-depth information about the practice for use in cost reviews or contract projections, longer surveys are more appropriate. (These are often best done using phone interviews, Kettlewell says.) Or try focus groups. To conduct a focus group invite about 10 patients into your office for a light meal and a lengthy discussion about practice issues. Focus group discussions can be videotaped for future review.

---

*P.O. Box 5251, Akron, OH 44334, 216-929-9944, 800-830-4919.

William C. Fiala, a group practice administrator and a MEDI consulting team member, has been tracking patient satisfaction for his group for the last three years. Says Fiala, "We've tracked patient satisfaction because it fits our patients' and managed care partners' needs."

He likes the idea that his group has a record of tracking over several years and can show that it has taken action to respond to survey results. This demonstrates to managed care organizations that the group is aware of and responsive to patient concerns. The greatest benefit of doing surveys, according to Fiala, is that "it gives you some feel for what your patients are going to say about you when HMOs and PPOs implement their own tracking mechanisms." (For more information on managed care report cards and your profile see Chapter 35.)

HOW MY PRACTICE SURVEYS PATIENTS

There are many different ways to survey patients. We give each patient a card (Exhibit 8-1) to fill out at every visit. On one side are survey questions we ask the patient to answer, and on the other side there's space for the patient to write the three questions he or she would most like me to answer. This removes the mind-reading component from our interaction and improves the efficiency of our practice: I can review the questions and answer them very quickly. In addition, it prevents situations where the patient forgets to ask a question and calls back later or, worse yet, does not call back and never receives an answer. On average, well over half our patients fill out this card. When they do, it makes my time with them far more productive, because I start the interview knowing about the top three issues of concern.

I have seen questionnaires designed by some of the professional associations, and they're all three to five pages in length. In my experience, that's too long—few patients will fill them out. Kettlewell agrees that surveys that look like IRS forms are often thrown away unread and unanswered. They are perceived as cold and impersonal.

We use our response card on a daily basis for all patients, and we respond to comments or suggestions immediately. We thank the patients for completing the card and for suggesting ways we can improve our service. We also let patients know whenever their suggestions are implemented. They took the time to respond to our questions, and we feel it's only right to take the time to thank them.

Occasionally, we want to know the answer to a specific question. We will add this question to the card and give it to the next 100 patients who visit our practice. We evaluate the response and take appropriate action immediately. For example, we wanted to know if patients wanted us to call in their prescriptions to their pharmacies so they wouldn't have to wait for the prescriptions to be filled. We

Exhibit 8-1 Patient Question and Satisfaction Survey Card

Neil Baum, MD
UROLOGY

What three questions would you like answered today?

1. _____

   _____

2. _____

   _____

3. _____

   _____

Please complete the back of this card.

Thank you for helping us to serve you better!

1. Was it easy for you to get an appointment in this office?
   ____ Yes   ____ No

2. Is your general impression of this office favorable?
   ____ Yes   ____ No

3. Was the office staff friendly and concerned?
   ____ Yes   ____ No

4. Did the doctor adequately answer your questions?
   ____ Yes   ____ No

5. Would you recommend this office to someone else?
   ____ Yes   ____ No

6. Do you have any additional comments?

   _____

   _____

---

found that most of them did, and we provided that service. We also queried patients about whether they wanted their weight and blood pressure to be taken on each visit. We found that most of them weren't interested in this service. We did post a sign stating that if a patient wanted his or her blood pressure measured, we would be happy to do it. These findings were useful and we wouldn't have known our patients' wants without surveying them.

In addition, we send all our patients a two-page questionnaire at least once a year. It arrives together with a nice letter explaining that the survey is part of an attempt to serve them better. They are welcome to sign the questionnaire or can return it anonymously. We include a stamped self-addressed envelope so it's easy for them to just fill out the questionnaire and slip it in the mail.

It isn't often that we get a negative comment, but when we do, we follow up with a phone call, from myself or someone else on the staff, because we really want to know what our patient's experience was like. If there was a problem involving me or the staff, we follow up with a letter addressing the complaint.

Kettlewell recommends a mail-in survey using a two-panel, two-color folded postcard measuring 6½" wide by 4½" high (its unfolded dimensions are 6½" by 9"). The card is mailed in an envelope or handed out as patients leave the office (see Exhibit 8-2 for a sample). This particular postcard design provides an outside cover sufficient for a headline and graphics, two interior panels for a personal message from the physician, and a panel that can be filled out by patients, detached, and mailed back to the physician postage paid. The size allows ample room for four or five questions and a line for additional comments.

You may elect to investigate any areas you think are especially important for your practice. However, the focus naturally will be on patient satisfaction, so the questions should be devised accordingly. A word of caution: if you are unwilling to take action to deal with a specific issue, do not ask for input on that issue.

THE COST OF DOING A SURVEY

Expect to pay somewhere between $1,800 and $3,200 (including concept, copy, design, and printing) for a professionally designed two-color survey, quantity 1,000. A typical price breakdown follows:

Envelopes	$175
Strategy	$350
Copy	$400
Design	$400
Printing	$375
Photo	$175
Misc.	$100
Servicing	$800
	$2,775

Your survey is an extension of your practice and it should look professional. Professional designers are trained to create visuals that are balanced, present information with high impact, and produce materials that exude a feeling of qual-

Exhibit 8-2 Mail-in Patient Survey Postcard

Questions:
Circle YES or NO
with comments, if you'd like

1. Were you satisfied with the scheduling of your appointment?

      YES   NO

Comments _____

_____

2. Is the physician care you receive to your liking?

      YES   NO

What do you like best? _____

_____

What do you like least? _____

_____

3. Did our support staff provide you the considerate care you deserve?

      YES   NO

Comments _____

_____

4. Did you receive the kind of help with insurance forms and billing you expected?

      YES   NO

Comments _____

_____

5. What do you like best about the care you receive with us?

_____

_____

6. What is the area you feel we have most room to improve upon?

_____

_____

medi
MEDICAL MARKETING SERVICES

Tell Us . . .

                   Confidentially

Source: Kittlewell Associates, Akron, Ohio.

ity. Professional copywriters communicate ideas clearly and in a convincing manner. Use them both to ensure you get a good result.

BENEFITING FROM COMPLAINTS

Marshall Field, founder of the famous department store in Chicago, used to say, "Those who enter to buy, support me. Those who come to flatter, please me. Those who complain teach me how I may please others so that more will come. Only those hurt me who are displeased but do not complain. They refuse me permission to correct my errors so that I may improve my service." We need to have the same mindset as Mr. Field and welcome complaints. It is only then that we can serve our patients better.

If your practice has problems and you survey your patients, you will hear about the problems. You will get complaints. This is just fine. You should embrace complaints. Think of every complaint as an opportunity to improve your service to your patients. If you only get pats on the back, you will just keep doing things the way they've always been done.

However, you can only carry out so many major changes at once. Target your efforts and implement changes in stages. You may say, I think we should concentrate on our current patients first. That's usually what I recommend. After all, if your current patients aren't happy with the services that you are providing, the new ones that arrive are likely to be disappointed also.

What can you do to make patients' experiences more positive? Perhaps you do a survey and learn that your patients want to be seen on time. That means the first thing you need to do is improve scheduling procedures. If scheduling is an area you would like to tackle, then I suggest that you refer to Chapter 23, which deals with developing an on-time medical practice.

Let's say you've learned from your survey that your hours are inconvenient because there are more two-earner families today. You might decide to start at 7:30 AM instead of 9:00 AM one or two days a week so people could come in before they go to work. Of course, you would also have to reschedule shifts so some of your staff would come in and leave earlier. This type of adjustment will endear you to managed care organizations since it demonstrates a willingness to alter your practice style in ways that might benefit their members.

The implementation of such a change should occur in stages so you can judge responses as you proceed. You might send out information about the change in your newsletter and as a bill stuffer. (Remember to thank the person who made the original suggestion.) Post a sign in the reception area that says, "Due to patients' requests, we will now offer early morning hours once a month." If the response is enthusiastic, you can increase the offering of early hours to once a week.

A survey may demonstrate that you have patients concentrated in several areas, who have to travel long distances to reach your office. This may indicate that you need to have a satellite office.

A survey might inform you that many of your patients are having problems with their insurance forms. Although it is not the physician's responsibility to file insurance claims, you can make your practice more user-friendly by having an insurance clerk to assist your patients with the paperwork.

One man complained that there were no hangers in our waiting room behind the door. When we got some hangers, they made too much noise. He said, "You should get padded hangers," so we did, and sent him a note of thanks for calling this to our attention.

Once I learned from a survey that a physician who was covering our practice had failed to return calls. I was able to talk with him, and the situation did improve; if we hadn't surveyed our patients, I would never have known about the problem.

Although it is important to survey patients, there is one question that is pointless to ask, namely, whether your fees are appropriate. Why? Because you'll always hear that they are too high!

A medical practice, like any other business, should never be put on automatic pilot. You always have to make changes and fine-tune the system. Patients aren't the same today as they were a few years ago, nor are you using the same medications and diagnostic skills as you did several years ago. The same also applies to the way you run your practice. You need to ask questions, measure the response, and then take action based on what you discover. Find out what patients want by surveying them on a regular basis. That's the first part. The second is to give the patient and the managed care plans more of what they do want and to avoid what they don't want. If you can do that, you are guaranteed to have a successful and enjoyable practice.

9

Develop Effective Communication Skills

P hysicians generally don't win stellar marks as communicators. In fact, the average doctor interrupts a patient after only 16 seconds of discussion.

Your goal is to ensure good service and make every patient's experience with you and your practice a positive one. As Sam Walton put it, there is only one boss: the customer. The customer can fire everybody in the company, from the chairperson on down, simply by spending his or her money somewhere else.

It seems to me that the most important ingredient in good service is good communication. Although we know poor communication can lead to loss of patients and malpractice suits, few physicians take measures to ensure effective communication and patient satisfaction. Furthermore, many physicians are very sympathetic and concerned individuals, but unfortunately they often are not perceived to be caring. I think this is another result of physicians' poor communication skills. Physicians unintentionally give patients mixed messages when they don't demonstrate interest or involvement, both verbally and nonverbally.

The first 15 seconds of a meeting are the most important in terms of building a relationship and making the patient feel at ease. If the average physician interrupts the patient after just 16 seconds, you can imagine how many physicians don't allow the patient to talk at all.

Begin each meeting by shaking hands and looking the patient in the eye. Let's not forget the power of human touch. Why do you think that chiropractors, acupuncturists, and reflexologists are so successful? It is probably because they understand the importance of human touch and know that nothing else is an adequate substitute for it.

Ways to show that you're listening include leaning forward slightly and responding to the patient's comments. Be attentive and display interest and concern through appropriate facial expressions or by nodding your head. To avoid giving the wrong impression, pay more attention to the patient than to the patient's lab and X-ray reports.

It is commonly believed that the quality of communication is proportional to the time spent with patients and that physicians simply don't have the time to invest in communication. The truth is that physicians can communicate effectively in a short period of time if they focus on being good communicators and listeners.

WHY COMMUNICATION IS SO IMPORTANT

"Often it's not what you say or where you say it, but how you say it that counts." Communication is especially important today, in this era of health care reform and managed care. Managed care plans will be surveying their members. The questions they will ask include "Did your doctor communicate with you and answer all of your questions?" and "Do you feel the doctor spent enough time with you during your visit to his or her office?" How your patients answer these questions will be a measure of your communication skills. This is one test you can't afford to fail.

If you ever join a group, you will find members of the group will not tolerate anyone who loses patients because of a failure to communicate. In addition, nowadays patients are more likely to act on their frustration with the lack of communication from their physician. In the past, they hesitated to complain or to speak badly about their doctor to someone else. Well, they don't hesitate any longer.

Newspapers have articles every day about the ways patients are aggressively pushing for the kind of care they believe they should receive from their physician. There are even classes available intended to teach patients how to talk to their doctor. These classes emphasize that patients have rights and can be assertive if they feel they are not getting what they or their managed care plan is paying for. Lawyers advertise that they are available and eager to file malpractice lawsuits— many of which result from miscommunication. One recent study of malpractice suits found that 71 percent of the time the plaintiff cited communication issues, such as the way the doctor or nurse discussed the diagnosis with the patient and family. The findings suggest that doctors and other caregivers "should be attentive to their communication style with patients and families as one means to decrease the likelihood of being involved in malpractice suits."[1]

Today, although patients may be limited to the physicians who are part of a managed care plan, they often feel free to move from one physician to another within the plan. They don't feel that they have to have a permanent relationship with their doctor, as they often did in the past. Failure of communication is sometimes the major reason a patient leaves a practice.

In addition, many patients don't take prescribed medications or follow the regimen their doctor recommends because they don't really understand what they are supposed to do. This is an example of a communication problem that can have very serious consequences.

WAYS TO IMPROVE COMMUNICATION

The following suggestions for improving patient communication are based on the work of Kittie W. Watson, Executive Vice President of SPECTRA Communication Associates*, and coauthor of books such as *Effective Listening: Key to Your Success* and *Relational Communication*.

We often forget how it feels to be a patient. For one thing, patients generally don't like to admit that there is something wrong with them that they can't fix. They also don't like to admit their ignorance. Instead of asking for clarification, many patients who are intimidated or afraid to ask questions remain quiet. Erroneously, we assume they understand everything we say. We forget how long it took us to learn the acronyms and jargon of the medical profession. We need to remember to "translate" medical terminology into language patients can comprehend.

Patients look to physicians for advice and solutions but often feel insecure and out of their comfort zone when they walk into a physician's office. They may feel embarrassed to discuss personal issues, uncertain whether what they say will really remain confidential, or shy about exposing their bodies. Can you imagine how you might feel if you went to visit a stranger, had to reveal such personal matters as your bowel habits and sexual activities, and then had to get undressed to expose all areas of your body to a fully dressed man or woman? The chances are you too would feel out of your comfort zone and a bit intimidated. In addition, it is unlikely you would remember everything you were told to do in order to solve your medical problem.

As physicians, we need to learn to recognize nonverbal cues that indicate discomfort, a lack of understanding, or confusion on the part of our patients. A patient who begins scratching his arm, pulling on an ear, gazing into space, and/or touching his face while you're talking is probably feeling some anxiety. These cues also suggest some sort of internal emotional conflict. Other patients may avoid eye contact, clear their throats, fidget in the chair, furrow their brows, or tense their facial muscles.

---

*P.O. Box 5031, Contract Station 20, New Orleans, LA 70118, 504-831-4440, fax 504-831-0631.

When you notice one or more of these behaviors, think about what you can do to make the patient feel more comfortable. Consider asking a question, rephrasing what you said, or asking for patient feedback. For example, if a patient is giving you one or more of these nonverbal signs and is talking about shortness of breath and sweating, you might say, "What I hear you saying is that you start sweating and get short of breath late in the afternoon. Are there any other times of day that you experience these conditions?" Keep in mind, similar nonverbal messages can have more than one meaning. A patient may have her arms crossed in front of her because she feels defensive, scared, cold, or uncomfortable.

Check with each patient to make sure that you're interpreting a nonverbal signal correctly. You might say, "I think you may be uncomfortable with that? Can you share with me what you are feeling?" When checking for understanding, avoid asking questions that can be answered with a simple yes or no. Rather than asking, "Do you understand?" ask, "Which options are you willing to try?"

There are effective techniques for building rapport with your patients. Get as much information as possible about patients before seeing them for the first time. Get your office personnel to ask specific questions and create patient information files that will help you save time and build relationships more quickly. In our office, we mail a questionnaire to each patient before the first visit. (See Exhibit 6-1 on page 45.)

During your first meeting with a patient, note down specific information, including personal information such as marital status, number of children, hobbies, occupation, and even the location of the patient's last vacation. Note the name of the referring physician, the patient's preferred pharmacist, and his or her other health care providers (for example, dentist, podiatrist, or chiropractor). Review the patient's file before each appointment and use the information in patient meetings. A quick review will remind you whether the patient likes to chat for a few minutes before giving medical information or prefers discussing symptoms and progress immediately.

Learn to adapt your communication style to the individual needs of each patient. You can only learn which style is appropriate through trial and error. Assume that most patients want to ease into a discussion of their problems. Instead of "How are you feeling today?" try "That's a beautiful bracelet. Is it a family heirloom?" A useful rule of thumb is to talk to new patients for three to five minutes about nonmedical topics and to talk to current patients for one to two minutes before launching into a discussion of medical problems. This is where your notes come in handy. You can refer to them before you enter the room and begin discussing one of the topics that you know will be of interest to the patient. Chatting about such topics is an excellent way to connect with patients, help them to relax, and let them know that you are concerned about them as complete individuals.

I also use the social progress section of the chart to record the name and telephone number of the patient's pharmacy so when somebody calls and asks us to phone in a prescription we already have the information on file. If patients express any wishes about what they would want done if they were on life support, I record that discussion in this section of the chart, too. I don't find this subject comes up often in my practice, but I assume that physicians who often see older patients or more seriously ill patients probably deal with this issue more frequently.

HOW TO SHOW RESPECT TO PATIENTS

Add a Personal Touch

Use patients' names whenever possible. The most pleasing sound in the human language to each and every one of us is the sound of our own name. When a patient calls you, try to use his or her name at least twice during the conversation. For example, your receptionist might respond to a patient making an appointment, "Mrs. Smith, we look forward to seeing you. . . . Please do give us a call, Mrs. Smith, if you need us."

Getting your staff to use patients' names requires more than suggesting this policy at your next staff meeting. You will need to train, encourage, and remind your staff for several weeks before use of names becomes an automatic habit.

It is a nice courtesy to ask patients whether they prefer to be addressed by their first or last name. I once introduced myself to a patient as "Neil Baum" and referred to her by her first name. She was appalled and promptly corrected me. I then circled her last name on the chart as a reminder to always use her last name. Elderly patients often prefer "Mr. Jones" or "Mrs. Smith" because they perceive these as respectful forms of address. Some patients, like physicians, have titles they prefer to use, such as Colonel or Doctor. Patients in their forties, on the other hand, may prefer to be called by their first name because they grew up in a less formal society. In the case of a name that is difficult to pronounce, I suggest that your staff ask the patient for the correct pronunciation of the name and then write the name phonetically at the bottom of the chart.

Another way to show respect for patients is to provide privacy for office conversations. Make sure patients can't overhear confidential discussions in the examining rooms, hallways, or business office. Patients lose confidence in their physician if they feel another patient's privacy has been violated.

For example, a patient once complained to me that the receptionist specifically mentioned his injections at the checkout counter. He was embarrassed and concerned that others might overhear and realize that he was using injection therapy for his impotence. Although it is unlikely anyone in the reception area would know the purpose of prostaglandin, the patient knew what it was used for and he was uncomfortable. And that's the bottom line. If some type of behavior makes one patient feel self-conscious, then that type of behavior is likely to cause the same reaction in other patients. It needs to be changed to avoid creating a negative experience for patients.

Say "Thank You"

Say "thank you" to your patients often. There are many situations where a thank-you is in order. If you issue a refund because a patient overpaid the bill or because the insurance company sent a check after the patient paid the bill, encourage your office manager or billing clerk to include a thank-you note in the refund envelope. When a current patient refers a new patient to the practice, he or she should receive a handwritten note of appreciation. Every gift or card a patient sends should be acknowledged. Never take your patients graciousness and support for granted.

Welcome Complaints

Constructive criticism provides you with an opportunity to improve the services that you provide your patients. Chronic complainers keep you on your toes. I have one patient who was very influential in the community and had already seen seven other urologists—all competent physicians. I had nothing to offer her but my ability to listen with compassion. She was very difficult and demanding, often calling on weekends and after hours for prescription refills and dropping in for visits without an appointment. I told my staff that we would do everything reasonable to keep her happy and that our goal was to keep her in the practice. We all agreed that if we could make this patient happy, satisfying other patients would be a "slam dunk."

Consider these statistics. A typical business hears from only 4 percent of its dissatisfied customers. The other 96 percent just quietly go away and 91 percent will never come back.[2] That represents a serious financial loss for companies whose employees don't know how to treat customers and a tremendous gain for those whose employees do.

Successful practices encourage feedback from patients and even solicit it. The most common complaint from patients is that the doctor or staff were rude, didn't respect the patients' time, and offered poor service. Even if the goal of providing high-quality services is pursued energetically, there will still be people who have complaints.

Never forget that a complaint requires a twofold response. First, deal with the patient's emotions and concerns. Second, solve the actual problem. You can react to a patient's financial complaint by zeroing the balance or giving the patient a refund, but if you don't acknowledge the emotional component of the complaint, you may win the battle but lose the war. Tell the patient, "I know I would feel the same way if it happened to me." Admit you are wrong when that is appropriate. "I'm sorry" are magic words that can wipe the slate clean. Patients allowed to remain angry may leave your practice and go elsewhere or may voice criticisms of your practice to their employer or managed care plan. You can't afford to have patients spreading disparaging stories about you and your practice. Whenever possible, if you have a lemon, use it to make lemonade. It's cheaper and sweeter in the long run.

COMMUNICATION TECHNIQUES

Jacob Weisberg, President of Creative Communications* and author of *Does Anybody Listen, Does Anybody Care? They Will for You!* [3] says, "I believe you can improve communication skills the same way you improve any skill— whether it's communication, surgery, or driving a car. You read about how to do it. You attend lectures and seminars. You watch others. Then you practice." He also says, "Just as there are quality assurance committees, checking the quality of medical and surgical care, there should be and I believe there eventually will be quality assurance committees checking on the quality of communication be- tween the health care practitioner and the patient or between two health care practitioners."

All physicians believe they know how to communicate. The only problem is, they may not communicate in the best way. Weisberg has categorized the commu- nication process and identified a number of specific techniques that physicians and staff can systematically learn and practice.

- *Eye contact.* In face-to-face communication, the listener should look at the speaker. This means that the doctor should not be writing notes while the patient is speaking. The patient's perception is that the doctor really isn't listening when he's busy writing. Weisberg comments, "Even if the doctor says, 'I'm writing down what you're telling me,' the patient's emotional need for eye contact is so strong that it has a greater force than the doctor's logical explanation."

---

*31861 Via Pavo Real, Trabuco Canyon, CA 92679, 714-589-1723, fax 714-589-1627.

- *Body position.* Lean forward. Lean toward patients. Show them with your body that you are interested in what they're saying.
- *Verbal acknowledgment.* Say something like "Uh-huh" or "I understand, please continue" so the patient knows you have heard what he or she said. In phone conversations, these verbal cues are very important because visual cues are not available.
- *Facial expression.* Smile, look interested, or even frown. Respond with an appropriate facial expression to what the patient is saying.
- *Paraphrasing.* After patients feel listened to, their next need is to feel understood. There's a big difference! Eventually, patients need some sort of feedback or response that shows you understand what they have said. For example, if a male patient, in discussing his sexual problem, tells you he has trouble holding an erection, you might respond by asking, "Would it be correct to summarize your situation by saying that you find it difficult to maintain your erection? Is this the area you would like me to help you with?"
- *Appropriate use of* I *and* you. Use the word *you* to give some kind of credit. Use the word *I* to take responsibility. For example, if a patient is late, the receptionist should not say, "You are late." Instead, she should take responsibility for her own actions and say, "I wish you had been here at 9:00, when you were scheduled, because I could have taken you right in. However, under the circumstances, I had to give the time away." As Weisberg explains, she is "telling Mr. Jones that he won't be seen right now. But he knows he's late. He doesn't need [her] to remind him and scold him and smack his little hand, for having come late."
- *Words and music.* The words someone says and the way they are said should match. If they don't, pay attention and probe further to find out what is really going on. Suppose a physician says, "I've outlined this treatment program that I would like you to follow. Do I have your agreement now that you will start tomorrow?" Often a patient will say yes while betraying reservations through tone of voice or facial expression. The doctor who ignores such cues and says, "Well, fine, we'll see you in three weeks," will be disappointed in many cases. According to Weisberg, "If the doctor didn't focus on the words alone, then he would say to the patient, 'You said yes, but you seem to be hesitant. Let's talk about it.'" At this point the doctor will learn what is bothering the patient—it may be cost, his/her life style, or failure to understand the instructions; it may be vacation or work plans.

After this full discussion, the patient is much more likely to actually follow the doctor's suggestions. Taking the time to listen to a patient and probe feelings is obviously difficult when there is a full waiting room and a crowded schedule. That's why one of the most important communication skills Weisberg teaches is buying time.

- *Buying time.* It is possible for the doctor to write down what the patient is saying and allow the patient to feel heard at the same time. Key points: say the patient's name, say something to show you heard what was said, explain what you're going to do, and then go back to listening to the patient again. "Oh Mr. Jones, thank you for giving me this information. I'm not going to remember everything you said, so I'm going to write it all down now. Then I want you to continue."

While writing, the doctor says out loud, "Pain in abdomen on arising, disappears with exercise but then his back starts hurting. Walking does not seem to help." The patient, hearing the physician repeat back what was said, thinks, "Wow, the doctor listened to me and really understood me." One of the biggest frustrations for doctors is the way patients tend to repeat themselves. "In my opinion," Weisberg says, "they repeat themselves because they don't believe you listen to what they are saying. If you make the effort to really listen to what they say, and show them that you are really listening, you will find it takes less time and has far better results than if you act as if you're always in a hurry."

IMPROVING LISTENING SKILLS

The truth is that the most common activity we engage in is communication, and like any other essential activity, it merits our full and undivided attention. Physicians often underestimate how important it is to concentrate on listening. They tend to think that listening is a passive activity and that all you have to do is sit and nod your head and the information will load itself. That's not true, according to Deborah St. James, a medical educator and editor, author of *Writing and Speaking for Excellence: A Practical Guide for Physicians.*[4]

Listening is a skill, St. James says, one that physicians must learn and practice in order to improve. The first and most important thing to do is just stop talking. Next, you need to take specific steps to put the patient at ease. Put down your pencil, focus on the patient, make eye contact. If the patient seems nervous, you may want to reassure him or her with a pat on the shoulder, by holding a hand for a moment, or by smiling. You might even empathize with the patient, saying, "I know you are upset and I would be too if I had to tell my medical history to a stranger." Next, deal with the barriers to good listening (unfortunately, most physician offices are full of such barriers). If you are going to listen properly, you can't also answer the phone or talk to someone else or eat your lunch. Prepare yourself to concentrate. If possible, put all your calls on hold or transfer them to someone who can take messages while you are in a meeting. In some cases, where there are distractions that can't be eliminated, you have to train yourself to ignore them and focus instead on what the patient is trying to say.

In addition to ignoring outside distractions, you also have to recognize internal distractions that may interfere with listening to the patient. If by any chance you have negative feelings about the patient, you need to put those feelings on hold and concentrate on the message, not the sender. Also, listening takes energy and effort, and if you're very tired or have other problems on your mind, it's more likely you'll fail to be attentive. Be aware of internal noise or distractions. The average person speaks at a rate of about 150 words a minute, whereas it's possible to listen to and understand 300–400 words a minute. This means you may find yourself thinking about something else while you're listening—planning what you want to say or daydreaming about what you're going to do that night or next weekend.

"The amazing thing is that we learn by the first grade how to give someone the impression that we're listening to them with full attention when, in fact, we're miles away," St. James says. "Most people, because they haven't paid attention to this process, don't even notice what a habit it is. If you become more aware of these barriers, that will help you focus."

Be patient with your patients. Sometimes it will take a patient a while to say what is really on his or her mind. If the patient feels rushed, he or she will probably stop talking. Of course, it's a fact that many physicians have limited time to talk with each patient. How can they create an atmosphere of unhurried listening when the reality is that they are overly busy? "If you know you only have 15 minutes, you have to make every one of those minutes count," St. James says. "Devote the time exclusively to that patient. If physicians spend more time in active listening, they find they get fewer call backs and greater compliance. In the long run, it will save them hours and days and months."

Put your own beliefs on hold. Be aware of any anger or negative emotions and set them aside while you are listening. Avoid criticizing a patient's attitudes and beliefs: focus instead on listening to the patient's feelings.

Patients often feel frightened, frustrated, or anxious, when they come in for an appointment. When they start talking, what they have to say may not be clear and well organized. It's important to listen not just to the words but to the message behind the words. What is the main point, the central thought? "Physicians and other health care providers are often trained to listen for special words that trigger a diagnosis," says St. James. "Yet often they may jump to a conclusion because while focusing on the words, they haven't heard the entire message."

After reacting to what a patient says, you may find the patient exclaiming, "No, no, that's not what I meant at all." If the patient seems to have a hard time getting to the main point, it helps if you and the patient go back and forth in an attempt at clarification. Once you are sure you understand the patient's main concerns, then it's time to set down a few notes.

Many physicians don't know how to take effective notes, St. James says. "It seems to me that taking bad notes can be worse than taking no notes at all. People who attempt to write down too much of what someone is saying often wind up missing the point the speaker is trying to make. They may lose their emotional connection with the speaker."

There are many medical issues where emotional content is of primary importance, such as alcoholism, positive HIV status, or battery by a spouse. Often the patient has a message he or she hopes to convey to you without having to come out and say it. If you listen superficially, you may only get the tip of the iceberg, whereas if you put your pencil down, turn and face the patient, and act as if you're interested in listening to the whole story, you will get the whole story. Physicians and other health care providers should actively listen to patients, pay full attention, verify what they've heard, and only then make a few brief notes.

St. James has codified the above guidelines into a brief list, which she calls the Ten Commandments for Active Listening (Exhibit 9-1). This list begins and ends with "Stop talking." The reason for this, she says, is that keeping quiet is probably the hardest thing to do. "People are uncomfortable with silence," she says. "It makes them uneasy. However, it is very therapeutic, as any psychiatrist will tell you. Just be silent and listen, give your patients your full attention, and they will tell you what is on their minds."

One practical suggestion from St. James: to make it easier to remember active listening skills, post the Ten Commandments for Active Listening next to your desk.

USING VISUAL AND TACTILE MATERIALS TO GET YOUR POINT ACROSS

I hear and I forget. I see and I remember. I do and I understand.

Chinese proverb

The more ways that you stimulate different senses at the same time, the more likely it is that patients will be able to retain the information you give them. I find that when I involve my patients by using visual and tactile materials while talking with them, it makes it easier for them to remember important information.

Involve patients whenever you can. For example, when discussing lab results, show the patient the report. Indicate where the normal range is and where the patient's values fall. Ask if the patient would like to have a copy of the lab report. Most patients really appreciate this.

When I talk with a patient about a vasectomy, I often show how it's done using a rubber band. I let the patient apply a clip and cut the rubber band, allowing him to do his first vasectomy! This makes it easier for the patient to understand and remember the explanation. When I'm talking to a patient about the prostate gland, I'll make a fist and ask the patient to make a fist, explaining that the prostate

Exhibit 9-1 The Ten Commandments for Active Listening

1. Stop talking.
2. Remove distractions. If possible, forward the phone, turn off radio, etc.
3. Make eye contact. Speaker deserves your full attention.
4. Work to overcome negative emotional responses toward speaker or topic.
5. Be patient.
6. Help speaker clarify his or her message. "What I hear you saying is . . ."
7. Ask questions.
8. Keep a check on anger, frustration, criticism.
9. Empathize.
10. Stop talking.

Source: Deborah St. James.

gland normally feels like the base of the thumb: soft, rubbery, smooth, and easily movable. Then I explain that if I feel something stiff and hard, like a knuckle, I suspect it is a prostate nodule. I also use photographs (Figure 9-1) or a model showing a prostate nodule to make the explanation clearer. Similarly, an orthopedist could use a hinge to explain how a knee joint works, and a gynecologist could use a balloon and a clothes pin to describe the bladder and the urinary sphincter.

PROVIDING EDUCATIONAL MATERIALS TO PATIENTS

Given the recent focus on technological progress in medicine, many of us, myself included, frequently forget an important part of our mission—to be educators and teachers. The increasing pressure we feel to see more patients in the same amount of time makes the task of educating our patients seem even less of a priority. Ironically, new advances in audio, visual, and computer technology permit us to be better educators than ever before.

The general public is very interested in health and wellness. If people are given a chance to learn more about their medical conditions, they will take advantage of the opportunity. Today, computer programs that offer medical information in lay language are both available and affordable. For example, BARD Urology

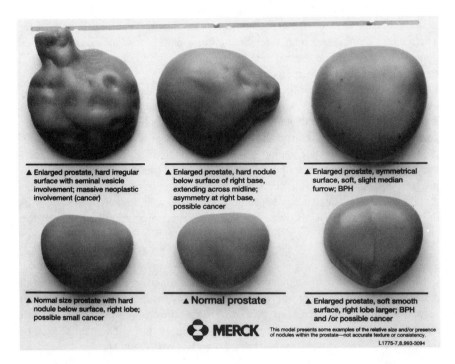

▲ Enlarged prostate, hard irregular surface with seminal vesicle involvement; massive neoplastic involvement (cancer)

▲ Enlarged prostate, hard nodule below surface of right base, extending across midline; asymmetry at right base, possible cancer

▲ Enlarged prostate, symmetrical surface, soft, slight median furrow; BPH

▲ Normal size prostate with hard nodule below surface, right lobe; possible small cancer

▲ Normal prostate

▲ Enlarged prostate, soft smooth surface, right lobe larger; BPH and /or possible cancer

MERCK

This model presents some examples of the relative size and/or presence of nodules within the prostate—not accurate texture or consistency.

L1775-7,8,993-3094

Figure 9-1 Photographs used in educating patients about prostate gland conditions. *Source:* Merck, Inc., Lafayette, Louisiana.

Division* has a program, DISCussion, that gives patients educational material and instructions on every urologic condition and procedure. Patients have access, at the touch of a computer key, to information on every operation, test, and drug commonly used by urologists.

For example, if a male patient calls my office for an infertility evaluation, we send him and his partner a five-page monograph on infertility, together with our usual patient history questionnaire, practice brochure, and newsletter. The monograph explains the importance of semen analysis and the technique to be used for the collection of semen. Offering patients this sort of written information before their office visit significantly reduces the number of questions that have to be answered by me and my staff.

When leaving my office, each patient is given educational information on the tests ordered and the drugs prescribed. This material is placed in a plastic binder

*8195 Industrial Blvd., Covington, GA 30209, 800-526-4455.

with the patient's name written on the front page. In addition, the patient receives a letter that thanks him or her for becoming a patient and includes additional educational material on the patient's condition. This sort of educational material makes patients more informed and more compliant.

Computerized medical information written in lay language is available for nearly every medical practice. My favorite is the Home Medical Advisor*, which is available on CD/ROM or diskette. It reviews medical problems by symptom, body part, and age. It contains information on nearly every drug listed in the *Physician's Desk Reference* and includes a module for patient records that creates a very impressive summary a physician can give his or her patients. The CD/ROM program also contains video segments photographed during operations and examinations. Patients can actually see for themselves what the physician observes during an arthroscopy of the knee or review an actual angiogram before and after angioplasty.

* * *

I have discussed many aspects of the physician and staff relationships with patients, probably the most important aspect of any medical practice. In order to serve our patients, we have to create a comfortable office environment and recruit and train staff who will provide outstanding patient services. The next section of this book will look at ways to develop a first-class office and staff.

NOTES

1. H.B. Beckman, et al., "The Doctor-Patient Relationship and Malpractice: Lessons from Plaintiff Dispositions," *Archives of Internal Medicine* 154 (1994):1365–70.

2. M. LeBoeuf, *How To Win Customers and Keep Them for Life* (New York: Putnam, 1987), 13.

3. J. Weisberg, *Does Anybody Listen, Does Anyone Care? They Will for You!* (Englewood, CO: Medical Group Management Association, 1994).

4. D. St. James, *Writing and Speaking for Excellence: A Practical Guide for Physicians* (Boston: Jones and Bartlett, 1995).

---

*PIXEL Perfect, 10460 South Tropical Trail, Merritt Island, FL 32952, 704-779-0310.

Your Office

10

Create a Mission Statement

I n order to meet patients' needs, physicians must be supported by a smoothly functioning office staff. The office team, including the receptionist, nurses, and office manager, will be key contributors to your practice's health and the perceptions that patients have about your practice.

This part of the book flows directly from Part I. Once you understand what your patients want and expect, you can adjust your office operations accordingly.

First, everyone who is part of the office staff must understand the basic mission of the practice. Drafting a mission statement and ensuring that every employee understands it is a technique that has worked for some of the industrial giants whose names are on everyone's lips. If it can work for Disney, Federal Express, and McDonald's, then it can work for medical practices too.

MISSION NOT IMPOSSIBLE

> Wealth, like happiness, is never attained when sought after directly. It always comes as a by-product of providing a useful service.
>
> Henry Ford

That advice worked well for Henry Ford and will work equally well today for any medical practice. One of the best ways to define the services you provide is to draft a mission statement. It serves as a road map of your practice. It defines your purpose, where you're going, and how you plan to get there.

You may recall that Alice asked the Cheshire Cat, "What road should I take?" "Where are you going?" the cat replied. "I don't know," said Alice. "Then any road will get you there," said the cat. If you don't know where you're going, if you don't know your purpose in having a medical practice, then one road seems just as good as another.

According to Michael LeBoeuf, a mission statement expresses a business's purpose.[1] Why does the business exist in the marketplace? This can be a difficult question to answer. It must be answered, however, because the answer will affect everything the business does and may well determine its success or failure.

For example, American railroads nearly went out of business as the airline industry expanded. Why? The railroads had decided they were in the railroad business. They didn't realize their mission was to move people and things from one place to another. They would have been far better off if they determined that they really were in the transportation business. Similarly, an insurance company doesn't just sell insurance. It sells peace of mind by providing financial security for its clients. Hair salons don't simply sell hair styling and beauty care products, they also offer their clients self-confidence and self-esteem.

Medical practices exist to serve patients, but the way they serve patients varies from one practice to the next. In developing a mission statement, each medical practice needs to ask certain vital questions:

- What is our purpose?
- Who are our patients?
- What do patients expect when they seek medical care from us?

KISS (KEEP IT SHORT AND SIMPLE)

Your mission statement should be so simple and brief—a couple of sentences—that it can easily be recited by any staff member anytime, anywhere. Too many businesses and medical practices have a mission statement that is seen by employees on their first day at work or during orientation and then never seen again.

Look at McDonald's mission statement: "Our pledge is to serve each person hot, tasty, quality food in a fast, timely and courteous manner in a sparkling clean environment." Isn't it a given that when you walk into a McDonald's restaurant you'll find good food, quick service, and a friendly atmosphere? Isn't it true that every McDonald's you enter is spotlessly clean?

Or look at Disney's mission statement: "We create HAPPINESS by providing the finest in family entertainment." Isn't that short enough and clear enough to serve as a guideline for any employee? Isn't it true that whenever you visit a

Disney theme park, you're rewarded with happiness and fun and receive good value for the dollars you spend?

DEVELOPING A MISSION STATEMENT

Here is the mission statement my staff and I developed:

We are committed to providing the best urologic health care possible for our patients. We are committed to excellence. We are committed to persistent and consistent attention to the little details, because they make a big difference.

To develop this mission statement, I first put the issue on our staff meeting agenda and explained in advance why we were going to talk about developing a mission statement. I described at length the function of a mission statement and noted that every successful business or organization has a one- or two-sentence statement identifying its purpose. I told the staff, "I want to develop a mission statement that we can use in this practice. It should be so simple that all of us will remember it. I could write it on my own, but something I write by myself is not necessarily something you will embrace. You're going to have to work with me so we can create this together—so it's *our* mission statement."

Then we sat down at a staff meeting and discussed what our practice was all about. Everyone participated. We set up an easel and on large sheets of paper we wrote down every idea that came to us. We did not reject or criticize anyone's idea. Our goal was to get as many ideas out as possible. We brainstormed like this for about 15 minutes at each of three meetings. In the end, after considering all the ideas, we agreed that excellent service, including paying attention to all the little details, was what distinguished our practice and made it unique.

USING A MISSION STATEMENT

What do you do with a mission statement after you've written it? First, you learn it by heart and ask every staff member to do the same. Next you make sure every patient has an opportunity to see your mission statement. It should be included on your stationery and in your practice brochure. Post it in your reception area, in the exam rooms, and even in the restrooms.

Our mission statement is printed on a banner hung right behind the receptionist. Every patient sees it on every visit during check in and check out.

Whenever we have a problem in our practice, I ask employees, "What's our mission statement?" When they respond, I ask, "Did we give the best health care possible to this patient? Were we committed to excellence? Did we pay attention to the little details?" If the answer to even one of these questions is no, then we discuss how we can correct or make amends for the current problem and how we can prevent similar problems from happening. In most situations we begin the problem-solving process by referring back to the mission statement.

HOW TO GET STARTED

How do you get started creating a mission statement? Ask yourself and your staff, What is the purpose of our practice? What are our patients' expectations regarding their health care experience? The answers to these questions will usually provide you with your mission statement.

According to LeBoeuf, a good mission statement defines the company in terms of the benefits that the customers receive and not just the services the company happens to be selling. Any physician asked to describe his or her practice will say it is a high-quality practice and offers excellent services. However, few physicians are able to list objective indicators to verify that their practice is one where people have positive health care experiences.

You must ask, how does our practice offer services to patients? What are the benefits to the patients? When you can answer those questions, you will have a mission statement that will serve as a guiding light.

Some medical practices define their mission in precise terms. For example, an obstetrics and gynecology practice might have the following mission statement:

> We provide state-of-the-art technology that is not available anywhere else in the community. We deal with infertility and high-risk pregnancies.

An orthopedic practice might use this statement:

> We provide state-of-the-art information and technology for management of sports injuries.

A primary care doctor who plans to shift the emphasis of his or her practice toward wellness and providing home health care might revise the practice mission statement to read thus:

> We are committed to preventive health and a growing appreciation for the home environment as a factor in recovering from illness. We will make every effort to ease the transition from the medical environment to the home in a compassionate and caring fashion.

Physical medicine and rehabilitation specialists might express their mission this way:

> Our purpose is to make patients as independent as possible from day 1 and help them function in society without the need for external support.

An emergency medicine department might adopt this statement:

> It is our goal to provide emergency medical care for everyone as quickly as possible, through our courteous, compassionate, and friendly medical staff. We coordinate follow-up care with the patient's primary care physician and provide it in a timely and appropriate fashion.

FEDERAL EXPRESS: A COMPANY WITH A MISSION

This is the Federal Express mission statement:

> Federal Express is committed to our People-Service-Profit philosophy. We will . . . provide totally reliable, competitively superior, global air-ground transportation of high priority goods and documents. . . . We will be helpful, courteous, and professional to each other and the public. We will strive to have a completely satisfied customer at the end of each transaction.

Isn't it true that whenever you deal with a Federal Express employee you meet someone who is courteous, energetic, and helpful? That has certainly been my experience. That's why millions of people worldwide use Federal Express when they want their letter or parcel to arrive the next day by 10:30 AM.

Last year I actually went to Memphis, Tennessee, where I watched 5,000 Federal Express employees sort two million documents and packages from 1:00 AM to 3:00 AM. I saw employees who were working hard, carrying out tedious, repetitive tasks with enthusiasm and excitement. Their sorting every night is 99.6 percent accurate. According to Kay Carter, the senior manager of employee benefits at Federal Express, its wonderful record all grows out of its mission statement. That statement clearly communicates Federal Express's commitment to people, service, and profit. Every manager, from the chief executive officer, Fred Smith, on down the hierarchy, believes that taking care of the employees is the key to having completely satisfied customers. And if the customers are happy, the profits will take care of themselves.

Wouldn't it be wonderful if we as medical professionals could have two million interactions with our patients and have a patient satisfaction record of 99.6 per-

cent? Well, that's exactly what Federal Express does on a daily basis. In my opinion, there is a great deal health care providers can learn from this giant of customer service. We can begin by emulating the methods used by Federal Express,
and that means we all should create mission statements to serve as the backbones
of our medical practices.

*   *   *

Once you have drafted a mission statement, the next step is to hire, train, and
empower a "dream team" to carry out that mission and offer exceptional service
to all patients. In the next chapter, I will discuss the best way to hire the right
employees for your practice.

NOTE

1. M. LeBoeuf, *Fast Forward* (New York: G.P. Putnam's Sons, 1993).

11

Hire the Dream Team

Walt Disney said, "If you can dream it, you can make it happen." If you hire the right people and properly train and motivate them, then your dream of an ideal practice can be a reality. It is no accident that outstanding practices have outstanding staff.

If you hire the wrong people, your mission will never be achieved. You just can't create "nice people" who want to go the extra mile for each other and for your patients. There are four important factors to consider in promoting a practice: your product, your price, your place, and your people. Of those four, I believe that the last factor, your people, is by far the most important.

Red Auerbach, the president of the Boston Celtics, said, "How you select people is more important than how you manage them once they're on the job. If you start with the right people, you won't have problems later on. If you hire the wrong people, for whatever reason, you're in serious trouble, and all the revolutionary management techniques in the world won't bail you out." This chapter describes techniques you can use to find the dream team for your practice.

READING A RÉSUMÉ

You need to hire the best staff. That sounds simple but it's not easy to do. Few physicians can read between the lines of a prospective employee's résumé or interpret the responses they get from previous employers. Remember, there are professional résumé-writing services that can make anyone appear attractive on paper.

In his book *Team Think*,[1] Don Martin provides useful suggestions for reviewing a résumé:

- Start at the end. Read the résumé from back to front. This way you learn the least flattering information first.
- Question a functional résumé. A résumé that has no dates, no job descriptions, and no qualifications may be attempting to cover up a lapse in employment or a history of job jumping.
- Don't get turned on by a lengthy list of educational attainments. Spending lots of time in school is no substitute for experience.
- Read between the lines. Terms like "involved with" and "knowledge of" often really mean "I haven't done it yet."
- Typos and careless mistakes are red flags. If a person can't take the time to make his or her own résumé perfect, how much attention do you think he or she will pay to the hundreds of details constituting physician office operations?

Hiring the right person for the right position is not like taking a history, performing a physical examination, and developing a treatment strategy. Hiring is "soft science." It requires practice and attention to detail, just like any other skill.

The Employee Management Association*, in Raleigh, North Carolina, found it costs an average of $443 to recruit a new hourly worker and almost $7,000 to recruit a professional or management employee, such as a nurse or office manager. Add in intangible costs and you've got a very expensive process. Consequently, you want to invest the time to do it right the first time.

FINDING THE RIGHT EMPLOYEE

We all like to think of ourselves as winners and to associate with winners. One of the challenges of daily living is to identify the winners and make them part of our team. Ross Perot referred to winners as eagles. When asked how to find the eagles, he said, "You don't find them in a flock because eagles soar alone; you carefully select them one at a time." Let's look at how to identify eagles one at a time.

Finding the right employee begins with writing a detailed job description for the position you are planning to fill. This is essential because the process of writing a job description forces you to rethink and clearly define the staff role. The

---

*4101 Lake Boone Trail, Suite 201, Raleigh, NC 27607, 919-787-5181, fax 919-787-4916.

job description should include a title and a general description of the work to be performed. I suggest that you start by considering what a typical day is like for a person in that position. I have asked all my current employees to write out descriptions of their jobs and have added them to our employee manual. They will serve as guides for the positions should they need to be filled by other employees. (See Exhibits 11-1 to 11-3 for sample job descriptions.)

When you write a job description, in addition to the duties you want the employee to perform, include desirable traits you want the employee to have. Often, when an employer creates a job description, he or she forgets that the personality of the individual being hired is almost as important as the skills and training needed to do the job. In fact, in a doctor's office, personality may be even more important than job skills. I don't believe it makes sense to hire smart people and train them to be nice. It's far easier to hire nice people and train them to be smart.

Here are some skills and personal characteristics I believe are especially important in a medical practice:

- *High self-esteem.* You want employees to like themselves. If they don't, then they surely won't be able to like the patients.
- *Communication skills.* Nothing is more important than that every employee be a good communicator—and a good listener.
- *A caring attitude.* Patients for the most part appreciate the fact that someone genuinely cares about them and demonstrates caring through touch as well as through verbal communication.
- *Self-motivation.* As an employer, you don't want to spend your time acting as a baby sitter. You want to be able to tell an employee to do something one time and know that it will get done.
- *Energy and enthusiasm.* Health care is not an easy profession. It is usually not a nine-to-five job. As Vince Lombardi put it, "If you aren't fired with enthusiasm, then you will be fired with enthusiasm."
- *A sense of humor.* Employees need to take their work, not themselves, seriously. They need to be able to laugh at themselves and create a relaxed, cheerful atmosphere in the office.

WHERE TO LOOK FOR NEW EMPLOYEES

First, consult your network ("Your net worth is directly related to your network," as the saying goes). If you have a substantial network, you can find new employees quite easily. Ask your present employees if there is anyone they would like to recommend. I offer existing employees a finder's fee based on a scale tied to the new employee's salary. This is a lot less expensive than using a headhunting

Exhibit 11-1 Practice Administrator Job Description

1. Be accountable to the physicians.
2. Coordinate all activities of the office.
3. Follow the plans and policies of the office—delegate when appropriate (follow up on delegation).
4. Create an efficient and harmonious working atmosphere.
5. Maintain knowledge of all aspects of the office.

Some Specific Tasks

1. Prepare agenda and conduct meetings with physicians and with department supervisors. Keep minutes of meetings.
2. Maintain personnel and payroll records and overview finances.
3. Prepare budgets, plans, and recommendations for physicians.
4. Ensure compliance with Medicare, PPOs, HMOs, etc.
5. Initiate interviewing, hiring, and dismissals (with specific physician approval).
6. Orient and supervise training of new employees.
7. Oversee maintenance of building; order supplies.
8. Schedule vacations.
9. Meet with attorney, accountant, bank, or others as necessary.
10. Review fee schedule periodically and make recommendations.
11. Oversee expenses, order supplies, and provide for cost control.
12. Act as a mediator between physicians and staff.
13. Help develop job descriptions.
14. Conduct employee performance reviews on a regular basis.
15. Keep office, physicians' liability, and other insurance current.
16. Monitor office staff for compliance with office policy.
17. Handle physicians' travel arrangements.
18. Handle tasks requested by physicians (delegate as indicated).

Source: N.H. Baum, S.L. Aytona, and F.J. Weinstock, *The Urology Office Manual* (Columbus, OH: Anadem Publishing, 1994).

firm or an employment agency. Ask colleagues and their office staff if they know of anyone interested in working in your office. If you have a reputation as someone who treats employees fairly, involves them in the practice, appreciates and rewards them for outstanding service, and pays a fair wage, then you won't have any trouble finding employees for your practice.

If you are looking for a nurse or nursing assistant, think about the nurses at the hospital where you practice and invite the best ones to apply for the job. Or if you need an insurance clerk, look at the business office of the hospital. If you need a transcriptionist, contact the medical records department.

Don't forget, your patients can be a resource. Some of your patients may be able to help you find candidates to interview. If you have a patient who is a bank

Exhibit 11-2 Appointment Secretary Job Description

Goals

"To make the patients feel they want to come here and to continue coming here to receive top quality health care. To increase patient volume and decrease no-shows."

Primary Duties

1. To give top-quality care to the patient.
2. Every morning, review schedule status for the rest of the week and the following two weeks. This will enable you to know what areas need to be worked on and to give input as to what can be done.
3. Make appointments.
4. Confirm appointments.
5. Cancel appointments.
6. Follow up on no-shows and canceled appointments.
7. Distribute daily schedules.
8. Send confirmation cards and recall cards.
9. Send new patient packets.
10. First person to answer phone.
11. Help file charts.
12. Open office, advance computer date, turn on support equipment.

Secondary Duties

Be able to handle check-in and check-out station duties as needed (especially during lunch hours). If you are scheduled for any of the other stations, you are responsible for the duties that go with that station.

Source: N.H. Baum, S.L. Aytona, and F.J. Weinstock, *The Urology Office Manual* (Columbus, OH: Anadem Publishing, 1994).

---

executive or works for an insurance company, you may mention to them that you're looking for a receptionist or a file clerk.

Another tactic is to place an ad in the newspaper. Make the ad brief but exciting. Here are some effective ads for medical practice staff:

> **Receptionist.** 55 WPM typist, with dictaphone, multi-line phones and 1C-key calculator exp. Computer a plus. Dependable team player with strong commitment, self-starter. EOE. Call 555-4444.

> **Medical Billing.** For home health agency. 1 yr exp., ICD-9, computer, medical terminology a must. EOE. Call 555-4444.

Exhibit 11-3 Medical Writer Job Description

1. The medical writer is to correctly document what the physician says during an examination. This includes the proper charting of the examination and the recommendations for treatment.
2. It is the medical writer's responsibility to observe the patient and the physician so as to be able to assist during the exam. The medical writer needs to be aware of the patient's verbal and nonverbal communication when he or she is being instructed by the physician. Often, the patient hesitates to question the physician when he or she does not understand instructions. It may necessitate the writer putting the information down on paper for the patient.
3. The patient's chart is a legal document, and if errors are made, one line is to be drawn through the mistake and the initials of the person making the error are to be written. The correct information can then be documented.
4. The writer is to remain as close to the physician as possible and should limit time away from the physician and his or her next patient. Often, the physician may ask the medical writer to remind him or her of something, have a chart copied, or get specific information. If this happens, it is the writer's responsibility to follow through on what is asked.
5. When in the room with the physician and a surgical instrument or any additional equipment is needed, the medical writer is to phone the tech station, and the tech station personnel or another technician will get it. If surgery is to be scheduled or a referral appointment is needed, the writer should communicate this to the tech station personnel and they are to follow through. The tech station coordinator is responsible for the flow of the back office, and the writer relies on him or her so as to be able to stay with the physician.
6. Each physician has his or her own personality and preferences. It will be the medical writer's responsibility to recognize these differences and abide by them when working with that particular physician. Experience will help the medical writer understand the exact requirements of each examination.

Source: N.H. Baum, S.L. Aytona, and F.J. Weinstock, *The Urology Office Manual* (Columbus, OH: Anadem Publishing, 1994).

CFO Assistant. B.S. in mgmt., organized and a self-starter. Know computer hdwr. & software, WP, Lotus, Excel, graphics. Health care a plus. Must travel. EOE. P.O. Box 321.

You might wind up deciding to consult an employment agency. Send the agency a job description and make sure it does a good screening job. Receiving dozens of names and résumés is not very helpful. Make sure the firm spends some time investigating your practice and your needs. Otherwise, if you say you are looking for a receptionist, you will get a stack of résumés to review and many phone calls saying that the agency has found the perfect match for the position. I also recommend that you put the agency at risk for its placement. For example, you might arrange to get a full refund if the employee doesn't last 90 days in the job.

Ask applicants to send a handwritten letter along with their résumé. Health care involves so much writing that you want to make sure the person you hire has legible handwriting.

I once received a résumé that had an origami frog taped to it. Next to the frog was this note: "This is symbolic of the 'jumping' energy I have and will provide your organization if I get the job." That applicant was hired because her résumé was exciting and creative.

HOW TO CONDUCT A HIRING INTERVIEW

Physicians, for the most part, are very skilled in taking a physical history and doing an interview to diagnose a disease. They are trained for this sort of interviewing and do it dozens of times a day. However, their ability to elicit medical information does not necessarily mean they know how to conduct a hiring interview.

During a hiring interview, you need to ask the right questions and also be an effective listener. Start with a few minutes of general conversation to break the ice. Then ask questions designed to find out about the person you are interviewing, such as these:

- What are your strengths? Your weaknesses?
- Why are you interested in this job?
- Tell me about your previous work experiences?
- What was your best boss like? Your worst boss?
- What do you want to be doing one year from now? Five years from now?
- What books have you read recently?

Try to use open-ended questions that can't be answered yes or no. Open-ended questions usually begin with *what, how, why,* or *where.* Try to use the same questions for each applicant so that you can compare candidates' responses.

Under current laws, there are many questions that are prohibited during hiring interviews. For example, you cannot ask the following:

- How old are you?
- Have you ever been arrested?
- Are you married? Single? Divorced?

- Do you have a disability?
- What is your religion?
- What is your native language?

I prefer to hire people who have healthy life styles. Other things being equal, I would rather not hire a smoker. I am in health care, and I need to surround myself with people who are leading healthy lives. You're not allowed to ask someone whether he or she smokes. However, you are allowed to ask, "What is your opinion about the 'no smoking' ban in this hospital?"

Ask the candidate, "What do you think your previous supervisors will say about you?" If the responses from the candidate and the previous employers do not match, you need to know why. Also ask the candidate if there is anything he or she would like you to know. Be suspicious if the candidate says nothing and prepares to walk out the door.

Be honest about the position. Don't make it sound better than it really is. Tell the candidate about potential problems and sources of stress and anxiety. Every practice has problems, and if you present them upfront, the candidate won't be blindsided later. No one wants to accept a job and discover hidden problems that weren't discussed during the interview process. For example, our insurance clerk left during the replacement of one software billing program by another. This was a difficult time, and our failure to mention potential problems resulted in a very unhappy new insurance clerk. Had we been honest and forthright about what was in store for her, we wouldn't have caused additional troubles for ourselves.

Also, discuss the salary with each promising candidate early in the interview process. It isn't fair to make a candidate wait until the end of the interview process, only to learn that the salary being offered is below what he or she can accept. You will have wasted the candidate's time and yours.

Ask for the names of past supervisors and written permission to contact them (Exhibit 11-4). Then fax the permission form and a cover letter (Exhibit 11-5) to each supervisor and follow up with a phone call. This strategy, in my experience, makes previous supervisors less reluctant to communicate with me, because they are less fearful of any sort of litigation. You can also learn more about a job candidate from previous coworkers than from supervisors or bosses. For example, when hiring an office manager who worked for another practice, ask to speak to the doctors in the practice but also ask to talk to the nurses and the receptionist. They will provide you with more information about what it is really like to work with the candidate.

During a second or third interview, I often ask curveball questions. For example, I ask candidates what they would do if a patient says, "I've got to see the doctor today, it's an emergency." Or what they would do if someone calls and says, "I am a friend of so-and-so," and asks a question about that person's medical

Exhibit 11-4 Letter to Job Candidate Requesting Additional References

---

Dear [name of candidate],

I and my staff enjoyed meeting you at the interview for the position of [name of position]. I am very impressed with your credentials and your previous work experience. I have contacted the references you provided and they all spoke very highly of you.

I have narrowed down our selection to a few and would appreciate the names of the last two supervisors that you worked with and permission to contact them for references. If you would send me their names and telephone numbers and sign the release at the bottom of this page, I or my office manager, [name of office manager], will contact them.

We plan to make our selection for [name of position] in the next five days and will call you shortly with our decision. I appreciate your cooperation in assisting us with the additional references.

Sincerely,

Dr. Neil Baum

_____ Permission is given to contact the references listed below

_____ Name   _____ Telephone number

_____ Name   _____ Telephone number

_____ Signature _____ Date

Source: Reprinted with permission from *Correspondence for the Clinical Practice* by Baum, N., McIntire, K., Osborne, L., Anadem Publishing, Inc., Columbus, OH, Copyright 1996.

Exhibit 11-5 Letter to Previous Supervisor Requesting Information

---

Dear [name of previous supervisor],

I have interviewed [name of interviewee] for a position in my medical practice.

He [she] has provided me with a release to contact you regarding his [her] previous employment.

I am enclosing a copy of the release for your records.

I would like to call you in a few days to discuss his [her] job performance with you and your company.

I look forward to talking with you for just a few minutes.

Sincerely,

Dr. Neil Baum

Source: Reprinted with permission from *Correspondence for the Clinical Practice* by Baum, N., McIntire, K., Osborne, L., Anadem Publishing, Inc., Columbus, OH, Copyright 1996.

records. In other words, I ask difficult questions to which candidates may not know the right answer. I want to see how they think on their feet. Health care is full of crisis situations, and staff have to be able to respond quickly to difficult situations.

I also try to ask questions that require some depth of thought or that are outside the standard interview format so candidates cannot resort to prepared responses. Following are a few examples:

- What would your last boss consider your greatest weakness and why?
- What was one of your greatest faux pas and how did it impact your career?
- If there was one thing you could do over again in your career, what would it be?
- How would you describe yourself in one word and why?

There's one other thing that I usually do, since I'm not an expert in hiring. When I am close to hiring a new employee, I ask someone in the hospital's human resources department to please look over the candidate's résumé and interview him or her on my behalf.

MAKING THE HIRING DECISION

When you are about to hire a new employee, ask yourself these questions:

- Does the candidate have the training, skills, knowledge, and personal traits required for the job?
- Will the candidate be a team player and work well with current staff?
- Would I like to be around this person eight hours a day?

If you can't answer yes to all of these questions, then you need to keep looking. If you can, then you are on your way to putting another member on your dream team.

WELCOMING THE NEW EMPLOYEE INTO THE PRACTICE

You're still not done when a candidate finally accepts the position. You have to help the candidate get acclimated to the practice and his or her job responsibilities. Set up a buddy system so that each new employee is assigned a coworker to help with orientation. The coworker should be in contact with the new employee even before the employee's first day on the job. The two should meet so that the new employee is prepared for the new position. The coworker should be there to greet the new employee, introduce the employee to the rest of the staff, and show the employee the ropes. The worst thing you can do is to talk enthusiastically to the employee about the team spirit that pervades your practice, then let him or her flounder about unaided. If you adopt a sink-or-swim policy, your potential dream team can become your worst nightmare.

Make every effort to make the new employee feel part of the team immediately. Supply a uniform with the employee's name on it before the first day of work, along with business cards imprinted with his or her name. Providing these will help the employee feel a sense of belonging.

I will never forget the day I joined the practice of a group of urologists in Houston. They had a white coat embroidered with my name, along with business cards and stationery printed with my name, and my name on the office door, ready for me on the very first day. They didn't wait until I came to work to order these essentials, and their thoughtfulness made me feel both proud and welcome. Because such a positive impression was made on me, I have tried to have a uniform and business cards ready for every new employee on his or her first day of work.

THE ULTIMATE RESPONSIBILITY RESTS WITH YOU

Many physicians in large and small practices delegate the hiring of employees to the office manager and do not take an active role in the hiring process. Think of yourself as a coach and assume the responsibility for selecting your own dream team.

If you think the responsibility of hiring and firing belongs to someone else, consider the example of Admiral Hyman Rickover, who as head of the U.S. Submarine Command personally reviewed the nomination of every single officer under his command. Or think of Alfred Sloan, Jr., the head of General Motors for more than 40 years, who picked every GM executive down to the master mechanics at the smallest accessory division.[1]

The best advice on hiring I've ever heard was given by the former provost of Stanford University, Frederick Turman, who said, "If you want a track team to win the high jump event, go out and find one athlete who can jump seven feet, not seven people who can jump one foot." Since you aren't building a track team, you need to go find that one best office manager, receptionist, nurse, or technician and then empower that person to provide a positive experience for your patients.

*   *   *

Once you have hired your staff, you must train them so they can offer stellar service. It is necessary to focus our hiring efforts to then set up an environment in which our employees can succeed and not only reach our expectations, but also reach for the stars and provide that stellar experience for our patients. What is required from physicians is vision, attention to details, commitment to open communication between physicians and staff, and trust. In the next two chapters, I'll discuss ways to train and empower your employees.

NOTE

1. D. Martin, *Team Think* (New York: Dutton, 1993), 82.

12

Training New Employees

You can dream, create, design, and build the most wonderful place in the world. But it requires people and training to make the dream a reality.

Walt Disney

Give new employees a copy of your mission statement. They need to be familiar with your practice's vision and purpose, so make every effort to see that they understand the mission statement. Ideally, they should memorize it before they come to work. A good mission statement should be on the tip of the tongue of every staff member, including the physicians!

Patients should never be expected to provide or be a part of the training process for new employees. Patients seldom volunteer to be guinea pigs for a clinical study, and they aren't excited about the thought of offering their office visit as a trial and error session to train a new employee.

You need to explain your practice's attitude toward patients, referring physicians, managed care plans, hospitals, and insurance companies. Make sure the employee understands that patients are doing the practice a favor by coming to the office, not the other way around. Also be sure that every employee understands that managed care plans, other physicians, and payers as well as the patients are customers. Without the support of those additional customers, you would soon be out of business.

In my practice, our philosophy is that the patient is always right (see Exhibit 12-1). We never want to win a battle with a patient only to lose the war—and the

Exhibit 12-1 Dr. Baum's Philosophy of Practice

In our practice we have these three rules:

    Rule #1—The patient is always right.

    Rule #2—If you think the patient is wrong, reread rule #1.

    Rule #3—All other rules are null and void.

---

patient. It is essential that new employees agree with this philosophy. If they do not, they will never be a part of our office team.

Always emphasize the importance of each and every patient. In our office, we have taken the L.L. Bean Company's customer service philosophy and modified it for our medical practice (Exhibit 12-2). We have put it on a prominently placed sign so it is visible to staff and patients alike, as it demonstrates our commitment to our patients and their value to us.

TRAINING EMPLOYEES TO BE PROBLEM SOLVERS

As part of your orientation of the new employee, explain the methods you use to manage patient complaints and problems. Even in the best practices, patients do get upset occasionally and come into conflict with the doctors and the staff. They may disagree with the bill, have difficulty scheduling appointments, or have

---

Exhibit 12-2 What is a PATIENT?

A PATIENT is the most important person ever in this office . . . in person or over the phone. A PATIENT is not dependent on us . . . we are dependent on him.

A PATIENT is not an interruption of our work . . . he is the purpose of it. We are not doing a favor by serving him . . . he is doing us a favor by giving us the opportunity to do so.

A PATIENT is not someone to argue or match wits with. Nobody ever won an argument with a patient.

A PATIENT is a person who brings us his wants. It is our job to handle them profitably to him and ourselves.

Source: Adapted with permission from L.L. Bean, Freeport, Maine.

---

problems with their records or lab reports. That means employees have to be, first and foremost, problem solvers. They must be empathetic, good listeners, and able to follow through. If an employee says to a patient, "I will get back to you on Wednesday" or "I will schedule the appointment with the oncologist next week," the employee must do exactly what he or she promised. Or if there is some problem, the employee must call the patient back and explain the new situation.

Patients complain most often about the long periods of time they spend waiting to be seen by physicians. Their second most common complaint is that physicians fail to return their calls in a timely fashion. None of us like the typical response of the phone company: "We'll be by to repair your phone sometime between 9:00 AM and 4:30 PM. It should be obvious that patients don't want to wait endlessly by the phone for their physicians to call back with test results or lab reports.

All your employees need to be familiar with your practice and all the services it offers. They need to know the background and training of the physicians and how to tell new patients the best way to reach the practice by car or bus. If a patient calls and asks about a procedure or test that you perform, the staff need to understand basic information about that procedure. That's why effective staff meetings are necessary—to make sure the staff are properly educated about your services and office procedures.

In the past, most patients didn't care about the cost of their health care since insurance companies paid all or nearly all of each fee. Today, patients who shop for the best price are far more common. You need to have your staff explain your policy on providing costs of procedures over the telephone when patients ask about this. Years ago we asked callers to make an appointment to see the doctor, and then costs would be discussed. Today, patients are asking for the costs of their medical care upfront, and a policy of not discussing fees will lose patients, especially those valuable fee-for-service patients. Also, it is very important for every employee to understand what patient information can and cannot be discussed over the phone to referring physicians, insurance companies, hospitals, Workers' Compensation, and attorneys. For example, patient information pertinent to a legal case cannot be given to an attorney unless a release of information form has been signed by the patient. Also, lab reports for a child of legal age, which differs in various states, cannot be given to the parents without the child's consent.

Every practice should have a policy manual, and every new employee should receive a copy before starting work. This will allow the new employee to become familiar with his or her job and with office routines as soon as possible.

EMPLOYEE ORIENTATION

The best programs have an orientation period during which new employees work together with an experienced member of your team when dealing with patients. It is not a good idea to allow brand-new employees to answer the phone unless you've trained them in proper telephone etiquette. Similarly, when you set standards for electronic billing, employees must follow those standards. Otherwise you will have many returned claims, which means the insurance company will hold your money for longer periods of time.

International Marketing Systems (IMS)* specializes in helping large companies develop a customer service corporate culture in line with their external marketing mission. This means IMS has a great deal of experience in training and orienting new employees. Lamar Berry, IMS chairperson and CEO, believes that when new employees come on board, the most important thing is for them to internalize the corporate culture. "They need to start understanding in an experiential way what the mission and vision of the organization is, so they have a realistic emotional buy-in to the long-term success of the company."

> From my viewpoint, the health care industry has gone through a paradigm shift over the last decade, in a way that is similar to other industries. They have shifted from a "supply" mindset to a "service" mindset. The leaders of the health care industry are now recognizing that the competitive forces and governmental forces are all leading to a much greater emphasis on service in health care than ever before. This means the patient's perception of customer service and attention to detail will be at the root of the ongoing success of the medical practice.

IMS has worked with Disney University in Orlando, the custodian of the corporate culture for Disney World. According to Berry,

> When an individual is hired at Disney World the first training they get is not on how to run the Monorail, or how to play a particular functional role as a member of the Indiana Jones attraction. The first training they receive is on the corporate culture and the mission of supplying guest relations. For two days they listen to lectures and stories about the values and spirit and history of the organization. They learn about some of the influential founding members of the organization and what made those people tick.

Of course, a medical office is a much smaller organization than Disney World and probably won't be able to set up a program that trains large groups of employees. However, the same basic principle—that it is essential to educate new employees about the culture and philosophy of the organization they have joined—applies just as much to small organizations as to large ones.

---

*3850 North Causeway, Suite 210, Metairie, LA 70002, 504-831-9400.

How can a medical practice orient new employees? A large group practice, with 100 or more employees, probably has enough turnover so that it can schedule formal orientation sessions every month or two. A smaller office can orient new employees by encouraging current staff to reach out and offer a helping hand.

Every practice can set up a mentorship or shadow program when someone first comes on board. "You have one of the older veterans team up with the new employee," Berry explains. "The new person shadows the older employee and listens to him talk about the company and its history and philosophy for three or four days. This team approach tells them that the practice wants them to understand the vision and the mission of this organization, what we're trying to achieve here—that it is really important to us."

Another suggestion from Berry: invite current staff to offer ideas on how to improve the orientation of new employees. If possible, take the whole office on a retreat for a half day and ask the staff what they would have liked when they first came on the job. Or else set up a small task force and invite it to plan the orientation process.

KINKO'S: TRAINING EMPLOYEES IN A SERVICE INDUSTRY

Kinko's is one of the best-known companies in the fast-paced field of printing and copying. They understand that the training of new employees plays a key role in any service industry. "In this day and age, we don't like to take chances with our business if we can avoid it," says Kathy Ruckstuhl, Regional Trainer for Southeast Kinko's Gulf States' Region.* "You know, someone may go to a restaurant a thousand times and get wonderful service and great food—then one time they get poor service and they don't go back to that restaurant. The same principle applies to other service businesses, too."

All new employees of Kinko's go through a four-day program called New Coworker Orientation. It includes two days of classroom training and two days of in-store training. "We don't put coworkers in a position where they will be overwhelmed and stressed, where our customers will receive subpar service, because they have a brand-new person on the floor. We have a high-stress business, so if you put someone in there who isn't trained and can't feel part of a team, then that person is very ineffective and morale in the store goes down."

The same principles apply in a medical office, Ruckstuhl says.

All customers in this day and age are looking for name recognition. They want personal service. They want to know that they are not just a

---

*400 North Carrollton Avenue, Suite 100, New Orleans, LA 70119.

number. It seems as if today everybody feels that there are so many people around that you may just get lost in the shuffle.

I would think when you're going to a physician it's even more important to be able to immediately establish that personal relationship. I come from a family of doctors, so I have a little background in the medical field. Patients want to feel that they're dealing with knowledgeable people who can answer their questions, that they are getting prompt and friendly service at a reasonable price.

Ruckstuhl's advice for physicians who are setting up a training program:

- Define your business philosophy.
- Have clearly stated expectations.
- Set up a mentor program in which current staff take new employees under their wing.

Anytime you want to have an effective training program, you must have an outline for the training. Employees need a precise definition of the expected work. "You can't just say to someone, 'You're going to sit at the desk and be the receptionist and we'll teach you things as they come up.' They need to know what specific elements are essential in order for them to be able to do their job well."

Kinko's has audits for new coworkers. Thirty, 60, and 80 days after being hired, their progress is checked. "We can see how our training is going and how employees are doing. I think in the medical field you could do the same thing, where you would check how an employee answers the phone or speaks to a patient in the reception area. One problem in too many training programs is the lack of follow-up."

CONTINUING EDUCATION

A physician's education is never complete. The skills that physicians need to provide high-quality health care are constantly evolving. Physicians must continue to take postgraduate courses, read journals, and attend regular meetings and seminars as long as they practice medicine. The same is true of staff. They, too, need to continually upgrade their skills and training. Your staff cannot be maximally effective if they are using outdated methods, technology, and skills. So in addition to orienting and training new employees, encourage staff to attend seminars and training programs on a continuing basis. I pay for all seminars and educational programs in which my employees participate. My rule is that if they pass the course, I pay for it. This obviates the risk of paying for a course that the employee quits after a few sessions. In fact, it gives employees a real incentive to pass.

Encourage staff to read and listen to tapes on communication, management, telephone skills, and motivation. We have a tape library in our office, and I provide educational tapes for all the staff. Often I will ask someone to summarize an interesting tape at a staff meeting.

Following are the titles of several tapes that we have found particularly useful:

- *How To Win Customers for Life* by Dr. Michael LeBoeuf*. This tape describes how to provide excellent customer service.
- *Seven Habits of Highly Effective People* by Stephen Covey*. The focus is on making life-style changes to improve your personal and professional life.
- *Raving Fans* by Ken Blanchard*. This is another tape on providing knock-your-socks-off service.
- *Marketing Where Your Competitor Is Not* by TomKat Productions†. This tape helps you identify your competition and focus on your strengths and weaknesses. It emphasizes Sam Walton's approach: "He didn't get where he did by being on the same street corner as everyone else. He went where the competition wasn't."

CROSS-TRAINING

Any long-term training program for a medical practice should include some efforts at cross-training (that is, training staff to do more than one job). If your practice is relatively small, the absence of one or two people because of vacation, illness, or family emergencies could cause operations to come to a grinding halt. One way to limit the risk is to have employees periodically assume other employees' roles while the other employees are there to assist and advise them.

For example, receptionists and appointment clerks should learn to fill out the super bill and post the bills and checks. The business manager should be able to put patients into the exam rooms or chaperon a male physician when he sees a female patient. If staff usually deal with patients on the front end, there's no reason they can't be cross-trained to deal with patients' financial concerns or their insurance questions. Similarly, employees who usually work on billing can be trained to deal with medical records.

---

*Available from Nightengale Conant, 7300 North Lehigh Ave., Chicago, IL 60648, 800-323-5552.

†Available from Success, P.O. Box 2535, Kearneysville, WV 25430.

You can never teach a pig to sing. It wastes your time and it annoys the pig. But what you can do is help your staff provide outstanding customer service through careful attention to the training of new employees. The employee pool that you have available is the same as that in the practice across the street, across town, or even in Rochester, Minnesota, at the Mayo Clinic. The difference in the service your staff provides can be attributed to the training they receive—beginning on their first day at work. Sam Walton said, "Communicate everything you can to your associates. The more they know, the more they care. Once they care, there is no stopping them." The same applies to *your* employees. If you select the right employees and then train them well, there's no stopping them when it comes to providing quality service.

*   *   *

In addition to training employees to deal with a wide variety of situations, it is even more important to empower them to always put the patient's needs first. In the next chapter, I will discuss how to create an exceptional experience for your patients by empowering your employees.

13

The Power of Empowerment

In the past, most physicians ran their offices by controlling the staff themselves. Today, however, office management is very complicated and time consuming. Few physicians have a thorough understanding of the business, management, and legal aspects of a medical practice. Consequently, most physicians have learned to delegate many of the responsibilities of running the office. The most successful have learned to empower their employees to take control and assume responsibility for the nonclinical decisions made in the practice. This chapter discusses the importance of empowering your staff and offers suggestions on how to help your staff perform nonclinical activities.

WHY EMPOWERMENT IS EFFECTIVE

Empowerment means giving employees the training and authority they need to manage their own jobs. What does empowerment demonstrate to your employees? That you trust their judgment and abilities. By empowering employees—by treating them with honesty, openness, and integrity and by training them and supporting them—you bring out the best in them.

This is my philosophy: I didn't go to medical school to learn how to buy a fax machine or photocopier, select office stationery, or evaluate the merits of a software program. As a physician, I am most effective when eyeball to eyeball with a patient, not enmeshed in office operations. Operational responsibilities are best left to my staff and I make every effort to empower my staff to make all nonmedical decisions. If staff come to me with questions or problems, I ask them what ideas or solutions they would suggest for those problems before I give them my opinion. I want to encourage my staff to think on their own and to make every effort to solve the problems themselves. When employees know that you trust them to make decisions and that office procedures are in their hands, they work harder to accomplish what is expected of them and to reach the practice goals and objectives. Furthermore, empowered employees are more creative than "do as you're told" employees.

Empowerment also gives employees a sense of ownership. I have given my staff the authority to use their best judgment on behalf of the patient at all times. Nordstrom's, the well-known West Coast department store, has a one-sentence policy manual: "Use your best judgment at all times to make the customer's experience a positive one . . . all other policies are null and void." Although my practice has an extensive employee manual, the best advice I give my staff is to think of the patient first. If they think of the patient first and make a mistake, there will be no repercussions. As a result, they are motivated to try new ideas and reach beyond their job description. Employees who fear punishment for making mistakes will take the safe path. A practice that relies on punishment and fear will have low morale and a high turnover rate.

When you give employees the freedom to make responsible decisions, you're letting them know that you care about their working conditions too. I believe it is appropriate to ask empowered employees what changes in the workplace they would like to see. After you hear their suggestions, you should implement those you believe will lead to more patients having a positive experience. For example, my employees wanted to see patients early in the morning after a survey indicated that patients favored having early access to the practice. That required me to change my operating schedule on the days that we planned to see patients in the morning. After a trial period, we found that it worked out best for the patients and really didn't alter the surgery schedule significantly. The employees were following our basic philosophy and were acting in the best interests of the patients. This is what we encourage, and it has meant that our practice is continuously progressing. It's true that if you accept ripe, you'll soon get rotten. But if you are green, you are growing. Empowering your staff makes you green and growing.

EMPOWERMENT IN HEALTH CARE

If people are going to spend large amounts of money with you and entrust their health care to you, you want to make them think, "Wow, am I glad I am here!" It's very important that people leave with the feeling that they got their money's worth, that they got more than they were expecting.

One advantage of empowerment is that your employees will not feel they are just robots doing mindless work. They will tend to embrace the responsibility you have given them. Empowered employees are likely to go the extra mile and exceed patients' expectations. They are likely to feel a part of the team and take ownership in the practice. They are less likely to be absent from work and less likely to leave and seek employment elsewhere (low employee turnover means lower overall costs).

Although managed care plans are proliferating in most metropolitan communities, at least 15 percent of the population is likely to remain in fee-for-service care. Fee-for-service patients will have very high expectations regarding the quality of the services they receive from their physician. It is unlikely that they will select or remain with a doctor who has a rude telephone receptionist, keeps patients waiting more than 30 minutes before being seen, doesn't answer patients' questions about their health care, and doesn't call back in a timely fashion. Fee-for-service patients will demand "Cadillac care" and will quickly leave any practice that doesn't provide exceptional service.

YOUR ATTITUDE DETERMINES YOUR PRACTICE'S ALTITUDE

It's very important for you to have a positive attitude. Unless you feel excited and enthusiastic and unless you are growing and setting goals for yourself and sharing information about this with your employees, how can you expect them to do these things?

According to an old adage that pertains to rearing children, "If you set the example, you don't have to worry about the rule." That adage also applies to acting as a role model in a medical practice. If you set an example of courtesy and respect for patients and are highly motivated yourself, you will find your staff will act the same way.

You can promote a positive mental attitude by surrounding your employees with motivational statements such as "It is not your aptitude but your attitude that determines your altitude" or "Attitudes are contagious. Is yours worth catching?"

In our practice, employees are given golden attitude pins* to be worn as part of their uniform. These pins serve as a reminder that every employee is expected to enter the office each day with a golden attitude. When an employee goes the extra mile for a patient, a referring physician, a fellow staff member, a hospital, or even an insurance company, he or she is given an additional golden attitude pin. We call these ABCD awards (above and beyond the call of duty awards). When an employee accumulates five golden attitude pins, then I send the employee and

---

*Available from 4817 Running Fox Drive, Shepherdsville, KY 40165.

spouse or significant other out for an elegant dinner or an overnight cruise on one of the Mississippi riverboats.

Another recognition system, used by Sunrise Medical, Inc., in Torrance, California, thanks employees who exceed customers' expectations by sending them an exceed-o-gram. An exceed-o-gram can be sent to any employee by another employee. In our practice, we use what we call an extra-mile-o-gram for the same purpose.

Napoleon said, "If I had enough ribbon, I could conquer the world." Sometimes all it takes is a few pins and some ribbon to say thank you to employees for a job well done.

EMPOWERED STAFF MAKE YOUR PRACTICE MORE EFFICIENT

If you are willing to invest the time to select, train, and reward a good team of employees, you will have more time to devote to providing medical care. Today more than ever before, physicians have to do what they do best—diagnose and treat diseases. They shouldn't spend their valuable time doing the things that their staff can do or that they can outsource to others at a reasonable price or fee.

I like to think I have an efficient practice. If it is efficient, the reason is that we organize and prioritize. Of course, we have problems and crises and make mistakes. However, we are all motivated to find solutions to problems and to make every effort not to repeat mistakes. We welcome constructive criticism and are constantly surveying patients about their experience with the practice. If we identify any problems in the practice, we discuss them during staff meetings and find ways to solve them. We interpret problems as stepping stones, not stumbling blocks.

When we offer a new procedure, we discuss it first at staff meetings, so if a patient calls and asks, "What's the new operation I heard Doctor Baum does for incontinence?" the nurses are able to give an explanation and answer questions on the phone. When a patient complains about an excessive delay in the office and appears to be very upset, the staff member hearing the complaint is empowered to make an on-the-spot decision not to charge the patient. I believe avoiding the potential damage that can occur when a patient talks negatively about his or her experience is worth losing the $35 office fee. Note also that a write-off policy such as ours will need to be used only rarely. (At least we have found this to be the case.)

I want my staff to be empowered to make immediate decisions, because the quicker problems are solved, the more patients appreciate it. For example, one patient complained to the nurse that the delay in the office resulted in her receiving a parking ticket. On the spot, without asking the office manager, the nurse gave the patient $15 from petty cash to pay the fine. When the nurse reported to me what had happened at the end of the day, I said, "Great, you did the right thing." The patient wrote us a nice note of appreciation, and I am sure she told her family and friends about our response to her problem. I doubt the reaction would have been the same if the nurse had contacted me at the end of the day or the next staffing meeting and we sent the patient a check days or weeks later. The "wow" occurs when you manage the moments of truth.

There are some practical steps you can take to empower your employees. Remember that no one has the title Chief of Patient Services. Improving the quality of patient services is everyone's job. Just imagine if you were a patient. What would make you feel satisfied with your health care experience? What would be the minimum you would expect and accept? And what would make you have a stellar experience that would lead you to come back again and also go out and tell others about that experience? The answers to these questions will give your staff some examples to illustrate what it takes to be an empowered staff focused on patients and their experience with your practice

A farmer bought a piece of rocky, wasted land and with hard work converted it into acres of grain, fruit, and vegetables. One day the town minister visited the farmer. He praised the farmer for creating such a productive farm but remarked that the farmer probably couldn't have done it without the help of the Lord. The farmer agreed that the Lord did have a lot to do with his success but commented, "You should have seen it when the Lord had it all by Himself." The same holds true for a medical practice. There are few physicians that can do it all themselves. We need the assistance of a well-trained and highly motivated staff. The best advice is to hire the best, pay and train them well, and then empower them to go the extra mile and exceed patients' expectations.

*   *   *

In the next chapter, I will look at how to create and use an office manual so that your staff has a broad view of the practice and its philosophy, and knows and understands the standard procedures for most situations.

14

Office Manuals Are Mandatory

E mployees will be ignorant of your dress code and how you want them to greet patients unless you define your expectations in writing in a policy manual. A detailed office manual is essential, because every medical practice has a large variety of work-related processes that must be done correctly. No one can remember all the details if they are not written down. This chapter discusses the importance of an office manual and how to create one for your practice.

In most organizations, new employees get a brief orientation, receive a policy manual, and are told to go to work. They are expected to be up to speed in a short time. However, employees are frequently unable to master their jobs without help. It is not that they don't want to work or succeed. They are simply unclear about what is expected of them. The policy manual gets placed on a shelf or in a drawer and never again sees the light of day. The expense of training skyrockets, the new employees get discouraged, and production deteriorates. There is a loss of morale in the practice, and the new employees may even quit because they cannot meet the expectations of the existing staff and the physicians. Then this painful, expensive cycle of training new employees repeats itself.

The difficulties of orienting new employees can be avoided or reduced if the practice has an office manual that deals with many of the problems and concerns that every new employee has when he or she joins a practice. A good office manual contains a comprehensive description of the practice and its philosophy, a welcome to new employees and an outline of their training, a detailed synopsis of financial systems, job descriptions, standard office procedures, and employment policies. It also contains the office dress code, a section on infection control, definitions of key professional terms employees need to know, and a phone directory.

Having all this information gathered together in one place saves time and money. It keeps all necessary details at employees' fingertips and ensures that routine but essential administrative tasks are not forgotten. It serves as a ready reference manual for the practice and will be one of the most useful items for the staff (veteran employees as well as new ones).

A good office manual allows new employees to understand what is expected of them from their first day on the job. New employees can come up to speed very quickly when they understand what to do, when to do it, and, most important of all, how to do it. The guesswork and uncertainty have been removed or minimized.

For example, the office manual should include a checklist of steps to take when closing the office. It might look something like this:

- There should never be an employee alone in the office. When closing, the last two employees should leave the office together.
- All patients' charts should be collected and placed in the appropriate place in the business office or on the nurse's desk.
- Do not turn off the modem.
- Backup computer tapes should be removed each night by the designated person and stored off-site.
- Use call forwarding to transfer incoming calls to the answering service.
- Do a test check of the answering system by calling the office to see that the answering service is now accepting calls from the practice.
- Make sure all doors are securely locked and all lights are off.
- Check that all equipment is turned off, including the radio, copy machine, and coffeepot.
- The last person to leave the building turns on the alarm system. Should you have any questions about the alarm, call the burglar alarm company at 777-4949.

With a list like this one, even if the person closing the office is relatively new to the job, everything important will get done.

ADVANTAGES OF HAVING A MANUAL

An office manual can facilitate the training of new employees. For instance, the section on ordering will include a complete inventory list and a directory of suppliers. You or the office manager can give new employees a list of needed supplies and train them in the standard way to place an order. This will allow new employees to be effective in ordering supplies from the very start.

An office manual also provides legal protection in a variety of situations. For example, the section on staff policies sets out clear expectations for employees and defines the process that will be followed when there is a problem with an employee: a formal warning, a probationary period, then dismissal if the problem continues. You need to set the ground rules for termination in writing. If somebody doesn't meet the standards, you should document his or her poor performance and your grounds for dismissal. When job requirements and policies are clearly defined in a manual and the policies are followed precisely, the practice is protected against frivolous lawsuits relating to wrongful termination of employment.

Having a manual also facilitates cross-training, which allows an employee to fill in for another employee in case of an absence or a work overload in one area or department. Every job in the practice is defined, described, and delegated. If someone is out of the office and another employee has to fill in, he or she can turn to the manual for an outline of the work that needs to be done. Having the manual available saves a great deal of time in setting priorities and dealing with difficult situations.

Many practices try to cross-train employees systematically so they can fill in for each other during busy periods or emergencies. Having a manual available aids employees in learning the nuts and bolts of other employees' jobs.

Every employee is out of his or her comfort zone when asked to perform a new role. Even though it is the same office, the employee is in unfamiliar surroundings, and this results in anxiety and often frustration. Much of the tension can be relieved if the employee can refer to a manual where all of the expectations for and functions of each position are clearly defined and described. You know you have an excellent manual when one employee can pick up the manual and assume a new job with no loss in productivity.

Many physicians use an office manual to structure staff meetings. The method is to discuss one chapter of the manual at each meeting. This focuses the discussion and allows the manual to be reviewed in small digestible bites.

What problems do offices face when they do not have a detailed manual? Karla Gale, managing editor at Anadem Publishing*, which specializes in medical office manuals, says, "They place both time and money at risk. It takes much more time to do things if you don't have a manual written down. If a practice is not well organized, it can lose a lot of money."

---

*3620 North High Street, Suite 310, Columbus, OH 43214, 614-262-2539.

For example, a manual that clearly explains the practice's vacation policy is likely to reduce absenteeism. A manual that discusses vendor selection and management of inventory will help reduce inventory and overhead expenses. Will Kuhlmann, President of Anadem, adds another example:

> A consultant told us about a surgery practice that was losing tens of thousands of dollars each year because they weren't monitoring their accounts receivable properly. It's so easy for physicians, particularly those who are making a good income and don't want to be bothered with details, to let these things slide. That's why you need a policy in writing, so all the administrative details are done correctly.

A TURNKEY OFFICE MANUAL

Anadem has worked with physicians and other health care professionals to develop a turnkey office manual, available as a notebook and computer disc, at a cost of $145 per practice. Specialized versions are available for family practice, surgery, dermatology, ophthalmology, urology, dentistry, and physical therapy.

Each manual is designed for easy customizing. For example, each practice would probably want to add details relating to its hours, the scheduling of vacation time, specific software systems, the vendors it uses, and its financial policies.

Anadem suggests that all the employees should participate in the process of reviewing and adapting the manual to fit specific practice needs. Staff typically have a thorough knowledge of the details of daily operations. In addition, participation gives them a sense of ownership in the project. Anadem recommends that all staff review the changes that have been made. Then a final version can be printed and a copy given to each staff member.

It is also important to set up a process to review the whole manual thoroughly at least once a year. Forms staff can use to suggest needed changes are available as part of the initial package. In addition, every time an issue is discussed at a staff meeting, someone should be responsible for making needed changes to the manual.

According to Kuhlmann,

> It seems as if every practice recognizes that they need an office manual, but the project tends to get put on the back burner. We tried to make our system easy to implement and adapt for a specific practice. We believe this ease of installation will overcome what we consider the major hurdle in the way of office organization. People tend to feel that it's just too hard to do. Well, this computer model is easy to do.

Anadem is currently developing an additional section of the manual on managed care, including patient evaluation forms and a checklist of issues to consider when negotiating a managed care contract. This section will be available as an addition to each of the standard manuals and will be updated regularly to meet managerial needs in this quickly changing field.

*   *   *

A manual by itself is only a stack of printed paper. One way to generate an atmosphere of positive expectations and patient service is to constantly offer positive reinforcement when your staff performs according to the manual or, better yet, goes beyond the written job description in the manual. In the next chapter, I will discuss some of the ways positive reinforcement for the staff can be built into every aspect of your medical practice.

15

For Positive Results, Use Positive Reinforcement

E ven if you find good employees and train them well, you will still need to continually monitor how your employees are doing. Monitoring is not something you can do just once a year when it's time for a salary review. Periodic, frequent performance reviews are necessary.

The rule I follow is to "inspect what you expect." That means, if you say to an employee, "I expect that all claims will be accurate," and in fact last month 10 claims were returned because of mistakes, someone needs to deal with the issue. That someone is not necessarily you; perhaps the best person would be the office manager. In any case, it is essential to have benchmarks—targets that you want employees to hit—then measure how well they succeed and reward them appropriately.

If mission statements and policy manuals are the road maps for your practice, then motivational tools are the grease and oil that keep your practice running. This chapter describes the advantages of using motivational techniques to encourage your staff to provide exceptional patient services and offers practical suggestions that you can easily implement.

THE CARROT VERSUS THE STICK

Guess what? People don't always do what you ask them to do. You can tell people what to do. You can show them how to do it. You can give them examples, write out detailed instructions in job descriptions, and even create user-friendly policy manuals. You can hold staff meetings and surround your staff with motivational sayings. You can have them read books and listen to tapes on excellence and quality, but these techniques seldom work by themselves. All of them need to be accompanied by positive reinforcement.

What is your typical response when an employee makes a mistake? Perhaps you tell the employee what to do again, only this time with more emphasis. If so, you may find that you can repeat yourself over and over without altering the level of performance. So then what do you do? Perhaps you try new ways of telling the employee what to do, only to find that they don't work either. The only change is a decrease in the efficiency, productivity, and morale of the entire office staff.

One study by the Public Agenda Forum on the motivation of nonmanagement workers found that 50 percent of employees do just enough work to keep their jobs. That means that half the work force merely goes through the motions every day. How can you break this pattern? How can you motivate every person on your staff to stretch and extend him- or herself and not just do enough to get by?

I've found that the best way to accomplish this goal is through the use of positive reinforcement. In most work environments negative reinforcement—that is, punishment—is the method used to keep employees in line. Think of typical comments to employees: "If you can't be here on time, we will have to find another person for your position." "If you can't get the patient properly scheduled for hospital admission, you will have to look for another job." Such remarks, besides being distressing to deliver and even more painful to hear, are not very effective. Often an employee will respond to negative reinforcement by doing the minimum amount of work necessary to keep the physician or office manager temporarily off his or her back.

Positive reinforcement, on the other hand, produces long-lasting changes in behavior and extraordinary effort on the part of employees. It can energize employees to go the extra mile. Here in New Orleans we use the term *lagniappe*— "something extra." Positive reinforcement causes employees to give that little something extra.

Every medical practice needs to have a motivated staff to help make operations run smoothly. You can be a world-class physician, have impeccable credentials, and develop a marketing program that generates hundreds of calls, but if your staff isn't motivated to answer calls with an enthusiastic voice and make the callers feel excited about coming to your practice, everything, including your wonderful clinical skills and all your marketing efforts, will be wasted. On the other hand, give your staff a reason to be emotionally invested in your practice's success and you'll see them go to surprising lengths for the good of the practice.

Aubrey Daniels, a training and management expert, refers to this sort of extra effort as "discretionary effort."[1] It's the level of effort that staff can give if they want to—a level beyond what is expected, demanded, or paid for. Physicians and office managers need to create an atmosphere in which the rest of the staff wants to function at this level all day and every day. Every medical practice is capable of getting staff to make an extraordinary effort, but it does require additional planning and attention on the part of the physicians and office manager.

THE MAGIC OF GOING THE EXTRA MILE

Going the extra mile ensures that your patients will have a positive experience when they visit your practice. It will make them eager to tell their family and friends about you and your staff and will generate invaluable word-of-mouth marketing. A truly outstanding practice has staff that make whatever effort is necessary to exceed patients' expectations.

Why do employees resist changing their behavior toward patients? The truth is that most employees don't resist change as long as they feel there is some benefit in modifying their behavior. According to Daniels,

> New behaviors require extra effort to learn, result in increased mistakes during the learning process, initially cause the performers to get behind in their other work, and create stress because people fear they won't be able to learn or perform as well under new conditions. In order to produce changes in behavior we need to be less concerned with the initial results and more concerned with applying positive reinforcement.[2]

Of course, there is still a place for negative reinforcement in managing a medical office. When employees fail to meet minimum standards and their performance affects others, then prodding and punishment are in order. However, negative reinforcement by itself is never enough to sustain a high level of performance. Furthermore, negative reinforcement is tough not only on staff but also on doctors and office managers. The practice of medicine is filled with stress, and physicians don't need the added anxiety of monitoring and correcting their staff. If work only means meeting deadlines and trying to make patients, doctors, hospitals, insurers, and managed care plans happy, then coming to work will never be something employees look forward to. Working around people who just want to punch the clock and do only enough to get by is not very much fun for doctors or office managers.

George Halas, the owner and coach of the Chicago Bears, said, "It's only work if you'd rather be doing something else." In other words, when you're doing work you really enjoy, it becomes fun. When positive reinforcement is added to the workplace environment, staff are excited and enthusiastic about their work, pa-

tients feel better about the services they receive, and the doctor has a more rewarding and gratifying experience practicing medicine.

WHY POSITIVE REINFORCEMENT IS SO EFFECTIVE

It would be nice if every employee was a self-starter and didn't need a pat on
the back. But in reality few employees, including physicians, can sustain a commitment to go the extra mile without some positive reinforcement.

Physicians routinely receive positive reinforcement nearly every day. Our patients tell us how wonderful we are, how we saved their life or eased their suffering, and how much they appreciate what we have done for them. Perhaps this
abundance of positive reinforcement is one reason why so many of us elected to
become physicians.

In order to bring out the best in staff, it is necessary to give them positive
feedback regularly. Too often poor performers get the largest share of our attention. Giving them instructions and advice on how to improve their performance
takes up substantial time and energy. Consequently, we leave the good performers
on autopilot, hoping that their work will continue to improve and that their behavior will have a positive effect on the other staff members.

I believe we need to shift our focus and concentrate on the average and outstanding performers as much as or even more than we concentrate on the poor
performers. If we lavish praise and attention on the good performers, then me-
diocre performers will try to rise to a higher level. When employees are asked
whether they prefer positive or negative reinforcement, they universally respond
that they appreciate and work better in an environment that rewards desired behavior.

STRATEGIES FOR PROVIDING POSITIVE REINFORCEMENT

As part of our scientific training, we all learned that positive reinforcement
given immediately after a desired action has more impact than reinforcement
delayed for weeks or months.

If an employee does something positive and a letter or memo describing the
action goes to the office manager and then is filed away to be discussed at the
next annual performance review, the employee will not feel a very strong desire
to repeat the action. You can't give an employee praise or positive feedback once
a year and expect that it will be enough motivation to change the employee's
behavior.

When an employee does something that deserves verbal recognition or other
reward, the sooner the reward is given, the more likely it is the behavior will be

repeated. As mentioned previously, in my practice we use what we call an extra-mile-o-gram (Figure 15-1) whenever an employee does something beyond the call of duty. Any employee can give an extra-mile-o-gram to another employee— or even to the doctor.

I find that employees light up and get excited when they are given a card with a single sentence recognizing the good work they have just done. It is a myth that employees only work for money. Psychic pay is just as important as, and sometimes more important than, monetary pay.

SOCIAL REINFORCEMENT AND TANGIBLE REINFORCEMENT

There are two main types of positive reinforcement: social reinforcement and tangible reinforcement. Social reinforcement can be provided simply by saying, "Good job," "Thank you," or "I appreciate your going the extra mile for the patient." It can also be provided by giving a note, a smile, or a pat on the back to an employee. All of these rewards and forms of recognition are inexpensive and available to every practice, and employees seldom tire of receiving them.

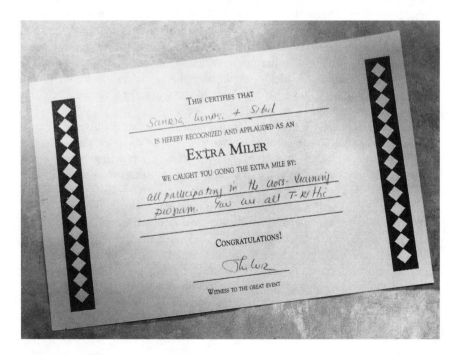

Figure 15-1 Sample extra-mile-o-gram.

Tangible reinforcement is provided by giving rewards that have a dollar value. In my opinion, such rewards only serve as a backup and are not a substitute for social reinforcers. However, they are important because they are a tangible expression of your gratitude and they also add variety. You cannot use one method and expect it to work all of the time. If you just say, "Thank you, thank you," all day long, that can soon become ineffective. And you can't offer monetary rewards continually, because then your staff will learn to expect them. You have to use a combination of tangible and social rewards. In addition to frequent positive social reinforcers, for example, you might occasionally offer good performers two tickets to a play or concert, pay for a dinner at a really nice restaurant, or arrange a weekend visit to a nearby vacation spot.

When one of my staff does something really exceptional, he or she gets a golden attitude pin.* A total of five pins entitles the employee to a weekend in my condominium on the Gulf Coast or a paid weekend luxury vacation in a hotel.

Strive to reward as many employees as possible. Consistently selecting just one winner will only motivate that one person and may negatively impact the rest of the staff.

You should also define benchmarks or criteria for success that must be met before rewards are given. For example, the insurance clerk might have to submit a given number of claims that are accurately filled out and are not returned for additional information. The receptionist might be required to consistently answer the phone within three rings. A standards-based system allows employees to compete against their own previous performance instead of against fellow employees.

According to Daniels, the ideal recognition system should allow for an unlimited number of winners, and employees should know exactly what is expected in order to get a reward or recognition.

Some employers believe that money is the main motivator for outstanding performance. In actuality, if an employee is receiving a fair wage and decent health benefits, then nonmonetary rewards may have a greater effect than monetary ones.

Show your employees that you care about them not just as workers but as individuals with their own personal lives. When my employees or their family members are sick, I call them at home to check on them and make sure that they've got access to adequate medical care. If an employee gets sick on the job, I call another medical office to make sure the employee is seen in a timely fashion. I also ask permission to call the doctor and see how the employee is doing or to call to get a lab report for the employee. This type of attention demonstrates that I am genuinely concerned about my employees' health and well-being.

One of my employees had a husband stationed in the Persian Gulf. During the war, we put up a big yellow ribbon on the inside of the office door, and all of us

---

*Available from Rich Wilkens, 502-955-7269.

started wearing yellow ribbons—to let her know that we cared about her and were sharing her worries.

DESIGNING AN EFFECTIVE REWARD SYSTEM

Here are some general principles to think about when designing your reward system.

Match the reward to the person. Start out by finding what the person wants. You don't gain points with an employee if you provide tickets to the opera for a job well done but he or she prefers country music. One of the easiest ways to identify what would be effective and appropriate rewards for your employees is to ask them to complete a survey about the rewards that would motivate them to go the extra mile for your patients. Then when you want to give a gift or reward, you can refer to the appropriate list and select something suitable for the particular person. In fact, my employees asked me to list my preferences so they can select a gift for my birthday that I will enjoy and use.

Match the award to the achievement. It doesn't make sense to give the same reward to an employee who collected a long overdue payment and to an employee who landed a lucrative managed care contract.

Be timely and specific. The most effective rewards are given as close as possible to the behavior you want to reinforce. A letter placed in the employee's file weeks or months afterward has little value as a reinforcer. When I see an employee do something outstanding, I immediately write a thank-you note.

Provide a variety of rewards and types of recognition. Use cash and noncash rewards as well as combinations of cash and noncash benefits.

Never miss an opportunity to tell an employee "thank you." Everyone likes to feel appreciated. I sometimes thank staff for going the extra mile by sending a "Thanks a Million Check" from Dr. Baum's Bank of Gratitude. I mail these tokens of appreciation to employees' homes so they can show them to family and friends. In fact, one employee's husband said, "That's such a nice thing to do. Now I know why my wife loves to come to work in your office."

Recently one of our employees was absent from the office for several days and the other employees worked extra hard during her absence so we didn't have to hire a temporary employee. I wanted to let everyone know how much I appreciated their assistance and sent them all an extra-mile-o-gram letter. I found that all of the employees posted these letters at their workstations, where they could see them as they worked and visitors and patients could see them too.

MORE METHODS FOR MOTIVATING EMPLOYEES

Make sure your staff has the tools and resources needed to do their work. Today nearly all practices are computerized, yet many of them are using antiquated equipment. Nowadays, it is not enough just to have a computer, you need a fast computer with plenty of memory, a Windows operating system, and a fast modem to electronically transmit claims. This doesn't mean you have to throw away your current MacIntosh, Unix, and DOS-based systems. It does mean that you need to check to be sure that your staff has modern equipment that shows them how much you value the work they do. In most situations, your staff will tell you what they need. They talk to employees in other offices and have their own network for learning what's available and what's necessary for efficient operations.

Share the gifts you receive from your patients and other physicians. Most of us couldn't and shouldn't eat and drink all the wine and cheese baskets that we receive at Christmas. It is nice to share these gifts equally with your staff. After all, without them, it is unlikely that you would have received these gifts. Offer each staff member money for a turkey for Thanksgiving and include a note of thanks for his or her service.

Make sure you tell your employees how important they are to the practice. Whenever I receive a compliment about one of my staff from a patient, I call the employee into the room and ask the patient to give the compliment one more time so the employee can hear it. We start every staff meeting by asking everyone to announce the best thing that happened to him or her at work since the last staff meeting. This is a nice way to publicly acknowledge staff members who have done a good job. (It also begins each staff meeting on a positive note.)

I'm a believer in the idea that praise and compliments are very appreciated. My credo is "praise in public, pan in private." Nothing is more motivating for an employee than for the physician to recognize his or her accomplishments. When you see that someone's job performance has improved, tell the person directly. You will be satisfying the employee's need for self-esteem and helping to improve his or her self-confidence. If an employee wins an honor or performs beyond expectations, post congratulations on the bulletin board for patients and fellow employees to see.

Congratulate employees when they receive an award or complete an important task or project. If the task or project is related to their work, such as taking a course or seminar on a health-related subject, you may want to mention their achievement at a staff meeting and possibly give them an appropriate gift certificate. If you have a newsletter, it is a nice gesture to mention awards and accomplishments there. For example, my office manager took a course on executive health care management at a local university. When she completed the two-year course, we celebrated with a party and reported her accomplishment in our newsletter.

Find occasions to celebrate together. Celebrating helps to create warm, friendly feelings and fosters team spirit. We try to celebrate the birthdays of all staff members and we often celebrate the anniversaries of their employment as well.

Set goals that are achievable and write the goals down. You can't hit a target that you can't see. We have a goal card that announces how many new patients we see each month. This card is posted in the employee lounge, and all new patients seen are posted on it. If we see more than 25 new patients a month, we all go out for lunch. If we see 50 new patients, I take everyone out for dinner. The month we saw a record 80 new patients, we all went out for a night on one of the gambling boats on the river, and I gave each employee $50 to spend.

Because we set the goals for new patients, my staff is excited about making contact with new patients. It affects everyone's attitude. If anyone calls, the staff enthusiastically say, "Oh yes, we can work you in. Dr. Baum will be able to see you. He'll come early or stay late." They never say, "No, he's booked solid today, he can't see you, we close at five." And of course it affects me just as much as the staff. I have to be willing to do my part too. When we all go out together, that builds camaraderie. We're a team, we've reached our goal, and now we're celebrating together.

Involve staff in most decisions that affect your patients and your practice. This makes them feel like part of a team. When your employees have a personal investment in problem solving and decision making, they are likely to be motivated to perform beyond expectations.

Be available to your staff when they want to talk. If my staff want to see me, I'm almost always available (occasionally a patient emergency occurs that makes it impossible to see a staff member right away). Usually your staff has interesting and important things that they need to talk about, and they sometimes suggest ways to improve operations.

In fact, most of the employees in my office have become friends and socialize together outside the office. They have become friends through work because we have attempted to make the atmosphere in the office pleasant and cheerful. A positive atmosphere builds upon itself, and people really like working with their friends.

*   *   *

In addition to creating an atmosphere of constant positive reinforcement, it is also important to sit down frequently with your staff to discuss your expectations and how well they are being met. A once-a-year salary review is not enough! In the next chapter, I will discuss how frequent performance reviews can aid your staff in providing outstanding service to your patients.

NOTES

1. A. Daniels, *Bringing Out the Best in People: How To Apply the Astonishing Power of Positive Reinforcement* (New York: McGraw-Hill, 1994), 52.

2. Ibid., p. 32.

16

Periodic Performance Reviews

S uppose you told your children once a year what kind of behavior you expected of them. Do you think a single annual discussion would result in the behavior you want to see? Clearly it would not. Your children need to hear about the behavior you expect over and over again. Repetition is, indeed, the mother of invention.

The same principle holds true for your staff. I don't mean to imply you should treat your staff like children. I mean your staff requires constructive feedback from you on a regular basis if they are to improve their ability to provide consistent and outstanding service to your patients. Help your staff develop positive, service-oriented attitudes by adding periodic performance reviews to your management tool box.

Maryann Ricardo, a marketing consultant in Redondo Beach, California,* believes that while reviews to discuss salaries are needed once a year, periodic performance reviews to discuss behaviors, goals, and interpersonal relations are needed two to four times a year. This chapter discusses techniques for conducting periodic performance reviews.

THE IMPORTANT ROLE OF FEEDBACK

Feedback, especially constructive criticism, is essential for the growth and development of your staff. Negative reinforcement, such as pointing to mistakes

---

*Healthcare Management Services, a division of Custom Management Services, Inc., 2115A Curtis Avenue, Redondo Beach, CA 90278, 310-370-6917.

and threatening staff with job loss, causes staff to change their behavior just enough to avoid punishment. It may get them to show up for work but it won't generate enthusiasm. Negative reinforcement produces responses like "That's not my job" or "I don't know." On the other hand, periodic positive performance reviews generate extra or discretionary effort on the part of the staff. They motivate the staff to function as a team. They produce responses like "I don't know but I'll find out" or "That's not my job but I will find someone who can help you." Once-a-year discussions with staff will not produce extraordinary effort. That takes regular and consistent fine-tuning of staff behavior.

Each of my employees has a review every three months. I schedule a private meeting, one on one. I think my employees need to know what I expect of them. They also need to have a clear understanding of the areas in which I would like them to improve. I, on the other hand, need to hear their concerns, problems, and obstacles and what I can do to assist them in reaching agreed goals and objectives. With rare exceptions, staff members are not self-starters, nor can they be put on autopilot. Annual meetings are insufficient to produce substantive behavior changes.

Periodic performance reviews can provide positive reinforcement for desired behaviors, correct deficiencies in performance, resolve problems, set goals, motivate employees to pursue continued improvement, and provide an opportunity to express gratitude for a job well done. In addition, performance reviews can help resolve general problems in the office. Suppose there is friction between two employees. They just rub each other the wrong way and tend to feel hurt over tiny incidents. I use their performance reviews to teach them how to resolve interpersonal conflict. I don't want to be a referee for my staff. That's not part of my job description, nor did I learn refereeing skills in medical school. The best thing I can do is encourage staff to develop their own conflict resolution skills so they can deal with interpersonal problems on their own.

Performance reviews offer an opportunity to make adjustments in job descriptions and practice plans. Most importantly, these reviews ensure that nothing in the annual salary reviews will be a surprise to you or the employees.

I believe in the sandwich technique of reviewing performance. That is, I begin with a positive comment to make the employee feel comfortable and relaxed. I often will mention something that the employee did in the past quarter that helped the practice or was beneficial to the patients. If I have corrective comments to make, I insert them after the initial stroking. For example, suppose I have an employee who is frequently late for work. I will discuss this after first making a positive comment. If the employee improves, three months later I will say, "I want you to know I've noticed that you are on time now, and you're doing a great job." This praise is a positive reinforcement for the behavior I want to see. Or if there has been no change, I will say, "You're not really showing much improvement, and unless we see a change soon, we're going to have to take more drastic measures."

Every performance review session should end with a positive comment or compliment. I want the employee to leave feeling good about me and the practice. By beginning and ending with a positive comment, I think that my corrective comments are softened and that the employee is given the impression that overall I am satisfied with his or her performance—if that is indeed the case.

HOW TO CONDUCT A PERFORMANCE REVIEW

Have the employee fill in a self-evaluation form (Exhibit 16-1) before the performance review. Maryann Ricardo suggests asking what the employee likes most about his or her job, what the employee likes least, and what the employee's goals are for the next 30, 60, 90, and 180 days. During the actual interview, ask the employee what you can do to aid in the achievement of his or her goals.

At the start of the meeting, set the right tone by spending a minute or two in social conversation. Many employees will be anxious about this meeting, so Ricardo suggests trying to begin with a positive statement or compliment. Both of these techniques will help the employee relax and reduce the chance of defensiveness.

Plan what you want to say ahead of time. Describe the employee's performance and how it compares to standards you have set. Try to describe specific examples that support your general comments. If a performance review is to be productive, you've got to devote some thought to the meeting before the employee arrives.

For example, suppose the employee under review is supposed to prepare the charts before the patients arrive but usually does not post the lab results, causing delays while the patients are in the office. You should explain that this type of oversight results in inefficiency and upsets patients and that in this era of managed care, patients will be reporting any discontent to their managed care plans and their employers. Unfavorable reports can lead to the loss of a contract, and that could mean hundreds or even thousands of enrollees would be denied the opportunity to become new patients.

Try to avoid referring only to the most recent or most negative incidents. Instead, focus on the general pattern of behavior that needs to be improved. Try to emphasize how poor performance on the part of this employee affects you, fellow employees, and the practice.

Demonstrate a positive attitude. Be enthusiastic—that will make the employee feel comfortable and be willing to talk honestly. Be sure that you, too, are not defensive. It is particularly important for you to be open to a real exchange of

Exhibit 16-1 Employee Evaluation Form

NAME: _____   DATE: _____

DEPARTMENT: _____   JOB TITLE: _____

PURPOSES OF THIS EMPLOYEE EVALUATION: to take a personal inventory, to pin-point weaknesses and strengths, and to outline and agree upon a practical improvement program. Periodically conducted, these evaluations will provide a history of development and progress.

INSTRUCTIONS: Carefully evaluate each quality separately. Place an "X" mark on each rating scale over the descriptive phrase which most nearly describes yourself or the person being rated. NOTE: Everyone has strong points and weak points. Raters should be critical in their judgment of each category. Do not judge by the overall picture.

1. ACCURACY—the correctness of work duties performed.

SELF-EVALUATION	RATING	EMPLOYER EVALUATION
_____	Makes frequent errors.	_____
_____	Careless; makes recurrent errors.	_____
_____	Usually accurate; makes average number of errors.	_____
_____	Requires little supervision; is exact and precise most of the time.	_____
_____	Requires minimal supervision; almost always accurate.	_____

2. ALERTNESS—the ability to grasp instructions, meet changing conditions, and solve problem situations.

SELF-EVALUATION	RATING	EMPLOYER EVALUATION
_____	Slow to "catch on."	_____
_____	Requires more than average instructions and explanations.	_____
_____	Grasps instructions with average ability.	_____
_____	Usually quick to understand and learn.	_____
_____	Exceptionally keen and alert.	_____

continues

Exhibit 16-1 continued

3. CREATIVITY—talent for having new ideas, for finding new and better ways of doing things, and for being imaginative.

SELF-EVALUATION	RATING	EMPLOYER EVALUATION
_____	Rarely has new idea.	_____
_____	Occasionally comes up with new idea.	_____
_____	Average imagination; reasonable number of new ideas.	_____
_____	Frequently suggests new ways of doing things; is very imaginative.	_____
_____	Continually seeks new and better ways of doing things; is extremely imaginative.	_____

4. FRIENDLINESS—the sociability and warmth which an individual imparts in his/her attitude toward patients, other employees, supervisor, and the persons he/she may supervise.

SELF-EVALUATION	RATING	EMPLOYER EVALUATION
_____	Very distant and aloof.	_____
_____	Approachable; friendly once known by others.	_____
_____	Warm; friendly; sociable.	_____
_____	Very sociable and outgoing.	_____
_____	Extremely sociable; excellent at establishing goodwill.	_____

5. PERSONALITY—an individual's behavior characteristics; his/her personal suitability for this job.

SELF-EVALUATION	RATING	EMPLOYER EVALUATION
_____	Unsatisfactory for this job.	_____
_____	Questionable for this job.	_____
_____	Satisfactory for this job.	_____
_____	Very desirable for this job.	_____

continues

Exhibit 16-1 continued

6. PERSONAL APPEARANCE—the personal impression an individual makes on others. (Consider cleanliness, grooming, neatness, and appropriateness of dress on the job.)

SELF-EVALUATION	RATING	EMPLOYER EVALUATION
_____	Very untidy; poor taste in dress.	_____
_____	Sometimes untidy, careless about personal appearance.	_____
_____	Generally neat, clean; satisfactory personal appearance.	_____
_____	Careful about personal appearance; good taste in dress.	_____
_____	Unusually well groomed; very neat; excellent taste in dress.	_____

7. PHYSICAL FITNESS—the ability to work consistently and with only moderate fatigue. (Consider physical alertness and energy.)

SELF-EVALUATION	RATING	EMPLOYER EVALUATION
_____	Tires easily; is weak and frail.	_____
_____	Frequently tires and is slow.	_____
_____	Meets physical, energy job requirements.	_____
_____	Energetic; seldom tires.	_____
_____	Excellent health; no fatigue.	_____

8. ATTENDANCE—faithfulness in coming to work daily and conforming to work hours.

SELF-EVALUATION	RATING	EMPLOYER EVALUATION
_____	Often absent without good excuse; frequently reports for work late.	_____
_____	Lax in attendance; reports for work on time.	_____
_____	Usually present and on time.	_____
_____	Very prompt; regular in attendance.	_____
_____	Always regular and prompt; volunteers for overtime when needed.	_____

continues

Exhibit 16-1 continued

9. HOUSEKEEPING—orderliness and cleanliness in which an individual keeps his/her work area.

SELF-EVALUATION	RATING	EMPLOYER EVALUATION
_____	Disorderly or untidy.	_____
_____	Some tendency to be careless, untidy.	_____
_____	Ordinarily keeps work area fairly neat.	_____
_____	Quite conscientious about neatness and cleanliness.	_____
_____	Unusually neat, clean, orderly.	_____

10. DEPENDABILITY—ability to do required jobs well with minimum of supervision.

SELF-EVALUATION	RATING	EMPLOYER EVALUATION
_____	Requires close supervision; is unreliable.	_____
_____	Sometimes requires prompting.	_____
_____	Usually takes care of necessary tasks and completes them with reasonable promptness.	_____
_____	Requires little supervision; is reliable.	_____
_____	Requires absolute minimum of supervision.	_____

11. DRIVE—the desire to attain goals, to achieve.

SELF-EVALUATION	RATING	EMPLOYER EVALUATION
_____	Has poorly defined goals and acts without purpose; puts forth practically no effort.	_____
_____	Sets goals too low; puts forth little effort to achieve.	_____
_____	Has average goals; usually puts forth effort to reach these.	_____
_____	Strives hard; has high desire to achieve.	_____
_____	Sets high goals; strives incessantly to achieve these.	_____

continues

Exhibit 16-1 continued

12. JOB KNOWLEDGE—the information concerning work duties which an individual should know for a satisfactory job performance.

SELF-EVALUATION	RATING	EMPLOYER EVALUATION
_____	Poorly informed about work duties.	_____
_____	Lacks knowledge of some phases of work.	_____
_____	Moderately informed; can answer most common questions.	_____
_____	Understands all phases of work.	_____
_____	Has complete mastery of all phases of job.	_____

13. QUANTITY OF WORK—the amount of work an individual does in a work day.

SELF-EVALUATION	RATING	EMPLOYER EVALUATION
_____	Does not meet minimum requirement.	_____
_____	Does just enough to get by.	_____
_____	Volume of work is satisfactory.	_____
_____	Very industrious; does more than is required.	_____
_____	Superior work production record.	_____

14. STABILITY—the ability to withstand pressure and to remain calm in crisis situations.

SELF-EVALUATION	RATING	EMPLOYER EVALUATION
_____	Goes "to pieces" under pressure; is jumpy and nervous.	_____
_____	Occasionally "blows up" under pressure; is easily irritated.	_____
_____	Has average tolerance for crises; usually remains calm.	_____
_____	Tolerates most pressure; likes crises more than average person.	_____
_____	Thrives under pressure; really enjoys solving crises.	_____

continues

Exhibit 16-1 continued

15. COURTESY—the polite attention an individual gives other people.

SELF-EVALUATION	RATING	EMPLOYER EVALUATION
_____	Blunt; discourteous; antagonistic.	_____
_____	Sometimes tactless.	_____
_____	Agreeable and pleasant.	_____
_____	Always very polite, willing to help.	_____
_____	Inspiring to others in being courteous, very pleasant.	

16. OVERALL EVALUATION—comparison with other employees with the same length of service on this job.

SELF-EVALUATION	RATING	EMPLOYER EVALUATION
_____	Definitely unsatisfactory.	_____
_____	Substandard, making progress.	_____
_____	Doing an average job.	_____
_____	Definitely above average.	_____
_____	Outstanding.	_____

EMPLOYEE SUMMARY:

_____

_____

_____

_____

_____

EMPLOYER SUMMARY:

_____

_____

_____

_____

_____

_____

COMPLETED BY _____ TITLE _____

A copy of this report has been given to me and has been discussed with me.

_____   _____
EMPLOYEE   DATE

Source: American Academy of Podiatric Practice Management, Spring Newsletter 1995, Robert C. Purdy, DPM, Editor, 6005 Monclova Road, Maumee, OH 43537.

ideas with employees. If they have constructive comments, make sure you listen carefully.

Try to see each issue in terms of the way it affects not only you but also the employee, other staff members, and, most importantly, your patients. After the employee gives you his or her assessment, demonstrate that you understand it by restating or summarizing it. This technique lets the employee know that you are actively listening to his or her ideas.

When you agree with an employee's point of view, say so. Always give praise where praise is due—never take good work for granted. Make certain the employee understands that his or her contribution does make a difference.

Asking open-ended questions can give you valuable insight into specific employee needs and the best way to deal with them. I remember one employee who informed me that what she liked least was attending our evening support group meeting on impotence. She said, "I give you 110 percent of my time and attention from 9:00 to 5:15, but at 5:15 I really want to go home and spend time with my husband and family. I don't want to stay in the evening." I was paying a bonus for overtime. She felt that she would rather not do it, and I respected that. Rather than demanding that she attend, I backed off, and somebody else came in her place. Had I not had this opportunity to talk with her, I might have "strongly encouraged" her to attend the meeting and she might have come unwillingly. It could have affected her outstanding daytime performance and even resulted in my losing a good employee. After the performance review, I knew her needs and wants and made an effort not to interfere with her personal life. I wouldn't have been able to uncover this important information if I only met with her once a year.

ENDING THE MEETING

At the end of the meeting, ask the employee to express any reactions he or she has to your assessment. Also ask if there are any personal problems affecting the employee that you may not be aware of. Don't go overboard here. Just let the employee know that you are available to discuss personal problems.

Sometimes there are special circumstances affecting an employee's performance that are really beyond the employee's control. I had one employee who said, "I just cannot draw blood." Another stated she could not catheterize another woman. And I said, "OK, I respect that." My point here is that everyone has some strengths and some weaknesses, and you don't want to push employees to the point they become uncomfortable or feel stressed.

I find employees' suggestions regarding goals and objectives very valuable in determining how to improve their performance in ways that suit their own personality and skills. For example, a typical 30-day goal might be to start learning the Windows software program. A six-month goal might be to enroll in an evening class two nights a week. Another employee might decide to get more involved in public speaking and join the local Toastmasters group. I try to get employees to pick a goal and set their own deadline. Some of my employees initially resisted this idea, but I emphasized the importance of personal and professional growth. As a physician, I can't practice with the same skills, methods, techniques, drugs, and procedures that I used 5 or 10 years ago. Medicine is changing too quickly.

Be sure to ask the employee for possible solutions to performance problems. Ricardo notes that when you ask your employees for ideas and are willing to respond to their needs, this helps create an open and trusting atmosphere and frees up energy so the employees can work more effectively. In fact, employees often come up with worthwhile suggestions for changes in procedures or methods that will solve performance problems, attract new patients, help keep current patients, and improve operational efficiency. No one knows the problems and potential solutions better than your employees.

Toward the end of the performance review, ask the employee to agree on an action plan. If the employee's performance has been less than optimal, the action plan should include specific steps the employee will take, the date by which you expect the preferred behavior to occur, assignments you expect the employee to complete, a "to do" list, and careful documentation of your discussion.

Ricardo suggests that you ask the employee if he or she agrees the action plan is acceptable. If the answer is yes, then you and the employee should both sign the plan. Give the employee a copy as a written record of the agreement. Hopefully this will help to create the feeling that the agreement is a binding contract and that the employee should work hard to achieve the stated goals.

At the very end of the meeting, you should summarize the plan and thank the employee. Close on a positive note by expressing your recognition of the employee's value to the practice. Mention the areas where the employee's performance is excellent or above standard and then set the date for your next meeting. Of course, each meeting should be documented in the employee's file.

Periodic performance reviews allow the identification of opportunities for performance improvement and personal development. There is no better way to fine-tune the performance of your staff than by conducting such reviews. I find the reviews each take only a few minutes but yield tremendous rewards.

REQUESTING FEEDBACK FROM YOUR STAFF

Because it is so important to create the feeling that we are all a team, I meet every quarter with my employees in a role-reversal session. I allow my employees to critique my performance as a physician and as their employer. Each of them takes a turn leading the meeting, and it is their chance to say what is on their minds. I find I obtain valuable information, and, just as important, it is appropriate for me to be subjected to the same scrutiny that I'm asking my employees to undergo.

Therefore, I complete the same evaluation form that I ask them to fill out. I also complete an action plan and sign it at the end of the evaluation. I set specific goals for myself. Completing this book was one goal for me. I shared with my staff that we were going to get a new bar-code computer program and I was going to try to have it functioning within 90 days. I promised them that I would come to the office 15 minutes early to make patient callbacks before the start of the afternoon appointments.

My participation in this sort of review process allows me to hear frank opinions of my performance and gives me an opportunity to improve my relationships with my employees and my patients.

During these meetings, my employees have sometimes given me accurate, valuable criticism. I have made changes in my behavior because of their critiques. For example, once they pointed out that I was taking nonmedical calls while I was seeing patients and was thus causing delays. They also felt that when I came from the hospital I should immediately change from my scrub suit into my slacks, white shirt, and tie because that was part of creating a professional atmosphere. I saw their point, especially when the office manager mentioned that I wouldn't accept any one of them being dressed in the equivalent of a scrub suit. The meetings provide an opportunity for me to let employees know that constructive criticism goes both ways. It has been said that the best way to understand other people is to walk in their shoes. There is no better way to walk in the shoes of your staff than to let them periodically review your performance.

*   *   *

As important as positive reinforcement and frequent feedback is salary. Paying a fair salary will gain the sort of performance you expect. In the next chapter, I will discuss how to set salary levels and bonuses to have the greatest motivational impact.

17

You Get What You Pay For

I f you want to have a successful practice, you need to recognize how important your staff is and compensate them appropriately. This means that if the practice is financially successful, all of the staff should share in the financial gains. In many medical practices, employees aren't given adequate rewards for taking care of patients.

I want my staff to offer patients first-class, top-notch service. That means I need to pay salaries that are somewhat above the average for our area, type of practice, and type of work performed.

There are a number of resources available with information on current salary levels for both physicians and nonphysician employees.

The Medical Group Management Association publishes an annual report on typical costs based on a survey of their members.[1] Information on "non provider expenses per full time equivalent (FTE) physician" is given separately for each geographic section of the country, for multispecialist practices, and for many kinds of single-specialty practices. Information on support staff salaries is broken down into various categories, such as "general administrative," "registered nurses," "medical receptionists," and "laboratory."

Woody Allen said that "90 percent of success is showing up." Most people are inclined to act on that principle, and so if you pay average wages, you can expect your employees to show up, punch in, go through the motions and look busy, and at the end of the day punch out. However, if you pay slightly more than the average for the community, you can expect your employees to earn the extra amount by providing outstanding service.

Every one of your employees knows how his or her salary stacks up against those of other employers in the community. How the local salary network gets the word out is not always clear, but you can be sure that if your employees feel underpaid, they generally will perform at a low rate of productivity. The converse is also true. If they know they are receiving higher salaries than those paid by a practice across the street, they will work a lot harder to keep their jobs. By paying more than the going rate, you can anticipate less employee turnover and better patient services.

USING FINANCIAL INCENTIVES TO ADVANTAGE

In addition to paying good salaries, you need to offer other types of financial incentives to motivate enthusiastic, superior service. Good employees don't come cheaply.

J. Landy Damsey, of Damsey and Associates, routinely checks policies on performance reviews and salary increases. He says,

> We walk into a lot of practices and find out that they routinely do an across-the-board annual 5 percent increase for everybody. We strongly recommend that they do merit reviews instead. We do not think that everyone should get the same raise every year. Salary increases should be based on merit and not seniority.

William Abernathy, Ph.D., of Abernathy and Associates,* a company that specializes in designing employee payment systems, also criticizes standard payment arrangements:

> The conventional payment system is a compound-growth fixed expense. When it became established, right after World War II, much of the world's industries had been destroyed and we were the only sellers, so revenue was constantly increasing in most companies. This compound-growth fixed expense didn't bother anybody. An annual salary increase for all employees in every industry could be easily hidden or covered in the large profit margins which were enjoyed right after World War II. Today things are different. Many companies in health care now have decreasing, not increasing, revenues. Most businesses and industries, including physicians, cannot raise their prices, due to competitive forces.

---

*665 Oakleaf Office Lane, Memphis, TN 38117, 901-763-2122.

There are many types of incentive payment systems. In recent years, managerial consulting firms such as KPMG Peat Marwick have done a great deal of work analyzing and testing different systems to see what works best.

According to Steven Berman, KPMG Peat Marwick National Practice Director of Employee Reward Systems,* it is important to distinguish between base pay and variable, performance-based pay.

Base pay is compensation for the skills and experience an employee brings to the job. In general, the more skills employees have, the greater their base pay will be.

Performance-based pay is determined by an individual's actual performance. An increase in salary due to performance, such as a three-percent "merit raise," is an example of performance-based pay. However, Berman says,

> Merit increases have become much less important because the funds available for merit pay have decreased so much in recent years. Twenty years ago merit pay could mean a 10-percent increase in salary. Today a good performer may receive a 3-percent annual increase, while an outstanding performer only receives an increase of 4 percent. The difference is so small it does not motivate people to try for outstanding performance.

In addition to rewarding specific skills, a payment system should also reward employees who develop what Berman calls "self-management techniques," such as leadership, teamwork, innovation, and giving personal attention to problems as they arise.

Often a relatively small financial incentive, such as a 5-percent increase in pay, is sufficient to motivate a 30-percent increase in performance. Berman says,

> When we design these incentive systems, we don't know what the specific outcome will be in each situation, but we do know that 1 or 2 percent is not sufficient to really have an impact on people. This amount is considered a paltry sum by most employees and will not result in desired behavior changes. The optimum amount for motivation and generating first-class service would be about 8-percent incentive pay, which is equivalent to one month's base pay.

Berman notes, "When we're setting up an incentive system and we use numbers like 5 percent or 8 percent, we're just trying to create a reasonable expectation of what the employee may have to produce in order to receive the incentive

---

*1600 Market St., Philadelphia, PA 19103, 215-299-3100.

payment. But who says that an outstanding employee couldn't receive 20 percent, if his or her performance warranted it."

In addition to financial compensation, which follows negotiated, defined standards, organizations also need to use rewards and recognition as incentives and motivators, Berman says.

IMPLEMENTING A VARIABLE COMPENSATION PROGRAM

Berman emphasizes several key points for those intending to implement a variable compensation program.

Develop clear objectives. This means identifying the behaviors you want to encourage. Also, develop a strategy and an action plan for achieving this year's key organizational goals. Then review your incentive program on a regular basis to be sure that your incentives support the achievement of your most important goals. In designing the plan, look at the following: available funding; performance periods; key performance indicators; threshold, target, and maximum award levels; timing of payout; and type of payout (cash, stock, other).

You may want to consider having a fixed element of compensation for each employee as well as a variable element determined by how well the employee performs. It is advisable to make incentive awards as quickly as possible after the measurement period ends. Berman recommends setting the base salary below the median base salary in your area, while setting the variable incentive compensation substantially above the median. This means that someone who does the minimum will end up with an income below the median and someone who meets or exceeds the incentive goals will do well financially.

Most importantly, after designing and implementing a variable compensation program, continue to monitor it to see that it works well and supports your organizational objectives. "Many companies monitor their performance objectives quarterly to determine if performance objectives are reasonable, i.e., not so modest as to offer little or no motivation to employees, nor so ambitious that employees become demoralized by the inability to achieve success."[2]

THE ABERNATHY INCENTIVE SYSTEM

Abernathy and Associates, of Memphis, Tennessee, has developed an alternative to traditional salary increase systems that is designed to pay people on the basis of their personal performance as well as officewide profitability. Rewards are based on performance in areas that employees can affect (criteria might include how many new patients are seen each month or how many billing claims are returned because of errors).

The Abernathy system defines an organizational threshold that typically covers all the fixed expenses of an organization plus a desired return to the owner or stockholders. Above that threshold, employees receive a share of all additional income. The system uses measurements of two to five key objective measures for each position (or in some cases each department). The possible return is calculated on a monthly basis so employees who perform well are rewarded quickly for their performance.

Abernathy says, "The built-in incentives of the Abernathy system motivate employees for success, and they want to be involved in all the details of the business." He reports that the average improvement in productivity for companies using the Abernathy system is about 12 percent or 13 percent the first year.

USING FINANCIAL REWARDS TO GENERATE SAVINGS

Reward your staff for reducing expenses. If one of your staff comes up with an idea that saves the practice money, give him or her a bonus. My policy is to give a bonus amounting to about 10 percent of the savings that result.

For example, my practice was paying a medical transcriptionist from the hospital's medical records department $2.50 a page for medical dictation. One of our employees found a legal secretary who was interested in doing medical dictation at home. She charged $1.50 a page. This saved our practice $100 to $150 a month in transcription fees. The employee who found the new transcriptionist received a bonus equal to one month's savings.

We also found that we were paying high prices for printing forms and patient education materials. Our office manager designed the forms and educational materials on the computer and took the master to a copy store, thus considerably reducing our printing costs. The office manager received an immediate bonus for the significant savings achieved.

Set up a suggestion box and pay a reward for any suggestions that are implemented in the practice. I give monetary awards for any suggestion that retains current patients, attracts new ones, decreases overhead, or increases efficiency. We thought we needed a new autoclave recently because our old one was broken and replacement parts were not available. A new autoclave costs $2,000. My nurse took our old autoclave to the biomedical engineering department of our local hospital and they fixed it for $50. I was happy to give her a $100 check for her practical, money-saving idea.

Another practice purchased a DEXA (dual energy X-ray absorbtimetry) machine to measure bone mineral density to test for osteoporosis. First the doctors ran the test on all the women who worked in the practice, thinking they would be motivated to tell others about this test. No one came. I suggested they offer a five-dollar incentive payment for each family member who came in for the test. Within a week, they had 25 or 30 new patients referred by the employees.

MY BONUS SYSTEM

In my practice we tie our incentive plan to our financial success. I don't believe in an automatic Christmas bonus. I do believe that the staff should earn their bonuses, and therefore have an active role in the success of the practice. A bonus should mean that things are going well.

One key measurement is quarterly net collections minus patient refunds. I discuss with each employee his or her role in generating revenue. My accountant has created quarterly statistics for my practice that have been averaged over the past three years. With these statistics he has set goals or benchmarks that we are to reach on a quarterly basis. When quarterly collections are less than the goal, there is no bonus. If quarterly collections exceed the goal by 15 percent, each employee receives a bonus equivalent to 8 percent of their quarterly salary. If the goal is exceeded by more than 20 percent, the bonus is 10 percent of their quarterly salary.

Another key measurement is the number of new patients that are seen each month. For example, you might consider a bonus of one dollar per staff member if the average number of new patients exceeds 30 per physician per month.

*   *   *

Salaries and bonuses are an important part of the management techniques that motivate medical staff. Equally important is having a standardized process for setting and working toward goals for improvement. In the next chapter, I will look at continuous quality improvement methods and how they can assist your practice in setting and exceeding goals.

NOTES

1. Medical Group Management Association, *Cost Survey: 1994 Report Based on 1993 Data* (Englewood, Colo.: Medical Group Management Association, 1994).

2. S. Berman, "A Process for Implementing Variable Pay," *Issues in Performance and Compensation Management*, April 1995, p. 6. See also S. Berman, "Grain Management Makes Productivity Soar at GST Steel," *National Productivity Review* 13 (1994): 503–515.

18

Measure and Improve Quality: It's Not a State of Mind

A s a physician, you don't make your reputation. Your patients do. You only give them the material to work with.

Every physician instinctively feels that he or she has a superior practice and provides excellent care. Every physician will claim, "My practice is terrific, my patients love me, I have a happy staff, nobody waits to see me, I have good clinical results and above average outcomes, and I'm making a lot of money. Of course, I have a superior practice."

Even if you can truly say this, there is always room for improvement. This chapter discusses some practical methods to enhance the quality of your practice. It also describes how to demonstrate to managed care organizations that you have an excellent practice and that their members will be cared for by outstanding physicians who consistently achieve desired results.

MEASURING QUALITY

What gets measured gets done.

Today it is not enough to say, "I practice high-quality medicine." You will be required to demonstrate the excellence of your practice. Managed care plans and accrediting organizations are putting a yardstick to quality. They are using objective criteria, such as the number of children who receive immunizations on schedule or the number of women who get Pap smears and mammograms on schedule, to measure how well a practice is caring for its patients. They are looking at lengths of hospital stay for certain conditions and measures of morbidity and mortality to see if a practice is offering cost-effective, high-quality care.

Major managed care organizations and accrediting organizations, such as the National Committee for Quality Assurance,* are starting to publish "quality report cards" that list measures of health care. Employers use quality report cards in deciding which plans to offer their employees. Health plans use detailed quality data to select or deselect physicians for their panels. You can anticipate that you and your practice will be judged against local and national standards of care. If you don't measure up, you'll be out of the managed care business.

Even more important, consumers are beginning to base their health care decisions on quality data. *Health Pages,*† a consumer magazine, offers this sort of information in several major cities. Major companies like GTE and Xerox are making detailed quality information on various health plans available to employees during the open enrollment season. In the past, patients knew how long they waited, what the bill was, and what the incision looked like. That was it. Now, or very soon, ordinary customers will have access to a wealth of statistical information about outcomes, morbidity, mortality, and costs of tests and procedures as an aid in choosing their physicians. The general public is better able to judge the quality of medical practices than ever before.

What this means for us as physicians is that we must measure how well our practices meet patients' needs and report this information back to managed care plans, employers, and consumers. The switch to a focus on quality is in its early stages, but the direction is clear. Those of us who take a proactive stance and measure our practices now will certainly have the jump on those who let others do the measuring for them.

WHAT IS A QUALITY PRACTICE?

A quality practice is one where patients are satisfied, doctors are doing what they do best (which is practice medicine), staff is highly motivated and enjoys the work, and fair compensation is received for services rendered. A quality practice is one that measures the processes of care and works to continuously improve them. A quality practice is efficient and profitable and is constantly searching for ways to cut costs and increase productivity. Finally, a quality practice is responsive to the needs of patients, staff, suppliers, payers, other physicians, and the community where the practice is located.

In many situations, improved quality of medical care results in improved outcomes and decreased costs.[1] Years ago when people had heart attacks, they would

---

*2000 L Street, NW, Suite 500, Washington, DC 20036, 202-955-3500, fax 202-955-3599.
†135 Fifth Avenue. 7th Floor, New York, NY 10010, 212-505-0103.

stay in the hospital two or three weeks. Today, once patients are out of intensive care, they are ambulating—and the results are better. Years ago, people who had coronary artery bypass surgery were often hospitalized 10 to 14 days. Now they are out in 3 or 4 days. We are seeing more one-day surgeries and morning admissions to reduce hospitalization. Patients have their gallbladder removed or their hernia repaired using a laparoscope and go home the same day. A good part of the decrease in lengths of stay is due to technological advances. In fact, we are learning how to control costs and at the same time improve results.

When quality improvement is the focus of a practice, the employees have an interest in all aspects of the patients' interaction with the practice. No one knows the process of patient care better than the staff on the front line. When their opinions are taken into consideration and their suggestions are acted upon, they become more involved and committed to the practice. You don't need an MBA to know that if your employees are allowed to define their own jobs, encouraged to do whatever is right for the patients and the practice, and rewarded for positive results, then you will have a motivated staff that likes to come to work and that you will enjoy working with.

Improving quality will help reduce waste. It has been estimated that today, waste accounts for 20 to 40 percent of the total cost of health care.[2] While it is possible to debate the exact percentage, and we all believe that we're doing our best to be efficient, I believe that every practice, if it looks closely, will find opportunities to cut waste and improve efficiency.

For example, the Texas Heart Institute, in Houston, offers package deals for coronary artery bypass surgery. The global fee, which covers hospital, doctor, and anesthetist services, is 30 to 50 percent less than fees at other hospitals. Why? Because of economies of scale. The doctors at the institute perform the operation 10 to 12 times a day, and as a result of their experience they were able to find ways to reduce expenses. In addition, the outcomes of the surgery are as good as or better than those achieved at other facilities in the community. Because they focused the attention on fine-tuning the procedure, they were able to both increase quality and cut costs.

In this era of reduced reimbursements and spiraling overhead costs, there's no better way to improve the bottom line than to cut inefficiencies in all areas. A quality practice that "does it right the first time" will be more efficient and will better utilize available resources.

Let's look at the issue of quality from another angle. Poor quality has many hidden costs. Patients unhappy with the service they receive will leave your practice. If you fail to achieve outcomes comparable to those of other providers, managed care plans are likely to deselect you. Higher costs will certainly lead to a loss of patients. Finally, you won't have the personal satisfaction of knowing that your practice serves patients effectively and efficiently.

Most physicians are fully occupied with taking care of patients, doing the necessary paperwork, and attending meetings. Very little time is left over for them to step back and take a look at their situation. They are thus unable to identify the problems that are making it more and more difficult to practice medicine.

There is a common saying: "If it ain't broke, don't fix it." Many physicians do not feel that the health care system is broken. However, the public is telling us a different story. We need to recognize that we have a good system but not a perfect one. We need to make it better.

When the media reports that 30 percent of medical care is inappropriate, unnecessary, and wasteful, then we must address the question of waste and find ways to become more efficient.[3] Patients are losing trust in hospitals and in the health care system in general. They read reports that one in ten hospital admissions produces avoidable, medically created harm.[4] They read that more than 90 percent of hospital bills are inaccurate.[5] Reports and articles like these damage people's confidence in the medical profession. They indicate that our system is in need of repair. Given this, physicians would be far better off taking the initiative to repair it instead of waiting for the government to mandate the repair process. True, the system may not be broken . . . yet. But it is in need of an overhaul and heavy-duty maintenance work.

LEARNING FROM INDUSTRY

Quality improvement programs have been used successfully in industrial organizations for many years. General Motors and other major car manufacturers, for example, have reduced the number of defects per car to a smaller number. Federal Express sorts 2 million parcels each night in Memphis and has a 99.6-percent accuracy rate. Wouldn't it be wonderful if health care providers had comparable success rates? Don't patients have a right to expect virtually flawless care? After all, having reliable health care is definitely more important than being able to buy a defect-free car or receive a package the day after it was sent. We would not be facing a health care crisis if our patients had a favorable experience 99.6 percent of the time.

HOW TO DEVELOP A CONTINUOUS QUALITY IMPROVEMENT PROGRAM

There are a number of different ways to set up a continuous quality improvement (CQI) program. One way is to use the FOCUS method.[6] This method involves the following:

- Finding a process to improve,
- Organizing a team that understands the process,
- Clarifying current knowledge of the work process,
- Understanding the causes of process variation, and
- Selecting improvement methods.

Begin with focusing on a problem. There isn't a practice that doesn't have problems that need to be solved. Ask your patients what causes the greatest frustration, the most anxiety. Ask your staff what causes the heaviest loss of productivity, patients, or income. Problems may be as simple as keeping the exam rooms and restrooms clean or as complicated as achieving acceptance by a managed care plan.

Perhaps you should start with a small project, one where results can be clearly seen in a short period of time. You want your first quality improvement efforts to be successful so you can build on your success and get others in the practice of buying into the CQI program. If people see that early, CQI efforts are successful, they will be more willing to tackle major improvements in the future.

Organize a team that understands the relevant work process. Be sure to include staff who deal directly with the patients. The office manager, supervisors, and physicians should also be part of the team.

Sometimes it is difficult to get physicians to participate in quality improvement. Some may object that CQI does not follow a rigorous scientific method. Others will look for a magic bullet or quick fix in order to save time and energy. However, the reality is that if the physicians don't buy into CQI, it will not work. The CQI process requires involvement of everyone in the practice, physicians as well as file clerks.

Clarify current knowledge of the process. In this phase of CQI, data are collected that will serve as standards for comparison once changes have been instituted. The object is to find out, for example, when, where, and how often. This step moves the CQI team beyond a gut feeling that things aren't going well to the specifics of what is happening and how it affects the practice.

It also involves an analysis of the problem. Possible causes of the problem and possible solutions are identified. The generation of causes and solutions can often be accomplished in a brainstorming session. In this type of session, withhold judgment regarding possible causes and solutions, since negative reactions will stifle the process.

The next step is to try to understand the causes of process variation. At this point the team selects the most probable major causes and what seems to be the best solution. The selection of a solution to test is a difficult task. The practice must be careful to continue to monitor results so the solution does not create a new problem that is worse than the original problem. Don't forget to compare the cost of fixing the problem with the cost of leaving it alone.

After the agreed solution is implemented, continue to collect data and compare them to the data collected before any changes were implemented. You can thus learn if the solution has fixed the problem identified in the beginning, fixed a portion of the problem, or had no effect. If the problem has disappeared, the members of the team will feel a sense of gratification and will be more than ready to start the next project.

MY EXPERIENCE WITH CONTINUOUS QUALITY
IMPROVEMENT

I've personally seen the value of using the CQI process. To take just one example, like many other practices we frequently failed to file lab data and reports in patients' charts prior to their visits. A patient might wait 30 to 45 minutes while we tracked down the relevant lab data or X-ray reports. We decided to use this problem to start our CQI program.

We formed a CQI team, which included the nurse, the office manager, the person assigned to file reports in the charts, and myself. In order to gather accurate information about the problem, we measured and recorded the number of charts each day that didn't contain all the appropriate reports before the patients arrived in the office. We also calculated the number and length of delays caused by the failure to file the reports.

Next we got together and spent some time thinking of all the possible causes of the problem. We did not focus on finding solutions at this point or on blaming anyone, we simply tried to be sure that our list included *everything* that might be causing the problem. Our list included the following:

- Doctor took the chart home.
- Chart not in the file cabinet.
- Information not received from the hospital.
- Doctor did not review the report before it was placed in the chart.
- Patient's visit was scheduled too soon to get the report back.
- Lab did not report back in a timely fashion.
- Reports were not filed.
- A combination of the above factors.

Next we brainstormed possible solutions to the problem. Our suggestions included these:

- Doctor to sign out charts he takes home, so staff will know where the charts are.
- Ask hospital and vendors to return all data within 24 hours after they are received.
- Doctor to review reports daily so reports can be filed in a timely fashion.
- Doctor to initial the reports on all actions to be taken.
- Clerk who pulls charts for the next day's patients will review charts to be sure all needed reports are in the chart. If they are not, she will place a Post-it note on the front of the chart so the receptionist or nurse can request the reports first thing in the morning.

We then considered which suggestion would be most likely to result in success if implemented. We unanimously agreed that requiring the file clerk to check the charts on the next day's patients was the best place to start. Within two days the number of problem charts plummeted from 10 to 2 incomplete charts a day. The average time for patient visits not requiring an office procedure dropped from 45 minutes to 25 minutes.

We also used the same process to decrease the time patients spent waiting to be seen. We used it to improve scheduling between our office and the hospital. Now that we've learned how CQI methods work on relatively small problems, we plan to use them to make our practice more user-friendly for managed care plans.

ASSISTANCE IN IMPLEMENTING CONTINUOUS QUALITY IMPROVEMENT

When my practice was ready to learn CQI methods and philosophy, we took courses offered by the hospital. There are many potential sources of information on CQI, including your local hospital, professional societies, and management consultants. Since CQI has become such an important part of today's health care process, many consulting organizations offer conferences and written materials on and training programs in CQI philosophy and methods. Among the best known are the following three:

Institute for Healthcare Improvement
One Exeter Plaza, Ninth Floor
Boston, MA 02116
617-424-4800

GOAL/QPC
13 Branch Street
Methuen, MA 01844
508-685-3900

Juran Institute
11 River Road
P.O. Box 811
Wilton, CT 06897
203-834-1700

CONCLUSION

As we all know, the U.S. health care system is going through a process of rapid change. What this means for most of us is that we must relinquish some of the control that we have traditionally had and allow others a greater share in the process of caring for our patients. Some key health care decisions are now out of our hands.

Many of the changes are being instituted for a good reason—to help eliminate the waste and inefficiency in our health care system. My personal feeling is that we need to be open to new ideas and experiment with ways of improving our practices.

Working together with large managed care organizations will bring us benefits as well as opportunities. We will have access to a growing body of statistics showing how each practice compares with similar practices locally and across the country. We can use this information to continuously improve our practices and seek to provide better quality care and reduce costs for our patients.

* * *

But let's not be too serious about this. In the next chapter I will discuss the ways a sense of humor can revitalize your medical practice and help both patients and staff have a little fun when they walk in the door.

NOTES

1. J. Harkey and R. Vraciu, "Quality of Health Care and Financial Performance: Is There a Link?" *Health Care Management Review* 17, no. 4 (1992): 56.

2. C.P. McLaughlin and A.D. Kaluzny, *Continuous Quality Improvement in Health Care* (Gaithersburg, Md.: Aspen Publishers, 1994), 41.

3. R.H. Brooks and K.N. Lohr, "Efficacy, Effectiveness, Variations, and Quality: Boundary Crossing Research," *Medical Care* 23 (1985): 720.

4. T.A. Berman, et al., "Incidence of Adverse Events and Negligence in Hospitalized Patients: Results of the Harvard Medical Practice Study I," *New England Journal of Medicine* 324 (1991): 370.

5. H. Kim, "Unethical Behavior a Concern among Revenue Recovery Firms," *Modern Healthcare* 19, no. 51 (1989): 41.

6. McLaughlin and Kaluzny, *Continuous Quality Improvement in Health Care*, 20.

19

Putting Mirth into Medicine

The best doctors in the world are Dr. Diet, Dr. Quiet, and Dr. Merryman.

Jonathan Swift

Ask any patient on the way to the doctor or dentist if he or she is looking forward to the experience. You can be sure that almost everyone will say no. However, if the doctor and staff inject a sense of humor (in addition to antibiotics) during a patient's office visit, I believe they can transform the usual negative experience into a positive one.

Medicine is a high-stress occupation. Physicians are dealing, not with inanimate objects, but with real people suffering from real diseases, some of them life threatening. In addition, many physicians are trying to run a small business, an endeavor for which they are not necessarily well equipped. Finally, new regulations and changes in the health care system create uncertainty and discomfort.

Is it any wonder that physicians often suffer from burnout and are anxious and upset? The danger is that we will pass this anxiety to our staff and their anxiety will get passed on to our patients. There is no better way to relieve the tension and pressure of our work than to inject a small dose of humor. Humor is not only socially acceptable in a health care environment, but it is also actually welcomed. Your staff and your patients will enjoy being in an atmosphere of fun rather than one of doom and gloom.

A sense of humor makes work fun. Most people prefer working in a light-hearted environment. Of course, your staff want to get all their work done, they want to use their skills, but they also want to have fun while they're working. They won't be able to have fun if you are too serious or dour and morose. However, if you do not take yourself too seriously, then this will allow your staff to find ways to infuse humor into their work.

Humor can be an aid to communication. We are in a profession that demands a very high level of communication between patients, physicians, hospitals, payers, and managed care plans. Health care providers will never be replaced by computers or robots as long as we make an effort to be good communicators. At least for the present, no computer can think and interact with a patient. Even when the day arrives when computers can think, there will always be a significant number of patients who want a real live doctor to touch and communicate with—especially a physician with a sense of humor. Remember, there are still plenty of bank customers who want to carry out bank transactions with a live teller rather than an ATM. Similarly, some patients will want a physician who can listen to them, who communicates clearly, who is compassionate, and who does not take him- or herself too seriously.

This chapter explains why it is important to incorporate humor into your medical practice and describes how you can accomplish this without having to be a stand-up comedian.

THE MANY BENEFITS OF HUMOR

Humor is medicinal. Voltaire said, "The art of medicine consists of amusing the patient while nature cures the disease." A 13th-century surgeon, Henri de Mondeville, told jokes to his patients as they were coming out of surgery because he felt laughter would aid their recovery.

We now know that humor is good for us, both mentally and physically. Norman Cousins documented the medicinal value of humor in his book *The Anatomy of an Illness as Seen by the Patient*. Cousins, a former editor of *Saturday Review*, had ankylosing spondylitis, a debilitating and life-threatening condition associated with severe pain and limited activity. With the assistance of his doctor, he checked out of the hospital and into a hotel and began to treat himself with large doses of laughter. He watched comedy videos like "The Three Stooges" and "Abbott and Costello" for hours at a time. He noticed he received three hours of pain relief after watching comedy videos but only half an hour of pain relief after taking oral analgesic medication. He also found that laughter actually decreased his erythrocyte sedimentation rate, which is an indirect sign of a decrease in the inflammatory response associated with his disease.

Mr. Cousins used humor as a form of pain relief. Later his responses were verified. Researchers found that humor does release endogenous endorphins, which provide more potent pain relief than equivalent amounts of morphine.

Physicians need to find ways to harness the power of humor to aid patients. Try recommending that your patients read a joke book, watch comedy videos, or just smile at themselves in the mirror. Dr. Phil Williams, a neurosurgeon in Dallas, Texas, will actually write out a prescription for patients that recommends laughing out loud three times a day. After all, humor is one tonic that anyone can afford. And your managed care plans won't deselect you if you overprescribe it!

Steve Allen, Jr., M.D., an assistant dean for student affairs at the State University of New York Health Science Center in Syracuse, has long understood that humor can be a valuable asset to the health care provider and that tasteful humor can improve the rapport between physician and patient. In addition to observing the communication between humor and health in his own practice as a primary care physician, he has also had the opportunity to observe the connection during his work providing medical care each year to the Zuni Indians of New Mexico.

In Zuni culture there are three different kinds of healers: medicine men and women, bone pressers (the equivalent of orthopedists), and finally clowns. Zuni clowns use face and body paint, wear funny costumes, and have a social license to carry out humorous and silly activities in public. A Zuni Indian who is ill can ask a clown to pay a house call. More often than not, a visit from a clown works wonders. Zuni Indians have understood for centuries that humor has an important role in the healing process. Perhaps we can learn from Native Americans that it's really medicinal to "send in the clowns."

Humor is a terrific aid in reducing conflict and anxiety. Allen recalls being on an airplane that was delayed at the gate for 45 minutes. The pilot spoke to the passengers over the loudspeaker: "Ladies and gentlemen, will you please take your seats so I can see out of the rearview mirror and back this plane out!" This was all that was needed to relax the passengers, release tension, and improve the mood of passengers and flight crew.

Allen believes that the patient as well as the physician contributes to the success of the healing process. Each has to contribute 50 percent to the healing equation. Humor is a way to say to the patient, "I know more about the science of medicine, but you know more about you than I do. Help me understand you and I will help you understand the science behind your problem." Both the physician and the patient have special knowledge, which means they need to work together for the patient's benefit. This is especially true for the patient with a chronic or debilitating illness such as cancer, diabetes, or heart disease.

Physicians have to remember that, unfortunately, most patients consider themselves to be inferior in terms of qualifications and education. Therefore, patients don't start out understanding the importance of their own contribution to the healing process. Allen believes that humor is helpful in generating trust between patients and physicians, and in demonstrating to patients that physicians are just people, not beings from a higher order of existence.

Another advantage of humor is that it stimulates creativity. Avner Zvi, of Tel Aviv, Israel, demonstrated that individuals who watched humorous videos were able to provide more creative solutions to problems than a matched control group without access to the videos. Recently, positron emission tomography (PET) scan data have revealed that the area of the brain responsible for humor is the same area responsible for creativity.

Allen recalls a situation where a husband was upset with his diabetic wife because she wasn't taking good care of herself. Allen suggested that they try a role reversal: the husband would take responsibility for managing the diabetes, including diet and insulin, from sunup to sundown. After just two days he called Allen and asked to be relieved of this responsibility. Through Allen's clever strategy, the husband gained a greater understanding of his wife's chronic illness. Ingenuity and humor can cause eye-opening experiences that ultimately benefit patients.

Here's an example I can contribute. During a Southwest Airlines flight I was on, an attendant pushed a roll of toilet paper down the aisle from the back of the airplane all the way to the front. The attendant asked everyone to guess how many sheets of toilet paper there were in the strip. All the passengers wrote down estimates and submitted them to the flight attendant. Several passengers were given segments of the strip to count and helped to prepare the final tally. The winner received Southwest Airlines luggage tags. What a great way to use humor to amuse passengers and advertise the airline. It was a plane ride that few of the passengers will ever forget.

WAYS TO SPREAD HUMOR

Most people think that being humorous means being a stand-up comedian or being able to tell jokes. Well, there are some people who are naturally funny and can entertain a crowd with one-liners. However, joke-telling skill is relatively rare. Fortunately, that's not the kind of humor that is necessary in a medical practice.

Instead, I am talking about a sense of humor that can be easily learned. Amusing people is a skill like tennis, golf, public speaking, or even surgery. You don't have to be able to perform on stage, but you do have to let people know you and your staff are cheerful and relaxed. They shouldn't be met by sour faces, frowning and worrying, but by people who smile and like to exchange jokes.

Everything you do adds to the ambience of your practice. For example, I wear a tie that shows Charlie Brown, the cartoon character, exercising and working out with weights. When new patients look at that tie, they already feel that they know a little bit about me. I have another tie one of my patients had hand-painted for me—it has kidneys all over it. (There are not many organs associated with urology that can be painted on a tie!) Again, that tie sets a certain humorous tone.

Patients often comment on the two ties, which provides an opportunity for a nonclinical discussion.

Little humorous distractions will make patients less uncomfortable. I have a koala bear that hugs the tubing on my stethoscope with clothespin-like claws. The bear makes the patients, adults as well as children, smile when they first see it.

I always carry an empty matchbook with me. On the inside cover I write, "You are matchless!" When I come across patients who are feeling somewhat discouraged or depressed about their medical conditions, I hand over the matchbook and suggest they open it. Their frowns change to smiles as they read the message inside the cover.

Often a patient asks about my family, and I tell them, as I reach into my pocket for my wallet, "I'd like to show you a picture of my pride and joy." Then I show them a card with a photo of bottles of the furniture polish Pride and the dishsoap Joy. When the laughter and comments subside, I turn the card over and show them a picture of my wife and children.

When you open the door and walk into my practice, you see a globe of the earth hanging from the ceiling like a hot air balloon with *Around the World in 80 Days* characters on it. That globe says, "Humor as well as medicine is practiced here." The books in the bookcase, the drawings on the wall, the magazines on the table, the funny letters I've received—all help create a relaxed atmosphere. We know that patients are anxious when they come to visit a physician. Tasteful humor can reduce that anxiety and subliminally indicate that the patient is going to have a surprisingly enjoyable time.

BUILDING A SENSE OF HUMOR

Once you start looking, there are dozens of opportunities to exhibit a sense of humor in every room of your practice. We have signs in every exam room that emphasize the value of humor, such as

A merry heart doeth good like a medicine.

Proverbs 17:22

By laughing you put WOW into your here and NOW.

He who laughs, lasts!

Occasionally we show reruns of the Little Rascals or a Marx Brothers video in the reception area.

In the restroom, which nearly every patient uses during his or her visit, we have cartoons on the wall (Figure 19-1). We have a sign on the ceiling over each exam

" I'M GETTING IT AGAIN, HOWARD — THAT
FEELING THAT YOU'RE EMBARRASSED WHEN I'M AROUND."

Figure 19-1 Cartoon hanging in bathroom.

table that says, "Smile! You're on Candid Camera." (I promise you that patients will relax as soon as they see a sign like this, and you will be able to perform pelvic exams more easily.)

Some of our patients have a large repertoire of jokes and funny stories. I ask them to remember jokes and tell me one on each visit. This is a nice way of getting patients to relax. It also adds to my repertoire, since I write down these jokes and file them by categories such as "medical," "age," "children," "religion," and "bawdy."

We wear humorous T-shirts on April Fool's Day and dress up for Halloween.

Humor has to start from the top down. You might place a Gary Larson cartoon calendar on your desk and paste up appropriate cartoons for everyone to see, start staff meetings by asking everyone to tell a joke or funny story, send humorous faxes to colleagues and insurance companies (maybe when they're laughing, you'll get paid sooner), and encourage staff to find humorous stories and cartoons in the newspaper and post them on a humor bulletin board in the office. When all else fails, call your office and ask for yourself (at least you'll hear what your patients hear when they call your office).

On fax cover sheets I include several different cartoons that give patients something to laugh at and still leave room for a short message (Figure 19-2). In the

Attention: _____

Company: _____

Tel: _____

Fax: _____

Date: _____

CLEAVER & CHOPOFF
A cut above the rest!

CONFIRMATION OF YOUR
FORTHCOMING VASECTOMY

(Now that I *really* have your attention . . .)

From: _____

Company: _____

Tel: _____

Fax: _____

Figure 19-2 Sample fax cover sheet.

reception area, we have a joke journal containing jokes we've collected to share with patients. It's called Dr. Baum's Collected Quotes and Jokes on Humor and Success. There's a sign on the cover that says, "If you would like copies of any of this material, please let us know and we'll be happy to make them for you. More importantly, if you have a contribution, please tickle our funny bones as well and share it with us."

One physician colleague who actually is a stand-up comedian always tests new material on his patients. He has even created a humor chain letter. He writes out a few one-liners or jokes and sends them to 10 friends who appreciate humor, together with a letter asking them to add a few additional humorous items to the list and then send it on as a chain letter. He says through this method he has generated hundreds of new jokes for his routine.

If you want to develop a repertoire of funny stories, start a humor journal. Whenever you hear a funny story or joke, jot down a word or two that will remind you of the buildup and then write down the punch line. You can fill in the rest of the story when you enter it into the humor journal at the end of the day.

For example, I heard about an interview with the great hotelier, Conrad Hilton. The host said, "We'll take a station break, and when we get back, Mr. Hilton will give us his final advice." When the commercial break was over, the host said, "We have just a few seconds. Mr. Hilton, what is your final advice for our audience?" As all were waiting for the magnate's words of wisdom, he said, "When you take a shower, please insert the shower curtain inside the tub!" When I heard that story, I wanted to add it to my collection. I wrote down "Conrad Hilton" and "shower curtain" as reminders so that when I got home I could record the full story in my joke file.

HUMOR AND YOUR STAFF

Another advantage of humor in the office is that when patients are having fun, this energizes and invigorates the staff, avoiding the all-too-common problem of staff who start the day at 8:00 AM sharp and end it at 5:00 PM dull.

A sense of humor can help relax staffers as well as patients. Find time for a humor break every day. We often take a general break for five minutes in the afternoon and tell a joke or two or read something from the comics in the newspaper or the "Laughter Is the Best Medicine" section in Reader's Digest. It's normal to experience a midafternoon slump, so we take a few minutes in the lounge together (with one person on duty at the business desk) and just tell a couple of light stories. It's amazing how a couple of laughs can pump us back up. It only takes a minute or two. My staff prefers a comedy break to a coffee break anytime.

Buy gag gifts for employees. They don't have to be expensive. Funny coffee mugs and humorous badges and stickers let the employees know you are thinking of them. Send them funny postcards when you are on vacation.

A CUP OF HUMOR AND A TABLESPOON OF TACT

Use humor tactfully. Humor is contagious. Make sure yours is worth catching. Your goal is to help your patients and coworkers relax. Avoid any jokes that might offend people. Avoid sexist and racist jokes and jokes that use profane language. You don't want to be humorous at someone else's expense.

Steve Allen, Jr., describes a case where a patient, immediately after a mastectomy, told her doctor, "My husband won't look at me and won't touch me." The doctor responded, "You tell him that you are as beautiful as the *Playboy* centerfold and you have the staples to prove it!" Perhaps that physician had good intentions, but he should have realized that levity was not appropriate in this situation. Tasteless humor at the expense of the patient will diminish rapport and even cause the patient to seek health care elsewhere. Inappropriate humor can cut deeper than a scalpel.

Perhaps the best jokes are the ones you tell about yourself. Here's one story I sometimes tell: I was running late, and when I entered the exam room to see my next patient, I apologized by saying, "Mr. Jones, I am so sorry about the delay. I hope you didn't mind waiting so long." Mr. Jones replied, "It's okay, Dr. Baum, but I think it would have been easier for you to have seen my urologic problem in its earlier stages!" Now I find that a really funny story. We all need to be secure enough to poke fun at ourselves. It creates a relaxed environment that allows staff to work efficiently and patients to tell you what is really on their minds.

You don't want to come on like Don Rickles, but you do want to create an atmosphere that indicates it is possible to really have a good time here. At our staff meetings we talk about the good things that have happened each day. One of the staff members quoted a patient who said, "You know, I always feel so good when I come here." We want that. That's the goal.

SETTING STRESS ASIDE

When a physician and staff walk into the office, it's almost like they're going to be on view or on stage. If something is bothering them, they have to set it aside while at work because it is part of their job to create a pleasant, cheerful atmosphere. We have a sign in the employee lounge that reads, "Every night is opening night. There's an audience of patients waiting to see you give a great performance. Even if you are tired or blue, go out there and light up the room. Remember, that's what the patients are here for."

This serves as a reminder that we can't allow ourselves the luxury of having a bad day. Patients don't care about our personal problems. All of us need to have a positive attitude every day and go out of our way to ensure our patients have a good experience during their office visits.

I've noticed that when I, as the physician in the office, am not having a good day, that tends to set the tone of the office and affects the whole staff. The other day, I went out to run an errand and my car wouldn't start. While I was trying to jump-start it, I chipped my tooth. All of a sudden I was thinking, "Oh boy, this is one of those days!" I walked upstairs to call AAA, and within a few minutes I could see how the way I was feeling was affecting all the people who work with me. Then I said, "Wait a minute, I apologize, I'm only in this bad mood because my tooth hurts." But I could see that even though I apologized, the atmosphere in the office wasn't the same. It didn't feel like the same congenial place to work in because I wasn't feeling congenial.

The point of this story is that the person who heads the office has to set the example. Patients come to a physician's office to find solutions to their problems. They need a compassionate person to listen to them and a little levity to loosen them up. Everyone has down moments. Physicians need to find methods to recognize and deal with those moments. They need to present their cheerful, upbeat side to their patients.

I find it interesting that the word *silly* is derived from the Germanic word *selig*, which means "blessed, healthy, innocent, carefree." U.S. health care is going through a period of enormous change and nothing short of magic can bring back the "good ol' days," but by adding a little humor to our practices, we can still have fun and get enjoyment from our wonderful profession. There is both wisdom and therapy in laughter. I can guarantee that if you hire Dr. Merryman, you and your patients will both benefit enormously.

HOW WE USED A GAG TO BRING IN NEW PATIENTS

In my office I have a realistic human leg and foot wedged between the cupboard doors in one of the exam rooms (Figure 19-3). Most patients ask about the foot sticking out of the cupboard. We give responses such as, "That was a patient who was late for his appointment" or "That patient didn't pay his bill."

We had a contest to guess "what the foot is doing in the closet." The contest was mentioned in a bill stuffer, which also had a photocopy of the foot. We said that the winner would get a copy of my book "Impotence: It's Reversible" or would

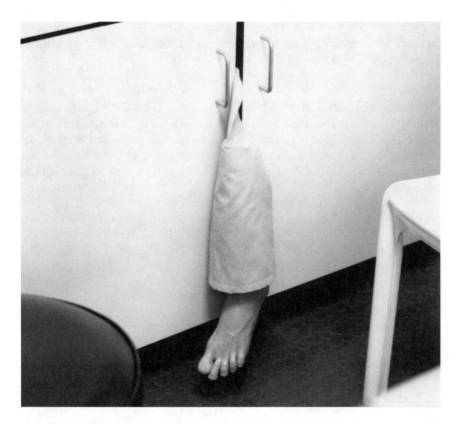

Figure 19-3 Fake human foot and lower leg used as a gag.

have his or her next prescription filled free of charge. The response was incredible. Patients asked to go into that exam room. Several brought their friends to see the foot. It was a great way to demonstrate levity in the office. The patients liked it and so did the staff. Lots of additional people were brought into the office, and many learned that I had written a book on impotence. How many more benefits could one ask for from a simple gag or joke?

By the way, the winning entry was,

> Anyone with a sore tootsie
> Should visit Dr. Baum's office and play footsie!

Humor props, gags, and toys that you can use to spice up your practice are available through the "Whole Mirth Catalog," 1034 Page Street, San Francisco,

CA 94117. Readers are also referred to *Humor and the Healing Professions*, by Dr. Vera M. Robinson, published in 1977 by SLAK, Inc., 6900 Grove Road, Thorofare, NJ 08086.

*   *   *

While we endeavor to create a lighthearted environment that patients and employees will find pleasant and enjoyable, we also need to be certain that we are dotting every i and crossing every t. This requires a high level of professional expertise, so it is wise to call in outside advisors as consultants for accounting and legal services. In the next chapter, I discuss how to find and use outside advisors.

20

Advice on Advisors

T oday, running a medical practice is like running a small business. In addition to treating patients, physicians need to manage expenses, create a business plan, sign contracts, hire and fire employees, supervise their staff's work, manage a pension plan, and supply required information to the government. Very few of us went to medical school with intentions of performing these tasks, and our medical training provided us with only a few of the nonclinical skills needed to run a small business. This chapter describes how to find outside consultants who can assist in the performance of business-related activities.

FINDING RELIABLE ADVISORS

Robert Katz, CPA, a principal and health care specialist in the accounting firm of Katz and Asher* and author of *The Physician's Survival Guide to the Business of Medicine*,[1] warns,

> Don't confuse a good personality and a firm handshake with competency. In fact, you need to be very, very careful. It's difficult to find a good insurance agent, accountant, attorney, or financial planner. Take your time in choosing the people you will rely on for all of your nonmedical decisions. Just as patients feel free to request a second opinion,

---

*1515 Poydras Street, Suite 1800, New Orleans, LA 70112, 800-622-4127, 504-525-8524, fax 504-525-8547.

173

don't be afraid to check out the advice your consultants give you if things aren't working out.

Katz suggests asking your colleagues to recommend advisors. Your hospital's physician services department may have suggestions. If you already have long-term relationships with trusted advisors, like an attorney or a banker, ask them who they would recommend. "I'm often told that if you do that, the same two or three names will keep popping up," Katz says. "Then you need to interview all three, get an idea of their professional skills, and also see if you can establish a rapport with them. There aren't any shortcuts. You're making an important decision, and you have to invest the time and energy to make such an important decision."

INTERVIEWING CANDIDATES

During the first interview with a candidate, discuss in general terms the work you need done. Then ask the candidate if there is anything else he or she would suggest for you and your practice. Discuss expected fees in some detail. Does the candidate expect a monthly fee or work by the hour? In either case, ask the candidate to estimate the annual cost for the services you will need. If you are dealing with a large firm, make it clear that you want experienced individuals working on your account, not novices. At the end of the interview, ask for the names and numbers of three physicians who have previously used the candidate's services and for permission to contact them. Call them and ask for their frank opinion.

After you have interviewed your "possibles" and have decided whom you would like to employ, have another meeting with the chosen candidate to define in more detail the scope of work you have in mind. After this meeting, the candidate should send you a proposal letter (Exhibit 20-1) describing the work that will be performed, the approximate hours required, and the expected fee.

DEFINING THE SCOPE OF WORK

One determinant of the job description will be the set of laws you must comply with. For example, you will have to generate periodic financial statements, file tax returns, and file pension and administrative reports.

The scope of work will also be partly defined by the size of your practice. For example, a large group practice may need monthly financial statements, whereas a small office with a few physicians may need quarterly financial statements.

Besides routine business services, you may occasionally need management advice. At times you will want to view your practice as a whole and make plans for the future. There's no hard and fast rule about when you need management advice, but you can develop a feel for the situations in which an objective outsider's

Exhibit 20-1 Sample Engagement Letter

Dear Dr. _____:

This letter is to confirm our understanding of the terms and objectives of our engagement and the nature and limitations of the services we will provide.

We will perform the following services for (company):

1. Compile from information you provide the monthly statement of assets and liabilities–tax basis and the related statement of revenue and expenses–tax basis. We will not audit or review such financial statements. Our report on the monthly financial statements is presently expected to read as follows:

   We have compiled the accompanying statement of assets and liabilities–tax basis of (company) as of (date) and the related statement of revenues and expenses–tax basis for the year then ended, in accordance with standards established by the American Institute of Certified Public Accountants. The financial statements have been prepared on the tax basis of accounting, which is a comprehensive basis of accounting other than generally accepted accounting principles.

   A compilation is limited to presenting in the form of financial statements information that is the representation of management. We have not audited or reviewed the accompanying financial statements and, accordingly, do not express an opinion or any other form of assurance on them.

   Management has elected to omit substantially all the disclosures required by generally accepted accounting principles. If the omitted disclosures were included in the financial statements, they might influence the user's conclusions about the company's financial condition. Accordingly, these financial statements are not designed for those who are not informed about such matters. If, for any reason, we are unable to complete the compilation of your financial statements, we will not issue a report on such statements as a result of this engagement.

2. Prepare the federal and state income tax returns for the above named company for its appropriate year end.

3. Aid you in your administration of a pension plan, preparing, as needed, annual tax filings, participant statements, summary annual reports, and trust accountings.

4. Prepare federal and state individual income tax returns for the physicians (and their children) of (company).

5. Attend your bimonthly meetings and present a management report.

6. Prepare necessary payroll tax returns.

7. Develop and aid the corporation in monitoring internal accounting controls.

8. Develop a management information system that establishes goals, monitors them, and places specific expectations on key employees.

9. Provide sundry business discussions, phone calls, and the like.

Our engagement cannot be relied upon to disclose errors, irregularities, or illegal acts, including fraud or defalcations, that may exist. We will inform you of such matters that come to our attention, however.

We will provide the services above for 1 year at $XXXX/month beginning (date). This fee includes travel expense.

continues

Exhibit 20-1 continued

In addition to the above, we will complete the following one-time projects over the next 12 months:

1. Accounts receivable management: The management of accounts receivable would initially require staff training in coding systems (i.e., CPT, HCPCS, ICD-9, evaluation and management, and modifiers), redesign of hospital and office superbills, restructuring of fee schedules, staff training in computer management capabilities, and design of daily, weekly, and monthly collections policies and procedures. Additionally, formal and fiscally responsible policies for adjustments and write-offs, past due accounts, and insurance claims follow-up need to be redesigned for optimal reimbursement. Once these policies are implemented, accounts receivable management would include continuous monitoring for procedure compliance, problem solving, crisis management, and attainable goal setting to reduce the size of the total accounts receivables and to shift the weighted percentages from having greater than 50% past–120 days to greater than 50% pre–90 days.

Total estimated hours over 12 months	300 hours
2. Fee schedule analysis	20 hours
3. Medical records quality control system implemented	20 hours
4. Risk management systems implemented	20 hours
5. Coding reimbursement policies	20 hours
6. Staff training	30 hours

These projects will require approximately 400 hours of staff time. We will spend no more time on a project than is absolutely necessary. Our fees are as follows: partners, $115–$145 per hour; consultants, $100 per hour; accountants, $65–$90 per hour; clerical, $55 per hour. Additionally, we will invoice you for basic travel expenses at our cost. Project work will be billed on a separate monthly invoice. Payment of our invoices is due and payable within thirty (30) days of the date of our statement.

Your returns are of course subject to review by the taxing authorities. Any items resolved against you by the examining agent are subject to certain rights of appeal. In the event of examination, we will be available to represent you and will bill you for additional services at our standard rates for them.

We shall be pleased to discuss this letter with you at any time.

If the foregoing is in accordance with your understanding, please sign in the space provided and return this letter to us.

Sincerely,

Robert W. Katz
Katz & Asher, Ltd.

RWK/rhl
Acknowledged:

_____   _____
(Physician)   (Date)

Source: R.W. Katz, *The Physician's Survival Guide to the Business of Medicine* (Gaithersburg, Md.: Aspen Publishers, 1994, pp. 92–93).

opinion will be useful. You certainly need to consult advisors if you face declining revenues or increasing accounts receivable or are thinking about merging with another practice.

HOW MUCH CAN BE DONE IN-HOUSE?

When it comes to legal and financial work, there are certainly routine tasks that can be done by your existing staff. A practice should be able to do all the single-entry bookkeeping. The staff should keep track of accounts receivables and payables and do the payroll and basic bookkeeping. An accountant uses this basic information to generate financial statements and then does the tax returns.

Similarly, the basic legal work of maintaining minutes of official meetings and records of hiring and firing can certainly be done in-house. You need to have an attorney review your legal records and provide advice when you face an unusual or potentially difficult task, such as evaluating a managed care contract, checking your lease, or creating a contract binding together your practice and a new associate.

"Some practices will insist on trying to do complicated work in-house," Katz says. "In my experience, they frequently make major mistakes. If they screw something up, it costs more for the advisors to unscrew it and do it right than if they'd just let them do it in the first place." This is an example of being penny-wise but pound-foolish.

What advisors do you need to manage your practice effectively? Certainly a lawyer and a CPA, and perhaps a management consultant, a banker, and a stockbroker.

ESSENTIAL ADVISORS

Lawyers

Every practice needs legal help. Your lawyer can assist you in determining if your practice should be a corporation, partnership, or sole proprietorship. Whenever you sign a contract, be sure your lawyer reviews it. Do not skimp on legal advice, because a molehill in a contract can become a mountain costing thousands of dollars in legal fees and penalties. For example, a contract that agrees to pay reasonable travel expenses for an associate without setting a specific dollar limit may lead to intense disputes regarding the definition of "reasonable." Or failing to formally record a lease at the county recorder of mortgages may lead to the invalidation of the lease.

Katz recommends that every physician who is incorporated should have at least one meeting a year with his or her attorney to cross the legal t's and dot the legal i's. Health care law changes every year. An annual legal checkup is just as important as an annual physical, but many physicians tend to skip it (as perhaps they also tend to skip their annual physicals).

A corporation must have its annual meeting minutes on file. The attorney needs to review the basic bylaws, articles of incorporation, and employment agreements. OSHA and Medicare regulations may have changed. A good health care attorney will review all those issues with you annually and keep you and your practice out of legal hot water.

In this day and age, when you want to fire somebody, it's beneficial to pick up the phone and bounce the idea off your attorney. Make sure that you're not vulnerable to a charge of discrimination or liable for a suit for wrongful dismissal. Discuss these issues before you take action, not afterward.

Basic legal work will cost $1,000 to $5,000 per year for most practices. Of course, more complicated legal advice, such as that required for the creation of an independent practice association, will be more expensive.

Accountants

A certified public accountant (CPA) will assist you in obtaining all your tax identification numbers, such as federal and state employer numbers. Most CPAs can also advise you on a computer software program for your office.

Accounting firms range in size from solo practitioners to large international firms. However, local firms are much more likely to seek out medical practices and be aware of their special needs. If possible, try to find a CPA who specializes in health care. "Too many CPAs are generalists and can't give physicians the meaningful advice that they need," Katz says.

Basic accounting for a small practice, including quarterly financial statements, tax returns, and basic consulting services, may run $5,000 to $10,000 per year. A larger practice will probably use more consulting services and should expect to pay $10,000 to $20,000 per year.

Management Consultants

A practice management consultant can assist you in every aspect of your practice, from budgets and marketing to personnel and finance. He or she can provide the business and management skills many physicians lack, especially when they are beginning a practice.

A reasonable fee for a practice management consultant is $80 to $100 per hour, depending on experience. Some consultants charge a flat fee, typically $2,000 to $5,000 per year.

Bankers

In most large cities, the bigger banks have special departments that cater to doctors and other professionals, and the personnel in these departments are aware of the unique needs and concerns of professionals. "Those I've met tend to be very sharp people, fairly insightful," Katz says. "You may find it useful to develop a relationship with your bankers and use them as a sounding board for certain decisions that occur in your practice."

For example, a banker probably has a good overview of the local accountants and lawyers who specialize in health care. He or she can suggest possible referrals. A banker will be able to help with basic investment decisions and explain why taking out a loan in a given situation is or is not advisable. Bankers have a good sense of "the pulse" of the community. They can provide balance when it comes to making nonmedical or business decisions.

A banker will also encourage the physician to keep annual personal financial statements and will be willing to review them with him or her. "A banker has no axe to grind—he's not getting paid a commission or a fee. What they do, they do for free," Katz says.

Stockbrokers

A stockbroker is not mandatory. However, setting up a retirement plan is recommended for most medical practices. If you have a retirement plan, you need investments and a good stockbroker.

Stockbrokers receive a commission on what they sell. Today brokerage commissions vary widely, so you should check the range of services you plan to use. Even full-service firms will negotiate fees with their better customers.

There are also discount brokerage firms, like Charles Schwab. With a little work, you can set up a retirement plan and run it without a full-fee broker. However, many physicians feel more comfortable relying on a broker—they don't want to take the time to make their own investment decisions. Katz recommends checking a broker's advice with "first tier" advisors, such as your lawyer, accountant, and banker.

THE IMPORTANCE OF STAYING INVOLVED

Advisors can offer advice, but the final responsibility still rests with you. That means you must dedicate time to business decisions. In a large group practice, only some members of the group may deal with these issues; their partners are often more than happy to leave business matters in their hands. In every medical practice, a physician must supervise the financial decisions that are the lifeblood of the practice.

*   *   *

One important role outside advisors can play is to help a medical office find innovative ways to cut overhead expenses. As financial pressures increase, this becomes more and more important. In the next chapter, I will examine ways to limit overhead and increase financial stability.

NOTES

1. R.W. Katz, *The Physician's Survival Guide to the Business of Medicine* (Gaithersburg, Md.: Aspen Publishers, 1994).

21

Reduce Overhead

Whan are the wants, needs, and concerns of practicing physicians today? Most of my colleagues, when asked that question, answer that
they need to see more patients, attract more new patients, improve
office efficiency, increase office staff morale, make managed care more manage-
able, and reduce overhead. This chapter focuses on simple, effective ways any
practice can cut overhead substantially. We will discuss practical techniques to
reduce the cost of lab fees, telephone expenses, printing costs, and service contracts for office equipment and computers.

There is no question that overhead costs are unfortunately continuing to rise
despite the fact that revenues continue to decline. You don't have to have an MBA
to understand that this means a loss of net income for each and every one of us. I
was concerned about my spiraling overhead and thus contacted Robert Katz, CPA,
of Katz and Asher.* The following discussion is based on his experienced advice.

Katz predicts that we will most likely continue to see flat or declining revenues. On
the other hand, fixed costs such as salaries, rent, insurance, and postage will remain stable or increase slightly. That means reducing overhead is one of the few
remaining options for controlling costs and increasing profits in our practices.

WHY IS OVERHEAD A CONCERN?

Overhead can slowly cripple and stifle an otherwise healthy and vital practice.
A practice lacking the time, staff, or expertise to monitor expenses consistently

---

*1515 Poydras Street, Suite 1800, New Orleans, LA 70112, 800-622-4127, 504-525-8524,
fax 504-525-8547.

will see rising costs obstruct cash flow and eat into profits. Given the increased pressure from HMOs and capitated health plans, the only way to maintain (or increase) your income will be to improve efficiency and decrease overhead. Cutting fixed overhead items such as salaries or rent is often difficult or impossible. Fortunately, finding innovative methods to reduce variable expenses, such as printing, telephone, laboratory, and travel expenses, is not. Most of us are paying 15 to 20 percent more for variable expenses than we need to. This usually translates into $15,000 to $25,000 in savings for a solo practitioner and hundreds of thousands of dollars in savings for larger group practices.

Many physicians spend more than required on office and medical supplies. It's easy to order office supplies from someone who comes by and chats with the secretaries, even though buying from a discount office supply store would save a considerable amount of money. It's convenient to buy drugs from a pharmacist, even though the cost is greater than it would be if you bought from a discounter. Katz estimates that outlays for office and medical supplies are 30 or 40 percent higher than they need to be.

There are many items whose cost can be reduced by creative shopping and large-volume buying. They include stationery, superbills, and other printed materials; air fares, hotels, and other travel costs; long-distance telephone service (and sometimes local service); computer equipment, computer maintenance, office supplies (copier paper, toner, etc.), and computer supplies; and lab fees (for practices that directly bill patients for lab services). A small group practice or solo practitioner can pool orders with a few other practices in order to obtain volume discounts.

It is helpful to assign one person in the office to do the work of ordering supplies. Usually the office manager serves as the purchasing agent. Remember, all prices are negotiable. Our practice was able to save $20 for each dose of an LH-RH agonist to treat prostate cancer because of the volume we used. Your purchasing agent should always inquire about the possibility of a price break for various products or services. Although the savings on any one item may be small, they can add up to thousands of dollars each year. Finally, have someone in the office check purchase orders against received shipments.

The costs of some items are surprisingly negotiable. Even so-called fixed expenses may be negotiable in certain circumstances. For example, don't try to save on rent by compressing your practice into a smaller space; instead, try to renegotiate the price of the space you are already in.

Katz tells a story about one client in California who was able to negotiate a 40-percent discount on rent. "Granted, once you've signed a lease you're committed to it, but in some parts of the country where the economy is really depressed we're able to go to the landlord in some cases and say, 'Look, we signed this lease when times were good. Now times are bad, and this is what we can afford to pay you now'—and they're accepting these offers. In one case, we won a rent reduction from $25,000 a month to $15,000 a month. The landlord wasn't too happy, but $15,000 was still above the current market rate, and he accepted it."

One rough rule of thumb is that rent should represent 6 to 7 percent of gross revenues. A rent greater than 7 percent of gross income should be renegotiated if possible.

WHERE TO LOOK FIRST FOR COST SAVINGS

The most significant savings are normally found in high-expense areas. Practices that spend $15,000 per year on superbills (this expense level can occur in practices with as few as 100 patients a day) will see big savings in superbills and other printed materials. Practices that incur heavy long-distance phone charges or travel expenses frequently can realize significant savings in those areas.

In some instances, it makes sense to pay a premium for high-quality service. For example, if your office manager likes and trusts your printing vendor, it may make sense to pay a little more, especially if the vendor provides one-day service or pickup and delivery. However, it would not make sense to pay 30 percent more. You must determine if the extra level of service justifies the price premium. Liking a vendor and paying a little more is one thing. Liking a vendor and paying an extra $5,000 per year is an entirely different matter—especially if you are not aware that you are paying a significant premium.

Of course, staff salaries usually constitute the biggest expenditure in any physician's office. The nonphysician payroll generally represents approximately 16 percent of gross revenues. Unfortunately, you can't cut staff. In today's health care environment, you need more staff than ever before to manage all the necessary paperwork, authorization forms, and communications with managed care plans. You need an office manager and an insurance person. Such staff are highly skilled and therefore very expensive. Your greatest expense will be your office staff, and while you may be able to save a little by looking more closely at your benefit package or the amount of overtime worked, your greatest expense will continue to be your staff.

One way to reduce or control staff expenses is to reduce overtime. In most states, it is legally necessary to pay each staff member 1½ times his or her hourly rate for all work over 40 hours a week. One way to limit overhead is to stagger staff hours. For example, if you offer early morning hours, have some staff arrive at 7:00 AM and leave at 4:00 PM and have the rest arrive at 9:00 AM and leave at 6:00 PM. Another way to decrease overtime is to have some staff convert to a four-day, 10-hour-a-day workweek so they can work longer daily hours without violating overtime laws. You should also cross-train staff to allow your receptionist to function as a nursing assistant in a pinch or a secretary to work the front desk if necessary. Finally, if you have a practice where the workload typically increases during a particular period (such as flu season), consider using some temporary or part-time employees to share the load.

Another way to reduce staff expenses is to select health insurance with a higher deductible and copayment. Also consider using an HMO or PPO for employee health care instead of a traditional indemnity plan. After all, most other businesses are taking these steps to reduce health care costs.

LEARNING TO NEGOTIATE LOWER PRICES

In order to cut overhead costs, you need to take a fresh look at your current suppliers, even if you have been with them for a substantial period of time. For example, J. Landy Damsey, M.B.A., M.H.S., head of the medical management consulting firm Damsey and Associates,* recalls one group practice of nine physicians that needed to buy a new computer. Damsey suggested a new supplier, and by switching from its old system, the practice cut maintenance costs by $15,600 a year.

The easiest way to reduce expenses is to solicit bids from at least three vendors for the same exact product or service. Your request should be in writing and you should get written responses.

For example, if you want bids on your superbill or letterhead, attach a copy of it to the bid request. If you want bids on a continuous form, include several pieces, including the attached pin-feed. When getting air fare bids, include a copy of a ticket from a prior flight or a future flight to verify your fare category and restrictions.

Securing the best price is easier than you think. It does take time and energy but usually yields a substantial return on investment. Prices normally continue to drop after a series of negotiations, which can take place over several weeks or even months, in the case of high-ticket items. Remember, polite persistence pays.

If you lack the time, staff, or willpower to deal with salespeople, you can do price shopping over the phone. Calling to find out prices is a quick method to determine if your existing prices are completely out of line. In most instances, however, this method rarely yields the best results. Vendors need to negotiate eyeball to eyeball before they offer their very best price.

To get the best price, you must first know what a good price actually is. Experienced consultants have an advantage because they deal with numerous busi-

---

*444 Crawford Street, Portsmouth, VA 23704, 804-399-5977.

nesses, practices, and vendors. They will know what a fair price is long before they enter into negotiations. For example, a consultant would be aware that your present average long-distance cost of 22 cents per minute is actually 25 percent above the "usual and customary fee." The consultant would look for vendors to offer you at least a 25-percent discount, whereas you or your staff, not being familiar with typical rates in your area, might think you're getting a great deal when a new vendor offers you a 10-percent discount.

By knowing the true industry margins, experienced consultants can secure the best possible prices for your practice. Some physician offices are paying $86 per thousand sheets for a raised letterhead. How does $75 per thousand sound? Better than the initial $86 per thousand, but still too high, even for limited quantities. A fair price would actually be $68 per thousand, a reduction of almost 30 percent. Over a year's time, that reduction will result in roughly $1,500 in savings for a group practice of five doctors.

PRACTICAL NEGOTIATING TIPS

If you or your office manager plan to do your own negotiating, here are some practical tips:

- Always let vendors know that price is going to be one of your crucial selection criteria.
- Try to give vendors your requirements in writing and request responses in writing.
- Include samples of the product whenever possible.
- Use recognized vendors whenever possible. Don't use a "fly-by-night" as a benchmark.
- Compare apples to apples. Do your homework up front. Determine quantity, color, shape, size, weight, delivery time, and so on, before you ask for pricing.
- Make sure your RFPs (requests for proposal) are simple, short, and easy for vendors to respond to. This will mean they will likely come back in a simple and easy-to-read format for you to review.
- Lastly, make sure you understand terms, conditions, and warranties. It may be better to get a toner cartridge that costs 30 percent more if it contains 50 percent more toner. By the same token, it may not make sense to spend $1,000 a year maintaining an older computer if for $2,500 you can purchase a new model that comes with a three-year warranty.

It takes a few phone calls and a few letters to achieve savings. Don't forget, a savings of $12,000 per year translates into a whopping $120,000 over ten years. These days, that's a lot of money to leave on the table.

REFERENCE MATERIALS THAT CAN AID IN CUTTING COSTS

One way to find the most fruitful areas to achieve savings is to compare your overhead expenses to those of other practices. The Medical Group Management Association publishes an annual reference book, *The Cost Survey*, that lists various overhead expenses by specialty, size of group, and geographic region.[1] It offers data on benefits, phone services, medical and surgical supplies, housekeeping and maintenance supplies, and furniture and equipment. If your expenses for a given category are higher than they would be in most other comparable practices, that is a clear signal to search for opportunities for savings in that category. A newsletter called *The Physician's Advisory* also periodically publishes useful information on physicians' overhead expenses.[2]

SALARIES AND BENEFITS

Employee health insurance is another rapidly increasing expense, and physicians, like other employers, may need to consider setting higher deductibles, limiting coverage, or requiring employee cost-sharing.

According to Damsey, when it comes to benefits such as health, life, and disability insurance, solo practitioners often offer better benefits than Fortune 500 companies. "In general, the smaller the practice, the better the benefits," Damsey says. "The staff is small, the physician feels close to the staff, and they all feel like family, so the practice just naturally evolves into a very generous benefit package."

Katz claims that many practices are paying too much overtime and that this is a fruitful area for renegotiation. "Almost always the overtime is unnecessary—it is just a way for employees to stretch eight hours' worth of work over ten hours. If a physician says, 'I really need you to stop working overtime,' there may be lowered staff morale in the short term, but I've never had one physician or staff complain a year later. Once a practice is run like a business, both the doctor and the staff are less stressed."

USING CONSULTANTS

My feeling, after communicating with many of my colleagues and their office staff, is that few practices have the time and money to secure money-saving results on their own. While a practice could decide to do all the legwork in-house, I suggest hiring a temporary cost-saving specialist instead. Many consultants do not charge an hourly fee but instead take a percentage of the estimated annual savings. If there are no verifiable savings, there is no charge. It's just that simple—no savings, no scratch. If there are savings, the practice pays a one-time percentage-based fee.

When using a consultant, you need to submit to the consultant for review sample invoices, data on use, and, if possible, a sample of the product you wish to buy. Should you want to reduce your stationery expenses, you would provide the consultant with the monthly (or annual) volume purchased, a copy of at least one invoice, and a sample of the letterhead. The consultant would then secure the pricing information and send an analysis to you so you or your office manager could select a vendor.

How do you measure the results of using a consultant to reduce costs? Savings are estimated in a simple and straightforward manner. Let's go back to the printing example. Let's say that during the consultant's initial meeting with your office, you state that you typically order 2,500 superbills a month. At an average cost of 40 cents each, the amount your current vendor charges, your estimated annual superbill expense is $12,000 a year ($.40 × 2,500 × 12 months). After securing bids from printing vendors, the consultant finds a printer willing to charge only 30 cents for exactly the same superbill, for a savings of $3,000 a year. The consultant could also go back to your original printer on your behalf and ask the printer to match the bid. If the printer agreed to match the bid, you would probably continue to order from that printer. If not, you could order from the low-bid vendor.

The consultant's fee is usually 35 percent of the overall savings (in this case, $1,050 [35 percent of $3,000]). Your overall savings would be almost $2,000 the first year and the full $3,000 a year thereafter. If for any reason you became unhappy with the selected vendor during the first year, you could expect your consultant to redo the analysis without charge and find an alternate vendor. An effective consultant normally can negotiate savings of at least 20 percent on printing, 15 percent on travel, 30 percent on lab services, and 15 percent on telephone charges. In some cases savings as high as 50 percent are obtained.

My personal experience using a consultant was very favorable. I still use most of the vendors he found. If problems develop and you don't keep the new supplier or vendor for at least 90 days, then ask for a refund or give the consultant the responsibility of finding a replacement. A reputable consultant will want to maintain his or her reputation and get a good recommendation from you, so it is in the consultant's interest to make sure you get high-quality goods and services and are satisfied with your suppliers.

WHEN TO INCREASE OVERHEAD COSTS

David Gans, Director of Survey Operations at the Medical Group Management Association, notes that it may make sense for a practice to boost overhead expenses if the increase adds to its overall economic viability. "Cut unnecessary expenses but don't starve your practice," he advises.

A decision to set up one or more satellite offices will certainly create a need for more staff and more supplies, not to mention the additional office space that will be required. However, it may still be a good idea to open new branches if it increases the practice's market share in a geographic area and makes the practice a stronger competitor for managed care contracts.

To optimize the economic viability of your practice, you must see as many patients as possible. For any medical practice, effective use of physician time is critical. If you can expand your facility so that the physicians each have four exam rooms instead of two, naturally they will be able to see more patients. But remember those four exam rooms will increase utility, rental, equipment, and staff expenses. "You may find that expenses as a percentage of revenue will increase from 40 percent to 45 percent," Gans says. "However, at the same time, you're seeing more patients and the practice's total revenue after expenses increases, which means there's more money for distribution as physician income and/or to be retained in the practice for expansion and capital improvement."

FUTURE SHOCK

Alvin Toffler defines future shock as the stress and disorientation that occur when individuals are subjected to too much change in too short a time. I think, at present, all of us in medicine are experiencing too much change occurring too quickly. One way to respond to this change is to be proactive and to identify creative ways to manage our practices. One of the best and easiest methods is to reduce overhead expenses. In most instances this can be easily accomplished without reducing the quality of care provided to patients. The goal should be to maximize the time physicians spend with patients and hire others or use technology to do everything else.

*   *   *

Just as important as cutting overhead expenses and practicing in a cost-effective manner is making your patients feel welcome. Creating a friendly environment will help your patients feel at home. In the next chapter, I will review some of the ways you can set up your office and train your staff so patients have a positive health care experience when they turn to you for care.

NOTES

1. *The Cost Survey* (Englewood, Colo.: Medical Group Management Association, published yearly).

2. *The Physician's Advisory*, P.O. Box 97113, Washington, DC 20090, 800-771-8154, fax 301-559-5167.

22

Create a Patient-Friendly Office

The way you organize and decorate your office lets patients know the type of experience they can expect to have with you and your staff. The place where patients are received should be called a "reception area," not a "waiting room," and it should provide a welcoming atmosphere. Four of the five senses should be pleasantly stimulated. The reception area should have attractive furnishings and interesting artwork on the walls. It should smell good. There should be potpourri or fresh cut flowers. There should be pleasant sounds to listen to and comfortable seats to sit on. Pleasant background music is available from Muzak™ or by tuning in to one of the "easy listening" stations. Your reception area provides an opportunity to create a "wow" experience for patients the moment they open the door.

READING MATERIALS

Augment the usual reception area reading fare with appropriate reading material for your patients. For example, if you have a practice that caters to businesspeople, provide the *Wall Street Journal, Barron's,* and *Forbes*. If your practice caters to senior citizens, provide *Modern Maturity* and the large-type version of *Reader's Digest*.

If you have written articles or there are articles in certain publications about you or your practice, place them in the reception area as well. I suggest that you enclose the articles in plastic cover sheets and put the sheets in a three-ring binder. This almost guarantees that the articles will have an indefinite shelf life. You might include a note at the front of the notebook saying that your secretary will be happy to provide copies of the articles upon request.

In addition, you might consider creating a notebook that contains information about your staff. Include photos of your secretary, nurse, and office manager along with brief job descriptions, their backgrounds, and their interests and hobbies. This will help patients feel at ease with your staff when they first begin to interact with them.

We have a book in the reception area we call the "warm fuzzy" book. It includes complimentary letters from our patients regarding their experience with our office. "Dear Dr. Baum, thanks for seeing me on your day off." "Dr. Baum, thanks for the wonderful care you and your staff gave me while I was in the hospital." "Dear Dr. Baum, we want to tell you that your staff is terrific." Of course, we always request permission before placing a letter in this book, but people are usually very happy to have their letters on display. We have three volumes of complimentary letters, and they are the most looked-at books in our reception area.

DECORATING YOUR WALLS

You can't just hang your diplomas on the wall and hope that's enough to keep your patients interested. A few diplomas might be appropriate, but don't stick up every piece of parchment you have ever received. If you went to a prestigious medical school such as Harvard, you do want to let your patients know this. However, most patients don't really care what organizations you belonged to, what meetings you attended, or what division in the army you served in. Let's take the physicians' honorary fraternity, Alpha Omega Alpha—very few patients or even nurses know what that is. Numerous diplomas filling up all the space just looks like the doctor's ego talking. Instead, put up pictures of your family and something that relates to your hobbies and recreational activities.

If you do want to exhibit your diplomas, one nice way to do it is to gather them together and have them professionally reduced in size into one attractive display. They take up less wall space and all the important information is readily available. You can have copies of this composite placed in all the exam rooms so every patient can see your credentials, society memberships, and awards.

But I think you want to reserve your wall space for other topics that will be more interesting to your patients and create the right atmosphere and image for your practice. We like to post inspirational statements. For example, we use a quotation from W. Mitchell, a Colorado businessman who received burns over 90 percent of his body in a motorcycle accident and then became a paraplegic as a result of an airplane crash. He said, "It's not what happens to you but what you do about it that counts." That reminds patients that regardless of the magnitude of their problems, they can persevere and make the rest of their life meaningful.

We use another quotation from Winston Churchill: "Never give in, never give up, never, never, never, on anything great or small, never give in."

We want patients to know that regardless of their problems, their physician and his or her office staff will not give up on them. If someone is fighting a serious illness, one of these sayings may be just what he or she needs to see—it may be the motivation to assume part of the responsibility for getting well.

It may be of interest to note that in nearly 20 years of practice I have never had a patient ask for a copy of any of my diplomas. However, I do get frequent requests for a copy of one of these motivational quotations.

Another interesting way to use your wall space is to post informative articles and diagrams relating to health issues. Many offices post anatomical drawings. Since I write regularly on health care, I often post a selection of my most recent articles. On the wall right now we have an article on PSA tests that appeared in *USA Today* in August 1994. We find people often ask us for copies of that article, and of course we're delighted to offer them (which include the name, address, and telephone number of our practice just in case they give this article to a family member or friend). We hand out nearly 50 copies of articles on health care every week.

The walls should contain pleasant distractions. I prefer artwork that will interest or involve the patient, like prints by M.C. Escher. These prints will often occupy a patient's attention while alone in the exam room. I also like to hang prints by the popular artist T.E. Breitenbach. His "Proverbidioms" contain well-known proverbs and idioms expressed by means of the characters or background of the painting (Figure 22-1). The viewer tries to guess the appropriate proverb or idiom.

I provide puzzles and three-dimensional optical illusions so patients can amuse themselves in the exam rooms. Each room also contains a health care–related cartoon and joke book. Books you may want to have available include *Medicine Is Not Pretty*, by Bill Andrews,[1] *The Original Missionary Position*, by Brian Moench and Chauna Moench,[2] and *Tales from the Bedside*, by John Wise.[3]

ACCESSIBILITY AND OTHER MATTERS

Make sure your practice is accessible to your patients, especially if most of your patients are employed. Do they need to see you before or after work? Do you have senior citizens in wheelchairs or using walkers? Make sure that your practice can accommodate the disabled.

Figure 22-1 A Proverbidiom by T.E. Breitenbach. In each Proverbidiom, a proverb or idiom is expressed pictorially and the viewer's task is to guess it. Can you find "People in glass houses shouldn't throw stones" and "Too many cooks spoil the broth"? *Source:* T.E. Breitenbach & Company, P.O. Box 538, Altamont, NY 12009, 518-861-6054.

I think it's important for staff morale to have uniforms that are distinctive—not the customary white ones. Everyone in my office has a uniform that is color coordinated with the wallpaper, the stationery, the rugs, and my uniform. I pay for the uniforms and let my staff pick them out. Make your uniforms distinctive and people will remember you for your signature colors.

Supply coat hangers for patients' clothes in the reception area and each exam room. Often patients go to the doctor and have to get undressed and lay their clothes over a chair or hang them on a hook. Providing coat hangers is a way of showing that you pay attention to the little details. If you're worried about coat hangers making noise, get padded coat hangers.

You can tell a world-class practice by its restrooms. If you walk into McDonald's, you know that the restrooms are going to be clean, you know that the tiles are going to shine, you know that there will be plenty of toilet paper. Don't you think it should be the same in a doctor's office? If you walked into the restroom and saw pieces of toilet paper on the floor or spilled urine specimen cups, how eager would you be to let that doctor take care of you?

This means that various staff members must take the responsibility to check the restroom several times a day. Similarly, staff should regularly walk out into the reception area to straighten the magazines, pick up any stray food and wrappers, and rearrange the chairs. The patients who arrive at 4:00 PM should have just as nice a view of the reception area and the restroom as the patients who arrive at 9:00 AM. Take care of these two vital areas throughout the day.

WELCOMING PATIENTS OVER THE PHONE

Patients are often uneasy when they first call a doctor's office. Thus it's important to create a welcoming impression over the phone, before the patient even steps in the door. In my office employees are trained to say, "Good morning/ afternoon. This is Dr. Baum's office, this is so-and-so speaking. How may I help you? . . . Oh, yes, we knew you were going to be calling for an appointment. We got a call from your primary care doctor, and we're looking forward to seeing you. We're going to send you some information because we know you may have lots of questions before you come in."

When my staff answers the phone, they have a script in front of them. Another detail that I think is important: use the caller's name at least twice during every phone conversation. Everybody loves to hear his or her own name. By using it, you personalize the conversation.

In addition, there's a sign on every telephone reminding the staff to smile. There's a mirror in front of each staff member to give feedback. You may think that no one can hear a smile over the phone, but I believe the opposite. Each call is an opportunity to create a good first impression long before the caller opens the door to your office.

USING YOUR HOLD BUTTON TO MARKET YOUR PRACTICE

Ideally no one should be put on hold. But even the most efficient practices with the most attentive staff will occasionally need to use the hated hold button. To avoid situations when the caller hangs up and does not call back, you may want to use a Marketing on Hold* program. Remember a hang up may mean a lost patient, and today few of us can afford to have a current patient leave because of poor telephone etiquette or lose the opportunity to attract a new patient.

In the past many practices have used Muzak™ or piped-in local radio broadcasts. Piped-in music is better than silence, but it does involve rebroadcasting a

---

*5311 Kirby Dr., Suite 115, Houston, TX 77005, 713-522-4333.

licensed radio program without permission, which creates the risk of a lawsuit. Also, piped-in music offers the practice no control over the content that callers hear. In the worst-case scenario, they could hear an advertisement from a competitor!

Any particular sort of music will only appeal to a small percentage of a given listening audience. Piped-in music may be unappealing to some callers and lead them to form a negative opinion of your practice. Mixed with the music selections are news programs that focus on crimes, violence, and natural disasters, which can put callers in a negative frame of mind.

A program such as Marketing on Hold combines music with informational messages that specifically relate to your practice and the health issues your patients deal with. It provides information to your callers for pennies—information that would cost thousands of dollars to deliver through print, radio, or television. You can advertise additional services that your practice offers and that callers were not aware of. The information is subliminally retained by the callers and will often generate questions about the topic or message.

The music-message format reduces your callers' perceived time on hold. The program can also answer frequently asked patient questions. It will significantly reduce caller anger and frustration and reduce by 95 percent the number of people who hang up before they get through.

My staff has commented that since we began using an information on hold program there has been a noticeable change in patients' attitudes. Our own surveys indicate that patients prefer to hear the recorded messages rather than the different types of music and radio talk shows. We find the patients respond in a friendly, courteous, and positive fashion after listening to our information on hold program.

Several of my colleagues who have heard our program have implemented their own. One physician used his program to notify patients that he was moving his practice to a new location. Another used his program to announce the addition of a new physician to the practice.

The taped program should be at least 24 minutes in length. If you use a short 4-minute program, repeat callers may hear the same program several times. And if, heaven forbid, a caller is left on hold for more than 4 minutes, he or she will hear the same program again. With a 24-minute program, patients learn new information each time they phone in.

The script should be written by professional copywriters who have both medical and marketing experience. You want the announcer to have a good voice and previous radio experience. You want your information given to callers in a courteous, friendly manner.

The best companies offering information on hold services allow you to change your message whenever you want. For example, during September, which is Cancer Prevention Month, I add a message offering a free PSA test.

Your company should offer prompt exchange of equipment if it becomes defective, preferably within 48 hours. You also need a backup tape if the current tape becomes defective from overuse. You should change messages at least twice a year, although more often than that would be even better.

*   *   *

Once patients arrive in your office, it is essential to show them that you value and respect their time and will treat them well. In the next chapter, I will review creative ways to adjust your schedule to see patients with maximum efficiency.

NOTES

1. B. Andrews, *Medicine Is Not Pretty* (Houston: Bill Andrews and Associates, 1987).

2. B. Moench and C. Moench, *The Original Missionary Position* (Midvale, Utah: Seagull Printing Service, 1992).

3. J. Wise, *Tales from the Bedside* (Clearwater, Fla.: John Wise, 1993).

23

On Time Means on the Ball

A few years ago an ophthalmologist in Lake Worth, Florida, "caught the wrath of a patient made to wait" when he was taken to small claims court and sued for breach of verbal contract. The patient, who had endured a wait of several hours, later told his story on the *Tonight Show* to millions of Americans. This sort of story may occur more frequently in the future unless physicians make an effort to develop an on-time mentality. Cartoonist Gary Larson has even devised a standard form a patient can complete to bill the doctor for excessive waits.

The number one complaint of patients is that they have to wait too long to see their doctor. In fact, about three years ago Ann Landers wrote a column titled "Patients Should Tell the Doctor If Tardiness Is Causing Anger." Excessive waits without explanation send the signal that your time is more valuable than the patient's. Two-hour waits, which might have been tolerated several years ago, are no longer acceptable. In today's hurried world, patients who spend a long time waiting for the doctor are likely to find another doctor.

I remember a story about a patient who invariably had to wait one or two hours to see his orthopedist. One day, the patient arrived an hour late for his appointment. The nurse admonished him for his tardiness and said, "Mr. Smith, you're an hour late today. Why is that?" He answered, "This time I decided to do my one hour of waiting at home."

In my opinion, most of the waiting done by patients is unnecessary—it's primarily due to traditional but ineffective scheduling methods. This chapter examines ways to improve the appointment process.

199

GATHERING DATA ON THE WAY YOU MANAGE TIME

I suggest that you begin by surveying your patients about their perceptions of time management in your office. Have them fill out a written form during office visits or do a random sampling by mail.

One question you should ask: "When you schedule an appointment with the doctor, are you seen on time?" If the answer frequently is no and your staff says patients are complaining about excessive waits, then I suggest you conduct a time and motion study.

A time and motion study should cover a ten-day period. You attach a time and motion sheet (Exhibit 23-1) to the front of each patient's chart. Record the time the patient arrives, the time of the scheduled appointment, the time the patient was seen, and the time the patient left the office. When you summarize the data, you will be able to identify problem areas and find potential solutions.

Examine your scheduling procedures. Does your staff "double book" in an effort to finish up early for the day? Do they fail to triage patients adequately and allow a non-emergency to create excessive waits? These issues should be reviewed at a staff meeting. If you find that most days have two to three emergencies that throw off the appointment book, then allow emergency slots. Also, allow for call-backs. Tell patients an approximate time when you'll be able to return their calls so they don't wait next to the phone for hours.

Exhibit 23-1 Time and Motion Sheet

PATIENT NAME: _____

DATE: _____

_____ Scheduled appointment

_____ Patient arrival time

_____ Time patient was brought into exam room

_____ Time physician spent with patient (minutes)

_____ Total time in office

CUSTOMIZED SCHEDULING

Most physician offices use linear scheduling: one patient follows another and every patient is booked for 15 minutes. We believe that linear scheduling results in excessive waits and unhappy patients. Instead we use a form of "customized scheduling" that allows us to see patients for appropriate lengths of time and still stay on schedule.

In a typical practice, when patients call with emergency problems, the schedule is already double and triple booked. That ends up producing what I call spasms in the schedule. Some patients are seen immediately, some are hurried through their appointments, and many end up waiting. The net result is an atmosphere of hurry and hassle that affects not only the patients but also the physicians and staff.

How can you avoid these problems and give your patients the feeling that you care about them and value their time? How can you reduce the number of complaints about long waits?

In my practice, we try to schedule patient visits based on each patient's specific clinical needs. When a person comes to visit us, we estimate how much time the visit will take. For example, a new patient with impotence takes about 35 minutes, but a new female patient with an acute urinary tract infection takes only 10 to 12 minutes. A patient who just needs an injection or blood drawn for a lab test takes only 2 or 3 minutes. We schedule half an hour for a patient newly diagnosed with prostate cancer. Obstetricians tell me a first visit for a primigravida will take about 40 minutes, while a first visit for a woman having her fourth child runs about 15 minutes.

We've developed a detailed set of patient standards for appointments (Exhibit 23-2). Based on what patients say about their condition and on our past experience with them, we usually can estimate how much time each patient will need to spend in the office. Occasionally someone does need extra time, but usually we can estimate visit lengths fairly accurately.

WAVE SCHEDULING

Another option is the modified wave scheduling method recommended by practice management consultant David Hunt, of Doctors Management Services.* This method makes it possible to avoid long waits when most patients require the same amount of time. Here's how it works: three patients are scheduled on the hour. On average, one will be late and two will be on time. One patient is seen immediately,

---

*1105 Wooded Acres, Suite 220, Waco, TX 76710, 817-776-5548.

Exhibit 23-2 Estimated Visit Time for Various Types of Patients and Conditions

New patient	20 minutes
Established patient	12 minutes
Recent postop patient	7 minutes
New patient with UTI symptoms	15 minutes
New patient with hematuria	25 minutes
New patient with impotence	35 minutes
New patient with incontinence	25 minutes
New patient with infertility	25 minutes
Patient with diagnosis of prostate cancer	35 minutes
Follow-up PSA and symptom check	7 minutes
Follow-up infertility	10 minutes
Patient to receive testosterone injection	3 minutes
Follow-up patient with UTI	3 minutes
Patient to get penile injection	45 minutes
Patient to get flow rate	5 minutes
CMG and flow rate	20 minutes
Transrectal ultrasound and biopsy	25 minutes

while one waits for a few minutes; the late patient also waits a few minutes, but being late he or she will usually accept the short delay without fuss.

Two patients are scheduled at 20 minutes after the hour, and one or both may wait a few minutes. One patient is scheduled at 40 minutes after the hour. This means the physician has 20 minutes to finish the last three patients and get back on schedule before the hour ends.

This method of scheduling means no patient has to wait any longer than 20 minutes. Most patients will wait for 15 minutes or so without any problem. If they have to wait 20 minutes or more, then they are likely to become anxious and upset . . . and start asking for their records so they can go elsewhere for their medical care.

PREPARING FOR PATIENT VISITS

In addition to customized scheduling and wave scheduling, we employ several strategies to make the appointment process more efficient.

First, we prepare our new patients before they come to the office. We invite our patients to write down needed information, such as name, address, and telephone numbers, ahead of time and encourage them to bring insurance information with them. We also mail them a patient history questionnaire asking questions about their current medications, allergies, previous surgeries, and chief complaint. We ask them to fill out this form at home and bring it with them on their first visit to the practice.

We send new patients information about the practice before they arrive. The packet includes the practice brochure, a newsletter, and a map with directions to the office and the location of nearby parking facilities.

Whenever a patient calls for an appointment, the receptionist tactfully asks about the reason for the visit. In addition to general information about our practice, every patient receives information about his or her medical condition. For example, a patient coming for a physical examination receives an article or brochure about the importance of an annual examination and what to expect on the first visit. The more knowledgeable and educated the patient is, the less explaining I have to do. In addition, patients who know what to expect are less anxious about their visit.

Sometimes a patient's illness may be a particularly sensitive subject. In my practice, we see people for problems related to sexuality. Therefore, we ask patients ahead of time for permission to mail them material and make sure to have their preferred mailing address. We find that almost everyone wants to know more about their condition—they are hungry for information—and, again, having relevant information makes their first visit proceed much more efficiently.

Since I'm a urologist, we always require a urine specimen during the first visit, but often new patients, because they are anxious, urinate before they arrive. To ensure getting a specimen, we send them an introductory letter explaining why we need one and asking them to drink extra fluids ahead of time. This simple notification can have a significant impact on the daily schedule. If we didn't do this, our reception area would be full of people drinking fluids and waiting for their bladders to fill—and for elderly patients with decreased renal function, the wait can be in excess of 60 minutes.

Associated with every specialty are similar pieces of information patients need before they come to the office. An infertility specialist might ask patients to start collecting their basal body temperature. An ophthalmologist should let new patients know their eyes will probably be dilated on the first visit, they'll need to wait for more than an hour afterward, and they may have difficulty driving home. New patients might also be asked to avoid wearing contact lenses for a day or two before the visit so that accurate corneal measurements can be taken.

When a patient is coming for a second opinion, ask him or her to collect and bring along previous X-ray reports and lab studies. Tracking down a single report can take half an hour, while the patient waits in your reception area or in an exam room. Unfortunately, it's natural for the patient to assume that the delay is your fault. My staff is trained to ask patients to gather their records from other doctors and hospitals and bring them in. They also tell patients that if they can send these materials to us beforehand, I can review them prior to their visit.

INFORMING PATIENTS ABOUT YOUR ON-TIME PHILOSOPHY

As you move toward implementing an on-time philosophy, you need to educate patients about the change. Write an article in your practice newsletter or send all patients a personal letter. Say something like this:

> We are making every effort to see patients on time. We know that many of you have tight schedules and work deadlines. Some of you are driven to your appointment by a family member or have carpools you need to meet. Therefore, we want to make every effort to see you in a timely fashion. It is our goal to see you within 15 to 20 minutes after the time of your arrival. To help us achieve this goal, we ask that you arrive at the designated time of your appointment or a few minutes early.

Post a sign in the reception area that says, "If you haven't been seen in 20 minutes, please inform the receptionist." This lets patients know that you are serious about being on time and avoids situations in which a patient forgets to sign in and continues to wait indefinitely.

There are some people who always arrive 5 or 10 minutes late for their appointments in spite of all their good intentions. In my experience, if people are late, it is usually for one of two reasons. They might be late because the doctor is always late—and that is usually the case. If the doctor is not on time, what motivation do patients have to be on time?

Second, they might be late because the practice lets them get away with it. Note, for example, that nearly everyone who wants to catch the 7:30 flight from New Orleans to Atlanta arrives at the airport on time. Why? Because there is a federal law saying that plane has to pull out at 7:30. It cannot wait.

PLANNING FOR EMERGENCIES

Sometimes a patient calls and says, "I must have an appointment today." On most days our schedule is full, but we do save some time for emergencies. I give my staff thorough training on how to differentiate people who need to be scheduled right away from those who can wait for a few days, and I give them the authority to decide who gets an emergency appointment. A sign near the telephones lists the types of patients who need to be seen the same day (for example, patients with blood in their urine; patients with fever, chills, and flank pain; women patients with stinging and burning on urination; patients unable to urinate at all; patients who may have a kidney stone; and men patients with a pain in their testicles). When we schedule emergency patients, we explain they may have a 30 or 45 minute wait because of the other patients who were previously scheduled, but we assure them they will be seen within a reasonable time.

Some people state they need to be seen immediately but disclose upon questioning that they have had the pain they are calling about for a couple of weeks. We work them in as soon as we can but we don't consider them true emergencies.

Sometimes we have to say to a new patient that we can't schedule an appointment for them for at least ten days. In such cases, we volunteer to take the person's number and promise to call back if an opening develops. We always honor that promise and make every effort to get the new patient in as soon as possible. We find that new patients are always impressed when we call back to inform them of an opening in our schedule.

MANAGING DELAYS

Even if you manage time according to the principles I have just described, there will still be some occasions when you are running late. You can develop methods to cope with those situations when they arise. Here are some techniques that work well in my office.

Obtain a daytime telephone number for each patient. As soon as you realize that a delay will occur, have your staff contact patients and explain the situation. Similarly, contact them immediately when cancellations cause slots to become available.

If you are delayed and patients are already in the office, have a staff member walk into the reception area and explain the nature of the delay and give them an estimate of how long they can expect to wait.

Consider providing patients with refreshments such as coffee or bottled water.

If there has been an excessive delay and you detect hostility on the part of a patient, you might offer a discount on the standard fee.

ENTERTAINING PATIENTS

Patients don't like to wait. Anything you can do to capture their attention will make the wait seem less painful and the overall experience more pleasant. Disney is the master of the queue or the wait line. Next time you are at a Disney theme park notice that in many instances there are things to do or watch while you are in line. Of course, it is not possible to make the wait in the doctor's reception room like a Disney experience. But the wait in the doctor's office should be at the very least pleasant, and when possible, interesting.[1]

You want the time patients spend waiting in the exam rooms to be as short as possible. The reason is, there's usually nothing on the walls but the doctor's diplomas and anatomic drawings. Patients end up snooping around, looking in containers, and opening up the cupboards out of boredom. If you're going to have them wait, they should wait in the reception area and not in the exam rooms.

I provide reading material in the exam rooms so patients who are waiting have something to occupy them. There should be appropriate reading material related to your particular practice or to their particular medical problem.

It's the little things that make a big difference. It's the little extras that are most appreciated by the patients and will make them talk about you and your practice in a positive fashion and keep them returning for more services.

MAKING TIME FOR PATIENTS WITH SPECIAL NEEDS

Now, there are times when going to the doctor is scary, and patients may be dealing with difficult emotions. They may be told that they have cancer. There are always a few patients with special needs who want to continue talking with the doctor.

We leave a block of time free at the end of the day for this situation. Every doctor must learn to explain to a patient that the appointment time is over. "We have an on-time policy for this practice. I know you have more questions and I want to answer them for you, but on the other hand, my 3:30 appointment is here, I need to see her on time, just as I saw you on time. Perhaps you would go out and get a cup of coffee and come back at 4:30. We would then have more time together. Or if you prefer, I can call you at home tonight."

*   *   *

In addition to scheduling patients' appointments in a user-friendly way, it is also essential to find ways to communicate with patients and answer their questions fully. In the next chapter, I look at ways to use practice brochures to help patients understand your practice and take responsibility for their own health.

NOTE

1. T.S. Cross, *Positively Outrageous Service* (New York: Warner Books, 1991), 91.

24

Build a Brochure That Builds Business

Physicians and practices are often advised that they need a practice brochure. Yet when you talk to colleagues who have actually created a brochure, they often say it wasn't effective—they tried to use it for marketing purposes and then stopped. Most of them tell you their return on investment was nil.

Is there any point in trying to swim upstream? My answer is, yes and no. Yes, you should create a practice brochure, but no, you should not follow the example of your colleagues and create a brochure that is worthless as a marketing tool.

This chapter provides clear guidelines for creating an effective practice brochure, one that is sure to generate new patients and strengthen your bond with your current patients.

Creating an effective practice brochure is not easy and it is not cheap. But if you are willing to invest the time, energy, and funds, you can create a marketing tool that reflects all the good features of your practice.

REASONS FOR CREATING A PRACTICE BROCHURE

Why do you need a practice brochure? It will tell your patients about you and your practice. It will probably increase your practice's name recognition. In addition, it can, if it is well designed, enhance the image of your practice.

207

To develop a practice brochure, first ask yourself two important questions: What is the purpose of your brochure? Who is the intended audience?

If you need a brochure primarily to inform your existing patients about new services, a new address, or new office hours, you can accomplish this with minimal effort and expense. They are already acquainted with you and know your level of competence and ability. You don't need to impress them with thick paper and sophisticated graphics. A simple brochure that describes your practice and your services will meet their needs. Expect to reprint your brochure about once a year, because there will always be new information that should be included.

If, on the other hand, you want to have a brochure that will attract new patients and inform directors of managed care plans about your special qualities, then you'll need to invest more energy and funds. You need a brochure that exudes confidence and class, and makes it apparent that patients receive special benefits when they select your practice. A brochure of this type should be absolutely impeccable in terms of layout and design and have no typographical errors. Use of thick, stiff paper will convey an impression of solidity and reliability. You'll want to include your logo and use color printing and catchy headlines to attract readers' attention. You may want your brochure to include photos of your office and staff.

WHO SHOULD WRITE AND DESIGN YOUR BROCHURE?

In my previous book, *Marketing Your Clinical Practice Ethically, Effectively, and Economically*, I recommended writing and designing your own practice brochure. I did the writing and layout for my first brochure, with assistance from the public relations and marketing directors of the local hospital. With the benefit of hindsight, I would give that brochure a C– for effectiveness, a B+ for expense, and an A for time investment.

I now think that the time and energy that a physician must devote to creating a good brochure would be better spent talking with patients, referring physicians, and managed care plans. That's where the biggest bang for the buck will be, not sitting and slaving over a practice brochure.

When a colleague tells you his or her practice brochure was ineffective, ask who created it and you'll probably find it was written by the doctor, the office manager, or the doctor's spouse. Since none of these three is likely to have a background in graphics, copy writing, or marketing, you can easily understand why the response to that brochure was meager. The fact is, very few physicians have the skills to create a practice brochure that generates visible results.

Let me put it this way: writing your own practice brochure is definitely better than having no brochure at all. However, if you take on this sort of project, it will require a lot of your time and energy. After creating my own brochure, I didn't think the return I got was worth the time I put into it.

The next time I needed a practice brochure, I relied on expert assistance, and I ended up with a much more effective brochure. So I personally believe that physicians, with very few exceptions, need outside assistance to create an effective brochure. The company that currently assists me with my practice brochure is Doctor's Press,* and I think they do very good work.

FINDING CREATIVE ASSISTANCE

If you are really serious about creating a brochure that will make an impact, I suggest you consider hiring a professional writer and a graphic designer with experience in the health care field. Look at the brochures in medical offices in your area and at brochures displayed at health fairs. When you see brochures that are really well done, ask the people distributing them who did the work; they will almost always be happy to share this information with you.

Once you have found a professional writer and graphic artist, ask for additional samples of their work. Call physicians or hospitals who have worked with the designer and writer you are considering. Did they produce work you would accept? Would the physician or hospital use them again? Show their samples to your staff, patients, and family. Do they like the work?

According to David Kettlewell, founder and president of MEDI Medical Marketing Services, a division of Kettlewell and Associates,[†] 1,500 copies of a two-color brochure will cost $2,500 to $3,000. Here is a listing of typical costs:

Concept	$350
Service	$600
Copy	$450
Design	$375
Photos	$250
Printing	$535
Miscellaneous	$150
Total	$2,710

Next, schedule a meeting with the writer. Have plenty of information ready about yourself and your practice, including résumés for all physicians and samples of articles written by them, especially any that appeared in lay publications. If the

---

*Wentworth Publishing Co., P.O. Box 10488, Lancaster, PA 17605-0488, 800-233-0196.
[†]P.O. Box 5251, Akron, OH 44334, 216-929-9944, 800-830-4919.

practice has been in the community for a long time or has enjoyed a particularly interesting history, be sure to provide historical information as well.

The graphic designer will help create the "look" of the practice brochure. The cover should catch the reader's attention. It might display the name of the practice, the logo, or an appealing photograph (such as a physician interacting with a patient). Bring samples of available photos to the first meeting with the graphic designer.

One of your first decisions will be to select the physical format you want to use. Kettlewell observes that most of his clients choose a two-color brochure, 3⅝ inches wide and 8½ inches high when folded, which will easily fit inside a standard letter envelope. Normally Kettlewell and Associates does not recommend using four-color or oversize brochures, since that will increase production and mailing costs.

A 3⅝-by-8½-inch finished or folded size allows several design options (Figure 24-1):

- A two-sided card. Usually printed on high-grade coated and glossy white paper stock, this is an excellent option when the information you want to communicate is short.
- A trifold brochure. This common brochure consists of two folds in an 8½-by-11-inch sheet of paper.
- An eight-panel double-parallel brochure. This brochure begins as a single sheet of 8½-by-14-inch paper, then it is folded once in half and once again. The format provides a considerable amount of space for information at a relatively low cost.
- A 16-panel booklet. This is a more costly option, using eight pages stapled together along one side. The format provides considerable space and is excellent when there is lots of information to share with patients.

Bring samples of all the handouts and educational materials that you give your patients. Bring materials from the hospital, your local medical society, and your specialty society. If possible, bring samples of practice brochures that you find especially attractive or interesting to give the designer and writer an idea of the type of brochure you admire.

In addition, take the writer on a tour of your practice and introduce him or her to your staff. You may even want to allow the writer to interview some patients. If you have "before" and "after" photos (assuming you provide services that can have visually dramatic outcomes) and can get the patients' permission to use them, make them available.

Be prepared to discuss the benefits your practice provides. Think ahead of time about specific features that set your practice apart from others in the community.

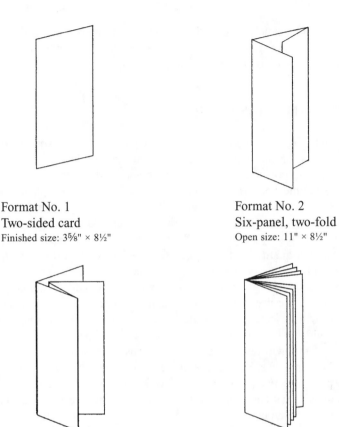

Format No. 1
Two-sided card
Finished size: 3⅝" × 8½"

Format No. 2
Six-panel, two-fold
Open size: 11" × 8½"

Format No. 3
Eight-panel, double-parallel
Open size: 14" × 8½"

Format No. 4
Sixteen-panel booklet
Finished size: 3⅝" × 8½"

Figure 24-1 Four different formats for printed circulars.

For instance, if you are an ob/gyn physician who practices natural childbirth and your hospital has a birthing room, mention that. If yours is a multispecialty group practice and it has an unusually full range of services, you should include that information. As a urologist, I emphasize that I make every effort to use conservative medical treatment in the management of benign prostatic hyperplasia, impotence, and incontinence. If you are a family practitioner and make house calls or weekly visits to nursing homes, then this benefit should be included in your practice brochure.

When you contact the printer, order as many copies as you think you will need—and then order a few more. It is far less expensive to overprint than to order even a few extra copies if you run out six months later.

TARGETING MANAGED CARE PLANS

If you're trying to encourage managed care plans to include you in their directory or put you on their panel, a brochure can be very helpful in letting them know about your practice. Right now most practices don't have a brochure. That means the minute you print a brochure for distribution, you place yourself a cut above the rest. Having a brochure doesn't necessarily mean your medical services are better than those of other providers, but it does show you are trying to inform patients about your practice. When a managed care plan director sees that you have a high-quality brochure, you are more likely, other things being equal, to be chosen for a spot on the managed care panel.

If managed care plans constitute one of your target audiences, then your brochure should emphasize that you do as much surgery as possible on an outpatient basis—this will indicate you are trying to limit costs while maintaining quality of care. It should mention that you provide samples for all patients starting on a new medication—this will also indicate you are cost conscious (you wait to see if patients develop side effects or allergic reactions before requiring them or their plans to pay for a full prescription). If you offer early morning and weekend hours so working patients don't lose time from work, be sure to include that information. If you use a physician's assistant or nurse practitioner, be sure to include that information—this also implies you are sensitive to the need to cut health care costs while maintaining quality of care.

CHECKLIST OF TOPICS

Here is a checklist of topics that might be included in your practice brochure:

- office hours
- location
- nearby parking lots
- map (if the location is not well known or if patients come from great distances)
- services offered
- managed care plan affiliations
- policy on refilling prescriptions by telephone

- how the practice returns patient calls
- policy on discussing health care problems with family members
- patient recall policy
- answering service number
- physicians who cover for practice when necessary
- appointment scheduling policy
- cancellation policy

Here are additional elements that may be useful to include in your practice brochure:

- business reply card
- tear-out containing commonly used telephone numbers in the community, including the practice's number
- offer for a free first visit or consultation
- nutrition card
- card outlining how to prevent common sports injuries.

It's a good idea to include a map and emergency phone numbers, because this gives your patients a reason to hold on to the brochure. Put maps, phone numbers, and addresses on the back panel, so this information is readily available.

FINANCIAL POLICY INFORMATION

Whether to discuss your financial policies in a practice brochure is a difficult question. You may have policies in place that require that the copayment must be paid at the time of a patient's first visit or the deductible and copayment must be paid in advance for elective surgery. My feeling is that when you are trying to attract new patients, a financial discussion may send the wrong message. Prospective patients may feel on a subliminal level that you are more interested in monetary gain than in providing health care services.

On the other hand, if financial issues have been a problem for your practice, it may make sense to state your policies clearly in the practice brochure so everyone knows what to expect. If many patients arrive for their first visit without a way of paying, and you are spending lots of money on accounting fees as a result, you might want to mention your payment-at-time-of-service policy in the brochure. In my practice, we discuss our payment policy when someone calls for an appointment. We simply say, "Please plan to make the copayment at the time of your visit. We accept cash, check, or credit card."

HOW TO USE YOUR PRACTICE BROCHURE

There are many different ways to use your practice brochure. You can send it to your current patients, together with a note that says, "We are glad you continue to choose us." You can also send it to inactive patients with a note that tells them you are still thinking of them. When you give a presentation, make the brochure available for the audience to take home afterward. Distribute it at health fairs. Leave copies in a rack in the reception area and exam rooms and put up signs that encourage patients to take some home and give them to family and friends.

Send your brochure to new patients in a "welcome to our practice" package (this is a particularly good tactic for primary care physicians, pediatricians, and ob/gyns).

Include your brochure in the package you send to managed care plans. Include it in a press kit when you communicate with the media. Send it to referring physicians—you can include one with each referral letter. Send your brochure, with a friendly note, to members of other professions who are in a position to refer to you. For example, send it to attorneys if you want to attract workers' compensation cases. Head and neck surgeons can send their brochure to dentists, orthopedists can send theirs to chiropractors and podiatrists, and ophthalmologists can send theirs to optometrists.

*   *   *

To facilitate communication with other physicians and managed care plans—and for many other reasons as well—it is essential to have a well-designed computer system. In the next chapter, I look at important questions to consider as you upgrade your computer equipment.

25

Use Computer Power To Boost Your Practice

I f you're using your office computer primarily for billing and accounting, you're using only a small percentage of its capacity. Computers have a far larger role to play in today's medical practice.

One cause of their increased importance is the advent of managed care. Computers can help you monitor your practice and generate the information that managed care plans rely on in selecting physicians. This chapter reviews the benefits of increased computerization and describes how to select a computer and software.

Bob Katz, a certified public accountant who specializes in health care, says,

> I don't know how a practice can run today without computers. They offer a very inexpensive way to make a practice more efficient and accurate. In the future, health care will be more and more data driven. That means, any physician who can capture, interpret, and use the data is going to find himself more successful than the physician who can't. And computers are vital in that process.

SUPPORT IS ESSENTIAL

What sort of support should you look for when buying a computer system?

If essential practice routines are based on the use of your software, reliable support is crucial. If you're only using the computer for batch jobs, like billing, then you can afford to be down for three days, says Paul D. Clayton, Ph.D., professor of medical informatics at Columbia University. Today, however, medical practices rely increasingly on computers for essential daily functions.

When you buy hardware, look for an arrangement that includes the provision of on-site support within a short time after any failure. When you purchase software, be sure that training and over-the-phone technical support are included—and test the support phone number to be sure you're not placed on hold for 20 minutes.

Katz notes that consistent support is more important today than ever before. "In the past, physicians used software primarily for repetitive tasks, such as appointment scheduling, billing, and tracking receivables. Now, with managed care and all the changes in health care, physicians are asked for many different reports on practice patterns and outcomes." That means you've got to have software that is on the cutting edge. Look for a vendor who will periodically send you updates so you can improve your system and provide more data to managed care companies as well as run your practice better.

CHOOSING A VENDOR

What should you keep in mind when choosing a vendor of software programs? Katz says,

> Go slowly. References are very important. Speak to other doctors, or better yet their office managers. Find out what your peers are using, and you'll find that in your specialty probably the same three or four packages are recommended over and over again. Get those [software manufacturers] to send their representatives to make a presentation to you or ask your office manager to go over to their facility and try their software.

Clayton suggests,

> The stock market probably reflects a company's financial stability better than anything else. So you can look at a company's sales growth and how the stock market values a company as a way of evaluating if they will be around for the long term.

To get the right system you have to go through a fairly complicated process, analyzing what you want to do now, what you may want to do in the future, and how it will all fit together. The individual modules themselves are relatively inexpensive and easy to use. The most important questions are systemic: do you want a DOS-based system or a Windows-based system? How are you going to link individual workstations together? Each choice you make today will limit the choices you can make in the future.

"But once you get through this initial process and make a good choice, you and your staff will be very happy that you've computerized," Katz adds.

COSTS

Katz estimates that a solo practitioner could obtain state-of-the-art hardware and some good basic programs for about $10,000. A small- to medium-size practice could do it for under $30,000, and a large practice with multiple sites should expect to spend $70,000 to $80,000.

MANAGED CARE SOFTWARE

The collection of data on how physicians practice medicine is growing ever more important. Given current trends in the health care industry—significant growth in managed care and new constraints on physician reimbursement—it is vital for physicians to be equipped with the financial tools necessary to evaluate and monitor profits.

Throughout the 1980s the profitability of a medical practice was almost a given. Unfortunately, the decade of the 1990s presents a very different picture. Physicians are no longer assured of profits simply by placing an announcement in the newspaper and offering good service.

According to David Hoehne, president of the Hoehne Group* and an expert in managed care software programs, two factors account for much of this change. The first is the set of reimbursement constraints introduced by Medicare's Resource Based Relative Value System (RBRVS). The second is increased cost consciousness related to growth in the managed care sector of the health care industry. Both of these can have a significant negative impact on a physician's bottom line.

According to Hoehne, the profitability of capitated managed care contracts is a function of four factors:

1. the revenue received per member
2. the percentage of members actually seeking treatment
3. the quantity and mix of services provided to members
4. the costs incurred providing those services

---

*Salt Lake City, Utah, 801-647-0103, fax 801-647-0104.

Physicians can evaluate capitated managed care contracts by making simple, rule-of-thumb calculations using data already available in most practices. That's the good news. The bad news is that the figures arrived at are only guesstimates.

For example, an ophthalmologist might estimate that she will see 25 percent of an HMO's enrolled population (30,000 members) each year. For these 7,500 members, the doctor will anticipate one office visit per patient, or 7,500 office visits. Included will likely be 200 cataract surgeries, 4 retinal repairs, and so on down the CPT code list.

The doctor multiplies each service or procedure by the current fee to arrive at the total price of the contract, then multiplies the total price by a reasonable discount the doctor can live with. The discounted price is then divided by the total number of covered lives (30,000), and the result is then divided by 12 (the number of months in a year) to arrive at a per member per month (PMPM) price for the contract.

According to Hoehne, there are three critical question marks involved in this sort of calculation:

1. the estimate of the percentage of the capitated population who will seek services
2. the estimate of the services that will be provided to the average patient in the population of covered patients
3. the guess as to whether the discount will be acceptable to the HMO

At present it is very difficult to accurately estimate the amount of services that will be provided to the average patient because of the lack of data. Most HMOs and practices have only been collecting detailed data for a short time.

In addition to problems due to guesswork, there is generally no attempt to take account of the costs associated with providing medical services to members of a plan. Without calculating costs it is very difficult to predict the profit to be gained over the life of the contract.

Although this approach has numerous drawbacks, it is better for physicians to use these calculations than to simply accept whatever figure a plan offers or select a number out of thin air. They can now acquire, however, new managed care software that will do these calculations and many more, allowing them to arrive at an accurate figure they can use in negotiations.

Managed care software is not the same as medical care software. The current software most of us use is patient based; it is able to generate claims and bill patients and insurance companies and assist in scheduling patient visits. Managed care software, on the other hand, is profit based. It measures trends, evaluates the practice and the physicians, and identifies the services provided and related costs for each patient encounter. New managed care software programs are able to monitor each minute of physician and staff time and assist the practice in determining which physician and staff procedures are the most productive. It can analyze to what degree physicians and staff members need to modify their work levels in order to contribute fully to the practice's profitability.

MINIMUM REQUIREMENTS FOR MANAGED CARE SOFTWARE

To be effective, a managed care software program must be able to track patients by plan, eligibility status, benefit limit, copay, referral rule, and withhold. It must be able to identify the contact person, claim-filing addresses (postal and electronic), and payment structures for third parties. It also must be able to track diagnoses, referral patterns, services (by CPT codes), demographic patterns, capitation payments for each patient, medications, overhead, supplies, and payments made to all other physicians and ancillary providers. The program should have the capacity to produce reports and summaries, including the following ratios: encounters per member per year, referrals per thousand patients, revenue per member per month, revenue per visit, and the capitation to fee-for-service ratio.

Of course the program should include a patient scheduling and patient recall system. Ideally it should allow easy connection to the hospital and permit electronic networking with colleagues in other offices.

The program should allow you to connect your office computer with your home personal computer so you have access to data and patient records whenever you wish.

A high-end or luxury program also includes automated charting, dictation codes, and a cross-checking system to assign CPT and ICD-9 codes for every procedure and confirm that all office visits have been charted. State-of-the-art but expensive features include optical scanning and voice transcription.

In summary, a managed care software program is not a tag-along module for your medical program but should complement your existing patient-based billing program. Its purpose is to provide you with the same sort of accounting information used by managed care plans to manage the physicians and thus put you on an equal footing, in terms of data, with the plans with which you have contracted.

*   *   *

Computers today play an essential role in increasing efficiency in the medical office. So do well-trained assistants known as physician extenders, who can dramatically increase the physician's ability to spend high-quality time with each patient. In the next chapter, I will look at the role of physician extenders in the modern medical office.

26

Team Up with Physician Extenders To Increase Your Office Efficiency

oday there are more demands on physicians than ever before. We have more paperwork and dictation to do, which leaves us with less time to meet our primary care responsibilities and to devote to our families and our personal interests. Frequently the pressure to work constantly leads to physician dissatisfaction and burnout.

I feel that in this era of managed care, managing time is *the* way to build a successful and enjoyable practice. One helpful strategy is to employ one or more physician extenders. This chapter discusses the advantages and disadvantages of physician extenders and describes how to find and train them.

What are physician extenders? They are employees whose function is to increase a physician's efficiency and make the time he or she spends with the patients more productive. They may handle some telephone work and paperwork and are frequently used to double-check details. They perform clinical and nonclinical tasks and thus free the physician to do what he or she does best.

Many physician extenders, such as physicians' assistants, nurse practitioners, and certified nurse-midwives, have specialized medical training. Others do not have specialized training but learn on the job how to aid physicians and increase their efficiency.

PHYSICIAN EXTENDERS IN AN OTOLARYNGOLOGY PRACTICE

Sidney Christianson, M.D., an otolaryngologist from St. Joseph, Missouri, has successfully used physician extenders for the past five years. He believes physician extenders can increase the efficiency of doctors, decrease the paperwork they handle, and allow them to spend quality time with each patient. A doctor may spend only two to five minutes with each patient, but if he or she can give the patient undivided attention during that time, the patient will feel satisfied. The patient actually will believe that the physician has spent more than this small amount of time with him or her.

Christianson's current physician extender interacts with the patient from the moment she accompanies the patient from the reception area to the examination room. She takes an initial medical history and completes a questionnaire on allergies, current medications, smoking and alcohol use, and previous surgical experiences. Christianson has trained his assistant to ask key questions pertinent to the eye-nose-throat specialty. Since his physician extender does not have formal medical training, she writes down the chief complaint in the patient's own words. Christianson feels that patients often relate their history to the physician extender, in a more frank, relaxed fashion than they would to him. After all, they are communicating with another layperson, and this is probably less threatening than an encounter with a physician. They may be more willing to discuss stressful situations at work or in the family, problems with alcohol, or their sexual history.

First Christianson reviews the findings of the physician extender before entering the examination room. Then he takes his own history and performs the physical examination in the presence of the physician extender. During this time the physician extender records the responses to Christianson's questions as well as Christianson's examination findings.

A good physician extender can read the physician's body language, Christianson says. For example, she records the physician's positive findings; she also soon learns what is normal (by the absence of any comment) and records that as well. The physician describes positive findings to the physician extender in medical language after informing the patient that this information will be translated into lay language in a few minutes.

Toward the end of the interview, the physician extender selects appropriate educational materials for the patient to take home. She may provide a video for the patient (and family) to view in the office's audiovisual room. She prepares lab and X-ray requests so they are completed by the time the patient is ready to check out at the business office. She will also write out prescriptions, including the name, date, medications, dosage, and directions. The physician reviews all prescriptions before they are given to the patient. A physician extender who works for a surgeon can also prepare consent forms for surgery and discuss the preoperative and postoperative course with the patient. Studies have shown that patients who receive good pre- and postoperative education have shorter lengths of stay, better outcomes, and fewer complications.[1]

The physician extender also transcribes all letters to referring physicians and to managed care plans after reviewing the office notes. Christianson believes the physician extender is more efficient than a transcriptionist since she is familiar with the patient, the history, and the treatment plan. In addition, a physician extender can have the letter typed and mailed much quicker than the standard process of dictation, transcription, and mailing, which can take up to two weeks.

A physician extender can also be used as an assistant in the operating room. Whenever a surgeon has an assistant who helps him or her on a regular basis, there is a more efficient process and less likelihood of missing equipment and supplies. Usually a physician extender who assists in the operating room needs to have credentials that qualify him or her for this role (for example, certification as a nurse technician).

A physician extender can help with progress notes and hospital medical records, provided the physician signs the records. Every hospital has rules and regulations determining what nonphysicians can and cannot write on hospital medical records. However, if your hospital does allow physician extenders to complete your medical records, you can save many hours in the medical records department—probably the area physicians least like to spend time, even if they are fed and offered prize trips and restaurant vouchers!

A physician extender can also call patients at home after surgery or outpatient procedures and diagnostic tests. Patients really appreciate this simple courtesy. It gives the physician extender an opportunity to answer their questions and allay their anxiety, and reduces the number of calls from patients to the physician. Again, this is another example of how the physician extender allows the physician to make better use of his or her time without sacrificing quality.

Many practices searching for ways to increase efficiency are using "midlevel providers," such as physicians' assistants, nurse practitioners, and certified nurse-midwives to expand services for patients while keeping the lid on costs. For example, a physician's assistant can take a history, give injections, draw blood, and prepare the patient for an examination by the doctor. Then the doctor can enter the exam room, spend a few minutes with the patient, answer the patient's questions, and allow the assistant to complete the visit by providing educational material, prescriptions, and answers to any final questions.

Today nurse practitioners and physicians' assistants are often responsible for their own caseload of patients and work in collaboration with physicians. Using practice guidelines and clearly drafted protocols, nurse practitioners and physicians' assistants can care for routine or simple acute illnesses and achieve good outcomes and high levels of patient satisfaction. In fact, studies have demonstrated that nurse practitioners and physicians' assistants are well accepted by patients. They can facilitate communication between patients and medical practices and at the same time provide high-quality care.

Look at a case where a patient is seen by a primary care physician for a problem with obesity and high blood pressure. The doctor enters the exam room and suggests that the patient lose weight, exercise more, and use less salt in his diet.

The likelihood of a patient actually following these suggestions and making life-style changes that will reduce his body weight and blood pressure is virtually nil. However, if a physician extender were to follow up by describing specific techniques of salt restriction, devising a diet that is acceptable and palatable to the patient, providing the addresses of the YMCA and other local venues that have exercise programs, and promising to call the patient at home in 10–14 days to check on his progress, the chance the patient will alter behavior patterns is much greater.

ADVANTAGES OF USING PHYSICIAN EXTENDERS

They say that in real estate three things count: location, location, and location. In the practice of medicine, the three most important things today are efficiency, efficiency, and efficiency. By using a physician extender, a physician is able to maximize his or her time with the patient. The physician extender is able to take care of many small but significant details, and the patient perceives the physician as efficient and dedicated.

The physician extender also serves as a double-checker. Nothing is left to chance or memory. Each patient is fully processed with the physician and physician extender both present. Christianson says his medical records are more precise and accurate since he began using a physician extender—and pharmacies no longer call to say that they cannot read his writing!

Christianson believes that a physician extender allows him to see one or two more patients every hour. With some exceptions, he rarely touches a pen or pencil when he is examining a patient. He never fumbles for a prescription pad or sorts through folders to find educational materials for the patient. Consequently he never looks away from the patient. All his time is spent in direct, focused contact with the patient.

Christianson summarizes the disadvantages in a single word: none!

HOW TO SELECT AND TRAIN PHYSICIAN EXTENDERS

Christianson suggests that a physician extender should be someone who is comfortable with the public and can handle the type of stressful situations that occur in every medical practice. He looks for individuals who like to be around people, are enthusiastic, and have a ready smile. He has located physician extenders through ads and word of mouth, but his best physician extender came from the transcription pool at the hospital. Transcription pools are good places to look because transcribers have a medical background, are familiar with medical terminology, already possess transcription skills, are efficient, are familiar with hospitals and patients, and usually work evening and night shifts and are delighted to accept a day job and take off the headset.

The training of a physician extender should be individualized. Christianson suggests creating a clearly written job description, including a description of the physician's expectations. He suggests breaking down the job into daily, weekly, and monthly duties. It has been his experience that a physician extender can become efficient and useful after only one month's training, but certainly the necessary training period will vary with the nature of the practice.

*   *   *

Important as it is, health care is only one aspect of a successful medical practice. The other equally important side of the coin includes all the normal functions every business must carry out—purchasing, billing, managing employees, and negotiating all sorts of business decisions. In the next chapter, I discuss how a management audit can review the way your office carries out these necessary functions, and show you ways to save thousands of dollars.

NOTE

1. L.A. Headrick and D. Neuhauser, "Quality Health Care," *JAMA* 273 (1995): 1719.

27

Give Your Practice a Checkup

I n order to improve office operations, the first step you need to take is to analyze where you are now. The best way to do this is to conduct a practice audit. This chapter describes how to conduct a practice audit, what it will include, how to find appropriate consultants, and what their fees are likely to be.

Just as your patients need to get a regular checkup, so does your medical practice. A few years ago, many physicians felt comfortable putting their practices on automatic pilot. Today, when every physician needs to be aware of the rapid growth of managed care, new coding techniques and procedures, and methods to cut spiraling overhead costs, such complacency is likely to result in an erosion of the bottom line.

One definition of *audit* given by the *Random House Dictionary of the English Language* is "the inspection or examination of a building or other facility to evaluate or improve its appropriateness, safety, efficiency, or the like." According to J. Landy Damsey, M.B.A., M.H.S., head of the medical management consulting firm Damsey and Associates,* which specializes in medical practice evaluation, a management audit of a medical practice is a comprehensive and systematic review of the practice's systems, policies, and day-to-day functioning. "It's a top to bottom, inside out, detailed review of all nonclinical aspects of the practice, from A to Z," Damsey says. "We look at everything the practice does, asking, 'Is there a better way to do it? Is the practice meeting its organizational objectives, and is it making a profit?'"

---

*444 Crawford Street, Portsmouth, VA 23704, 804-399-5977.

WHY AUDITS ARE NEEDED

In any system, policies, procedures, and practices are based partly on factors that no longer have any force. Therefore, they must be continually reviewed to make sure they are appropriate. Many people feel comfortable with familiar, time-tested systems and resist changes even if they are clearly improvements. Their motto is, if it's not broken, don't fix it. "That attitude doesn't move the practice forward," Damsey says. "That just maintains the status quo. Our motto should be, if it's not broken, make it better. You can always find ways to make improvements. Good management is about the constant evaluation and revamping of the system to make it better."

Here's one example where improvement is called for. Many practices are still filing hard copies of insurance forms in the medical records. This definitely represents waste: the practices are buying duplicate claim forms instead of single forms, and someone has to pull the medical records and file the piece of paper, which is very labor intensive. Maybe it made sense five years ago but now computer billing is standard. Some people don't really trust computers, so they're still doing it the old way regardless of the expense and lack of benefit.

Another example: in most practices, the historical pattern has been to have secretaries make appointments for the doctors. Today many practices have computerized scheduling—everybody has a computer and access to every physician's schedule. However, patients often wait for one particular person to make an appointment. With computers on everyone's desk, it's much more efficient to train all staff who take calls from patients so they can all make appointments for the physicians.

These are examples of the kind of habitual patterns that can decrease efficiency and increase costs. By having an audit—by having an experienced outsider come into a practice and look at its operations—it will be able to identify more effective and efficient ways of practicing medicine.

WHAT TO EXPECT

At the typical small to medium physician practice (1 to 15 physicians), two consultants will generally spend two days visiting the practice and examining every aspect of its operations in detail.

A typical practice management audit looks at the following:

- cash control procedures and audit trails
- how accounts receivable are managed and controlled
- insurance processing

- CPT and ICD-9 coding
- third-party payer audit liability
- personnel administration
- wage levels and benefits
- ways to maximize reimbursement
- personnel records, including necessary signatures on forms
- documented personnel policies
- regular staff meetings
- regular performance reviews
- office efficiency and productivity
- patient flow
- job structure
- department locations
- fee schedule

It's not uncommon to hear this said: "We had a consultant come in and his report is still on the shelf." In today's environment, mere report writing is not an adequate form of consulting. Consultants must make practical suggestions, train the staff, and assist them in the first steps of implementing change. Suppose an audit finds that 75 percent of the accounts receivable are more than 120 days old. With further scrutiny, the audit determines that the practice was only submitting claims on the 15th and 30th of each month. Once claims are submitted daily instead of twice each month, accounts receivable will decrease considerably.

When Damsey and Associates conduct an audit, they compare the practice statistically with similar practices in the same part of the country, in terms of the number of patients seen, gross charges, receipts, and overhead expenses (broken down into administrative supplies, clinical supplies, rent, and so on). "We look for items which cost either much more or much less than in comparable practices, and then we investigate further to find out why that is so," Damsey says.

An audit uses employee opinion surveys to find out what the staff think about the practice, and it also investigates the management environment. Are the physicians actively involved in the management of the practice? Do they meet regularly to discuss business issues and make business decisions?

At the end of the audit visit, the consultants hold a two- to four-hour summation conference that focuses on the practice assessment thus far. A week later the practice receives a written report intended to function as a blueprint or road map for needed changes. It identifies the problems, states why each problem is a problem, and gives recommendations for correction. The practice reviews the list of problems and says, for example, "You've sent us 20 recommendations; we agree with 18 of them but we aren't going to follow 2 of them. Of the 18 we want to implement, we can handle the first 10, but we are charging you with responsibility for the remaining 8."

Improved computer processes are something most practices can implement on their own. The computer system should be closed out every day, with a separate closing report. Some responsible person, such as the office manager, should take a set of backup tapes off site so that the practice's records will be preserved if there is a fire or other unforeseen emergency.

On the other hand, developing personnel policies is a more detailed project, takes more time, and may require more assistance from the consultant. Many practices don't have personnel policies, benefits, or job descriptions in place. A full-service consultant will supply prototype policies that the practice can adapt to its own situation. "We charge $350 for a personnel manual," Damsey says. "If you prefer, you can invest $5,000 worth of time and effort writing your own."

How does an audit find ways a practice can become more efficient? In one case, a practice was using fee-for-service health insurance for its own employees, even though all the providers used by employees were part of a network PPO option with reduced health care premiums. The consultant pointed out that the practice would benefit by shifting from the fee-for-service indemnity plan to the network for its health insurance, and it saved $18,000 the first year.

Many practices use a bank to act as trustee of their pension fund. This will typically cost a five-physician practice $15,000 a year. The trustee simply has to ensure that the pension plan is administered in accordance with the pension documents, a minor task, hardly worth $15,000 per year. "I say to them, unless you're planning to embezzle from yourself, act as your own trustee," Damsey says. "Have all five of the physicians serve as trustees, which requires five signatures for anything you do. Then do a small amount of paperwork, and boom, you've saved $15,000 a year."

In another practice, four physicians were practicing in a building built for two physicians but said they couldn't afford additional space. Damsey and Associates found coding errors in the bills that totaled about $50,000 a year. The practice moved to a new location, and each doctor now has three exam rooms, allowing more patients to be seen every day.

FINDING A CONSULTANT

The main factors to consider in hiring a consultant to conduct an audit are qualifications, credentials, and experience. There are a number of societies and organizations that credential and select consultants for physicians based on academic background, practical experience, and letters of recommendation. For example, the American Medical Association has the Doctors Advisory Network, a network of attorneys and practice consultants throughout the country, and the American Academy of Family Physicians has its Network of Consultants. Also, the Medical Group Management Association has developed its own management consulting service.

Some practices attempt to conduct an audit using staff members, such as the office manager and the accountant. Although staff are certainly able to bring about improvements in the system, it is difficult for them to perform a full-fledged audit because managing a practice is a full-time job. More important, every organization by its nature tends to be a closed system, with an accepted body of knowledge. Bringing in outside people who are familiar with many other organizations means bringing new knowledge and innovative viewpoints.

Damsey recommends conducting a management audit at least once a year "because in today's environment things are changing that fast."

COST AND COST-EFFECTIVENESS

The cost of an audit will vary depending on the geographic region and the specialty and type of practice, but a price of $1,000 to $3,000 per physician is fairly typical. Damsey says the payoff is usually five to ten times the cost of the audit.

The cost of a follow-up audit runs 70 to 80 percent of the cost of the first year's audit because the consultant is already familiar with the practice. The second audit probably won't result in dramatic savings, but there will always be aspects of the practice that can be improved because the practice has to change to keep in step with the constantly evolving health care environment. Damsey says, "An audit every year is very cost effective; however, the second year you rarely see the enormous payoffs you get the first time around."

HOW TO PREPARE FOR AN AUDIT

When a practice prepares for an audit, the physicians and staff shouldn't change anything they're doing or the way they're doing it. "The key to a successful audit is communication," Damsey says. "The organization must communicate internally with *everybody on staff* to explain what an audit is, why it's needed, and why everybody's input is necessary to make the audit successful." Aside from that, it should be business as usual. Staff members need to understand that an audit is not designed to evaluate or criticize individuals; it is designed to evaluate systems and procedures.

When Damsey and Associates do an audit, they ask for data from the practice before the consultant's visit. Typically the data includes

- profit and loss statements for the last three years
- tax returns
- several computerized reports (assuming the practice is computerized), including CPT frequency and aging analyses
- letterhead
- patient information brochure
- samples of all marketing materials
- Yellow Pages advertisements
- all advertisements placed within the last year
- meeting minutes for the past six months
- health insurance bills
- malpractice insurance bills
- bills for supplies
- personnel policies

MARKETING AUDITS

A management audit deals with some elements of marketing. However, it is also possible to do what is called a marketing audit, which specifically targets marketing issues. According to Heidi Isom, a marketing audit will look at three main areas:

1. Markets. Several markets must be studied: the community, referral sources, patients, and payers, among others.
2. Services. Critical areas of the practice should be studied from a marketing standpoint, including the way business is generated, volume levels, profitability, patient and referrer demographics, and patient and referrer satisfaction and attrition.
3. Competitors. The audit should examine real and perceived competitors (i.e., both providers who perform the same services and those who do not but are perceived as doing so). According to Isom, you need the same sort of information on competitors as you would gather on your own practice.

REASONS FOR CONDUCTING A MARKETING AUDIT

A marketing audit can help prepare a practice to launch a new program, physician, paraprofessional, service, or product. It also can serve as a preventive check for any yet-to-surface marketing problems. An effective marketing audit will ensure a practice is able to maintain its current volume of patients. Most importantly, an audit will help the practice to continue to grow in an ever-changing marketplace.

Most practices, regardless of their success or their maturity, should undergo a full or partial marketing audit every 12 to 18 months, depending on the amount and regularity of the data to be gathered and examined.

The cost of a marketing audit is determined mostly by the assistance required. Expect to pay health care marketing consultants $50 to $125 an hour. According to Isom the cost of an audit for a solo or small group practice is $1,000 to $2,500.

THE ROLE OF THE CONSULTANT IN A MARKETING AUDIT

Physicians frequently ask, "Can a marketing audit be done in-house?" Even though most practices do not have a full-time marketing person on staff, there are a couple of options available to them. One is to find a consultant who will work with your staff to retrieve the information and to prepare and interpret the data. This is the least expensive option. However, it does not provide the close-up view often necessary to identify problems and solutions.

The other option is to use a consultant to do everything. This gives you the opportunity to generate the most objective data. However, it is also the most expensive option.

KNOW THYSELF

Every practice needs to know as much as possible about its referral sources, payers, and patients. Its future will depend on the satisfaction of these three groups.

Today, more than ever before, it is imperative that physicians begin to think like business people. The more we know about our own practices, the better we can meet the needs and wants of our patients and other customers. Businesses that offer services, like the health care industry, may find that it is difficult to achieve consistent and outstanding quality. Unlike widgets produced on an assembly line, health care services depend on many different circumstances and variables, and there is lots of room for variation and error.

In this era of managed care, audits are more important than ever. The information gathered in a practice or marketing audit is essential for positioning your practice to take advantage of the trend toward managed care. Among other things, it allows you to sit at the negotiating table with managed care plans as an equal.

Practice audits are appropriate whenever you are planning to make a change or implement a marketing strategy. Not doing one is like treating a patient's symptoms without thoroughly diagnosing the problem and identifying its underlying conditions and secondary complications. How would you know what to prescribe? The old aphorism, "Prescription without diagnosis is malpractice" also holds true for the business component of a medical practice.

Under managed care, new skills are essential. Managed care organizations are gathering all sorts of data on health care practitioners. They are developing practice guidelines and asking practitioners to follow them. They are conducting surveys of patients, asking whether they are satisfied with the care they receive. They are negotiating prices designed to cut all the fat out of a medical budget. Surviving and serving patients in this new health care environment requires a host of new skills.

*   *   *

In the next section, "Managing Managed Care," I will discuss proven ways to be successful in the new world of managed care.

III

Managing Managed Care

28

Putting "Manage" into Managed Care

Managed care is growing rapidly throughout the United States. It can take many forms, ranging from tightly controlled HMOs to point-of-service plans that offer patients additional options to preferred provider networks. Even fee-for-service insurance has some elements of managed care these days, with prior authorization required for many costly procedures.

Managed care is growing so fast that today no physician can afford to ignore it. Dealing with managed care organizations means that physicians have to develop new skills, new marketing methods, even new attitudes about which sort of care is most important.

Part III of this book looks at methods and ideas for functioning successfully under managed care. Below is an overview of managed care based on the ideas of three experts in the field.

In the spring of 1995, the National Managed Health Care Congress,* which conducts national and regional conferences on all aspects of managed care, invited three keynote speakers to address the question "Where is the humor in managed care?"

The three speakers, all highly respected experts in the field, doubted whether there was any humor to be found in managed care—but they did describe the current situation.

---

*70 Blanchard Road, Suite 4000, Burlington, MA 01803, 617-270-6000.

A THREE-TIERED HEALTH CARE SYSTEM

Uwe Reinhardt, Ph.D., professor of political economy at the Woodrow Wilson School of Public and International Affairs, Princeton University, said that the defeat of the Clinton health care reform plan indicates that for the foreseeable future there will be a three-tiered health care system in the United States. The bottom tier consists of uninsured patients served by public hospitals and clinics, the middle tier consists of patients served by managed care organizations, and the top tier includes those people who continue to demand fee-for-service care and have the money to afford it.

TWO MODELS OF MANAGED CARE

Alain Enthoven, Ph.D., professor of public and private management at Stanford University, commented on the rapid growth of managed care. He recalled the days when he consulted on health care issues for Joseph Califano and the Carter administration, back in the late 1970s.

> When I discussed managed care then, people regularly talked to me as if I were a stupid child. They'd say, "Can't you understand, this will never happen on the East Coast. It may be okay for you kooks in California, but never, never, never will it happen on the East Coast." I get a real chuckle out of that these days, because today Massachusetts is *the* leader in the percentage of the population enrolled in HMOs, and we in California are struggling to figure out how we can match them.

The term *managed care* actually covers a wide variety of health care organizations that differ dramatically in the incentives offered to physicians and the methods used to control utilization. Enthoven finds it useful to distinguish the "command and control" model and the "empowerment" model of managed care.

The Command and Control Model

The command and control model is based on the assumption that doctors need to be micromanaged because they will not take responsibility for managing the cost and quality of care. A managed care plan of this type requires physicians to obtain prior authorization before many procedures and sets rigid standards for allowable lengths of inpatient stays.

The Empowerment Model

The empowerment model is based on the assumption that health care providers are intelligent people who with the right organization and information will generally do the right thing for the patients. Under this model, doctors accept responsibility for managing the costs and quality of care. They are willing to accept the financial risk involved in providing all necessary health care services for a fixed per member per month payment. They have more freedom in determining the specific care offered to individual patients but have correspondingly more responsibility for developing cost-effective practice patterns.

"These doctors are empowered; they are satisfied with their enhanced role," Enthoven says. "They may be dissatisfied with the capitation rates that the market is offering them now, but they see the expanded professional role in which they've accepted these larger responsibilities as one which can lead us to better, higher quality care."

INCREMENTAL INNOVATIONS ADD UP TO BIG CHANGES

In California and some other states, managed care is motivating organizations to make significant changes to reduce costs while maintaining or improving the quality of care. "They are consistently finding ways to give customers better care at lower cost—something that not very long ago people said was impossible," says Enthoven.

He believes that hundreds and thousands of incremental innovations are occurring as part of a process of continuous quality improvement. Managed care organizations are finding ways to shorten inpatient lengths of stay and increase preventive care for many illnesses. "This would not happen without strong economic incentives," Enthoven says. "That is, people wouldn't make these innovations and lay off unnecessary personnel unless the economic incentives were really powerful, unless they understood that the survival needs of the institution require that they do that."

For example, the Permanente Medical Group has developed information systems that allow it to study practice variations throughout its entire system, including the lengths of stay for various operations and conditions. They are finding out which practices work best, and then spreading appropriate guidelines and protocols throughout the system.

Its clinic in Stockton, California, guaranteed members a same-day appointment if they wanted one and found that the rate of visits actually declined by 25 percent. It seems that people had been scheduling visits in advance whenever they thought they might need one. Once they were sure that, when really needing an appointment, they could get it the same day, they stopped making so many appointments in advance.

Friendly Hills Medical Center in Southern California is exploring the use of aggressive programs to prevent illnesses. For example, nurses regularly contact frail elders, monitoring their progress and looking for problems at home so they can reduce the likelihood of acute episodes that would require hospitalization. By doing home safety inspections, they prevent people from slipping on rugs or tripping on wires and breaking a hip. In a capitated reimbursement system, it is more cost-effective to pay a nurse to check on a patient's environment and keep him or her well than to pay for repair of a fractured hip.

The Palo Alto Medical Foundation has developed a voice mail telephone management system to answer patients' questions and help solve problems so they don't have to make a costly appointment just to get an answer to a simple question.

Enthoven described his own experience with a managed care cardiologist who relies on this sort of over-the-phone consultation:

> My cardiologist is actively caring for me, but when I have a question, I call him and leave it on his voice mail, and he calls back with an answer and leaves it on mine. It's so much more convenient. At one point I needed a number of diagnostic tests, and they were all set up by voice mail and telephone. After I took the tests, and my cardiologist got the results, we discussed them over the phone. Under the old fee-for-service system he would not have been able to bill for just talking with me on the phone. I found the new system enormously more economical and convenient.

Doctors are going to have to accept telemedicine (Figure 28-1) as a method of caring for patients. Of course, it's nice to be eyeball to eyeball with a patient, but that will not always be possible. Medicine will soon include guidelines delineating when it is medically acceptable to care for patients using phones and fax machines and modems. Physicians who recognize and accept the trend toward telemedicine will have practices that are more efficient and patients who are grateful they don't have to interrupt their busy schedules to go to a physician's office.

Enthoven is confident that under the empowerment form of managed care, there is an incentive to maintain high quality in health care. "Of course there will inevitably be negative anecdotes," he remarked. "You can't get away from that, but I think looking at the whole issue of managed care, there have been remarkably few. If people were getting bad care in HMOs, I think we would hear about it—but instead people in California are flocking to them."

Figure 28-1 Telemedicine is on its way.

A DIFFICULT PERIOD OF TRANSFORMATION

J. Ian Morrison, Ph.D., president of the Institute for the Future, Menlo Park, California, agreed that managed care is growing rapidly, but warned of a difficult transitional period ahead:

> We may get caught on the horns of a dilemma—what I call the two-curve problem. You're going along quite nicely on the old curve, let's call it fee-for-service medicine. You have a sneaking suspicion that a new curve is going to emerge, let's call it capitation. The problem here is that there is a tendency to believe that capitation is going to happen next week. Actually it won't work out that way. It may take a lot longer than you think, and we may get caught between two curves, with people behaving as if they are capitated long before it actually happens.

Morrison describes what he calls a "transformation in the health care food chain," where the institutions that used to be in the best position and have the greatest prestige now find themselves in the opposite situation. "The big academic health centers are at the bottom of that food chain now, not the top." He said that at-risk contracting, where physicians are financially at risk for all the costs of care, is growing very rapidly, and he predicted it would reach 30 percent of the population nationally (and 60 percent in some markets) by the turn of the century. "Those of you in the big, overbedded teaching hospital markets of the East Coast, look out," he warns. "Medicare risk contracting is coming to you."

In closing, Reinhardt mentioned that his own son is planning to be a physician. "I tell him, go ahead, it's an honorable and wonderful profession. Physicians, of course, are nervous now. My feeling is that at the moment you are experiencing a great deal of turbulence, but you will land safely sooner or later."

He cited a brass plaque his wife placed in their entrance hallway, listing Confucius' three rules of prudent living:

- Always praise the Buddha, or the Lord.
- Never stand between a dog and a lamppost.
- Exploit the inevitable.

And that was Reinhardt's final comment on managed care: "This is happening, you cannot stop it, so exploit it, turn it your way."

*   *   *

Many managed care organizations receive capitated payments from members, and some also pay their physicians on a capitated basis. Capitation reverses the incentives physicians formerly experienced under fee-for-service medicine. In the next chapter, I will review what capitation means for you and how you can deal with it.

29

Don't Get Caught in the "Cap Trap"

F irst it was *managed care*. Then it was *managed competition*. Now the buzz word is *capitation*. Years ago, when a physician started a medical practice, he or she hung up a sign, sent an announcement to the local newspaper, and waited for word-of-mouth marketing to deliver patients to the front door. Today, a lot more is required in the way of marketing and promotion. And in the very near future, physicians will have to assume the risk of caring for covered lives by accepting capitated patients. This chapter explains why capitation is so attractive to managed care plans, how to prepare for capitation, and what capitation will mean for your practice.

According to Sue Lynn Schramm, a managed care and capitation expert and president of Integrated Health Strategies Consulting,* capitation offers payers and managed care organizations strong incentives to reduce the cost of health care. In fact, capitation is the first reform that has significantly decreased the cost of care.

Capitation involves the advance payment of a fixed fee to cover a defined package of health benefits for plan members. If the costs of providing care to members are lower than the amount accumulated through regular payments, the physicians and hospitals who provide the services make a profit. However, if the costs of providing care are more than the amount, they operate at a loss. A capitation agreement is called a "risk contract." Physicians and physician groups may negotiate a wide variety of capitation agreements. They may be "at risk" for their own

---

*2824 Summerfield Road, Falls Church, VA 22042, 703-538-6152, fax 703-538-7186.

services, or they may share the risk for all health care services with the hospital. Some physician groups are taking responsibility for managing all aspects of the patient care and bearing all the risk, but this type of arrangement is still relatively rare.

In the old fee-for-service system, physicians had an incentive to offer all the care that patients needed or wanted. Physicians were not expected to let the relative costs of different treatments affect their decisions.

Under capitation, physicians have a completely different set of incentives, since they receive the same monthly payment regardless of the number of services patients receive. Thus it makes sense for them to offer preventive services, like flu shots, mammograms, and vaccinations, and detect illnesses at an early stage. They must take long-term health care costs into account and try to achieve favorable outcomes at a low cost.

At present, managed care organizations use a mixture of payment methods for physicians. Among HMOs, capitation is already the most popular method, with 62 percent of HMOs using it. Fee-for-service is also still widespread, with 60 percent of HMOs using it (they generally negotiate a discount from standard fee-for-service fees). About 21 percent of HMOs pay physicians a salary, 18 percent offer a bonus program, and 6 percent have a profit-sharing program. (These percentages total more than 100 because many HMOs use more than one method of physician compensation.[1])

You can anticipate that in the very near future capitation will be the most popular method for reimbursing medical practices. The health care marketplace has not witnessed anything else that is able to bring down provider costs as quickly and efficiently. Capitation, unlike other mechanisms, enlists physicians as contributors to cost-saving efforts, and payers can objectively see dramatic decreases in hospital admissions, hospital days, and surgical cases.

For example, in 1992 the average number of inpatient hospital days was 751 per thousand for the U.S. population as a whole, while it was only 362 per thousand for those enrolled in HMOs. The average length of stay was 6.2 days for the U.S. population in general, while it was 4.5 days for HMO members.[2]

The rate of certain surgical procedures declined dramatically. In Worcester, Massachusetts, C-section rates were 24 percent under indemnity insurance, but less than 15 percent in a capitated HMO.[3] Managed care even cuts the amount spent on prescription drugs, with an average cost in 1993 of $101.21 in a typical group practice, compared to $72.97 in an HMO, a 28 percent differential.[4]

According to Schramm, the bulk of the savings will come from decreasing hospital admissions and from decreasing use of specialists and their expensive procedures. On the West Coast, primarily California, there was a 69-percent reduction in inpatient hospital days in one year following the introduction of a capitated system of reimbursement for primary care physicians. There was also an overall reduction in health care costs of 25 percent in the first three years.

The greatest reduction was in payments made to hospitals, but the reduction in payments to specialists was a close second. If the savings realized under capitation were extrapolated nationally, they would equal more than $130 billion. That's a significant reduction even though the health care budget totals nearly $1 trillion.

From the vantage point of the HMOs, capitation results in a dramatic rate of change. At one integrated system on the West Coast, there was a decrease in the Medicare average length of stay from 6.6 to 5.1 days in a single month. There also was a 50- to 60-percent reduction in the number of Caesarean sections and a 50- to 70-percent reduction in surgical services.[5]

We need to recognize that capitation is a payment method that is here to stay and that the traditional indemnity system of reimbursement is going to be slowly but certainly phased out with only 10 to 15 percent of patients existing as fee-for-service.

WHY FEE-FOR-SERVICE WILL NOT LAST

Capitated care has a distinct and measurable pricing advantage over standard indemnity care. Consequently, indemnity care is noncompetitive from the economic standpoint. As soon as a capitated system is available in the marketplace, young, healthy patients gravitate to it because of its lower costs. Those that are left, the older and sicker patients, are now using indemnity care at a cost disadvantage and are paying higher premiums for their health care. With a continued movement of relatively young and healthy patients to capitated care, indemnity care becomes more and more expensive, resulting in an unsustainable cost differential. Ultimately this leads to the collapse of indemnity plans.

The changeover to capitation began in California with the capitation of primary care doctors. Capitating these providers is a very powerful and simple approach managed care organizations use to reduce costs significantly. They make capitation attractive to primary care physicians by giving the physicians a share in the risk pool savings. If there is a reduction in referrals to specialists, hospital admissions, and overall utilization of services, the physicians receive a financial reward. As a result, they have an incentive to reduce costs.

According to Schramm, it will take just a few years to fine-tune the capitation of primary care physicians. The next target for capitation will be the specialists. In California, specialists began to be capitated two to three years after the primary care physicians were capitated. Schramm predicts that interval will be shorter in the South and the Midwest.

Another possible scenario is that HMOs may capitate only the primary care physicians and be able to control the utilization management process without having to capitate the hospitals or specialists. In this scenario, the HMOs will maintain control over the covered lives.

It has been documented clearly and objectively that capitation does work—that is, capitation quickly decreases the cost of health care. But in order for capitation to work, the physician must make a giant mental switch from traditional fee-for-service medicine. In the past, the more patient visits, hospital admissions, and procedures, the greater the profits. Under capitation, less is better—less translates into higher profits. Every activity reduces net income. The more procedures done, the greater the expenses and the lower the profits. The ideal situation is an open appointment schedule and an empty reception area.

PREPARING FOR MANAGED CARE

If we accept that managed care and capitation are here to stay, what can we do to prepare for the capitated system that we will all have to deal with? The sooner we accept the capitation concept and begin to develop ways to implement a capitation strategy into our practices, the more successful we will be in making the transition from a fee-for-service to a capitated system. The sooner we are able to understand the capitated system and calculate the economics of the system for our practices, the more comfortable and ultimately the more profitable we will be.

Remember the first time you took a history and a physical from a real live patient or the first time you were given the scalpel and told to make an incision? You were probably nervous and uncomfortable because of the greater risk and responsibility. No doubt you were out of your comfort zone. But by taking more histories and doing more operations, you gradually were able to accept the added risk and responsibility. The same holds true for capitation. By jumping in and getting your feet wet, you will soon learn to be comfortable with the new system and make it work for you (instead of wasting your time looking for reasons why it will fail).

Believe it or not, there are some advantages to being a capitated provider. First, you will experience a predictable cash flow and a decrease in the overhead expenses related to billing and collections. Second, you will have access to patient populations that you might not have if you did not participate in capitated arrangements. It is also possible that caring for capitated patients will offer you an opportunity to interact with new physicians in the community and be a referral source for their fee-for-service patients. Finally, succeeding as a capitated provider demands that you learn methods to become more efficient and decrease expenses. The process of becoming more efficient will impact your entire practice.

THE BENEFITS OF FORMING A GROUP PRACTICE OR A NETWORK

According to Michael Naslund, M.D., M.B.A., at the University of Maryland,* now is the time to form networks with other colleagues. In a shrinking market, it is important to maintain market share and best to increase it. Assuming that marginal revenues are greater than expenses, a provider will garner increased profits as long as the provider's market share increases. These increased profits and the resulting lower cost for each patient encounter give the provider a future competitive advantage vis-à-vis other providers. On the other hand, if the provider loses market share, the result will be a decrease in profits and a higher cost per patient encounter. As managed care contracts become available, the provider will be in a less competitive position to bid on these contracts than providers who have been gaining market share and lowering their cost structure.

Both Schramm and Naslund suggest that the best way to attract full-risk capitated business is to form partnerships or networks with other physicians in the community. An organized network of physicians will have greater access to contracts, capital, and assistance with cost management and will be better able to develop a system to measure cost-effectiveness and quality of care. Networks also provide physicians with an opportunity to attract managed care business. The individual members will benefit from using common fiscal and accounting services and payroll administration and from the economies of group purchasing. In short, a network will allow the physicians to do what they do best—practice medicine.

Hugh Greeley,† a well-known health care management consultant, believes that managed care plans prefer to contract with tightly organized physician groups because it is easier to work with one small group than many independent contractors. "A group will share the responsibility and deal with issues such as on-call coverage, quality, credentialing consistency, and referral patterns," Greeley says.

An alternative view is offered by Joseph Aita, M.D., medical director and executive vice-president of Lifeguard Inc., a Northern California HMO with 140,000 covered lives. Aita says, "We prefer to have individual contracts with our physicians, even if they have an affiliation with a medical group or an IPA." The plan actually uses a variety of contracting arrangements, including individual contracts with about 4,000 physicians as well as contracts with another 1,000 or more in IPAs and 1,500 in integrated medical groups. But the plan prefers individual contracts, according to Aita, because then there is direct communication between the plan and the physician. "If we have a concern about quality or utilization, it

---

*22 South Greene Street, Room S8D18, Baltimore, MD 21201.

†President, Greeley and Associates, 28220 Silver Lake Road, Salem, WI 53168, 414-889-8189, fax 414-889-8483.

doesn't have to go through a filter of the IPA, which may have its own internal issues that affect interaction with its physicians."

Lifeguard's preference, however, is a somewhat unusual one and is influenced by its desire to position itself as the most inclusive health care provider in the area. Although some managed care plans are willing to contract directly with individual providers, the trend does seem to be toward increasing integration of the health care system.

The reality is that preparation for capitation requires time and money that most solo practitioners don't have. To a certain degree there is strength in numbers, and a solo practitioner has little or no bargaining power. Most attractive to managed care plans will be those groups or networks that are strategically located and provide cost-effective care. Ultimately, your decision to remain in solo practice depends greatly on both your specialty and the degree of managed care penetration in your market.

USING CARVEOUTS

In contracting with managed care plans, you may need to use carveouts. Carveouts are parts of a specialty capitation contract for which your practice does not take responsibility. Separate contracts are made with other providers for these services. In some instances, you or your practice may not have the expertise or the desire to provide a full range of services (e.g., you may wish to exclude renal transplants or complex oncology cases).

In general, managed care plans take responsibility for arranging the additional necessary contracts. In some cases, especially if they do not want to grant carveouts, they may propose that you take responsibility for the services and contract with physicians that are interested in providing those services. This opens you up to legal, administrative, and utilization risk and should be avoided.

READING THE FINE PRINT

According to Schramm, a Sacramento physician who belonged to a managed care organization was deselected from the IPA without cause and with only 30 days' notice of contract termination. The doctor had more than 500 patients through that plan, and he mailed them all a letter explaining what had happened.

This doctor, like many physicians, was in a market heavily penetrated by managed care. He stopped reviewing all the details of the contracts he was given to sign and signed on a "good faith" basis. Thus he didn't realize he had signed an exclusive contract that resulted in a 25-percent reduction in his income.

The lesson to be learned here is that it is imperative to read all the fine print of these contracts. If you don't read them yourself, you need to hire someone who will review them on your behalf. Today many state medical societies will provide names of attorneys with health care experience who will review managed care contracts for about $300 to $500 per contract. The Sacramento physician would gladly have spent that amount of money to avoid experiencing the tremendous financial impact one bad contract had on his practice.

ANTITRUST ISSUES

Groups sometimes get together and attempt to dictate the financial terms and capitation fees to the managed care organizations. According to Schramm, this will not work or remain effective for very long. The reason? All the physicians must join the network. If some are left out, when the contract comes up for negotiation the next time, those left out of the contract will find a way to come up with a lower, more attractive price, and the network will collapse. On the other hand, if all physicians join the network, this might constitute a violation of the antitrust laws. Signing a managed care contract with a fee schedule is not in itself considered to be "price fixing" as long as the providers in the network have not colluded with one another on prices. One caveat: the network's pricing should not spill over to each doctor's non-network patients. Also, any antitrust risk is reduced when other networks are available for excluded providers to join. If some physicians are excluded, the network must show that there were grounds for their exclusion, such as documented evidence that their performance falls below community standards.

Recently safety zones have been created by the Department of Justice (DOJ) and the Federal Trade Commission (FTC). These government organizations have stated that they will not challenge networks that fall within these safety zones. A network may lie outside of a safety zone and still be in compliance with the law. The legitimacy of a network can be demonstrated if the providers have substantial financial risk or if the network allows providers to offer a new product that produces substantial efficiencies or cost savings. To qualify, the network must accept substantial financial risk sharing. The DOJ and the FTC are unlikely to challenge an exclusive provider network that includes no more than 20 percent of the physicians within any specialty who practice in the network's market and who share financial risk. Non-exclusive-provider networks will not be challenged if no more than 30 percent of the providers are included in the network.

According to Peter Pavarini, a lawyer and chair of the Health Law Department at Schottenstein, Zox & Dunn,* the DOJ and FTC, when analyzing networks, take into account the relevant market, anticompetitive effects, procompetitive effects, and any collateral agreements that involve spillover. They also look for the

---

*41 South High Street, Suite 2600, Columbus, OH 43215, 614-221-3211.

presence of other viable, sizable networks within the relevant market. Other issues of concern to the DOJ and the FTC include whether or not the network's providers participate in and earn substantial revenue from other networks (the providers must be free to compete against the network), evidence of substantial withdrawal of participants from other networks, and evidence of price fixing among the networks.

Given that the DOJ and FTC will continue to be on the lookout for antitrust violations, how can physicians in a network protect themselves? They must make sure their network is properly designed and implemented. They should use legal and business advisors who have expertise in antitrust law.

If they are accused, they shouldn't panic. They need to get the facts and devise a reasonable plan of action.

Above all, they must be accurate and clear when talking with competitors and patients. Most DOJ and FTC investigations begin when a private citizen or an excluded provider approaches one of these organizations with information about illegal business activities.

MANAGED CARE MEANS MANAGED EXPENSES

A proactive practice will make an investment in information systems and programs that measure quality. If you are thinking about purchasing new information software, be sure that it includes a system to track data and generate reports so that your practice can be accurately evaluated by the managed care organizations.

In a capitated system, managing care means managing money. You will need to know where the money is coming from and where it is going . . . down to the last penny—probably not a very exciting challenge to you. You will need to add *IBNR* (incurred but not reported) to your list of current acronyms. IBNRs are expenses that assigned capitated patients incur by going elsewhere. For example, suppose a primary care physician is capitated for all the health care that a patient receives. Now every doctor visit that the patient has, including visits to specialists, must be paid out of the per member per month fee that the primary care physician receives. If the patient goes to a dermatologist who is in the capitated system, the dermatologist will send a bill to the primary care physician, who is now responsible for payment of that bill. Anything that happens outside the physician's control is a potential IBNR and an additional expense to the practice. IBNRs need to be recorded and measured. Consequently, an accounting system or software program that allows for IBNRs is an essential tool.

You should begin collecting your own data so you don't have to depend on data from your hospital or from insurance companies. You will need to know the demographics of your practice—the age and sex of your patients, the most common diagnoses (by CPT codes), and the most common procedures you perform. You will also need to record the outcomes, complications, and lengths of stay of your hospital admissions. If you are presented with a capitation rate and you feel that your patients are sicker than the capitation rate allows, you will have to back up your feelings with data. The best data will be the data that you collect from your practice.

You will also want to compare your practice style to those of the physicians already in the capitated system. For example, you need to know the ratio of your referrals to patients seen in your practice and compare your referral statistics to those physicians already in the capitated system. If your referral rate is much greater than those of your colleagues, you might find that you don't qualify for inclusion in the system. You can at least assume that the plan's utilization review committee will be taking an especially close look at the way you practice and will make suggestions on how to reduce referrals. (Exhibit 29-1 is an appropriate referral evaluation form.)

To get ready for capitation, you will need to update yourself on new clinical procedures and new technologies. You don't necessarily have to buy the latest and most expensive widget, but you do need access to new procedures and technolo-

---

Exhibit 29-1 Appropriate Referral Evaluation Form

Patient name: _____

Primary care doctor: _____

Managed care plan (HMO): _____

	Yes	No
Was this referral necessary?		
Were the appropriate tests done before the patient was referred?		
Was the patient referred as soon as was medically indicated?		

Please explain any "No" answers below:

Source: Alvin Merlin, M.D., New Orleans, Louisiana.

gies that reduce length of stay, decrease the cost of care, and improve the outcomes of care (examples include laparoscopic procedures that return people to
work sooner than traditional surgery and pharmacologic alternatives to expensive
surgery).

Many physicians hear that the key to preserving the bottom line under capitation is to reduce overhead expenses. Of course, you need to be sensitive to overhead and make appropriate changes, but don't waste time trying to cut corners to
improve the bottom line. It is far more useful to consider altering your methods of
practicing medicine. Using new procedures that reduce average lengths of stay
and decreasing the number of tests and procedures you order will provide much
greater savings than simple overhead reduction. In fact, creating an attractive
office and buying computer systems to capture the data needed in a capitated
system—two requisites for attracting managed care business—may cause your
overhead to rise temporarily.

SUGGESTIONS FOR DECREASING UTILIZATION

A telephone triage system can significantly reduce utilization, as demonstrated
by a large capitated system in Southern California. The system monitored patients who called on the telephone for "emergency appointments" with their primary care physicians. These patients wanted to be seen immediately but instead
they were triaged by a nurse. The study revealed that 50 percent of the patients
didn't need to be seen at all, 25 percent needed to be seen within a week, and
25 percent had a legitimate emergency and needed to be seen that day. If given
reassurance and education, most patients will accept being seen at a time that is
appropriate for their medical problem.

Another good strategy is to send all new plan members a letter containing suggestions on utilization of services (Exhibit 29-2).

Copayments are an effective method of avoiding overutilization of office services. Numerous studies have found that when the required copayment increases,
utilization of services declines, especially for primary care practices. It is important that the copayment be collected at the time the service is provided; you don't
want to have to send out an expensive bill to collect $5 or $10. Your staff can
mention your policy when patients call for an appointment or it can be communi-
cated in the letter to new plan members.

Physician retraining and participation in continuing medical education courses
have been helpful in reducing costs. It is important that primary care doctors
learn that they can often take care of a medical problem at a lower evaluation and
management level and at a lower cost than a specialist. That doesn't mean that
primary care doctors should not refer patients to specialists. It does mean that

Exhibit 29-2 Introductory Letter Containing Managed Care Rules

You have joined a managed care health plan. Your physicians are trying to control the cost of your care so you and your employer can afford the coverage you need. You can help by following some simple guidelines.

1. When you call for an appointment, we need to know exactly what's bothering you. That lets us give you the time you need, when you need it. I have told my scheduler to ask questions that will help her do a good job for me and for you. She may ask you to talk to a nurse. It could save you a trip to the office.
2. We want you to stay healthy and we encourage preventive care like flu shots, back-to-school care, and annual physicals. Please schedule them well in advance, because we need to save time each day for sick patients.
3. As an HMO subscriber, you shouldn't make any unauthorized visits to specialists. If you do, it will cost you more. Call me first and we will decide together what care you need.
4. Using the Emergency Room is discomforting and expensive unless there is a crisis. Even then, you should call me first to make sure the trip is necessary. You can always reach a physician who is on call and who will either see you or authorize a visit to the appropriate location.
5. Bring your copayment for each visit. Since you know the amount, it's easiest for you to take care of it when you check in rather than waiting in line on your way out.

Source: Jeffrey J. Denning, Practice Performance Group, Long Beach, California.

specialists need to improve their communication with primary care doctors and develop guidelines for appropriate referrals.

For example, mild to moderate benign prostatic hyperplasia can be treated easily by a primary care doctor. If the doctor takes a history of urinary symptoms, performs a rectal exam, and obtains a PSA test on all men over 50 years of age, then he or she will be able to select those that need a urologic referral. All the others can be managed initially with medication by the doctor. Another example is that, through education and retraining, a primary care physician can take care of simple dermatologic and rheumatic conditions.

THE FUTURE OF MANAGED CARE

Since the election of President Clinton, there has been an insatiable interest in capitation throughout the United States. The truth, however, is that it remains too early to predict with confidence the eventual prevalence of capitation nationwide. An estimate that 50 percent of all Americans will be in a capitated system by the year 2005 is based on current compelling evidence that capitated systems and physician groups enjoy a meaningful cost advantage.[6]

When capitation arises as a topic of conversation among physicians, someone usually argues that it will result in the deterioration of quality of care. However, to date there is no peer-reviewed study that documents that there is a compromised standard of care among capitated providers. On the contrary, studies exist that demonstrate at least improved service quality in a capitated system. For example, a study compared the hospital length of stay and time spent in the intensive care unit for 58 pediatric patients who underwent surgical treatment for congenital heart disease at an HMO with the statistics for a matched group of 58 patients who received standard cardiac surgery care at a university hospital by the same surgeon. The only difference was the preoperative preparation, including family education, that the HMO group received. The study showed that the 58 patients treated at the HMO with critical pathway methods experienced significantly shorter lengths of stay in the hospital and intensive care unit than the matched patients treated at the university hospital with no significant difference in outcomes.[7]

Capitation can result in improved quality since those physicians that are concerned about reducing costs are also interested in measuring quality. Although the era of meaningful quality tracking is still ten years away, outcomes tracking is clearly warranted and the methodology will soon be available. At the moment, most quality tracking is not really about quality. Current measuring focuses on cost, access, and service quality.

TERMINATION OF MANAGED CARE CONTRACTS

There may occur situations where you will need to terminate your arrangement with a managed care plan. In most cases, a contract provides that either party may terminate it for any reason a stated number of days after notification, usually 90. (Exhibit 29-3 is a sample letter for terminating participation in a managed care plan.) It is important to remember that termination of a contract will not necessarily end your relationships with enrollees, nor will it typically release you from liability if enrollees are deemed to have been abandoned without medical care.

To assess the advantages of continuing your contracts with managed care plans, I suggest that you keep a file on each plan and record the fee for each procedure, including office visits and in-office lab tests. Also include the CPT code, a description of the procedure, the relative value unit (RVU) for the procedure, the fee quoted by the plan, and the fee received from the plan. This file should also con-

Exhibit 29-3 Letter Terminating Participation in a Managed Care Plan

---

For the last (number) years, I have treated patients from (name of managed care organization). I enjoyed the working relationship I developed with a number of people in your organization.

I regret that at this time I must sever my relationship with (name of managed care organization), effective (date—at least 60 days' notice or per contract). My staff has identified the plan members we currently see, and we have attached a list to this letter. On (date) I am sending these patients a letter notifying them of my decision to discontinue my participation as a plan physician. A copy of the letter is attached; please note the phone number I am referring them to for assistance in choosing a new physician.

If you have any questions, or wish to discuss my decision in more detail, please give my office a call and my receptionist will schedule a time we can meet.

Thank you.

Source: Reprinted with permission from *Correspondence for the Clinical Practice* by Baum, N., McIntire, K., Osborne, L., Anadem Publishing, Inc., Columbus, OH, Copyright 1996.

---

tain the deductible required per year or per illness, the copay that is to be paid by patients, the percentage of the covered fee that is to be paid by the plan, and the contact person at the plan's office. Using a system such as this, you can easily evaluate a managed care plan and a capitated fee arrangement and make an objective decision to renew or drop the managed care plan contract. Today there are software programs that organize this information for you.*

Schramm believes that primary care physicians can anticipate stable or improved incomes if they negotiate a good capitation rate and that specialists will need to get used to less income under capitation. The physicians that sit on the sidelines and opt to practice only on a fee-for-service basis will experience a sharp deterioration in their profits. For these few diehards there are no guarantees.

* * *

In the next chapter I will discuss ways physicians can serve as advocates for their patients within the managed care system.

---

*Main Street Software, 292 Glen Drive, Sausalito, CA 94965-1848.

NOTES

1. *Marion Merrell Dow Managed Care Digest*, HMO ed. (Kansas City, Mo.: Marion Merrell Dow, 1994), 12.

2. *HMO Industry Profile* (Washington, D.C.: Group Health Association of America, 1994), 23.

3. "Worcester's Model HMO," *Worcester (Mass.) Telegram*, 25 October 1992.

4. *HMO Employer Data and Information: A Special Report Measuring Utilization, Quality, and Value at Group Health Cooperation* (Seattle: Group Health Association, 1993).

5. The Advisory Board Company, The Governance Committee, *Capitation Strategy* (Washington, D.C.: The Advisory Board Company, 1994), 27.

6. Ibid., 32.

7. K. Turley, et al., "Critical Pathway Methodology: Effectiveness in Congenital Heart Surgery," *Annals of Thoracic Surgery* 58 (1994): 57–65.

30

Act as a Patient Advocate

There are occasions when a managed care plan that relies on prior authorization to control utilization refuses to authorize a procedure that the physician feels is clearly indicated. This chapter describes several situations where the doctor and staff need to serve as patient advocates.

If authorization has been denied for a procedure or test that is medically necessary, it is appropriate for the physician to take on the role of patient advocate. This may involve making a phone call to the nurse reviewing the case or sending supporting documentation. If going higher up is necessary, the physician is usually able to reach the person supervising the nurse reviewer within a reasonable time to explain why this particular patient does need this procedure or test.

EXAMPLES OF PATIENT ADVOCACY

I had a patient who needed a penile prosthesis, and we wrote the insurance company to request authorization. The company wrote a letter to us saying that, while this procedure was usually covered, a final decision could not be made until *after* the surgery. When I called back, the reviewer said, "We can't give you our opinion until we get the operative report."

I said, "That's not acceptable to this patient. He needs to know now whether the surgery will be covered before he has the surgery. If it isn't covered, he may decide not to have the surgery."

"Well," she says, "that's all I can tell you. I can't tell you we'll cover it, I can only tell you that generally speaking it is covered in this plan. We won't determine whether the specific surgery is covered until after the surgery."

I said, "Responses and policies like yours are the reason Americans are so upset with the health care system."

And she kept saying, "That's all I'm authorized to tell you."

I finally told her I would advise my patient to write a letter to the insurance company's medical director and send copies to his congressional representatives and the state insurance commissioner. With my assistance, he wrote this letter. He explained what he needed done and said that it was covered by his insurance but the insurance company wouldn't give him authorization to go ahead. The insurer's medical director wrote back approving the surgery.

This story shows one way a doctor can be an advocate for the patient.

In order to act as a patient advocate, you have to be a good communicator. You can't take a "just do it because I said so" attitude. But if you present the reasons why a certain procedure is indicated and is really in the best interest of the patient, the managed care plan will generally go along. After all, the plan wants to limit costs but it also wants to limit its exposure to lawsuits.

Irene Prechter, M.D., an ob/gyn in New Orleans, was caring for a pregnant hypertensive woman who was at high risk for premature delivery. Prechter recommended fetal monitoring twice a week, which she felt was the appropriate standard of care. The insurance company denied her request for fetal monitoring. For three weeks Prechter kept suggesting it. She sent the company a chapter from a medical textbook that stated that fetal surveillance was appropriate for hypertensive patients during the last trimester of pregnancy because it would help the physician determine when the patient needed to deliver the baby or whether an early C-section was indicated.

Finally, after Prechter sent material documenting that this was the appropriate standard of care, the insurance nurse acquiesced and allowed her to monitor the woman. It was, in the end, a successful term pregnancy. This is another example where a doctor was a successful advocate on behalf of a patient.

The point I am trying to make is that, even in this era of managed care and treatment guidelines, we don't have to practice medicine that exposes the patient to increased risk. Whenever a payer's reluctance to approve a treatment or procedure could compromise care and negatively impact the patient, then that is the time to be a spokesperson for the patient. I believe that no managed care plan wants to see patients mismanaged in order to save money. After all, if the employers receive enough complaints from the plan's members, they will contract with another managed care plan.

Michael Alabaster, M.D., a urologist in Memphis, Tennessee, had a patient with prostate cancer who didn't want a surgical removal of his prostate because he feared the possible complications of impotence and urinary incontinence. Although cryosurgery was an alternative solution, the managed care plan turned it down because it wasn't FDA approved and was considered experimental.

Alabaster presented the medical and financial data to the managed care organization: cryosurgery costs $8,000, it requires the patient to spend less than a day in the hospital, and no blood is required. Radical surgery, on the other hand, costs about $15,000, it requires an average length of stay of 5.4 days, and the patient might need two units of blood. He was able to show the managed care plan that cryosurgery was cost-effective both for the patient and for the managed care plan. As a result, the insurance plan then approved cryosurgery as an accepted modality of treatment.

Alabaster also had a patient with a testicular tumor who needed a retroperitoneal lymph node dissection. Alabaster told the managed care plan he might do one of these operations a year, whereas Dr. John Donahue, in Indianapolis, Indiana, does two or three a month. He said, "Obviously, this guy would be much more effective in doing the operation than I would," and he was able to convince the managed care plan to pay for the patient to travel from Memphis to Indianapolis and have the operation.

There's another way a specialist can serve as an advocate on behalf of patients. Let's say a patient with back pain is sent to a urologist to determine if there is a urologic explanation. If the urologist doesn't find anything, instead of simply sending the patient back to the primary care doctor, he can dictate a letter suggesting that the patient be referred to an orthopedist. This letter primes the pump— pushes the primary care doctor to make the next referral in a timely fashion. It's more effective than just saying, "Go back and see your primary care doctor. I haven't found anything." It is better to be an advocate on behalf of patients.

GETTING BABY OUT OF THE WOMB AND MOTHER OUT OF THE ROOM

Another example where doctors acted as patient advocates resulted in state legislation that backed up the position of the doctors. Since the beginning of the era of managed care, the postpartum length of stay has become progressively shorter. In 1993, it was 2.4 days for all deliveries, down from 3 days in 1983 and 4.1 days in 1970. However, obstetricians and pediatricians have advised HMOs and managed care plans that short stays (less than 2 days) place the mother and infant at risk for such problems as bilirubin encephalopathy.

This was brought to the attention of the American College of Obstetricians and Gynecologists, which submitted a statement to managed care organizations claiming that "health insurers were conducting a large, uncontrolled, and uninformed experiment on mothers and infants." As a result of the college's position on short lengths of stay, Maryland and New Jersey approved legislation mandating a minimum 48-hour hospital stay for women delivering vaginally and a 96-hour stay for women undergoing a Caesarean section; other states are considering similar legislation.

In addition to helping patients gain access to the treatments they need, physicians and staff can also ensure that patients are aware of all the medical resources available to them.

Ben McGowan, office administrator for Orthopedic Associates in New Orleans, recalls a 72-year-old woman who had been on Medicaid for 12 years and had been turned away by medical practices that would not treat Medicaid-only patients. When she had a fractured ankle and was seen by Orthopedic Associates, the receptionist noted that the patient's card did indicate both Medicare and Medicaid. She called the Social Security department and made inquiries on the patient's behalf. It turned out that the patient was eligible for both Social Security benefits and Medicare. In seven years, no one had taken the time to read her Medicaid card or question the Medicare/Medicaid indicator!

McGowan also remembers a 53-year-old man who had a severe alcohol and drug problem and who could not afford admission to one of the private drug treatment facilities. Because of his condition, he lost his job, was evicted from his apartment, and ended up on the street.

When the office administrator learned of this situation through another patient, he investigated and discovered that this man had an honorable discharge from the U.S. Navy and was a decorated Vietnam veteran. The administrator contacted several state agencies and was able to get the patient into a Veterans Administration drug rehabilitation program. Today, three years later, he is a functioning member of society.

WHAT TO DO WHEN NECESSARY CARE IS DENIED

Under some state laws, plans may not be held legally liable for negligence if a utilization review decision results in a bad outcome. Since patients will not be able to recover damages from the plan, they may focus on the physician instead. Therefore it is important that you appeal any plan decision that denies authorization for a treatment you consider medically necessary. Unless you make a reasonable attempt to reverse the decision of the plan, you may end up being the sole defendant in the event of a lawsuit. It is absolutely crucial that you document in the record all information regarding any request for services or procedures and any appeal made to reviewers regarding patient care.

If a test, procedure, or treatment you recommend is not approved by a managed care plan, you should take the following steps in order to secure appropriate care for the patient and minimize your exposure to legal liability.

1. Inform the patient that the plan has refused to authorize the recommended treatment and that the patient may be responsible for payment if the plan continues to deny authorization of the treatment. Tell the patient of your intention to challenge the plan's decision. Inform the patient of the reasons supporting the recommended treatment and the potential risks of forgoing such medical care. Document the discussion in the chart.
2. Challenge the plan's decision. Contracts should, but often do not, spell out procedures for appealing the denial of recommended tests, procedures, and treatments. If such procedures do not exist, you must try to persuade plan principals of the validity of your opinion through discussion and writing. There may be an appeal procedure for the patient to follow as well, and you should assist the patient with this. Exhaust such procedures and carefully document your efforts in the medical record and in letters to the plan.
3. If the plan does not change its decision, provide the service as a noncovered service for which the patient may pay your usual (or an agreed) fee or assist the patient in seeking care from other sources. However, check your contract, as it may prohibit you from billing patients for services deemed medically unnecessary, experimental, or investigational.[1]

There are a number of legal decisions that uphold a physician's right and responsibility to act as advocate on behalf of his or her patients. For example, in *Wickline v. State*, decided by the California Court of Appeals in 1986, the court held that cost-containment and utilization review programs do not automatically invade a physician's authority. It went on to say, however, that these programs are not immune from legal challenges. Third-party payers will be held liable, the court said, if they establish a system with "defects in the design or implementation of cost containment mechanisms, as, for example, when appeals made on a patient's behalf for medical or hospital care are arbitrarily ignored or unreasonably disregarded or overridden."

In the *Wickline* case, a woman was hospitalized for ten days after repeated surgery on her foot. Her physicians then requested eight additional hospital days, but the Medi-Cal utilization reviewer only authorized four. The patient was discharged and then readmitted with blood clots and an infection in her leg. Eventually it was amputated. She sued Medi-Cal but lost the case because Medi-Cal did have an appeal process that the physicians hadn't used.

It is a good idea to designate one person in the office as the patient advocate (the best candidate is the employee who deals with insurance and the managed care plans). The patient advocate should serve as an intermediary between patients and payers. The patient advocate checks with an insurance payer and receives authorization before a patient is seen or before any procedure is performed on the patient. That avoids situations where the patient learns after the fact that a procedure is not covered and he or she is responsible for the physician's fee.

*   *   *

In the next chapter we will discuss techniques to improve communications with those who control much of the destiny of our patients.

NOTE

1. *Physician's Managed Care Manual.* (San Francisco: California Medical Association, 1994), 48.

31

Keep Your Gatekeeper Content

For specialists who serve managed care patients, forming good relationships with gatekeepers is critical to success.

In the past, many physicians used to make contacts by socializing—playing golf or having dinner together. Physicians used to do a lot of networking or schmoozing with other doctors, sending out special gifts at the holidays. For the most part, the good ol' days of getting patients by being a good ol' boy or girl are over. Doctors have less time available for socializing. Those physicians who are in the 30- to 45-year-old range are likely to have children and be deeply involved in their children's schooling and in family activities.

In the past, what mattered most was, did the patients like you? Were you a nice, kindly doctor? Today managed care plans want to know if you are current with your continuing medical education, if you provide cost-effective care, and if patients have easy access to your practice.

In the past you would run across another doctor in the hallway and he would say, "Hey, I'm going to send you a patient." That no longer works today. Now the doctor says, "Hey, I'd like to send you a patient. Are you on the ABC managed care plan's plan?" If your answer is no, the best you'll get from your colleague is "sorry."

THE END OF THE MEGAWORKUP

In addition to being a nice person and a good doctor, you have to be a cost-effective doctor. If every time you get a patient you spend thousands of dollars doing a complete workup instead of asking a few questions and doing a physical examination and a few inexpensive blood tests and a urine test, you will not be a managed care darling. A patient with a bruise or sprain does not need a whole battery of X-rays. A patient with a simple headache does not need EEGs and CT scans.

In the fee-for-service system, you made the decisions, together with the patient. Now you're going to have to justify your decisions and agree to follow guidelines and protocols set down by managed care plans.

When I had a patient with recurring urinary tract infections, I used to routinely order an intravenous pyelogram (IVP) and cystoscopy. Not too long ago a managed care plan called me. They said, "We'll authorize the IVP and a urine cytology, but if the IVP and the cytology are normal, we will not authorize the cystoscopy. If you do that cystoscopy, you won't get paid." And they made several calls and sent letters to remind me that I wouldn't get paid. It was very, very clear that they were watching over my shoulder. If I couldn't justify the very expensive ($1,000) hospital charge for looking at the patient's bladder, the patient was not going to have the procedure. We're probably going to see more of this sort of scrutiny in the future.

UNDERSTANDING GATEKEEPERS' NEEDS

In order to form constructive long-term relationships with gatekeepers, you need to put yourself into their shoes and try to understand their needs, wants, and concerns. What motivates them? What causes them to get upset? Once you understand all this, then you will understand how best to deal with them and get what you need.

You have to recognize that under many forms of managed care, gatekeepers have an incentive not to refer. (The exception is a form of capitation in which the gatekeeper is capitated for his own services and receives a fixed monthly payment, regardless of his referral rate to specialists.) The goal of gatekeepers is to see how much of the total health care needed they can offer patients without having to use expensive specialists. In the minds of gatekeepers, specialists are a liability: they reduce the bottom line.

There are various ways in which managed care plans track how often primary care physicians make referrals to specialists. Physicians who use more specialists than most other doctors may be questioned by managed care plans about their patterns of practice. Perhaps a physician with a high referral rate can provide objective evidence that he or she has sicker patients than the average and consequently must refer more often than the average. If not, the physician may well find that managed care plans no longer wish to use his or her services.

Thus, a gatekeeper has two strong reasons to limit referrals to specialists: every referral is money out of the gatekeeper's pocket, and the managed care plans are carefully tracking referral patterns.

WHAT GATEKEEPING MEANS FOR PATIENTS

Patients are going to receive fewer medical services than they did in the past. They will probably be followed for longer periods of time before they are referred and consequently might be sicker by the time they finally see a specialist. More telephone advice will be used to limit the need for an office visit. Physician extenders and physician assistants will take on a larger role in the care of patients. Office visits will be shorter and physicians will have to be more efficient. Managing care means, among other things, managing minutes.

More watchful waiting will occur before a referral is made. A primary care physician is more likely than before to say to a patient, "Well, let's evaluate your progress in a few weeks or a few months, and if it still bothers you, we'll make a referral." People are not going to be able to walk into a primary care physician's office and say, "I'd like to see a specialist." Patients will have to accept conservative treatments by the primary care doctor, and only if those fail will they be referred to a specialist.

COMMUNICATING WITH GATEKEEPERS

In the managed care system, primary care physicians play a key role. If you are a specialist, you need to convince the managed care organizations that they want to contract with you, but you also need to get the gatekeeper to actually use you. In short, you are going to have to demonstrate the benefits of your practice and communicate this information to the gatekeeper.

Gatekeepers want to hear that you have a cost-effective, high-quality practice. They want to hear that patients have easy access to your practice and that it offers early morning and late afternoon hours. You're going to have to demonstrate that your practice is user-friendly—that patients receive an appointment in a reasonable period of time and that emergency cases receive immediate attention. My office is able to give the managed care plans a list of emergency conditions and tell them that patients with these conditions will definitely be seen the same day they call.

There are several useful ways to communicate with gatekeepers. One is to prepare a practice analysis specifically designed for gatekeepers (Exhibit 31-1 is a sample table of contents for such an analysis). This type of analysis should present

Exhibit 31-1 Sample Table of Contents for a Practice Analysis Designed for Gatekeepers

MISSION STATEMENT

PART ONE: GENERAL INFORMATION
Dr. Neil Baum
    Medical Training
    Professional Affiliations
    Publications
    Presentations
The Office
    General Information
    Office Philosophy
    Patient Education
Types of Specialized Procedures
    Most Frequently Billed CPT Codes
    The "No-Incision" Vasectomy
    Radioactive Seed Implantation
Benefits to Managed Care Providers and Other Groups
Benefits to Patients
Cost Considerations

PART TWO: PATIENT SURVEY RESULTS
Patient Information
    Introduction
    Market Area Boundaries
    Patient Payer Source
    Results of Patient Satisfaction Survey

Appendix A: Curriculum Vitae

Appendix B: Selected Patient Letters

Appendix C: Selected Publications

Appendix D: Presentation "Managing Care, Time, and the Bottom Line"

Source: Gold Consulting, 5570 Jacquelyn Court, New Orleans, LA 70124, 504-488-2768.

a detailed picture of your practice. It should provide a demographic description of your patients, list the hospitals you practice at and the plans you currently contract with, and include patient satisfaction survey data and testimonial letters from patients. If you have statistics that indicate cost-effectiveness (for example, statistics that show your length of stay is at or below the national average or the community average), include that information. Of course, also show that you are on the cutting edge of your field by listing all the continuing medical education courses and seminars that you have attended. (Chapter 32 describes in detail how to put together a practice analysis.)

Someone from your practice, preferably the office manager or a comparable person, should hand-deliver the analysis to each gatekeeper and request an interview. This sort of thing works, partly because very few practices are doing it.

Another way to reach out to gatekeepers is to offer to give a talk on some subject of interest to them. For example, I might give a talk about the medical management of an enlarged prostate gland. I would explain what they, as primary care physicians, should look for, and the danger signs they should be aware of. When they need to refer a patient to a urologist, hopefully they will think of me because they've already met me and have a sense of how I practice.

In addition, I might follow up by sending a letter thanking them for allowing me to come and enclosing an article that is pertinent to the subject we discussed. Also, when I attend an interesting meeting or conference in my field, I summarize what I learned and I send the gatekeepers a letter describing the latest developments (Exhibit 31-2 is a sample letter of this type). See Chapter 44 for additional suggestions and examples of forms to use when communicating with gatekeepers.

HOW SPECIALISTS CAN WORK TOGETHER WITH PRIMARY CARE PHYSICIANS

In the past, urologists used to treat all men with prostate diseases such as prostatitis, benign prostatic hyperplasia, and prostate cancer. Today, however, there are effective antibiotics to treat prostatitis and medical therapy for benign enlargement of the prostate gland.

When these new treatments were first developed, urologists were concerned that they might lose a significant portion of their business to primary care physicians. Upon closer scrutiny, it became clear that it was more cost-effective for patients to be treated for mild to moderate lower urinary tract obstructive symptoms by a primary care physician and to see a urologist for more advanced or complicated diseases of the prostate gland, such as urinary retention or hematuria.

It is also in the best interest of the urologist to seek appropriately referred patients. One patient with a prostate nodule or an increase in his PSA level who needs a transrectal ultrasound guided biopsy generates as much income as 10 patients who need a history, review of symptoms, physical examination, and PSA test.

I've worked to educate primary care physicians on the evaluation and treatment of mild to moderate benign enlargement of the prostate gland and also provide them with suggestions about when it is appropriate to refer to a urologist. As a result of the kind of relationship I have with primary care physicians, the number of prostate surgeries that I do for benign enlargement of the prostate gland has decreased but the number of procedures I do to evaluate patients for prostate

Exhibit 31-2 Sample Letter Summarizing Trends in Urology

Dear [referring doctor],

I am providing a newsletter summarizing the latest developments and trends in urology. I hope you'll find this material useful and informative.

PHARMACOLOGIC MANAGEMENT OF BPH

The exact cause of BPH remains unclear, although the hormonal etiology is the most likely etiology. The two classes of drugs that are used to treat BPH are (1) antiandrogen drugs, used to decrease the size of the prostate, and (2) alpha adrenergic antagonists, used to decrease the tone of smooth muscle at the bladder neck and proximal urethra.

Androgens are known to be essential for BPH to develop. Testosterone is converted to the active metabolite dihydrotestosterone (DHT) by the enzyme 5-alpha-reductase. Until recently all drugs associated with decreasing the size of the prostate were associated with significant side effects such as impotence, gynecomastia, and hot flashes.

Finasteride (Proscar) is a 5-alpha-reductase inhibitor that reduces DHT to castrate levels. The drug decreases the size of the prostate 20 percent–25 percent. One-third of the patients will have statistically significant improvement of their voiding symptoms. The drug requires approximately six months to become effective. There are few side effects from finasteride, such as decreased volume of the seminal fluid. Since finasteride does not affect the testosterone level, less than 3 percent of the men using the drug will complain of impotence or a decrease in the libido or sex drive. Some men note a moderate decrease in the volume of the ejaculation at the time of orgasm.

Alpha-adrenergic receptors are present in the prostatic urethra and bladder neck. Nearly 40 percent of the prostate is made up of smooth muscle containing alpha receptors. Alpha-adrenergic antagonists such as prazosin (Minipres) or terazosin (Hytrin) result in a favorable response in patients with mild to moderate lower urinary tract obstructive symptoms. The dose is 1–2 mg/day of prazosin or 5–10 mg/day of terazosin. The side effects are dizziness, tiredness, and, rarely, postural hypotension. The postural hypotension can be controlled with stepwise dosing.

A large double-blind VA cooperative study is underway to evaluate placebo, terazosin, finasteride, and a combination of terazosin and finasteride. Theoretically a combination of these two drugs will be a more effective treatment than either drug alone.

At present, none of the pharmacologic methods cure BPH. They do reduce the symptoms of outlet obstruction. TURP still remains the gold standard in improving symptoms and in objective measurements such as flow rates.

NO WAY BABY OR INCISIONLESS VASECTOMY

A vasectomy is the most efficient and cost-effective method of permanent birth control. Now the procedure can be done in the office under local anesthesia without any incision. The new technique uses instruments developed in China. The procedure is performed through a single stab wound 3–4 mm in length. As a result, there is less intraoperative pain, bleeding, and postoperative discomfort.

continues

Exhibit 31-2 continued

CURRENT STATUS OF PSA AS A SCREENING TEST FOR CANCER OF THE PROSTATE

Cancer of the prostate is the most common malignancy in the United States and the second most common cause of cancer deaths. Since the April 1991 report in *The New England Journal of Medicine* that PSA was an effective screening test for prostate cancer, hundreds of thousands of PSA tests have been performed. Mild elevations of PSA also occur in most men with BPH. A normal PSA does not entirely rule out prostate cancer, as there have been reported cases of prostate cancer and normal PSA levels. Recently, the FDA has approved the PSA test as a screening procedure for prostate cancer.

Several modalities are available for early detection and screening. The digital rectal exam (DRE) remains the gold standard with which other tests are compared. The transrectal ultrasound examination is able to visualize lesions not palpated on DRE.

A recent study in the March 1992 *Journal of Urology* reported a study of 1,250 men who had a screening PSA; 187 (15 percent) had proven prostate cancer and 12/32 (37.5 percent) had elevated PSA and a normal DRE. Most of the patients with cancer had localized cancer and were amenable to definitive therapy.

Currently, I recommend a screening PSA in all men over age 50. Men in high-risk groups, such as Afro-Americans and men with a relative, especially a brother or father, that have prostate cancer, need an annual PSA and digital rectal exam after age 40.

The half-life of PSA is 2.2 days. I recommend that the blood be obtained prior to a DRE or 4 days after a rectal examination.

If you'd like additional information or articles on any of these subjects, please give me a call and I'll be happy to send them to you.

Sincerely,

Neil Baum, M.D.

---

cancer has increased. I find myself diagnosing an increasing number of cases of prostate cancer.

In a similar attempt to influence referral patterns, orthopedists and neurosurgeons could educate primary care doctors on the management of low back pain. After all, most patients presenting with low back pain can be successfully managed using conservative treatments. Only those patients with muscle weakness, atrophy, and neurologic changes in the lower extremities need a referral to an orthopedist or neurosurgeon. If the specialists can educate the primary care physicians on conservative management and what constitutes an appropriate referral, then they will have a more successful practice as well as better relationships with gatekeepers and managed care plans. One patient who needs back surgery is worth a whole lot more than a dozen or two who need office visits, checking of symptoms, and prescription refills.

The same also applies to endocrinologists. They would do well to inform primary care doctors about the management of early diabetes and identify which patients require referral. Most patients with adult onset diabetes can be managed through use of oral hypoglycemic agents, weight loss, and diet. If the primary care physicians refer only those who are difficult to manage or have complications or neurological changes, endocrinologists would be able to make the best use of their time.

*   *   *

In the next chapter I will describe methods to make your practice attractive to managed care plans.

32

How To Make Your Practice Attractive to Managed Care Plans

T he key to a successful medical practice used to be the three A's: availability, ability, and affability. Today, in order to make your practice attractive to managed care plans you have to demonstrate cost-effectiveness and high quality as well.

If managed care is just beginning to penetrate your community, almost any managed care organization will be eager to contract with you. Just completing the application and including a copy of your C.V., your medical license, and documentation of your malpractice coverage will ensure your inclusion on the panel of providers. However, if managed care has already invaded your area, then it will be much more difficult to join a plan. Now it will take energy and effort on your part to promote your practice and sell the plan on the advantages of adding you to its panel.

This chapter describes methods to make your practice attractive to managed care plans. It discusses the importance of preparing a practice analysis, the necessary ingredients of a practice analysis, and how to present the material to managed care plans.

The purpose of a practice analysis, in addition to demonstrating your practice's cost-effectiveness and quality, is to showcase the unique characteristics of your practice. The practice analysis should point out to managed care plans the benefits and advantages of your practice in an objective fashion.

DOING YOUR HOMEWORK

One of your first tasks is to prepare a list of all of the procedures and services you offer your patients. Provide the CPT code for each item on the list and the

271

relative value unit for each procedure (available in *California Relative Value Studies*).[1] You also need to note your fee for each procedure and the hospital cost for each diagnosis-related group (DRG) and ICD-9 code. Now the managed care plan can compare your charges to those of other physicians and practices that are already accepted or are applying to be included on the plan's panel.

You can demonstrate your cost-effectiveness by listing all of the procedures that you do in your office or in an ambulatory treatment center. Using these settings is less costly than using the hospital. For example, a cystoscopy performed in the office uses approximately $85 of disposable equipment, compared with a hospital charge to the third-party payer of more than $1,000. Most ambulatory treatment centers can operate 30 to 50 percent more efficiently than a hospital operating room, and many offer discounts for managed care business.

Also mention aspects of your practice philosophy that might result in cost savings to plan members. If you use conservative, nonsurgical treatments or cost-effective testing, be sure to include this information. For example, if you believe that an acute uncomplicated urinary tract infection can be successfully treated with a one-day or a short course of antibiotics instead of the traditional 10–14 days of medication, then be sure to point that out in your practice analysis.

Next you want to survey your current patients. Your questionnaire should ask patients how easy it was to make an appointment, how long they waited to see the doctor, how friendly the staff was, and whether the doctor answered all of their questions. (Exhibit 32-1 is a patient questionnaire I have used to survey patients, and Figures 32-1 and 32-2 graphically show the results for individual questions.) If you get responses from your patients that might make good testimonials about your practice, ask the patients for permission to include them in the practice analysis (see Exhibit 32-2).

If you are a primary care doctor, indicate your referrals per 100 patients seen. Also, it is a good idea to survey physicians you refer to. If you are a primary care physician, query your specialists and ask them if the referrals are appropriate. Are patients worked up prior to the referral? Are reports and documentation sent well in advance of the referral so that the specialist doesn't spend precious time tracking lab and X-ray reports? If you are a specialist, survey your primary care physicians about the completeness of your evaluations, about your promptness in communicating with them, and whether you obtain proper authorizations before you perform any procedure or test.

The practice analysis should also describe the setting and environment of your practice. Provide the number of full-time staff and the ratio of full-time staff to physicians. Since staff salaries constitute one of the highest components of overhead, this statistic will give plans some idea of your overhead expenses and the efficiency of your practice. Indicate your office hours, especially if you offer early morning, evening, and weekend hours for appointments. Offering extended

Exhibit 32-1 Patient Satisfaction Survey

To provide you with the best possible care, we need your feedback.

1. How did you decide to come to this practice?
   ____ Recommended by another patient   ____ Recommended by family
   ____ Recommended by another doctor   ____ Recommended by hospital
   ____ Physician referral service   ____ Local medical society
   ____ Yellow Pages   ____ Office close to work
   ____ Office close to home
   Other: _____

2. When you telephone our office, is your call answered courteously?
   ____ Yes ____ No Comments: _____

3. Are you able to obtain an appointment easily and timely?
   ____ Yes ____ No Comments: _____

4. During your last visit to our office, how would you describe your treatment by our staff?
   ____ Warm/friendly   ____ Cool/unfriendly   ____ Courteous
   ____ Professional   ____ Unprofessional
   Other: _____

5. How interested do we seem to be in you as a person when you visit the office?
   ____ Genuinely interested and concerned
   ____ Usually interested and concerned
   ____ Sometimes disinterested and unconcerned
   ____ Usually disinterested and unconcerned

6. Do you find our waiting room warm and comfortable?
   ____ Yes ____ No Comments: _____

7. Are the waiting room materials to your taste? ____ Yes ____ No
   If "No," your preference: _____

8. When you arrive at our office, how long do you normally have to wait after your scheduled appointment time? ____ minutes. If you wait longer than 30 minutes, are you given an explanation for the delay? ____ Yes ____ No

9. How would you rate the overall quality of care you receive?
   ____ Outstanding ____ Good ____ Fair ____ Poor
   Comments: _____

10. How would you rate the doctor on patience, warmth, and interest in your problem?
    ____ Outstanding ____ Good ____ Fair ____ Poor

---

continues

Exhibit 32-1 continued

11. Does the doctor fully explain your illness and treatment to you?
    ____Yes ____No Comments:_____

12. Are you comfortable recommending our services to your family and friends?
    ____Yes ____No Comments:_____

13. What other services could we offer that you would like available for you or your family?
    _____

14. Have the financial policies of this practice been completely explained to you?
    ____Yes ____No Comments:_____

15. During your last visit, were the charges explained to your satisfaction?
    ____Yes ____No Comments:_____

16. Is our superbill helpful in filing with your insurance for reimbursement?
    ____Yes ____No Comments:_____

17. Other:_____
    _____
    _____

Thank you for taking time to complete this information.
We value our patients' comments.

_____   _____
    Date   Signature (optional)

hours shows that you are really managed care–friendly and willing to see patients when it is convenient for them.

List your hospital affiliations, since the plans may already have contracted with one or more of the hospitals. If you do not have privileges with one of its hospitals, that will make it difficult for it to send members to you.

Analyze your existing patient base. Indicate the percentages of Medicare, fee-for-service, and managed care patients. If you already have a large percentage of managed care patients, that is an indicator that you understand the system.

Nearly every managed care plan is interested in utilization management and quality assurance. Plans will be particularly impressed if you have electronic medical records and provide patients with medical information electronically. Plans like to know whether you have an electronic patient recall system. This ensures that patients will not fall through the cracks and will be notified of important follow-up appointments. Plans want to know your system for documenting and

QUESTION 2: When you telephone our office, is your call answered courteously?

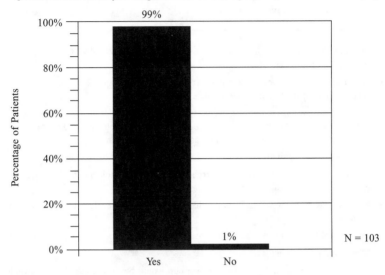

Figure 32-1 Graphic display of responses to Question 2 of the patient satisfaction survey.

QUESTION 9: How would you rate the overall quality of the care you receive?

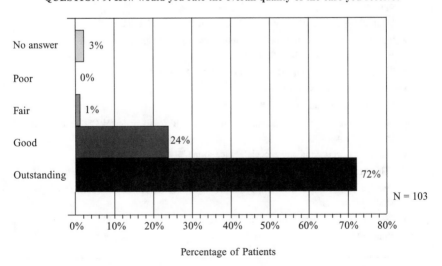

Figure 32-2 Graphic display of responses to Question 9 of the patient satisfaction survey.

Exhibit 32-2 Additional Comments Made by Patients in Response to Question 17 of the Patient Satisfaction Survey

- "It would be nice if you and your staff could teach your philosophy of office management to other staffs and doctors. . . ."
- "Dr. Baum and staff are always positive thinking people and relay that attitude to others. Wish all doctors had that attitude."
- "I am extremely pleased with the quality of care I receive from Dr. Baum and the outstanding support of his staff. I have never encountered such a relaxed openness and respect in a doctor–patient relationship as I do with Dr. Baum."
- "Stay as sweet as you are."
- "Dr. Baum's a great guy and runs a terrific business, personable and professional. I'm glad to avail myself of the services the practice offers."
- "I would like to know where I can purchase some of those puzzles in your examining rooms."
- "Would not let anyone else be my urologist."
- "You run a good show!"
- "I, as a senior citizen, feel that we as a group would be very grateful if you would accept assignment of our Medicare claims plus whatever else we might be able to contribute from secondary insurance to reach your gross charges."
- "Keep up the good work. Congratulations on your excellent staff."
- "Thank you for your care. The patient detail your office is committed to is evident even in this questionnaire."
- "Would have liked a little more in-depth discussion of condition and all treatment options."
- "Out of all the different physicians I see, Neil Baum is THE BEST!!"
- "Dr. Baum and the entire staff conduct themselves in a very professional, caring, and warm manner. I am extremely satisfied."
- "Very patient in dealing with insurance claims and delays."
- "Dr. Baum, you have given me the Best."
- "Great motivational literature."
- "It was a pleasure to be a patient at your office. Have a wonderful Christmas and a Happy New Year."
- "Jackie was very kind and especially nice to me."
- "This office is by far the most comfortable doctor's office I have ever gone to."
- "We are very satisfied with the doctor, the service rendered, and their staff. Thank you kindly for caring."
- "Sometimes too rushed/overbooked (not recently)."
- "Superb!"

charting lab and diagnostic tests. Nearly every one of us has had the experience of having a report filed in a patient's chart without it ever being read by the doctor. Plans want to be sure that this will not happen in your practice—that you have safeguards to prevent it.

Plans also want to know that you are a managed care team player and will adhere to guidelines and protocols. I have given managed care plans a copy of the "Suggestions for Urologic Referral" that I send to primary care doctors. These cost-saving suggestions outline what primary care doctors can do as part of the workup before seeking a urologic consultation. (Exhibit 32-3 is the cover letter I send to primary care physicians and Exhibit 32-4 presents the actual suggestions.)

For example, if a patient has hematuria, I suggest that a urine culture, an intravenous pyelogram, and a urine cytology be done before the patient is referred to the urologist. When a patient calls for an appointment and the receptionist learns that the appointment is for evaluation of hematuria and the studies have been completed, then the patient is scheduled for a flexible cystoscopy on the first visit. The information on the procedure, the consent, and the instructions for the

---

Exhibit 32-3 Cover Letter Concerning Suggestions for Urologic Referral

Dear [primary care physician],

In this time of change and health care reform, the relationship between the primary care physician and the specialist is being modified. In order to facilitate the transition, I would like to provide you with some suggestions regarding referrals to a urology practice. Of course, these are only suggestions and are not carved in stone.

It is my purpose to ensure each of your patients is seen in a timely fashion and receives a cost-effective workup and treatment and to improve the communication between your office and mine. Following a patient's visit to my office, I will provide you with an immediate report that contains the diagnosis, the medications that I have recommended, and the treatment plan.

I am including educational materials, appropriate consents, and drug information. If you need additional copies, please give my office a call and we will be happy to fax/mail them to you.

If you have any questions or comments on these suggestions, please let me hear from you.

Sincerely,

Neil Baum, M.D.

Exhibit 32-4 Suggestions for Urologic Referral

I. Referral for a man or woman with **gross or microscopic hematuria** that is not associated with a urinary tract infection

Please send patient with:
1) results of urine C & S
2) IVP report
3) urine cytology report

Please give patient:
1) consent for cystoscopy
2) the educational material on hematuria (note there is a different one for men and women)

II. Referral for females with **recurrent UTIs or complicated UTI** (fever, chills, or flank pain)

Please send patient to our office with:
1) results of urine C & S
2) results of IVP

Please give patient:
1) consent for cystoscopy and cystogram
2) information on recurrent UTI

III. Referral for **impotence**

A suggested evaluation by your office can in most instances differentiate psychogenic from organic erectile dysfunction. I recommend that you:

1) obtain serum testosterone, glucose—if the testosterone is at the lower limit of normal or decreased (<225 ng/dl), then include a prolactin level
2) provide the patient with a Snap Gauge band to determine the presence or absence of nocturnal erections

Please give patient:
1) sexual function questionnaire
2) educational information on impotence
3) results of the Snap Gauge test

IV. Referral for **BPH**

The Agency for Health Care Policy and Research (AHCPR) has developed guidelines that are based on symptoms and treatment according to patient preference. These are:

1) quality of life symptom score
2) physical examination/digital rectal examination
3) urinalysis
4) PSA
5) serum creatinine

---

continues

Exhibit 32-4 continued

Indications for urologic referral are:
1) moderate to severe symptoms unresponsive to pharmacologic management
2) urinary retention
3) possible neurogenic bladder (patients with diabetes, Parkinson's, multiple sclerosis)
4) recurrent UTIs
5) uninfected hematuria
6) PSA > 4 ng/ml, PSA rising more than 20 percent a year
7) abnormal digital rectal exam
8) azotemia

Please give patient:
1) results of PSA test
2) alternative treatments for the enlarged prostate gland
3) if patient has an abnormal rectal exam or elevated PSA test, provide the patient with information on the transrectal ultrasound/biopsy

V. Referral for **urinary incontinence**

Suggest that patient keep a voiding diary for 5 days.
Please give patient:
1) incontinence educational material
2) consent for cystoscopy and urodynamic evaluation
3) copy of urine C & S report

VI. Patient referred for **vasectomy**

Please give patient:
1) educational materials on no-incision vasectomy
2) consent for vasectomy
3) pre- and postvasectomy instructions

Source: Based on the work of Michael Alabaster, M.D., Memphis, Tennessee.

preparation are sent to the patient, who reads and signs the forms before coming to the office. This method, which allows the evaluation to be completed in a single visit, is a cost-effective way of evaluating many medical conditions and is thus very attractive to managed care plans.

If your practice performs weekly or regular random chart reviews to check for documentation and completeness of records, the plan will be impressed. Indicate that all allergies are noted on the front of any chart and that all patient telephone conversations as well as all prescription refills are noted in the chart.

You can demonstrate your attention to detail by including a copy of your employee manual. If your practice has regular staff meetings, send the plan a copy of the most recent notes from those staff meetings. You should also indicate whether you conduct periodic performance reviews of the staff and physicians and provide records of the last two years of continuing medical education for them (this shows their medical knowledge is current and up to date).

Finally, indicate the distinctive characteristics of your practice. List all its advantages for current patients and potential new ones. If there are any areas of particular medical interest or expertise that distinguish your practice as an innovator or leader in your field, then you want to note them in the practice analysis. For example, you will want to mention if you have written papers in peer-reviewed journals, made presentations at national meetings, conducted seminars, or taught postgraduate courses.

HOW TO USE PRACTICE ANALYSIS MATERIAL

Contact the provider relations representative of the plan you wish to join. Send the representative a letter of introduction saying you wish to join the plan and would like to present your practice analysis material. Request a meeting and mention that you will call to arrange a time.

When you meet the representative, show him or her the practice analysis and focus your presentation on cost-effectiveness and quality issues. If you merely send the analysis to the representative, you don't know if it will be reviewed or even looked at. At least this way you know the representative is aware of the highlights.

Ask about the current panel and inquire whether there are any obstacles to your inclusion on the panel. Conclude by explaining why it would be beneficial for the plan to contract with you. You might present the reasons in a one-page summary you leave with the representative. Indicate that you will follow up with a call in two weeks to learn of the plan's decision.

AFTER YOU ARE ACCEPTED

Once the plan has approved your application and has listed you in its directory, you must let the other plan physicians and the plan members know of your participation and availability. I suggest you write a letter to the physicians that introduces your practice and emphasizes your commitment to cost containment and quality (Exhibit 32-5 is an example of a letter to the physicians that are already on the plan).

SUPPOSE THEY SAY NO

Early in the managed care game, it was easy to gain entry into a managed care plan. Once managed care made greater inroads, doctors found that the panels

Exhibit 32-5 Introductory Letter Sent to Plan Physicians Announcing Participation in the Plan

Dear [plan physician],

As a new provider on your health care plan, I would like to take this opportunity to introduce myself and my practice.

I have been practicing urology in this community since 1978 and am on the staff at Touro Infirmary and Southern Baptist Hospitals.

In an era of cost containment I would like to mention my sensitivity to the spiraling cost of health care. I avoid the "mega" workup for common urologic problems such as recurrent urinary tract infections and prostatism. Whenever possible I do my diagnostic studies and even surgical procedures during a one-day stay or in an ambulatory treatment center.

My approach to prostate cancer in older men with disease confined to the prostate is to offer these patients radiation therapy using I^{125} implants. This is a very cost-effective method of treatment compared to radical prostatectomy.

I also offer collagen implants for women with severe stress incontinence due to intrinsic sphincter deficiency. This procedure can be performed on an outpatient basis and even under local anesthesia in the office in selected cases.

One of my areas of interest is the diagnosis and management of impotence. I have recently reported my results with several other colleagues and my success rate exceeds 95 percent with a two-year follow-up.

I make an effort to provide my patients with educational materials that inform them about measures they can take to prevent diseases and for early detection of urologic cancers. I provide all men with a testicular self-examination card encouraging them to perform self-examination on a regular basis. Patients are given a quarterly newsletter that discusses recent topics in health care. I also send a semiannual newsletter to referring physicians that reviews the latest developments in urology.

One of the most common complaints that patients have with managed care plans is that they can't obtain appointments in a timely fashion with the physician. I would like to emphasize that my practice will not discriminate or differentiate a managed care plan patient from a traditional fee-for-service patient. I reserve 30 minutes every afternoon as "sacred time" that is left open for the emergencies and urgencies that occur every day.

I also provide primary care doctors with a fax referral form that can be used to communicate with my office in an efficient fashion. This form will identify the patient with immediate needs. I can assure you that those patients with emergencies can be seen immediately and patients with urgencies can be seen in 24–48 hours.

I also recognize the importance of timely communications between the primary care doctors and the specialists. I have utilized a method of notifying you in writing within 24 hours of the urologic diagnosis concerning the medications prescribed for your patients and the treatment plan. If you have a fax machine and request a report immediately, it will be electronically sent to your office the same day your patient is seen.

I hope this letter gives you an overview of my practice and my office staff. I look forward to working with you and your physicians on the [name of plan].

Sincerely,

Neil Baum, M.D.

quickly became closed. They would receive requests from patients to have their records transferred to physicians who were on their plans' panels. After a number of such requests, the nonplan doctors would call the plans and ask for admission—only to find the panels closed.

If a panel is closed for your specialty, or the plan has enough physicians in your geographic area, then you have to mount a campaign to make your practice seem attractive to the plan. You have to tune into the plan's Station WIIFM (What's in It for Me?). You have to demonstrate that you have something to offer that will be of benefit to plan members.

Do your homework. Find out what the plan's needs and wants are and if there are any voids in its existing panel. If you have a service that is not being offered by the plan, then it can justify adding you on. For example, if you have special training in allergy and immunology and the plan does not offer allergy and immunology services, point this out when making your pitch.

Occasionally you will hear that the plan has all the doctors in your field that it needs. Ask to see the plan's directory, and when an existing member retires, moves, or is dropped from the plan, then act quickly and be the first to contact the physician representative with your new application.

Use your practice analysis to demonstrate your cost-effectiveness as well as your patients' satisfaction with their care. The plan does not want to hear any complaints from its members about their health care providers. If you can show your practice has a high patient satisfaction rate, the plan will not have to worry about the potential problems associated with patient complaints.

CARING ENOUGH TO SEND THE VERY BEST

Next consider organizing a letter writing campaign. Letters from old patients of yours who are members of the plan and can't see you because you are not on the panel will have some impact. I often ask patients to write a letter to their plan's patient representative and to their employer. Many of them would like to write a letter but don't have the necessary letter-writing skills. In such cases, I offer them a sample letter (Exhibit 32-6) and ask them to write it on their own stationery.

You can also ask employers to lobby on your behalf. Ask them to send a letter to the plan administrator or physician representative and ask that you be included on the panel. I gave a talk on incontinence and urinary tract infections to a local oil company's female employees. Many of those in the audience wanted to make an appointment but couldn't because I wasn't on the plan. I suggested that the health nurse send a letter to the plan requesting that I be included. Shortly thereafter I received a call asking me to join a plan that was previously closed to me.

Exhibit 32-6 Letter Supporting Physician's Attempt To Be Put on a Physician Panel

Dear [employer],

For the past five years I have been under the urologic care of Dr. Neil Baum. I called to make an appointment with Dr. Baum and learned that he is not on our new insurance plan. Dr. Baum informed me that he has submitted an application to [insurance plan] and has been told that there are too many urologists already on the panel.

I would like for you to consider recommending Dr. Baum to [insurance company]. Unlike the urologists currently on the plan, Dr. Baum takes early morning appointments and will allow me to come to his office after 4:30 PM. If I select one of the urologists on the plan, I will be required to miss several hours of work in order to see a doctor.

I also know that Dr. Baum's office conducts an annual patient survey in order to meet the needs of his patients. He is the only physician that I have been to that asks patients if they have any concerns relating to the doctor and the staff. Dr. Baum also emphasizes preventive care and provides all his male patients with a testicular self-exam card to check for testicle cancer.

I hope you will take all of these reasons into consideration and will recommend that Dr. Baum be included on our plan.

Sincerely,

Exhibit 32-7 Letter of Recommendation from a Plan Physician

Dear [medical director],

I am writing this letter to recommend a colleague, Dr. Excellent, to be a provider for [specialty] referral to the plan members of [managed care organization]. I have worked with Dr. Excellent for the past [number of years] and have found his performance to be exceptional. He presently is seeing a number of the plan's members, and I know that they are very satisfied with his services. He is a member in good standing with [hospital] and the local and state medical societies.

Dr. Excellent has been instrumental in organizing the physicians in his specialty into an independent physician association. He understands the concepts of managed care, guidelines, and cost-effectiveness.

I believe he will make a fine addition to our panel of providers and I recommend him highly.

Sincerely,

Exhibit 32-8 Annual Letter to the Medical Director of a Managed Care Plan

---

Dear [medical director],

As a member of your managed care plan, I would like to tell you about the activities in my practice that have taken place this past year.

I have received 75 hours of continuing medical education. This includes attendance at the American Urologic Association's annual meeting, a seminar in urodynamics, and a post-graduate course that describes a new technique for the treatment of urinary incontinence that will significantly reduce patient discomfort, length of stay, and costs.

I have had five articles in peer-reviewed journals published in the past 18 months. I am including copies for your review.

My practice conducted a patient survey (a copy of the survey is enclosed). This survey demonstrates that 94 percent of patients have found the services provided to be satisfactory and would recommend my practice to others.

I have compared my practice to other practices in our community, and I am including data on the length of stay, complication rate, readmission rate, and hospital costs for the 10 most common urologic procedures that I do in the hospital.

We have conducted a time and motion study on the time patients spend in my practice. We have demonstrated that the majority of patients spend less than 20 minutes in the reception room. Nearly all established patients are seen, processed, and discharged within 40 minutes of their arrival in the office. This means that plan members can be seen in a timely fashion and return promptly to their job.

My practice offers early morning hours two days a week and weekend hours once a month. This enables plan members to receive urologic care without losing work time.

My practice has a computerized callback system that notifies patients when they need to call for their next appointment. Consequently patients are contacted months later and re-minded when they need to return for their follow-up care.

Our practice is a believer in wellness and prophylactic urologic care. We encourage all men over 50 years of age (or 40 if they have a family history of prostate cancer or are African-American) to have an annual digital rectal exam and a prostate-specific antigen test.

All men are given a testicular self-examination card (enclosed) for their shower or closet. This card serves as a reminder for all men to examine their testes on a monthly basis to detect early testis cancer.

I am including a copy of my practice analysis. This handout reviews the above information in greater detail and includes a recent survey of my patients.

I know this is an interesting time for all of us in health care. It is my goal to make patients' experiences with my practice positive ones. I hope that my practice can continue to provide that level of service to your plan members.

Sincerely,

Neil Baum, M.D.

Finally, ask your physician colleagues who are on the plan to write a letter on your behalf. Have them emphasize that you are already seeing many of the plan's patients and that you enjoy an excellent reputation in the community. (Exhibit 32-7 is a sample letter from a colleague to a plan's administrator.)

Trying to get on a closed panel is a situation where strong-arm tactics seldom will work. However, polite persistence, along with lots of information, testimonials, and letters, will succeed over the long haul.

STAYING ON A PANEL

Getting on a panel is only half the challenge in modern health care. The second half is staying on the panel. You have to continually provide objective evidence that you meet the standards of the plan.

I suggest that you provide annual satisfaction surveys of patients, particularly members of the plan, and referring physicians. You will want to accumulate outcomes data and for this you will need a managed care software program. The goal is to gather and analyze data in a way that allows you to compare the quality of your practice to that of others in your community and throughout the nation.

Look at your inpatient and outpatient services. Identify your cost per DRG and submit your average length of stay for each DRG. For your office-based services, provide the charges for the most common diagnoses, the frequency of office encounters for each diagnosis, and the average charge for each office encounter by diagnosis. If you can identify complications, readmissions for each diagnosis, and the results of your clinical decisions, you will have information to give that is very useful—especially if the outcomes are favorable.

I suggest that you write a letter to the plan administrator once a year describing what has taken place in your practice. (Exhibit 32-8 is a sample letter of this type.) Let the administrator know of any continuing education courses taken, any awards received, and any articles published during the past year and what your plans are for the future.

NOTE

1. *California Relative Value Studies* (San Francisco: California Medical Association, 1974).

33

Prepare for Success in Managed Care

anaged care is growing rapidly, but there are large differences between various parts of the country, with the West Coast leading the way. Nationwide, 19.4 percent of the population are enrolled in an HMO. The percentages of people who belong to HMOs are given below for all regions[1]:

Pacific region: 33.4
Mountain region: 21.4
West north central region: 16.7
South central region: 9.2
East north central region: 17.9
Mid-Atlantic region: 21.0
South-Atlantic region: 14.5
New England region: 27.9

This chapter is based on interviews with leaders from two organizations in different parts of the country, in different stages of the managed care process, and using different but equally successful strategies to prepare for managed care. The chapter demonstrates that there are multiple ways of achieving success in the managed care arena.

MEDCENTER ONE

Medcenter One, in Bismarck, North Dakota,* was formed on January 1, 1994, when two 90-year-old institutions, a large multispecialty clinic and a tertiary care hospital, merged into a single organization. It now includes a hospital with over 200 beds, a large multispecialty clinic with approximately 110 physicians and about a dozen outreach clinics, a long-term care center, a home health agency, and a women's health center. It serves the entire western part of North Dakota, northern South Dakota, and eastern Montana.

North Dakota at this point has very little managed care but the hospital and multispecialty group decided to merge in order to be ready for it when it comes. "When it comes, they're going to look for systems that can provide the whole gamut of services at a capitated rate. Hospitals and physicians must work together as a team in this situation in order to provide all the services that they're going to be looking for," says executive vice-president Nick Brandner. Medcenter One still plans to contract out for some highly specialized services (for example, those required to treat pediatric anomalies and those used in heart transplants), but it can meet almost all its patients' medical needs.

In creating an integrated delivery system, Medcenter One faces the challenge of increasing efficiency by combining various administrative functions. It may combine hospital and clinic information and admitting systems, business office functions, and medical records. It now has nurses who function both as nurse managers of the oncology floor of the hospital and also as nurse managers of the oncology department within the clinic.

Medcenter One also realizes it probably needs to develop a whole new information system, but that issue has become so complex it is currently developing a job description for a chief information officer.

In general, does Medcenter One plan to hire new managers as it moves into managed care? No, says Brandner.

> I don't think that you need new people, but you do need people who are willing to update their skills. We've lived so long in this fee-for-service environment, but now things have begun changing. We have to find ways to be more efficient and more productive. In the future you will be paid on a per member per month basis, so it's going to take a different set of skills and a different way of looking at things.

Another step Medcenter One will take to prepare for the future: improving its cost accounting. "We have to get more sophisticated in actually knowing what all our costs are. There are many managed care systems that know how every dollar is spent and, I'll be honest, we're not at that point yet."

---

*300 North 7th Street, P.O. Box 5525, Bismarck, ND 58506-5525, 701-224-6000.

Brandner likes to quote a physician who is also a rancher. He summed up today's challenge this way: "Hospitals have to be like ranchers. They need to recognize the difference between nice and necessary—and the difference between nice and necessary is bankruptcy." Brandner adds,

> I think this adage about what's nice and what's necessary pinpoints a key issue for us right now. We know the primary care needs to be there, but we also need specialists available so that we're not constantly sending things out. As we plan the future of the organization, that's the fine line that we continually walk right now in terms of making sure that we have what's necessary and not just what's nice.

Medcenter One is preparing for managed care by forming continuous quality improvement (CQI) teams. One of the well-respected physician leaders of the group practice has been talking to other physicians about CQI methods and going to department meetings to discuss possible projects. "We actually have physicians now who are planning the processes that they as a department will look at, using quality improvement methods," Brandner says. "It's exciting to see the interest people have in doing that."

For example, one Medcenter One team will be looking at standardization of products used within the operating room, such as anesthetics and instruments. Another department is looking at dehydration of patients in radiation oncology, trying to find better methods to prevent it.

At present, Medcenter One uses fee-for-service reimbursement since that still dominates its area. Physicians receive a percentage of what they bill and actually collect, and the remaining percentage goes to group overhead. The organization is currently analyzing its payment system, and Brandner predicts it will end up with some sort of base salary plus bonus.

Under capitation, physicians will need to be much more conscious of the resources they use. The organization will have to give them data on their utilization patterns. If a physician is a high-cost utilizer, he or she will have to be willing to look at why his or her pattern of utilization is different from those of other physicians with a similar group of patients. For example, Brandner says, physicians who consistently use more lab tests or expensive X-ray services than others will have to be willing to discuss their level of use and hopefully modify their methods of practicing.

CALIFORNIA ORTHOPEDIC AND SPORTS MEDICINE ASSOCIATES

Medcenter One is at the very beginning of the process of preparing for managed care. California Orthopedic and Sports Medicine Associates (COSMA),*

---

*2001 Santa Monica Boulevard, Suite 1160 West, Santa Monica, CA 90404, 310-828-5441, fax 310-453-2245.

on the other hand, is an example of a specialty IPA that has learned how to survive and even flourish under capitation.

California moved toward managed care well ahead of the rest of the country. COSMA, based in Southern California, started in 1990 with six orthopedic surgeons and one capitated contract for 21,000 patients. In 1995, it had 207 orthopedic surgeons caring for half a million California patients.

"We decided at the very beginning that we had to get involved with capitation," recalls Thomas J. Grogan, M.D., formerly CEO of COSMA, and currently CEO of California-based Innovative Medical Consulting and Management.* "Our hypothesis was that if we could assemble five or six high-level orthopedic surgeons, each trained in a different subspecialty, and if we could keep our population of patients healthier, we would do less work and achieve higher levels of patient satisfaction."

COSMA felt that one key to success was managing time efficiently. It also decided to base physician compensation on relative amount of work performed. This meant that it needed some way to evaluate all the different sorts of procedures anyone might do.

It initially based its coding on a billing system called the 1974 California Relative Value Scale, which was really designed for general surgery. COSMA modified the scale to meet the specific needs of orthopedic surgery. For example, an initial complex office visit counts as 1 unit, while carpal tunnel surgery is equivalent in time and effort to 5 units (or 5 additional office visits). A total joint replacement is equivalent to 21 units. COSMA reduced the value previously given to total joint replacement and long bone surgery and increased the value given to hand, foot, and ankle surgery. It kept on fine-tuning and modifying this system until it could score every procedure any member orthopedist might do.

Although COSMA initially developed this system in order to have an accurate idea of who was doing how much work, it soon discovered that it could use the database to improve the efficiency and quality of the care it offered and to negotiate managed care contracts.

At present, COSMA has information stored on a total of 10 million member months. It knows exactly how much work is required to care for patients in different categories, broken down by patient age, payer (Medicare, Medicaid, or commercial), and procedure. For example, patients over 65 utilize orthopedic services 4.2 times more than those under that age, while the orthopedic utilization rate for Medicaid patients is half the rate of standard commercial patients. The average orthopedic surgeon can produce 400 units' worth of work per month.

When COSMA negotiates a capitated managed care contract, it knows exactly what the cost will be to care for a certain number of members. Suppose it is evaluating a contract to care for roughly 50,000 commercial patients and 10,000

*2001 Santa Monica Boulevard, Suite 1160 West, Santa Monica, CA 90404, 310-458-3865.

seniors. It knows, based on previous experience, that each commercial patient requires .135 units' worth of work per year, whereas each senior requires .61 units per year. After a little multiplication, it knows that the total contract would require 12,800 units' worth of orthopedic work per year, or roughly two and a half full-time orthopedic surgeons.

COSMA decided that the lowest rate its doctors would accept is a net income of $30,000 per month, which is equivalent to $75 per unit of work. Office expenses and other overhead average $25,000 per physician per month, or $62.50 per unit of work. Now COSMA knows its bid price needs to be about $137.50 per unit of work. That corresponds to $1.55 per member per month for commercial patients, and $6.99 per member per month for seniors. When COSMA meets to negotiate or renegotiate its contract, it has the data to justify its financial arrangement with the managed care plan. (See Exhibit 33-1.)

In addition to using the database to set prices, COSMA also uses the mass of data it's collected to evaluate and improve the process of care itself. "All of this just builds on itself," Grogan reports. "We started to learn about quality management, and we learned that, number one, you do not make money by denying care. We've learned that the way to make money in managed care is to just do a very good job. If you do a high-quality job the first time, you don't have to redo it."

COSMA developed extremely detailed records of previous utilization patterns, which allow it to predict expected utilization in the future. For example, it expects to do six total joint replacements per thousand covered seniors per year. It also expects to do .69 anterior cruciate ligament reconstructions per thousand commercial patients per year. That means if it has 50,000 commercial patients in a given area, it expects to do about 3 anterior cruciate ligament reconstructions per month. If it finds that in a given month it did six or seven, that triggers an automatic review by the quality management nurse, who pulls the charts to see what is happening.

COSMA has developed treatment algorithms for various procedures and conditions. Anterior cruciate ligament reconstruction, for example, is indicated for a patient under age 40 whose knee is giving way, who is unable to tolerate high-level sporting activities, and so on. The standard is, 95 percent of a doctor's choices should fall within the guideline parameters. If they do not, the physician is asked to meet with the quality management board and discuss with physician peers why the high rate occurred. "That doctor may have a perfectly good reason—we may have to shift our parameters a bit to include that situation," Grogan explains.

Sometimes it is unclear what the best practice pattern actually is. When COSMA looked at knee reconstruction surgery, it realized physicians in Northern California were sending patients for much more rigorous physical therapy than physicians in Southern California. Reviewing their database, it found that vigorous physical therapy did return patients to work sooner, but only by one day. "So we

Exhibit 33-1 COSMA Calculations on Costs and Income

Each orthopedic surgeon produces an average of 400 units of work per month, or 4,800 units per physician per year.

50,000 commercial patients multiplied by .135 units per year = 6,750. These patients will need 6,750 units of work per year.

10,000 seniors multiplied by .61 units per year = 6,100. These patients will need 6,100 units of work per year.

The contract will require a total of 12,850 units of work per year.

Physician net income of $30,000 per month divided by 400 units of work per month = $75 net income needed per unit of work.

Overhead expenses of $25,000 per month divided by 400 units of work = $62.50 for overhead expense needed per unit of work.

$75 plus $62.50 = $137.50 per unit

The practice needs to receive $137.50 per unit of work.

Each commercial member will require .135 units per year. Multiply .135 units by $137.50 per unit of work = $18.56 per year. To calculate the monthly rate, divide by 12, for a rate of $1.55 per member per month.

Each senior will require .61 units per year. Multiply .61 units by $137.50 per unit of work = $83.87 per year. To calculate the monthly rate, divide by 12, for a rate of $6.99 per member per month.

This means the fee for commercial members should be $1.54 per member per month, and the fee for seniors should be $6.99 per member per month.

The contract for 50,000 commercial members will bring in $928,000 per year, while the contract for 10,000 seniors will bring in $838,700 per year.

Source: Thomas J. Grogan, M.D., IMCM.

found that vigorous physical therapy was nowhere near as important as some of our doctors had thought," Grogan recalls. "We put doctors from both groups in the same room and showed them the data and asked them to come up with some reasonable guidelines. Now our physical therapy parameters for knee reconstruction surgery are very clear: we want patients to achieve a certain range of motion by three months' postsurgery, and if it takes the therapists one visit or 30 visits, that's up to them."

COSMA exhibits the kind of sophisticated use of data and physician-driven quality improvement that will permit physicians to flourish under managed care. At present, there are relatively few organizations at this level of sophistication. Grogan gets calls from physicians throughout the country asking him whether they can do the same thing. They can, he says. These basic principles apply to any physician's practice: gather detailed information and use that information to negotiate better contracts with managed care organizations and improve the quality of care patients receive.

If someone is a high-quality specialist, Grogan says, there is definitely room for him or her under managed care. "Don't lose hope, because as long as you take good care of patients and you do a good job, you're going to win. Your goal is good patient care, so organize good records and just be consistent. If someone is a good specialist, the system wants him."

*   *   *

Point-of-service plans are the fastest growing segment of the managed care marketplace. In the next chapter I will look at their special significance.

NOTE

1. *Marion Merrell Dow Managed Care Digest*, HMO ed. (Kansas City, Mo.: Marion Merrell Dow, 1994), 18–19.

34

The Power of Point of Service

We often hear that managed care is growing while fee-for-service care is shrinking. The implied suggestion is often that in the future cost will become paramount while quality of care will decrease in importance. This betrays a misunderstanding of modern managed care. In the physician-directed "empowerment" model of managed care, the goal is still to deliver high-quality, cost-effective care.

In addition, there will always be some people who seek the very best care possible and consider cost to be a lesser consideration. Most health care system projections predict that about 10 percent of the population will continue using fee-for-service medicine for the indefinite future.

Under what is called the "open-ended" or "point-of-service" option, members of managed care organizations can choose any physician they wish, including physicians not under contract with the managed care plan. In exchange for the added choice, the patient pays a higher deductible and a higher copayment or a percentage of the physician's fee. This option offers patients yet another way to select the highest quality care if that is their priority.

This chapter looks at the growth in point-of-service plans and how one medical group practice has positioned itself to serve patients who want the very best.

POINT-OF-SERVICE PLANS

The fastest growing segment of the managed care marketplace consists of point-of-service plans, which offer members all the standard HMO features combined with the ability to self-refer out of network by paying additional fees. Typically, there is no deductible for in-network care, but when a member chooses to go outside the network, he or she must pay a deductible that averages $500. If members use out-of-network inpatient care, most employers require them to pay 25 or 30 percent of the health care fee.[1]

At present only 5.8 percent of HMO members are enrolled in a point-of-service plan,[2] but the percentage is growing rapidly. Employers and health plans often consider the point-of-service option to be a user-friendly way to introduce members to managed care. The 1994 Foster Higgins survey of U.S. employers found that the percentage of large employers offering a point-of-service plan grew from 10 percent in 1992 to 15 percent in 1993 and 25 percent in 1994. About 52 percent of very large employers (with 20,000 or more employees) offered a point-of-service plan in 1994, and the use of such plans is growing rapidly among employers of all sizes.[3]

The number of HMOs offering a point-of-service option has also increased dramatically, from under 20 percent in 1990 to 59 percent in 1993. It is of interest that 16 to 17 percent of HMO enrollees use out-of-network benefits in any given year.[4] Consumer freedom to choose providers was the backbone of the traditional health insurance programs of the 1970s and 1980s. Before managed care became so widespread, its inherent limitation on choice was one of the reasons more employers did not offer HMOs to their employees. Now HMOs have brought back freedom of choice and flexibility in the form of point-of-service plans.

Some point-of-service programs are added to managed care plans that already exist, and employees can choose whether to sign up for the usual managed care option or the more expensive point-of-service option. In other companies, employees are able to sign up for the point-of-service option but do not have to pay extra unless out-of-network services are actually used. This is called a "dual option" program, meaning that employees have two options at all times. For example, an employee can use an HMO physician most of the time and a non-HMO physician only occasionally. When this second option is chosen, the employee pays a higher copayment for the physician's services.

Today most HMOs offer some kind of point-of-service option. Even though there are only 3.5 million HMO members currently enrolled in point-of-service plans, about 90 percent of them never use out-of-network services. The members of the plan just like to know this option is available if they ever need it.[5]

What this means is that if you position yourself as the very best doctor in your specialty in town, you can win additional patients who are willing to go outside their networks and pay more because they want the very best care.

SANSUM MEDICAL CLINIC

The Sansum Medical Clinic,* founded in 1924, is a world-renowned multi-specialty group practice of about 75 physicians, including 6 primary care physicians and 69 specialists covering 35 subspecialties. The founder, Dr. William David Sansum, was the first American to successfully isolate, produce, and administer insulin to treat diabetics. The associated nonprofit Sansum Medical Research Foundation continues to be active in diabetes research and other areas of medical research, including cancer, immunology, metabolic disease, arteriosclerosis, allergies, and arthritis. In a typical year, patients come to the Santa Barbara–based clinic from every state in the union and more than 20 countries. Today, about 35 percent of the patient load consists of traditional fee-for-service patients, although five years ago the figure was 68 percent. Ten percent of its patients are in HMOs, and half of those are capitated. About 30 percent are Medicare patients, and the remainder are in preferred provider organizations (PPOs). Many of its patients are acutely ill and travel hundreds of miles to reach the clinic's specialists. For example, Las Vegas, its fifth largest market, is 7½ hours away.

Like other institutions with an international reputation, Sansum came to managed care late. Organizations that draw on a diversified population base with good fee-for-service coverage have been somewhat slow to realize that the new focus on cost-effectiveness applies to them, too.

Going after the Local Patient

Santa Barbara has a highly competitive health care market, with three times as many doctors as it needs and a stable (not expanding) population base, according to Douglas A. Trigg, associate administrator and director of business development. Traditionally, Sansum drew the vast majority of its patients from outside the county. Five years ago, it began to position itself to attract more local patients.

Market research uncovered that in its local market Sansum had a reputation for providing high-quality health care but was viewed as relatively inaccessible. Local people knew that patients came from all over the world to the Sansum Clinic and thought that perhaps they would not be as welcome. The clinic's sterling reputation, which should have been an asset, made it somewhat intimidating to the local community.

---

*317 West Pueblo Street, P.O. Box 1239, Santa Barbara, CA 93102, 805-682-2621.

In response, it developed an in-depth local advertising program that emphasized how accessible and affordable the Sansum Medical Clinic is. The program focused on welcoming local patients. Initially Sansum directed its message toward the presidents and human resources directors of local businesses and organizations. Today, its local advertising is aimed at the individual patient; it ends by saying, "If you have further questions, give us a call or call your insurance broker or human resources director." Five years ago, people who lived within a 20-mile radius of the city of Santa Barbara probably constituted 10 percent of Sansum's patient population. Today, after a successful marketing campaign, they constitute about 25 percent.

The real challenge for Sansum today is maintaining a two-pronged marketing campaign, directed toward both local patients and those who are willing to travel long distances for health care.

The first step in successful marketing, Trigg says, is to keep good records. Sansum has a database for use in analyzing current and potential patients demographically, geographically, and psychographically. The demographic analysis looks at patients in terms of age, sex, college education, and so on. The psychographic analysis looks at patients' life styles (categories include "old money," "young mobile family," and "rural agricultural" life styles).

Because of its history of serving patients who travel long distances and are often acutely ill, Sansum specialists have developed a practice style that includes many referrals to other specialists and relatively long office visits.

In the past, Sansum developed a reputation for serving acutely ill patients who want the very best possible care. To continue to attract these patients, Sansum sends out a quarterly publication with articles written by its physicians to about 350,000 households nationwide, including former patients and others who have requested the publication from their direct mail program.

It has a separate quarterly publication written by physicians for physicians, and that goes out to about 6,000 physicians nationwide. When these doctors need to refer a patient to a top-notch specialist, they are likely to think of Sansum. Using its extensive database, Sansum has learned that the average physician-referred patient generates about $1,200 in additional revenue and has an average hospital stay 1.1 days greater than the average self-referred patient.

Contracting with Managed Care Plans

At the same time that Sansum positions itself to serve patients who travel long distances to seek the very best care, it also plans to seek out managed care contracts for local patients. Santa Barbara County has the seventh-highest concentration of PPOs in the nation, and Trigg observes a steady gravitation of patients from indemnity coverage to PPOs and from PPOs to HMOs.

"So the writing is on the wall," he says. "Those PPOs are going to become HMOs, and we are obliged to develop a strategy of seeking and serving HMO patients."

"What HMOs are looking for is a long-term relationship," he adds. "Particularly in California, I think we've gotten to the point where HMO prices are pretty similar now and everyone knows what the market is, so we've positioned Sansum as a 'quality institution' so to speak. Our background and history help make us more attractive to the provider groups."

When a plan does a site visit to the Sansum Medical Clinic, the clinic prepares a package of information on the history of the organization, physician qualifications, and its international reputation. The package includes research on the local marketplace and the clinic's favorable reputation among potential patients and employer groups. An HMO is going to find it easier to go sell its product when it can say that the prestigious Sansum Medical Clinic is available through its plan.

As Sansum has increased its involvement in managed care, it has had to make some changes to adapt to the new market environment. It has enhanced its wellness and patient education programs and is working closely with HMO and PPO patients to encourage them to enroll in plan-sponsored smoking cessation programs and dietary programs. It also acquired two primary care practices during the past year. Since it never offered obstetric and pediatric services, it is now contracting with other physicians to deliver those services and is thinking about adding an obstetrical and pediatric practice to the group. Through careful market research, it identified what the public wants and is making every effort to provide it.

Most importantly, it has discovered that under a capitated payment system the typical patient visit lasts about 10 minutes whereas a fee-for-service patient who drives from Las Vegas to Santa Barbara to consult a world-renowned specialist expects (and receives) an hour with the doctor. However, even if Sansum specialists wanted to see more patients in an hour, the physical setting, with one exam room per doctor and a small reception area, is not really suitable for increased patient flow. To top it off, the physicians have become accustomed to seeing only eight patients a day.

Sansum found that the gap between the traditional work pace and the quick turnover characteristic of managed care was too large to be bridged. Other organizations are retraining physicians to understand and practice under the new incentives of capitation and managed care. Sansum decided it was "more prudent to hire new primary care physicians who already have extensive experience in capitated programs," Trigg says.

He emphasizes that capitated programs can be lucrative and also offer patients high-quality care if they are correctly done—with an emphasis on preventive care and practice efficiency. But Sansum's specialists, who had been practicing in a different style for many years, were not interested in adapting to a change of this magnitude.

Today, Sansum's family practice and primary care physicians are housed in a different location on the Sansum campus from the specialists.

Advice for Other Practices

Trigg offers advice for group practices in other parts of the country that are not as advanced in managed care as California:

> You really have to identify your target audiences. Typically, health care institutions look at the patient as the target, but I think we have to extend our viewpoint beyond just the patient or potential patient. We looked at insurance companies and employers and human resource directors and our own employees, as well as patients, as people who need to hear and understand our marketing message.

In addition, he advises other health care providers to take a very close look at their information systems:

> There are so many different plans designed for different employers, each with slightly different provisions. It's essential when someone comes into your office to be able to identify that individual within a certain company, within a certain payer group, and a certain plan. If a patient comes into your office with a Blue Cross card, there may be 50 different Blue Cross plans which this individual could belong to. You also have to determine if, in fact, he's still current on that particular plan. So it's absolutely critical to be able to call up that information instantly and to get it right.

*   *   *

In the next chapter we will discuss the importance of report cards and how they will be used in the future to evaluate and measure your practice.

NOTES

1. *Foster Higgins National Survey of Employer-sponsored Health Plans*, 1994 ed. (New York: Foster Higgins, 1994), 27.

2. *HMO Industry Profile*, 1994 ed. (Washington, D.C.: Group Health Association of America, 1994), 16.

3. *Foster Higgins National Survey of Employer-sponsored Health Plans*, 24.

4. *HMO Industry Profile*, 13, 16.

5. M. Cafferky, *Managed Care and You* (New York: McGraw-Hill, 1995), 22.

35

Get a Good Grade on Your Report Card

B ecause health care costs have been increasing, employers and other purchasers have been searching for ways to cut costs and ensure they receive good value for the money they spend. Major employers have been leaders in the movement to increase the amount of information available on health care.

What does this mean for physicians? We can expect that managed care plans will be interested in gathering all sorts of data on the way we practice. They will use the data to determine which physicians they want to have practicing on their panels. The reason for this is very clear: major employers will be using similar data to determine which plans they want serving their employees.

At a recent quarterly staff meeting at my own hospital, the medical director, Dr. Stephen Newman,* made a presentation on current trends affecting physicians and hospitals. He emphasized the new and increasing emphasis on measuring quality, outcomes, and cost-effectiveness. Like almost all physicians, I believe that I practice high-quality medicine and achieve excellent outcomes, but I couldn't imagine how quality and outcomes could possibly be quantitated. I made an appointment with the hospital's quality assurance director, Fay Hernandez, and asked to see my own profile. I learned very quickly that physician profiling and health plan report cards will play an essential role in the future marketing of health care.

This chapter describes how hospitals, payers, and even patients will use report card information in making their health care decisions. It also looks briefly at

---

*Touro Infirmary, 1401 Foucher Street, New Orleans, LA 70115, 504-897-7011.

some facets of the current emphasis on report cards and member satisfaction surveys. Finally, it presents practical ideas that you can use to make your profile attractive to your patients, your hospitals, and payers.

HAVE YOU LOOKED AT YOUR PROFILE IN THE MIRROR LATELY?

Historically, medical marketing depended on providing excellent health care in a user-friendly fashion. Today, with health care costs rising faster than inflation and millions of Americans lacking access to medical care, cost and quality will be the most significant factors in obtaining and maintaining patients. In the past, it was considered difficult or impossible to measure quality and outcomes. Today, with the assistance of computers and database analysis, measuring outcomes and objectively comparing one physician to another has become a reality. There are still many difficulties in collecting the relevant information, but the pressure to cut costs while maintaining or improving quality is so great that we can expect to see health care data collection increase in the very near future.

How is the information obtained and used? To take just one example, the Medi-Qual National Database* contains information on 16 million cases from 524 hospitals collected over the past 8 years. Each patient you admit to a hospital can be graded or compared according to the admitting diagnosis and the severity of the patient's condition at the time of diagnosis based on objective criteria such as vital signs and laboratory and X-ray studies. The information is fed into a computer that assigns your patient an admission or numerical severity grade. The progress or the deterioration of the patient will be tracked until the patient is discharged, and your results will be entered into the national database. The outcomes you achieved will then be compared with those achieved by your peers, not only in your community but also nationwide.

For example, suppose I admit a patient who is septic with an obstructing ureteral calculus. The patient has several comorbid conditions, including uncontrolled diabetes and labile hypertension. The patient will be assigned an admission severity grade. How I manage the patient, including the length of stay and total charges, will be compared with how other physicians have managed patients with a similar diagnosis and similar comorbid conditions locally and nationally. Can you imagine the impact on my ability to attract patients and managed care contracts if my outcomes are consistently less favorable than those of my colleagues and if my charges are significantly higher? In those circumstances I won't be very attractive to hospitals or managed care plans and most likely will not be accepted on their provider panels.

---

*Medi-Qual Systems, Inc., Westboro, Massachusetts, 508-366-6365.

As a result of the new methods of gathering and analyzing data on physicians' practice patterns, managed care plans can now make sound objective decisions on behalf of their members. This will almost certainly be the trend of the future and will determine how we receive patients. Physicians who are sensitive to cost and quality will be the ones who have successful practices.

A STANDARD FORMAT FOR HEALTH CARE DATA

During the early 1990s a few health plans began to collect and release information on quality. One problem soon became obvious: in order to make valid comparisons of different plans, everyone needed to use the same definitions. For example, is a plan's mammography rate calculated using statistics for women aged 52–64 who have been continuously enrolled during the preceding two years or for just one year? Or does the calculation use some slightly different age range? In order to compare plans, everyone has to agree on the same yardstick. Apples must be compared with apples.

A working group that included representatives of health plans, major employers, and technical experts began meeting under the auspices of the National Committee for Quality Assurance (NCQA),* a Washington, D.C.–based accrediting organization for HMOs. The group analyzed which measures were most important and could be gathered relatively easily. In November 1993 they released a standardized data set, including precise definitions, known as the Health Employer Data and Information Set (HEDIS) 2.0.

HEDIS 2.0 includes approximately 60 measures in four categories: quality of care, member access and satisfaction, membership and utilization, and finance.

Member satisfaction is measured using phone and mail surveys. Access measures include the speed with which the phone is answered and the number of primary care physicians accepting new patients. Membership and utilization measures include enrollment data, inpatient utilization rates, length of stay for well and complex newborns, and readmission rates for chemical dependency and mental illness. Financial performance measures include liquidity, compliance with statutory requirements, and trends in premiums.

The measures that have generated the greatest interest are the nine quality measures:

- Preventive services
  1. Childhood immunization
  2. Cholesterol screening

---

*1350 New York Avenue, NW, Suite 700, Washington, DC 20005, 202-955-3500.

3. Mammography
4. Cervical cancer screening
- Prenatal care
5. Low birth weight infants
6. Care in first trimester of pregnancy
- Acute and chronic illness
7. Asthma inpatient admission rate
8. Diabetics receiving retinal exam
- Mental health
9. Ambulatory follow-up after hospitalization for major affective disorders

These nine quality measures indicate how HEDIS will affect practicing physicians. If plans are collecting data on the number of patients who have been screened for high cholesterol levels, the percentage of two-year-olds who have received all their immunizations, or the percentage of women who have received Pap smears and mammograms, then physicians will need to move to a new level of accuracy in reporting data of this sort.

In fact, HEDIS posed a challenge for many health plans. As they began to collect the data, they often found their current information system, while perfectly adequate for internal needs, was not able to collect all the HEDIS data easily. In spite of the difficulties, today more than 300 health plans are reporting data using HEDIS, and a substantial and increasing number of purchasers require HEDIS information from all plans they offer to employees. It seems likely that as health care organizations improve their computerized information systems, the amount and quality of data they collect will increase.

HEDIS: THE NEXT GENERATION

HEDIS 2.0 is not perfect. It was produced under severe time constraints, and the people most closely associated with its development seem to think of it as a first step in what will be a years-long process of developing accurate measures of health plan quality. Many of the quality measures in HEDIS 2.0 are straightforward measures of preventive care. It does incorporate two well-known enrollee satisfaction surveys, but plans are simply asked to report members' overall levels of satisfaction. It uses relatively few quality measures related to major chronic and acute illnesses.

In February 1995, NCQA released a revised version of HEDIS (version 2.5), which clarified technical questions relating to the definitions in the previous version. In July 1995 it released a draft version of HEDIS designed specifically for Medicaid beneficiaries.

In September 1995, a new Standing Committee on Performance Measurement held its first meeting. The broad-based committee includes representatives of major employers such as IBM and Xerox, health plans such as Kaiser Permanente and the Henry Ford Health System, labor and consumer organizations, and well-known medical researchers. Its goal: to develop a substantially revised version of HEDIS.

"This next generation of HEDIS will address a broader population (including Medicare and Medicaid), include chronic and acute care measures, consider issues related to risk adjustment, and incorporate a standard member satisfaction survey," said NCQA president Margaret O'Kane. A draft version of HEDIS 3.0 should be available by Fall 1996. Current plans call for field tests during 1996–1997 and the release of HEDIS 3.0 by the end of 1997.

HOW EMPLOYERS USE DATA TO SELECT HEALTH PLANS

Meanwhile, employer coalitions in major cities are using HEDIS data, NCQA accreditation status, and consumer satisfaction surveys to evaluate health plans. They are even conducting their own surveys to find out how their employees feel about the health care they receive. For example, in Chicago a dozen major employers and eight leading health plans cooperated in a consumer satisfaction survey of 75,000 employees. By cooperating on the project and using the same standardized survey, they were able to get far more accurate data than if they had each done their own survey.

Larry S. Boress, vice-president of the Midwest Business Group on Health, described the project as a "win-win-win opportunity for everyone involved. Employers will receive solid comparative data on which to make more informed purchasing decisions. Employees will have better information to meet their health care needs. The providers themselves will be able to pinpoint areas to strengthen services to their customer base."

The Bay Area Business Group on Health (BBGH), a coalition representing 20 employers who provide health benefits to over 2.5 million people, is also conducting annual member satisfaction surveys and using the results of those surveys, as well as other performance measures, in negotiations with health plans. In June 1994, 11 BBGH member companies negotiated rate reductions, standard benefit guarantees, and performance guarantees with 15 California HMOs. "We are asking HMOs to guarantee improvement in employee satisfaction," said BBGH associate director Tracey Rodriguez. "For example, if 70 percent of employees are satisfied with their physician care this year, we expect 75 percent to be satisfied next year."

REFORMULATING DATA FOR CONSUMER USE

Although HEDIS data will be studied in great detail by benefits managers at large corporations, it is not really suitable for consumers—it is far too detailed and intricate. However, employers, health plans, and consumer groups are working to develop ways to share this sort of information, in a simplified form, with consumers and employees.

For example, in 1993 the Northern California region of Kaiser Permanente released a 59-page "Quality Report Card" with a supplement on performance measure methodologies that is still a model for how to present data on health plan quality—it goes far beyond the HEDIS 2.0 measures. At the same time, they issued a 9-page booklet designed for consumers that summarized data on consumer satisfaction, maternity care, childhood health care, and the treatment of cancer and cardiovascular disease in a way the average intelligent consumer could easily understand.

During its 1994 fall open-enrollment season, GTE Corporation, headquartered in Stamford, Connecticut, mailed all its employees a "Consumer Guide" that gave the top 25 percent of plans a "superior performance" designation based primarily on HEDIS data. Every GTE employee received a factsheet on each health plan in his or her geographic area, and the plan with the best combination of quality and cost-effectiveness was designated a "benchmark HMO." GTE has decided to offer employees only plans that agree to submit HEDIS data annually. It has selected eight HMOs nationwide for an "exceptional quality" designation, saying they have the best quality in the country. GTE's evaluation was based on HEDIS data and employee satisfaction surveys.

During Fall 1994, Xerox, also based in Stamford and also a leader in the health information movement, gave its employees factsheets on each available plan. Unlike GTE, Xerox offered its employees each plan's score on eight of the HEDIS quality measures as well as other key data, including average waiting times for urgent and emergency care, the member satisfaction rate, and the percentage of members who would recommend this plan to others. GTE is following a strategy of analyzing the data and giving various plans a "gold star." Xerox is following a strategy of offering employees much more of the raw data on health plan quality and accessibility.

In addition to plans handing out data about themselves and large employers handing out data on plans to their employees, more information on health care is being channeled directly to consumers. A new consumer magazine called *Health Pages** is being published in Atlanta, Boston, Cincinnati, Denver, and Los Angeles, with many other cities under consideration. Each version offers

---

*135 Fifth Avenue, 7th Floor, New York, NY 10010, 212-505-0103.

consumers basic information about illness and about managed care in a particular city. It also includes a sort of guidebook to physicians in that city gathered by surveys of those physicians (i.e., the data are self-reported). At present, typical information published about physicians includes their location and years in practice, where they did their internship and residency, whether they are board certified, their hours of operation, their policies on credit cards and Medicare, and the managed care plans they are affiliated with. The guide even includes languages spoken by the physicians and the staff.

PRACTICAL SUGGESTIONS TO IMPROVE YOUR PROFILE

I asked Fay Hernandez, the quality assurance director at Touro Infirmary in New Orleans, what I could do to improve my profile. This was her advice.

1. Find out how you compare with your colleagues in a blinded fashion. Look at length of stay and average charges for each diagnosis-related group (DRG). This information should be available from the hospital quality assurance department. Your data will be compared with those of your colleagues but with their names omitted. Similarly, if a colleague asks to see data, he or she will not know which data comes from you or any other specific physician.

If you find that your costs are higher than your colleagues or your average length of stay is longer in a particular DRG, then it is time to re-examine the methods and approach you use in that DRG. For example, a cardiac surgeon looked at his profile and found he had a higher than average length of stay. By extubating his coronary artery bypass patients sooner than the routine 36 hours that they were on the ventilator, he shortened his length of stay and decreased costs by $10,000 per case.

When Hernandez reviewed my profile, she noted that I always typed and cross-matched my patients who were to have a transurethral resection of the prostate gland. She observed that I rarely gave these patients blood but incurred several hundred dollars of unnecessary expenses. She suggested that I use autotransfusions or else type and hold the blood, which would be considerably less expensive than typing and cross-matching, which is what I was doing.

She also reviewed the prophylactic antibiotics that I used prior to penile prosthesis surgery. I used an expensive aminoglycoside that costs $150 per dose. She suggested an oral medication that the patient could take with a sip of water just before surgery (at a cost of $2 a pill). By looking at your charges carefully, you will almost certainly find hundreds and maybe even thousands of dollars of savings for your patients and their insurance companies.

If your hospital isn't collecting physician profile data or they won't share them with you, then you may want to question your affiliation with the hospital. The "economic profile" that is being developed on you and me will be vital to our future. Many of the empowerment model managed care organizations share this sort of data routinely with their physicians, often on a quarterly basis. Sometimes the average physician receives a brief summary whereas those near the bottom, the lowest 10 to 20 percent, receive more detailed information. In any case, this sort of information is essential for physicians to understand their own practice patterns and to be able to search for the most effective and efficient methods of caring for patients. If you take a look at this information with an open mind, then your practice patterns are very likely to improve.

2. *Look at physician profile data in an analytical, questioning way.* Ask yourself and others what you can do to improve your profile. Your goal is to improve quality and decrease cost. It's not in your best interest to be defensive and argumentative. If your profile is substandard, consider what you can do to make the next profile more attractive. Remember, yesterday is a cancelled check but tomorrow is a promissory note. Don't try to deny past performance data, use them to improve your performance in the coming quarter.

3. *Compare your average length of stay with those of your colleagues and try to identify ways to shorten it.* The reason is that it will certainly reflect total charges and possibly quality of care. One way to shorten your average length of stay is to use same-day surgery whenever possible. Also, prepare your patients ahead of time by offering preadmission education. It has been my observation that an educated patient does better clinically and goes home sooner. If a patient has a special need for support after the operation, discuss this with social services as soon as possible.

For example, I do same-day surgery for the insertion of the penile prosthesis. During my preoperative discussion with the patient, I explain that he can go home as soon as he is taking fluids and has urinated. A urologic colleague, Dr. Jim Gottesman, from Seattle, does radical prostatectomies and has reduced his length of stay from 5–7 days to 2–3 days. He attributes this significant reduction to his providing educational material describing the hospital and the postoperative course to patients before they are admitted to the hospital. Now the patients are programmed for a short hospital stay even before they enter the hospital.

4. *If you are a primary care physician, look at your consulting habits.* Use only those consultants you and your patient really need. Remember, the more consultants you involve in the care of your patient, the greater the number of tests and the greater the expense. Using consultants will impact your profile as a primary care physician, not their profiles as specialists.

One way to use consultants in a cost-efficient manner is to ask them to call you and discuss their findings before they order tests or schedule procedures. You should decide together what is really needed and indicated. The days of the megaworkup are over. You are the captain of the patient's health care ship and know the patient's requirements best.

For example, when I request a consultation from another physician, I provide them with a form (Exhibit 35-1) that introduces my patient, provides pertinent background information, and indicates the necessary follow-up. I merely fill in the blanks and mark the response that I expect from the consultant. After all, I can't expect consultants to be mind readers and know what action I am requesting. Unnecessary tests and procedures can be avoided by the use of such a form.

5. *Probably the first place you should look to reduce costs is the prescription of medications, particularly antibiotics.* The latest-generation antibiotics are almost always the most expensive but do not always have special advantages that make them worth the cost. Reducing the prescribing of unnecessarily sophisticated antibiotics is a quick and easy way to cut costs. No one wants physicians to

---

Exhibit 35-1 Sample Fax Consultation Request Form

Date: _____

To Dr. _____

_____

_____

This will introduce my/your/our patient:

_____

For: ____ Evaluation   ____ Second Opinion

____ Treatment   ____ Provide Primary Care

____ Clear for Surgery   ____ Other

Remarks:

_____

_____

_____

Please:

____ Send Report   ____ Call After You See the Patient

____ Admit and Consult   ____ Other

Thank you,

sacrifice quality when prescribing antibiotics. The goal is to select the right drug, prescribe the right dose, and set an appropriate administration schedule.

You must check cultures and sensitivities. Then try to select the least expensive drug that provides the highest blood level and the one that is the most specific for the organ system(s) involved. Inquire about drug costs. If cost information is not available, ask the hospital pharmacy to provide it for you. You can be sure that the payers will soon be collecting prescription data on physicians. You can make your profile attractive by demonstrating that you are cost sensitive in your prescribing habits. Remember, generic ibuprofen is probably as effective as a third-generation nonsteroidal anti-inflammatory drug and is only a fraction of the cost. And if you really want to demonstrate your cost sensitivity, you'll recommend that the patient take aspirin first.

6. Don't order tests and procedures that are unnecessary for the diagnosis or treatment of your patients. Whenever possible, complete workups on an outpatient basis.

7. Talk with peers about cost-saving techniques and quality issues. Perhaps this type of discussion will be more productive than complaining about politicians, Washington, and health care reform. (One way of pursuing joint discussion of cost and quality issues is to participate as a member of hospital quality assurance and utilization review committees, something that Hernandez suggested I do.)

As physicians, we must recognize that costs do matter. Finding the best possible way to continue to provide high-quality care while taking costs into account is our responsibility. Smokey the Bear says, "Only you can prevent forest fires"—and only you can decrease the spiralling cost of American health care.

CONCLUSION

Although few of us are ready to calculate HEDIS scores and construct report cards, all of us need to understand that managed care plans will be looking for objective evidence to evaluate our practices. How soon use of evaluative data becomes standard will vary in different parts of the country, but in the next few years all physicians will have to find a method or a system to report back to the plans what they need to know in a form that allows them to compare medical practices.

There is probably very little that any single physician can do to impact decisions made in Congress. But each physician has substantial control over his or her physician profile. The current trend is toward demanding demonstration of superior outcomes and cost-effectiveness. Those who fail to recognize this trend will see not only a reduced number of patients but also an erosion of their income. So take a moment and check out your profile. You may soon find someone asking, "Mirror, mirror on the wall, who has the fairest profile of them all?"

36

Managed Care Contracting

In the coming era of managed care, physicians will need to be able to evaluate managed care contracts. They will have to calculate, for example, what level of payment will allow them to offer their patients appropriate care. This chapter looks at typical capitated payment rates and the key issues to keep in mind when negotiating managed care contracts.

KEY QUESTIONS TO ASK

What is the history of the insurance company or managed care organization? Is it financially viable? Look at its financial reserves and claims payment history. For insurance companies, you can review state insurance commission filings and A. M. Best reference publications.*

Analyze the plan's current subscriber base and its market growth objectives. What are the demographics of the currently covered population, including age, sex, and ZIP code? What is the current member satisfaction rate? If the plan has not surveyed its members, quality care is not likely to be one of its priorities.

Will the plan guarantee a minimum patient volume? After all, you are going to discount your fees. The trade-off should be more patients. A managed care contract should contain a guarantee of a minimum number of patients.

Best's Insurance Reports, Life-Health, available in most reference libraries or from A.M. Best Co., Oldwick, NJ 08858, 908-439-2200.

Which employers currently use the plan?

When are capitated payments typically made? At the start of the month or midmonth? For fee-based services, be sure the contract spells out reasonable time limits on the turnaround time for claims. This is an issue that may well be subject to negotiation.

Will the managed care organization provide a medical director? If so, request a copy of the director's curriculum vitae.

Ask about the methods the managed care plan uses to control utilization and monitor physician practice patterns. Ask to see a written document summarizing its quality improvement, risk management, utilization management, and credentialing programs.

Review policies on Medicare patients and negotiate separate rates for serving Medicare patients under a capitated risk contract. Typical payment rates for Medicare risk enrollees are three to five times higher than for commercial enrollees since the former typically use more services than the latter.[1]

Probably the best advice is to rely on lawyers and managed care contracting consultants with previous experience in managed care to double-check all the language in a contract and identify which points are likely to be negotiable, which are standard, and which signal potential trouble.

In addition to making sure that every i is dotted and every t crossed, you will also need to evaluate larger issues to determine whether there is a "match" between your organization and the managed care plan. Does the plan treat you as an equal and respond fully and frankly to your questions? Does its organizational culture convey respect for physicians' expertise and judgment? What role do physicians play in the governance of the managed care plan? How many physicians sit on its board?

NEGOTIATING A MANAGED CARE CONTRACT

Frederick J. Wenzel, F.A.C.M.P.E., executive vice president of the Colorado-based Medical Group Management Association,* warns physicians to be careful about signing too many managed care contracts with too many different organizations at once. Possible dangers: each plan has slightly different regulations and different formularies for prescriptions. "It can be tough on your financial people and your business people; you have to have somebody coordinating this entire effort," Wenzel says.

One rule of thumb: when considering a capitated contract, "It's generally not advisable to join unless there is a reasonable expectation that the plan will deliver

---

*104 Inverness Terrace East, Englewood, CO 80112-5306, 303-799-1111, fax 303-643-4427.

a minimum of 250 enrollees, or 3,000 (250 × 12) member months. A lower volume of patients will not financially justify the added administrative costs associated with participating with a new plan."[2] This is an opinion that Edward L. Grab, C.P.B.C., and Neil B. Caesar, J.D., voiced in the American Group Practice Association's journal. "One solution is to negotiate a fail-safe fee-for-service guarantee that if the number of patients is below the 250 member floor, then a minimum 85 percent fee-for-service equivalent will be provided."

Wenzel uses a similar threshold to evaluate which managed care contracts are worthwhile.

> More than one clinic has started an HMO, either on their own or with an insurance partner, only to find that in order to offer a competitive premium in the marketplace, the clinic has had to accept fee-for-service equivalents as low as 40 to 60 percent. These are levels at which losses mount rapidly. Prepayment at a level about 80 percent, with moderate changes in practice habits, is generally acceptable.[3]

Some managed care organizations may attempt to play hardball as they move into a new area. "Not infrequently an insurer will march into town and go to the doctors and say, now, we've signed up all the employers," says Wenzel. "Then they'll go to the employers and tell them they've signed up all the doctors, when the real case is that they haven't signed up either. You must be very, very careful here."

POINTS TO PONDER

According to Michael Naslund, M.D., M.B.A., a capitation contract is usually a complex document, so you certainly do have to read and reread every word of it before you sign it. In addition, your principal business advisor, a lawyer or accountant or consultant *with experience in this specific area of contracting*, should also review the contract.

Careful attention should be given to deciding whether laboratory tests, medications, and X-rays will be the responsibility of the practice. If your practice is able to perform some X-ray and lab work, it may be beneficial to capitate for these services. If you do not have that ability, it is generally best to carve them out.

Also consider whether supplies and durable medical goods should be covered in the contract. When deciding what aspects to cover, consider the potential for profit as well as the potential convenience or inconvenience to your practice if you furnish these services instead of having them contracted out. For example, if you have a laboratory in your office, you need to consider equipment and supply costs, staff salaries and benefits, and the hassles of Clinical Laboratory Improvement Amendments (CLIA) certification. You may find it easier and more efficient to contract out the laboratory testing.

It is critically important to accurately project the utilization of services by the patient population in question. The age, sex, and occupation composition of the covered population heavily influences utilization and should be taken into account. A claims history or actuarial analysis should also be used for predicting utilization. An HMO should have a claims history on the group of patients it is proposing be covered by capitation. Ideally the history should cover two or more years and show what procedures, office visits, X-rays, and so on, were needed. Get this information in writing and include it as part of the contractual record so that if the rate of services performed is very different from the predicted rate, you will be in a good position to renegotiate the contract.

If the group of patients is a new one, no claims history will be available. A new group of patients without a claims history represents a higher risk, and that should be reflected in a higher initial capitation rate. Another way to deal with a new patient population is to have a lower stop-loss level in place for the first year (see below).

The best approach to analyzing utilization risk is to have an actuarial analysis of the patient population performed. An actuary will consider the demographics of the population, the reimbursement system in place, referral policies for primary care and other referring physicians, and any previous claims history. He or she will be able to use all this information to make a good estimate of utilization. The actuarial analysis is usually valid with a population greater than 10,000 patients. There is, of course, a significant cost involved. An actuarial firm will typically charge $5,000 to $8,000 to analyze a patient population.

You need to consider the incentives driving potential referring physicians. For example, if the primary care physicians are also capitated, they may prefer to avoid seeing patients by referring them directly to specialists. In this situation, the specialists may be overwhelmed with trivial referrals that have not even been screened by the primary care physicians. If there is concern about the potential for abuse by referring physicians, the contract may need to be modified. For example, you might want the contract to state explicitly that any patient referred by a primary care physician must be seen by that physician prior to referral. Or the contract could state that if there appears to be many inappropriate referrals to the specialists (or a given number of referrals), any additional referrals will be paid on a fee-for-service basis.

If you are a specialist, you can monitor referrals by completing a chart (Exhibit 36-1) for each referral and submitting this to the managed care plan. This way the plan can see objective data on the status of the referrals sent to you.

Evaluate the withhold clause. The withhold is a portion of the per member per month (PMPM) payment that is put aside or withheld from providers until the

Exhibit 36-1 Appropriate Referral Evaluation Form

Patient name

_____

Primary care doctor

_____

Managed care plan (HMO)_____

	Yes	No

Was this referral necessary?

Were the appropriate tests done before the patient was referred?

Was the patient referred as soon as was medically indicated?

Please explain any "No" answers below:

_____

_____

_____

_____

_____

Source: Alvin Merlin, M.D., Metairie, Louisiana.

end of the year. It is a "reward" for physicians if they provide cost-effective care. There are several things to consider about withholds. First, they are important to the insurer because they protect the profit margin. If profits are low, the company does not pay withholds.

Second, for each dollar gained by the physician group from a withhold pool, the insurance company has usually saved $5 to $20 in decreased utilization.

Third, the criteria used to determine the payout of withholds vary a great deal. Some plans use cost or quality indicators and some use length of stay, number of hospital admissions, or number of consultations to gauge the efficiency of capitated physicians. Patient satisfaction surveys are and should be used to evaluate the quality of services provided.

When considering the validity of a withhold, you need to find out what percentage of the withhold goes to primary care physicians as opposed to specialists and how the proportions are determined. You also need to know what percentage of withholds went to specialists in the past. Another important issue is whether any of the plan's overhead expenses are paid out of the withhold pool prior to distribution. You should also ask, although you will probably not be able to find out the answer, how much the capitation rate is lowered to pay for the withhold pool.

A stop-loss provision in a capitation contract is critically important. It limits the risk of losing money to provide care to patients who have significant and costly medical problems. Most capitated contracts are for fewer than 30,000 patients. Since it is impossible to predict the risk of having a patient with serious problems when contracting for fewer than 30,000 patients, a stop-loss provision protects you by setting an upper limit for your financial risk.

Often an HMO will offer physicians stop-loss protection. You can choose to have an "individual patient stop-loss provision," where services for a patient above a certain threshold amount are paid for on a fee-for-service basis. Or you can have a "cumulative stop-loss provision," where physician services for all patients in the plan above a certain amount are paid for on a fee-for-service basis. In most instances, it is the responsibility of the practice to monitor utilization and inform the HMO when the threshold has been reached. You need to be sure that your managed care software program has the ability to let you know when the threshold has been reached so that you can notify the managed care plan and begin receiving fee-for-service reimbursements.

Threshold amounts tend to be $5,000 to $10,000 per person. Remember that physician fees account for a relatively small portion of outlier costs, so if the stop-loss provision for physician services is $10,000, only a small number of patients will exceed the threshold. This would suggest that a lower threshold should be considered. In the case of one large HMO, 92 percent of all patients had less than $3,000 in claims per year and 97.8 percent had claims of less than $10,000 per year. If the physician fee threshold is $5,000 to $10,000, relatively few, if any, patients will exceed the threshold for the physician component of their health care.

TYPICAL CAPITATION PAYMENTS

In a 1994 article in *Health System Leader*, Barry Bader and Meg Matheny analyzed the way a typical capitation payment is divided to cover various costs.[4] They suggested that a typical HMO member in Minneapolis, "Martha Median," may pay about $115 per month for comprehensive health care. Of that, about $9 to $18 goes to plan administration and about 7 to 10 percent or more goes to stop-loss insurance and carveouts for prescription drugs, mental health services, and diagnostic tests performed outside physician offices.

Now there's little more than $90 left from Martha Median's monthly premium to go to the provision of medical services. In Minneapolis, medical costs per member per month averaged $95.74. . . . A typical breakdown, or sub-capitation, might be $35 to $45 PMPM for professional services of primary care physicians and specialists [see Exhibit 36-2], and $45 to $50 for hospitals and other health care facilities. However, the exact amounts and methods vary depending on local market factors, the prevailing "generation of managed care" . . . and the degree to which local physician groups and hospitals have joined together to share risk.[5]

CALCULATING A CAPITATION RATE

How do you calculate the capitation rate? This is not easy, and few physicians have any experience in determining a figure that will keep their practices profitable. The challenge is to calculate a capitation rate today that will allow you to make a profit in the future. You need to have records on the past utilization of your services and the costs of caring for a defined population of patients. You will need to know your predicted future costs as closely as possible. Although actuaries have broad tables for large areas of the country and even for certain counties, you need to know the data for the specific panel of patients that you will be at risk for.

In order to preserve a healthy bottom line, you will need to be aggressive in cutting costs and overhead expenses. You will have to identify the marketplace standard for overhead and find ways to be competitive or even beat the standard by getting the fat out of your costs.

The first step is to find out how much it costs you to provide care per patient encounter. Perhaps the easiest method for accomplishing this cost analysis is to list all of the services you provide by CPT or evaluation and management (E/M) code. Multiply each CPT and E/M code by the existing fee for service and then multiply that total by how often you performed each service annually.

For example, the code for a Level 3 office visit is 99213. If your fee for this service is $70 and you do a total of 4,000 Level 3 visits annually, your income for this service is $280,000. If you then multiply that income by your standard percentage for overhead expenses you have an estimate of your cost for that procedure. For example, a 40 percent overhead for $280,000 of Level 3 annual visits costs your practice $112,000 in expenses for that service. Today, software programs are available that can make these calculations with just a few key strokes.

According to Naslund, the capitation rate can be calculated for your practice with data that you probably already have in your computer. To calculate it, list all services required under the contract by CPT or E/M code and then price each

Exhibit 36-2 Typical Specialist Services Breakdown of Monthly Capitation Fee
(Commercial Enrollees)

Ob/gyn	$5.48	Internal medicine	$1.04
Surgery	$2.56	Cardiology	$.83
Orthopedics	$1.47	Ophthalmology	$.62
Anesthesiology	$1.44	Urology	$.38
ENT	$1.38	All others	$5.98

Source: Health System Leader, March 1994, p. 10.

service using your existing fee schedule. Multiply your fee for each service by the anticipated frequency of services. The frequency data can be provided by the claims history or actuarial analysis of the managed care plan. (The plan should make the historic utilization rate available to you for the previous two to three years.) Add all these charges and divide by 12 to get a monthly charge. Divide the monthly charge by the number of covered lives to get the per member per month charge. This PMPM charge is then multiplied by your present collection rate. The result is a reasonable starting point for setting a PMPM range.

For example, if a plan contracts with your practice for services and procedures and gives you information on utilization frequencies for the past three years, you can determine a capitation range and thus will be able to negotiate from a position of strength rather than be tempted to accept any capitation fee thrown in your direction. Suppose your total estimated utilization would be $300,000 a year. If there were 10,000 covered lives, the average monthly charge per member per month would be $2.50 ($300,000 ÷ 10,000 ÷ 12 = $2.50). This amount represents 100 percent reimbursement, which is the most you would receive from the plan. However, if your existing collection rate is 75 percent, then $1.87 would be the amount you would receive under your existing fee-for-service system. Thus, a range of $1.75 to $2.50 PMPM would be a reasonable range to go to the table with in your negotiations with the managed care plan.

Of course "reasonable" range means different things to different groups. What is reasonable to the provider may seem exorbitant to the HMO. In general, capitation rates offered by a managed care company will be significantly less than the capitation rate calculated above.

The best advice is to find an accountant or consultant or actuary who understands managed care and have him or her calculate a figure for your practice and for the panel of patients that you will be at risk for. At the present time, the typical capitation rate for a primary care physician is $13 to $15 PMPM. The typical capitation rate for all specialists taken together is about $40 PMPM. According to

Sue Lynn Schramm, there will be a redistribution so that primary care physicians will average approximately $25 PMPM and specialists will average only $30 PMPM. The fact is that under capitation, income for primary care physicians will remain stable or increase slightly whereas income for specialists will significantly decrease.

According to Schramm, you can do as well under a capitated system as under a fee-for-service system of reimbursement but it will take more work. You may need to work longer, you may need to devote more attention to the details of your practice, you will need to look closer at your books, and you will need to be more aggressive about contracting with managed care plans. The prerequisite for all of this is having a system for accurate collection of data. According to Dr. Ray Painter, of Physician Reimbursement Systems in Denver, Colorado,* the Biblical Golden Rule of "Do unto others as you would have them do unto you" was changed in the 1980s to "Them that's got the gold, rules." In this new era of managed care, the Golden Rule should be "Them that's got the data, got the gold!"

There is no need to panic. Let's not forget that at the present time only 15 percent of the entire American population are enrolled in HMOs and only 40 percent of these people (or 6 percent of the American population) are capitated for all professional services. However, the forecast is that by the year 2005, 50 percent of the U.S. population will be fully capitated or at least fully capitated for all professional services.[6]

Because managed care contracting is such a complicated but important subject, you may want to review some of the books that focus on it. Recent publications worth reading are listed at the end of this chapter.

FORMING A PHYSICIAN NETWORK

As managed care increasingly dominates U.S. health care, physicians must decide how they want to respond to it, says L. Howard Wizig, a Kansas-based consultant for Towers Perrin.[†] "They basically have two options. They can do nothing and become a vendor to the system, a commodity, so to speak. Or they can band together, prepare themselves to manage risk, and become part of their own system. Each physician or physician group or association of physicians needs to address this issue."

Increasingly, physicians are joining together to form their own organizations. They may form an HMO but that is uncommon. More often, physicians join to-

*1675 Larimer Street, Denver, CO 80202, 800-574-1936.
†6900 College Boulevard, Suite 700, Overland Park, KS 66211, 912-451-3000.

gether to form an organization designed to contract with HMOs. The organization may be a specialty network (an IPA or group of specialists in different fields who contract en masse with an HMO) or a physician-hospital organization (physicians and a local hospital united together).

Wizig identifies several strategies that may motivate the formation of a physician-sponsored network. The members may be acting defensively (in response to a current crisis), proactively (in anticipation of future changes), or aggressively (to test the marketplace and to respond vigorously to any market demand).

The steps in forming an organization are actually similar under all three strategies. An aggressive strategy will begin with market research, and a proactive strategy, too, will benefit from it. Market research can be valuable in creating consensus among participating physicians and in designing the organization so that it meets market demands. In addition, market research can help determine what prices will be most effective.

The next step is to identify which physicians you want to be part of your network. There are a variety of ways to do that, but in essence you need to decide who you need in order to found your network. At the same time, or even before, you need to design the program. Typically you identify a few founders, just a handful, and work with them to figure out what the network should look like. Then you identify the additional physicians you need and recruit them.

"If you did your market research right in the very beginning, when you pull all of that back together, you'll have the product that the marketplace is telling you it wants," Wizig says. "You'll have the right product attributes, you'll have the right pricing, you'll have the right infrastructure and all the right design elements. None of us would jump in the car to drive someplace unless we knew where we were going. Market research let's us know where we're going, so we build something that, when we have it ready, will sell."

PRACTICE ANALYSIS SOFTWARE

In preparing for managed care, one of the things you most need is the ability to understand and summarize information about your practice. One excellent tool for analyzing all the details of a practice is the Physician Services Practice Analysis (PSPA) software developed by the Center for Research in Ambulatory Health Care Administration, the research arm of the Medical Group Management Association (MGMA). (The current price for the PSPA software is $875, which includes maintenance and support for the first year. Maintenance and support in future years, including updates, is available at $350 per year. The program runs on a 486 or better computer, with 8MB RAM preferred. For more information, call 303-397-7880.)

Doran Dunaway, a consultant with MGMA Consulting Services, which developed the software, says, "We believe it offers medical practices the same information that managed care plans have had for many years. It makes practicing physicians more powerful, because now they have the ability to capture information and verify that the information the plans use is accurate."

The PSPA software is based primarily on CPT-4 codes. It uses the resource-based relative value scale (RBRVS) as a unit of analysis; costs are determined based on the practice's historical productivity and cost information. The software is updated whenever the Health Care Financing Administration updates the RBRVS scale.

The cost accounting module analyzes cost per relative value unit of work performed and can separately analyze work, overhead, and malpractice insurance costs. It can track costs per relative value unit at the individual procedure level as well. If you were considering a discounted fee for service contract, it would allow you to compare your costs to the proposed fees and see whether or not you would make money at that fee level. If you were considering a capitated contract, the system could take your past experience and use that to generate a capitation rate. Then you could compare your experience to what the HMO is offering you and determine if the proposed rate will be profitable.

"You need to have that information in order to negotiate contracts successfully with managed care organizations and make sure that you're not losing your shirt," says Claude N. Cressy, M.A., project director for the Center for Research in Ambulatory Health Care Administration (CRAHCA).* "You've got to know what your costs are so you can negotiate effectively and make money, or at least break even in the worst case scenario. If your own analysis shows you're not breaking even, you need to reallocate your resources so that you can, at least, break even."

The productivity analysis module focuses on productivity at the group, specialty, and individual provider level. For example, after doing this sort of practice analysis, you might find that one physician is overusing ancillary services such as laboratory and radiology and offer him education on appropriate use.

The same software may find that certain physicians underutilize services. If a physician is dramatically below the standard utilization in the practice, that may mean this is a physician who holds onto patients inappropriately and also needs education on when to make referrals to specialists. If the patients do not receive an appropriate workup or treatment, they could incur illnesses that are more expensive to treat.

"The software can help you identify physicians who should be encouraged to see more patients," says Cressy. "In addition, it can help you identify whether you

---

*104 Inverness Terrace East, Englewood, CO 80112-5306, 303-799-1111, fax 303-643-4427.

need additional providers and what type of providers, whether they be physicians, nurse extenders, or PAs."

CRAHCA has a national Physician's Services Comparison program that allows you to take information from your PSPA program and download it automatically to CRAHCA, which then does an analysis of your data and compares them to data in a national databank. This allows you to look at median data and see how your performance stacks up to the performance of other practices nationwide.

* * *

With effort and attention to details, physicians will be able to negotiate contracts with managed care organizations that allow them to practice high-quality, cost-effective medicine. But negotiating a contract, important as it is, is only one piece of the puzzle. A continuing effort to market the physician and his or her practice to patients, managed care organizations, and gatekeepers is just as important. In Part IV I will look at ways of marketing within the managed care system.

NOTES

1. Advisory Board Company, Governance Committee, *Capitation Strategy* (Washington, D.C.: Advisory Board Co., 1994), 40.

2. E.L. Grab and N.B. Caesar, "Negotiating Profitable Managed Care Contracts for Your Group," *Group Practice Journal* 42, no. 5 (1993): 28–30.

3. F.J. Wenzel, "Managed Care," in *Ambulatory Care Management*, 2d ed., ed. A. Ross, S.J. Williams, and E.L. Schafer (Albany, N.Y.: Delmar Publishers, 1991), 374.

4. B. Bader and M. Matheny, "Understanding Capitation and At-Risk Contracting," *Health System Leader*, March 1994, 4–16.

5. Ibid., 5–6.

6. Advisory Board Company, Governance Committee, *Capitation I—The New American Medicine* (Washington, D.C.: Advisory Board Co., 1994), 37.

REFERENCE MATERIALS

Medical Management Institute. *Negotiating Managed Care Contracts.* New York: McGraw-Hill, 1994.

Beard, P.L. *How To Negotiate Capitation (Without Losing Your Head).* Shawnee Mission, Kans.: ProSTAT Resource Group, 1995. Tel. 913-722-1212; fax 913-722-1260.

The Doctor's Office. *How To Negotiate Managed Care Contracts (From the Standpoint of Your Personal and Professional Values).* Lancaster, Pa.: Wentworth Worldwide Media, 1994. Tel. 800-331-5196.

Mayer, G.G., Barnett, A.E., and Brown, N. *Making Capitation Work: Clinical Operations in an Integrated Delivery System.* Gaithersburg, Md.: Aspen Publishers, Inc., 1995. Tel. 800-638-8437. (Looseleaf manual, supplemented annually.)

McAdams, R.W., Jr., Gallagher, M.L., and Weller, C.D. *Managed Care Contracts Manual.* Gaithersburg, Md.: Aspen Publishers, Inc., 1996. Tel. 800-638-8437. (Looseleaf manual, supplemented annually.)

Youngberg, B.A., Ed. *Managing the Risks of Managed Care.* Gaithersburg, Md.: Aspen Publishers, Inc., 1996. Tel. 800-638-8437.

Physician's Managed Care Manual. San Francisco, Calif.: California Medical Association, 1994. Tel. 415-541-0900.

The Medical Group Management Association library provides thick packets of current information on various subjects, and their packet on "Contracting with Managed Care" contains a variety of recent papers from several sources. It is definitely worth reading.

IV

Marketing Your Medical Practice

37

Why Marketing Is a Necessity

The concept of marketing a medical practice is associated with many mis-understandings and myths. Most of us would like to believe that patients are capable of intuitively recognizing quality and will remain loyal to their current physicians, but in the 1990s this is no longer the case.

Many physicians think that marketing is just advertising—a quick fix for sagging revenues. In my opinion, marketing should be viewed as making the public and your peers aware of your services and your areas of interest and expertise in a professional and ethical fashion. The reality is that physicians have been marketing their practices for years by placing their names in the Yellow Pages or writing referral letters to referring physicians. These methods are considered both ethical and professional. But there are many other marketing methods available to all physicians that are equally legitimate.

Part IV presents some innovative methods you can use to market your medical practice. In addition, you may want to consult my previous book, *Marketing Your Clinical Practice: Ethically, Effectively, Economically*,[1] for more detailed information on how to become an effective public speaker, use targeted direct mail, create slides for public presentations, and set up a patient support group, among other topics.

Why should physicians market their practices? No physician needs to be reminded of the drastic reductions in the Medicare fee schedule and the possibility of more cuts in reimbursement. Under managed care and capitation, patients are now shopping for health care services and making their decisions based on cost and higher quality of service. At the same time, there is more consumer spending on health care services and products than on anything else, including cars, vacations, and TV sets. This means there are opportunities for physicians who offer services that patients need and want. Yet they must let patients know what is available so that the patients can judge for themselves where they would like to spend their precious health care dollars.

Setting goals is essential, and the first goal should be to establish a good, stable patient base. Marketing can help achieve this goal by informing the public of your areas of interest and expertise as well as any new services. Marketing can enhance referrals as well as target specific diagnoses, treatments, ages of patients, and socioeconomic status. Marketing allows you to sculpt the exact type of practice that you would like to have.

Marketing does not mean that you need to hire a consultant, design a brochure with a snappy logo, or engage in unprofessional advertising practices. The truth is that effective marketing can be done without advertising and without spending money on more staff. There are many effective marketing techniques I have used and tested in my practice that can be implemented inexpensively with your existing staff. The basic strategy is to take great care to keep the patients you already have, attract new ones, and motivate your staff to provide good service.

This section will provide you with dozens of practical ideas that you can easily, ethically, and effectively use in your practice.

NOTE

1. N. Baum, *Marketing Your Clinical Practice: Ethically, Effectively, Economically* (Gaithersburg, Md.: Aspen Publishers, 1992).

38

Market Shares and Market Niches

WINNING YOUR FAIR SHARE OF THE MARKET

Market share, a term commonly applied to the struggle between Coke and Pepsi or between different airlines, is now entering the vocabulary of medical practitioners. Ignoring market share will place physicians and their practices at a distinct disadvantage when coping with the rapid changes occurring today in the health care industry.

In the pages below, I define market share, describe its importance to your practice and explain how to create a market share analysis. As a help in preparing the information, I interviewed Charles Rose, administrator of Obstetrics and Gynecology Limited in Sioux Falls, South Dakota, who is a leading expert on the subject of market share analysis and its applications to private medical practice.

Simply stated, *market share* is used to refer to a share or percentage of a given market. Markets can be defined in various ways. As a physician, you will be interested in patient populations. One important market will consist of all the people (potential patients) residing in your geographic area. Other significant markets will consist of people who have common characteristics that allow you to distinguish them from the rest of the population of potential patients. These characteristics may include geographic location, sex, age, insurance coverage, income status, employer, diagnosis, medication use, treatment modality, and susceptibility to particular diseases. A market share analysis includes a profile of your current patients and a discussion of which segments of the population you currently serve.

THE IMPORTANCE OF MARKET SHARE ANALYSES

A market share analysis will help you make decisions for your practice. For example, if you are considering opening a satellite office for your pediatric practice, a market share analysis will tell you where the families with young children and insurance coverage are located. If you determine that you already have the majority of available patients in your practice, then a satellite practice will not be cost effective. If, however, the market share analysis suggests that the majority of available patients are traveling 15–20 minutes for their pediatric primary care, your decision to open a satellite office makes more economic sense.

Likewise, if you are targeting senior citizens with a newsletter or direct mail letter, you can find them easily with a market share analysis. If you are considering providing a new service, a market share analysis can tell you how many potential patients are in your area, and you can deduce how many you need to attract to make this new service profitable.

Perhaps you are considering a new associate for your ob/gyn practice. If you know the number of new births that occur annually in your geographic area, you can easily estimate the number of new patients that might be available to your new associate. As a urologist, I can estimate what percentage of my patients have impotence, benign prostate disease, urologic cancer, male infertility, and urinary incontinence. If I find that I have a smaller percentage of patients in one specific part of my patient mix, this will tell me where to concentrate my marketing efforts (assuming the compensation for that diagnosis and CPT code is profitable).

DEVELOPING A MARKET SHARE ANALYSIS

Initially you can use your own resources. Most practices begin by focusing on medical problems that interest them. Therefore, patients' medical characteristics are the first set of market factors to evaluate.

Rose suggests that you define a reasonable geographic area for your market. If you are a primary care physician, the distance from your office to the market area perimeter will be shorter than for a specialist. Specialists, who depend on referrals, will want to map the distribution of referring physicians and competing specialists. It can be discouraging when you see the number of potential competitors in your area as demonstrated by the number of pins on the map! Remember, just because someone else is in the community doesn't mean he or she controls the market. At this point, you are only investigating the market potential.

Next you need to define your share of the market. If you have a computerized billing system, the task is reasonably simple, as most contemporary software programs can provide this information. Your billing data already include each patient's address, birthday, sex, employment status, and insurance status as well as services rendered and the corresponding diagnostic codes.

You then need to formulate the data in a meaningful fashion so you can compare them to the data for the total market. Most managed care software programs have custom report generators that permit you to design your own reports from the data already available in the system. If you lack such a program, you will need to obtain the services of a consultant to devise a method of capturing the data and transferring them to a useful database. This is not difficult; once the program is established, the procedure becomes routine and you can generate reports and data at the touch of a key on your computer keyboard.

Where can you find additional information? Local and state government welfare services are sources of Medicaid and medical welfare recipient numbers.

Identifying market share is basically a process of finding the number of your patients who had a specific diagnosis and lived in a specific geographic area and comparing this number to the number of all patients who had the same diagnosis and lived in the same geographic area during the same time period. Dividing the former by the latter and multiplying by 100 will yield your share of the market.

In the past, physicians succeeded by providing quality care to each patient who entered through the practice door. The doctor-patient relationship was a sacred bond, and patient loyalty could be counted on to build and maintain the practice. Today, a successful physician must also be aware of each patient's origin and characteristics or run the risk of losing that patient to someone who has an active competitive strategy. A market share analysis performed annually or biannually will give you a better overview of where your practice is and help direct you to where you want to be. One of the best marketing strategies for the 1990s and beyond is to carve out a special niche that will allow you to offer services to your patients. The second part of this chapter examines the basic concepts of niche marketing.

IT'S NICE TO KNOW YOUR NICHE

Once a successful entrepreneur was interviewed on his techniques for business success. He said, "Find the unmet needs in the marketplace, learn your industry cold, then fill those unmet needs." That advice to businessmen and women is just as relevant to providers of health care. Nearly every community has health care niches (or unmet needs). Identifying those niches and matching them with your areas of interest and expertise is an effective way to market your practice.

Niche marketing provides your practice with many advantages and opportunities. By developing a local expertise in specific areas of medicine, you will receive referrals from physicians who would not ordinarily send you patients. Referring physicians who learn about your specialized expertise (through marketing) will refer patients to you since they want their patients' problems to be solved.

Niche marketing also makes it possible to generate intraspecialty referrals. For example, if you perform a procedure that many of your colleagues don't, you can let them know that you do the procedure and would be happy to work with them in the care of *their* patient. Emphasizing that the patient remains their patient is very important in generating intraspecialty referrals. When a patient is sent to you, make sure that your colleague is well informed about the progress of the case and that you offer him or her an opportunity to participate in the care of the patient.

DOES NICHE MARKETING WORK? YOU BETTER BELIEVE IT DOES!

When I moved my practice to New Orleans in 1978, business was very slow. Then I remembered my training in male sexual dysfunction at Baylor College of Medicine, where the inflatable penile prosthesis was developed. No other urologist in the community was particularly interested in treating patients with impotence. I was aware that approximately 10 million American men suffer from chronic impotence and only 100,000 had received surgical treatment for their problem, which indicated that there was an unmet need in the marketplace. I began by writing articles in the local newspapers and magazines and speaking to service clubs, hospitals, physicians, and operating room staffs. I also informed my urologic colleagues about my interest and training in this area and offered to see their patients and operate on their patients at their hospitals. I also organized a support group and participated in writing a book on impotence for laypeople.

Next I focused on informing the public that help was available for most impotent men—that no longer did they need to suffer "the tragedy of the bedroom." I spoke to local groups about this subject whenever I had the opportunity. Within three years I was seeing between 25 and 30 new patients a month, many complaining of erectile dysfunction.

Some exploitable niche exists for every specialty practice in every community. You simply need to find a service or procedure that you enjoy providing, that you have been trained in, and that your community needs. Then it is just a matter of informing the community of your expertise. Once you do that, the patients will be calling and filling up your appointment book.

Niche marketing can also increase the geographic area from which you draw patients. If you are considered an expert in a certain area of medicine, you can expect patients to be attracted to your practice from a wide area. Patients will travel great distances to be treated by respected experts. If your area of expertise is really well known, then you can expect patients from all over the country and even the world. My favorite example is Dr. Denton Cooley, from Houston's Texas Heart Institute, who has attracted patients from every corner of the globe because of his international reputation.

Niche marketing creates a positive image of you and your practice. Your expertise can make you a recognized figure in the community. The public, including your current patients, will have a sense of pride because they are associated with you and your practice.

Niche marketing attracts many patients who eventually will need other services your practice offers. For example, if a patient comes to my practice for treatment of erectile dysfunction, I might have an opportunity to do his vasectomy and treat his enlarged prostate gland as well. Unless he lives a great distance away or has another urologist, he will probably continue to see me for these other problems.

Another benefit of niche marketing is that patients who come for your advertised specialty and have a positive experience with you and your practice are likely to refer their family and friends to you.

Niche marketing allows you to reverse refer (that is, send patients to your colleagues and your referring physicians). For example, if a patient comes to you because of your recognized area of expertise, then you will be in a position to make referrals to colleagues who regularly and routinely refer patients to you. This is a much more appreciated thank-you than a fruit and cheese basket at holiday time.

Niche marketing allows your practice to profit from economies of scale. If you are seeing many patients who require similar procedures, you can expect that the utilization of equipment will increase and your staff will become more efficient doing their assigned tasks. Staff members will also become more efficient in dealing with paperwork, coding, insurance authorization, and billing when procedures are performed more frequently. Repetition generally increases efficiency and thus reduces overhead costs.

In addition, through improved efficiency you can make your practice more attractive to managed care organizations, since cost is one of their primary considerations in the selection of providers for their members (see Exhibit 38-1).

EXAMPLES OF NICHE MARKETING

Dr. Terry Habig is a New Orleans orthopedic surgeon specializing in sports medicine. Early in his medical career he apprenticed himself to his senior partner, who was the orthopedist for the New Orleans Saints football team. Dr. Habig is now the senior team physician for the Saints and has a large sports medicine

Exhibit 38-1 Ranking by Managed Care Organizations of Factors Contributing to Their Success

Price	69%*	Network affiliations	11%
Patient satisfaction	50%	Use of guidelines	10%
Access to doctors	31%	Publishing outcomes	9%
Quality improvement process	20%		

*The number listed is the percentage of managed care organizations that ranked the particular factor first or second in importance.

Source: Foster Higgins, *Survey on Outcomes Management*, 1994, p. 5.

practice. He has combined his interest in medicine and sports and estimates that 30 to 40 percent of his orthopedic practice is related directly or indirectly to his relationship with the Saints.

Dr. Brobson Lutz is a New Orleans internist with a special interest in politics and preventive medicine. He started out working for the city's public health department and has been appointed City Health Director. The media seek him out for comments on issues of public health, health insurance, malpractice, and sexually transmitted diseases. Because of his position as City Health Director, he has been invited to host a weekly television program on health-related issues. Although his area of special expertise is not intended to attract patients to his practice, he is in fact one of the most well-known physicians in the community.

Dr. Jerry Balanco is a member of a pediatric group in New Orleans. Since there was only one Ph.D. psychologist in the community with an interest in treating children with learning disorders, he identified this as a need in the marketplace and took a two-month leave of absence from his practice to work with a national expert on learning dysfunctions. Over the years he has attended postgraduate seminars and conventions on the subject and has become a local expert. He estimates that 50 percent of his practice is related to his specialty. He gets referrals not only from patients, parents, and school teachers but also from other pediatricians.

Dr. Joel Saper, a neurologist in private practice in Ann Arbor, Michigan, has developed a reputation as an expert in the management of headaches. He identified a common problem that did not interest many other neurologists. Through writing (he is the author of six books and puts out a monthly newsletter for physicians) and public speaking, he has informed the public and other health care providers about his expertise. He is now the director of a clinic that enjoys an international reputation as a leader in the management of headaches.

All of these examples of medical niche marketing show that it is important to provide state-of-the-art health care backed up by quality service. Note that it is possible to generate patients and referrals using ethical, accepted information modalities that are available to all physicians.

GETTING STARTED

Niche marketing means finding a medical need that you are competent and willing to deal with and that is not being adequately met in your community. If you hear that patients with a specific problem are leaving your community to receive health care elsewhere and you are trained to deal with that problem and want to work with those patients, then you have identified a niche.

The next step is to inform the public and your colleagues about your interest in treating the problem. In most cases, this will mean seeking out public speaking opportunities and writing articles for local newspapers and magazines. I suggest that you develop a first-class slide show (along with handouts, brochures, and follow-up letters) that you can present to target audiences. Draft articles on the subject for local and regional publications, and inform local TV and radio stations about your interest in discussing the subject on the air.

Next, educate your staff so they are knowledgeable about your niche. They need to be able to field most of the questions that patients and potential patients will ask. They also need to know about the training and qualifications you have in your identified area of expertise.

I have talked with numerous physicians who practice niche marketing, and they invariably report they get a high degree of personal and professional satisfaction and enjoyment from their efforts. I don't believe there is a physician who can't find an area of medical interest and match it with unmet needs in the marketplace and become successful at niche marketing.

A final caveat. Niche marketing is a slow process that requires persistence and patience. Paradoxical as it may seem, you need patience before you get patients.

*   *   *

In the next chapter, we will explore in detail how to create a medical practice marketing plan.

39

Create a Medical Practice Marketing Plan

C reating a marketing plan for a medical practice is no different from creating a marketing plan for any other business.

The purpose of a marketing plan is to serve as a road map or blueprint for the future. Here's an analogy: if you're planning to go on a trip, you prepare by buying maps and guidebooks. Similarly, in order to manage the future of your practice, you need a well-designed plan that includes future goals and a series of practical steps designed to reach those goals. A marketing plan is an analytic process designed to change amorphous concepts into clearly defined steps that lead to a desired result.

Stanley R. Levenson, A.P.R., chief executive officer of Levenson Public Relations,* agreed to share his public relations expertise.

A marketing plan has several basic elements:

- Situation review
  - External environment assessment
  - Internal environment assessment
  - SWOT analysis
- Objectives
- Target audiences
- Strategies

---

*600 North Pearl Street, Suite 910, Dallas, TX 75201, 214-880-0200, fax 214-880-0601.

- Tactics
- Measurement
- Budgeting

SITUATION REVIEW

The situation review is like a diagnosis of your practice. It comprises an evaluation of your current situation and an overview of your current market.

You begin by researching the internal and external environment. You will need to identify national trends, the competitive environment in your community, potential patients' needs, and current patients' perceptions and needs. You will use this information to identify opportunities and create the objectives of your marketing plan.

Below are the important questions to ask and data to gather.

External Environment Assessment

Begin with the big picture. What are the national trends in insurance, particularly managed care? Is there under- or oversaturation of physicians in your specialty? What are the effects of changing referral pathways on your specialty or type of practice? Which new technologies are affecting your patients' care?

Some key questions in this era of managed care are, What managed care plans are predominant in your community? How many enrollees are in each plan? How much growth is anticipated in managed care plans? Are you a provider on the panels of these plans? (If you are not participating in the right plans in your area, you are automatically eliminating a potential large patient base before you even begin to think about other aspects of marketing.) You can acquire information on the number of enrollees in managed care plans (both HMOs and PPOs) from insurance companies or state medical societies.

To assess your competition, find out how many physicians are in your community (both physicians in your specialty and potential referrers). Ask two vital questions: What is the competition doing? What are they not doing? When you uncover something they are not doing, you have identified an opportunity.

What are the demographics of your community? What are the current numbers and the projected growth over the next five years? Which groups are growing in number? Children, middle-aged women, the elderly? Your Chamber of Commerce probably can provide these data.

What are the current medical trends in your community? For example, is there a trend toward preventive care, increased use of ambulatory care, shorter hospital stays, or increased home health care?

Survey potential patients to learn whether they are interested in fitness, nutrition, sports medicine, or preventive medicine strategies. Is their main concern hours of operation? If so, do they require Saturday and evening hours?

Internal Environmental Assessment

How many additional patients could your practice handle currently? What is your capacity? (Nothing would be worse than to attract so many patients that you could not offer them quality service.)

What is your practice's market share in the community? Determine total projected number of visits based on the population (you can obtain the appropriate rate to use from your specialty's national organization), then determine what percentage of those visits are yours.

Is your practice computerized so that you can generate accurate demographic data on your patients? In what ZIP codes do most of your patients live? Should you consider placing a satellite office in one or more of these?

Can your computers provide a breakdown of patients in managed care plans and in Medicare and fee-for-service segments? (If you don't have a system that allows you to collect and analyze these data, be sure your next computer system does offer this capability.)

Regularly survey your current patients to assess their perceptions and attitudes. The tool can be as simple as a postcard with five or six questions that are easy for an office staff member to tally on a weekly basis. For example, ask patients whether they were seen within 15 minutes of their arrival. Ask if their calls are returned promptly. Leave space for subjective opinions and suggestions for improved service. If you are a small practice, for example, you may learn that personalized service is a strong desire—and that is something you could provide better than a large organization or a multispecialty group practice.

Not long ago, a group of pediatricians I know joined a large HMO. When one of their old patients called, she reached an answering service that said, "Please leave us your name and chart number and within one hour a doctor or nurse will call you back." In one hour a nurse did call back—a complete stranger who did not know how to handle the specific situation. The patient waited another two hours at home while the nurse gave the message to the doctor. Then a different nurse called back and answered the question. This patient never did get to speak to the doctor herself, and she still feels a certain uneasiness about the lack of personal attention.

That kind of story is a clue to a marketing opportunity. If I were a pediatrician in that city, I would position myself as someone who is available. "When you call our practice, you'll hear a familiar voice, ready to help you, and you'll be able to speak directly to the doctor when you need to."

A situation analysis is an opportunity to think about your strengths and capabilities and then base your marketing efforts upon the strengths you have to offer.

Ask your colleagues and referral base to tell you about their perceptions about
your practice. Ask for their suggestions—and be prepared to implement them if
you do! That will demonstrate that you are concerned and that you are listening.

SWOT Analysis

Using the data acquired in your external and internal analyses, you should be
able to write a quick list of your practice's strengths, weaknesses, opportunities,
and threats (SWOT). Using your SWOT list, you should be able to pinpoint marketing objectives or desired outcomes for your marketing plan. Sample SWOT
items are given below.

Strengths

- We have 40 percent managed care patients compared with the community's
  average of only 25 percent.
- We are an obstetric practice delivering patients in a major tertiary hospital,
  with all the benefits of high technology and capable of caring for high-risk
  pregnancies.

Weaknesses

- We are a family practice with only three providers, so we are at capacity and
  already have waiting lists, particularly because we act as gatekeepers in so
  many managed care plans.
- Our obstetric patients are increasingly moving out to the suburbs and say
  they would prefer to see a physician closer to home, even though they like
  the idea of delivering at a large downtown hospital.

Opportunities

- Recruit additional physicians, nurse practitioners, or physicians' assistants
  to handle the growing patient load.
- Open satellite offices in the suburbs in which the highest percentage of our
  patients live (as revealed by a ZIP code analysis).

Threats

- Younger, upscale families are moving into our community and insist
  on using a pediatrician instead of a family practice physician because

their perception is that a family physician is not as well-trained to handle children.

- More and more patients are seeking both obstetricians and hospitals closer to home.

By systematically listing all SWOT factors, you have constructed the foundation of your marketing plan. You are basing your plans on research and analysis, not on speculative ideas and gut feelings.

Shooting from the hip won't work in 1996 or beyond. You have to get the data and devise a systematic, informed research plan.

OBJECTIVES

You need to think in terms of different types of objectives—marketing and communications objectives as well as personal goals.

It is not enough to just set very general goals. Don't just say, "I want to build up my practice." You need to set specific goals that include numerical values and usually a deadline.

A typical marketing objective might be something like this: "We want to increase revenues by 15 percent and new patients by 10 percent within the next 12 months." Or you might say, "By the end of next year we'd like our clientele to be 40 percent managed care, 30 percent Medicare, and 30 percent fee-for-service." A primary care practice might set a goal of increasing pediatric patients by 10 percent, since pediatric patients are likely to stay with a practice for a long time.

In any case, you need to think carefully about your goals and objectives and write them down in clear, specific language, because they provide the targets against which you measure your success. Remember, you can't hit a target you can't see.

TARGET AUDIENCES

First, analyze all the potential patients and customers in the community you want to influence, including individuals and organizations.

Begin with your own employees. Are they satisfied? Do they feel good at the end of the day? Do they feel they are valued and appreciated and have opportunities to grow? Or are they stressed out? Do you have a high turnover rate?

Any marketing plan must start at the top, but the employees must buy into it for it to succeed, since they will play an important role in implementing it. If the employees don't buy into it, all your effort will be wasted.

Your current patients, both active and inactive, are another vitally important target audience. You have to look at ways to continue to satisfy your active patients as well as ways to reactivate patients who have drifted away.

Look at a wide range of important target audiences: new patients, potential patients, referring physicians, insurance companies and providers, and managed care plans. In addition, think of all the target audiences that are sources of referrals: pharmacists and pharmaceutical representatives, attorneys, social workers, clergy, civic and community organizations. How much of an impact have you had in the media, print and electronic?

STRATEGIES

A strategy is a general plan or method for accomplishing a goal.

Suppose, for example, that your target audience is your employees and your goals include ensuring that your employees experience pride and high morale, are loyal to the practice, have low turnover, are very productive, and have opportunities for personal growth. Your strategies might include trying to improve employer-employee communication, instituting a reward system, arranging for continuing education, and demonstrating recognition of exemplary performance.

If your target audience consists of current active patients and your goals include maintaining your relationship with these patients, promoting patient satisfaction and word-of-mouth marketing, and making these patients ambassadors of your practice, your strategies might include improving communication, service, and access to your practice and regularly surveying attitudes and perceptions. (Table 39-1 shows possible goals, key messages, and strategies for six target audiences.)

TACTICS

Tactics are the specific, detailed methods used to carry out a strategy and achieve a goal. For example, if your goal is to provide outstanding service, you might want to perform a patient service cycle and evaluate the way the patients are treated from the time they enter the practice until they leave. Based on this evaluation, you would develop a specific tactical plan for improved service.

Your tactics might include weekend, evening, and early morning hours if that's what your patients want. Develop effective scheduling so there is no waiting time. Provide patients a "no paperwork" service. Offer optional installment billing for elective surgery patients. Provide educational materials.

If your goal is to provide more services, you might want to set up a patient network where patients can talk to other patients about their experiences. You might consider offering the services of a nutritionist.

Table 39-1 Sample Goals, Key Messages, and Strategies for Various Target Audiences

Target Audience	Goals	Key Messages	Strategies
Employees	Increased pride High morale Staff loyalty High productivity Opportunities for personal growth Low turnover	The doctor is a "great" employer, is a leading-edge practitioner, is dedicated to patients, and offers advancement opportunities.	Communication Recognition Rewards Continuing education Include employees in developing practice's mission statement and standards of patient care. Post them and review them. Initiate regular (weekly) quality control meetings consisting of nurses, doctors, and office staff (cross-section). Determine root problems (not just symptoms); solve problems and recognize employees.
Active patients	Maintain relationship Promote satisfaction and word-of-mouth marketing Make active patients ambassadors of your practice	The practice renders professional care of the highest quality. The practice is a progressive one. Good health is important to the physician and staff. "We care about you."	Communication Service Technology Access
Inactive patients	Restore the participation of inactive patients in the practice Practice preventive medicine	"Give us the opportunity to continue to serve you." Regular checkups can prevent disease. Early diagnosis increases quality of life.	Communication Special events Office telephones to express concern and ask reasons for change or dissatisfaction
Managed care patients	Increase their endorsements of your practice to their colleagues	"We know managed care is confusing and new, and we want to help you understand how to access care to your advantage."	Provide information/education on the concept of managed care at first visits Instruct them on who's to obtain referral codes, when necessary, etc. Provide literature on preventing, identifying, and handling common ailments

continues

Table 39-1 continued

Target Audience	Goals	Key Messages	Strategies
Colleagues or referral base	Improve loyalty of referral base and increase referrals	"We listened to your suggestions, valued your opinion, and took action."	Ask for opinions/ suggestions Examples of tactics that may result: providing faxed reports on the referred patient in 24 hours; telephone response from physician within 30 minutes
Potential patients	Convert potential patients to active patients	"We have a quality practice." "We care about you and will take a personal interest in your health and well-being."	Specify the insurance plans for which you are a provider Emphasize board certification Provide and advertise discounted regular check-ups (e.g., for schools, etc.)

Source: Levenson Public Relations, Dallas, Texas.

If your goal is to be on the cutting edge in technology, your tactics might include buying new equipment or renovating and improving old equipment.

If your goal is to improve access, your tactics might include answering the phone within three rings, seeing all new patients within one week, and seeing emergency cases within one hour.

MEASUREMENT

In order to use a marketing plan, you need to measure how you are doing (before and after implementation) in terms of your specific objectives. If your goal is a 10-percent growth in new patients, and you're seeing 60 new patients a month, you would want to see 6 additional new patients next month. Your goal now is 66 new patients a month.

You measure your actual results against your forecast objectives.

BUDGETING

A marketing budget is traditionally based on a percentage of revenues. Typically a medical practice spends anywhere from 2 to 5 percent on marketing and communications—more if it is planning a particularly aggressive advertising campaign. For example, a one-physician orthopedic practice might spend $14,000 to $20,000 annually on marketing and promotion. An average primary care practice, with a gross income of roughly $200,000, might spend $4,000 or $5,000.

A budget of this minimal type does not include salaries for staff or investments in new equipment. It does include new projects and activities that will be part of your marketing effort. If you decide to hire a patient representative to welcome new patients and help them fill out forms, then you'll plan for that new staffer as part of your marketing budget. A patient representative would increase your marketing budget by $10,000 to $12,000 a year.

40

Practice Newsletters: How To Make Them Work

You probably receive several newsletters each month—one from your accountant, one from your stockbroker, and perhaps a few from pharmaceutical companies. Some of your colleagues may have practice newsletters, and perhaps you are considering whether to produce one for your own practice. If so, you are undoubtedly wondering whether it will attract new patients or help you keep the patients you already have. And even if it does have a benefit, will the benefit be worth the effort? As they say in the world of business, will you achieve a positive return on investment?

For this chapter I talked with Elaine Floyd, owner of St. Louis-based EF Communications.* Floyd is a national expert on newsletters and the author of *Marketing with Newsletters*. After reading this chapter you will be able to decide whether a newsletter is a worthwhile project for you and your practice.

WHAT ARE THE ADVANTAGES OF A NEWSLETTER?

A newsletter is a cost-effective, professional way to promote your practice. It offers your current patients valuable information and can serve as a vehicle to attract new patients. It can be used to pre-educate patients and prepare them for their face-to-face meeting with the physician. Doctors who have used newsletters for years believe that they improve the efficiency of their practices. Most doctors

---

*Newsletter Resources, 6614 Pernod Avenue., St. Louis, MO 63139, 314-647-0400, fax 314-647-1609.

don't have the time to talk about general health issues to their patients. A patient newsletter serves as an extension of an office visit.

For example, I have instituted a new procedure in my practice—use of a prostatic stent to treat benign enlargement of the prostate gland. When I mentioned this in my newsletter, patients who were possible candidates for the procedure were able to review some background information before they made an appointment. This saved me and my staff a small amount of time and energy.

Newsletters appeal to motivated, educated patients. A newsletter may serve to attract such patients and screen out price shoppers.

By describing services and procedures that you perform or symptoms or diagnoses that you treat, you can attract specific types of patients to your practice. For example, my specialty areas are impotence, incontinence, and infertility. My newsletter contains articles in these areas and tends to attract patients with those problems.

No matter what type of practice you have, you can target patients in specific age groups, socioeconomic categories, and ZIP codes through your newsletter.

Newsletters also serve the important function of informing your existing patients about the full range of your services and areas of interest and expertise. An informative newsletter serves as one of your best marketing tools. It also increases word-of-mouth advertising. When your patients are informed about your practice's services and share your newsletter with family members and friends, some of them are likely to become your patients.

HOW DO YOU MEASURE THE RESULTS OF A NEWSLETTER?

To measure the results of any marketing tool, it is essential to ask all new patients, "Who referred you to our practice?" Many practices include on the registration form a place where patients can mark the referral source. "Newsletter" should be one of the explicit options; do not rely on patients to check "other" and then explain.

To note the effect of the newsletter on current patients, ask your staff to record in their charts when they mention something they learned from the newsletter. For example, when a patient mentions a new test, procedure, or medical finding that was discussed exclusively in the newsletter, that should be documented as a newsletter referral.

Once I mentioned in my newsletter that I was able to do an incisionless vasectomy and got 20 requests for more information. In the next two months, I ended up doing six of the procedures. That tells me the newsletter is worth the relatively small effort and cost involved. A plastic surgeon described a silicone-free breast augmentation technique in his newsletter right after the recent implant scare. His office was flooded with calls, and he acquired several new patients as a result of that newsletter story.

Other techniques for measuring the effectiveness of a newsletter include the following. You can arrange to have a separate phone number for patients to call for appointments or for information offered in the newsletter. This allows you to record the name of every patient who responds to the newsletter and the amount of income generated. If you wish, you can even record the number of calls generated by each issue of the newsletter or by specific stories.

You can also enclose a postpaid reply card in the newsletter. (In newsletter lingo, this is referred to as a "bounce back reply card.") This makes it extremely easy for your staff to save the cards, pull the ledger cards from the computer, and calculate the income generated by each issue of the newsletter.

For example, in one issue of my newsletter I offered a free copy of my book *ECNETOPMI (Impotence)—It's Reversible* if the reader would send in a coupon. I saved those coupons and then calculated the income from the readers who responded. I found that the income from three patients more than paid for the cost of the newsletter.

Don't forget that new patients are attracted as a result of several factors, and the newsletter may play an important role even if a new patient does not mention it when making the first appointment. The patient may have received several issues of your newsletter and then seen your Yellow Pages ad. When asked how he or she heard about you and your practice, the patient may respond, "the Yellow Pages," yet the newsletter could have been an important part of the process that led him or her to your office.

The newsletter often serves as a reminder or a stimulator for current patients and motivates them to make an appointment even though they may not specifically mention it. Many practices will gather as much data as possible but end up evaluating their newsletter on the basis of "gut reaction."

HOW MUCH DOES A NEWSLETTER COST?

Most practices spend approximately $.50 per copy; that includes printing and postage. Typically, printing and mailing costs make up the bulk of the newsletter budget. Postage is now $.32 and climbing. If you mail within one or two ZIP codes and presort the newsletters, you can receive a bulk, presort rate that will reduce the mailing cost considerably.

If you rent a mailing list, you can expect to add $.05 to $.10 per name for a one-time use. The cost varies depending on how specialized the list is. For example, a list of people who have just moved into certain ZIP codes will cost less than a list of women who are over 40 and have two or more children.

There are newsletter services that will write a newsletter for you. However, your expenses will go up, and the final newsletter may not be as personal or as geared to the needs of your specific patients.

To save on printing, consider a shorter format than the standard four-page newsletter. According to Floyd, today most people spend much less time reading. Keeping your newsletter short may increase the chances that it will get read.

"MA, I WANT TO DO IT MYSELF"

The question of whether or not to use a generic applies to newsletters just as it does to medications. In both cases you get what you pay for. Generic newsletters have the advantage of saving time and money, since you're splitting the cost of production and of printing with other practices. Another advantage of generic newsletters is that they are written by professional writers, so you won't have to worry about deadlines, typos, and having your office cluttered with mailouts.

Should you choose the generic newsletter option, look for a company that has publishing experience with your specific specialty. You want the newsletter to be personalized as much as possible (that is, beyond the standard name and photo on the heading, along with address, telephone number, and office hours). You also want it to reflect your opinions and the philosophy of your practice. A good compromise is to have the front and back of the standard four-page newsletter written with your practice in mind and place the generic or standard material on the inside. (The reason for this is that the front and back pages are most likely to be read.) The Doctor's Press, in Lancaster, Pennsylvania,* offers a service where they customize the first and fourth pages and provide material for the second and third pages.

EDUCATING YOUR STAFF ABOUT NEWSLETTERS

I think it is very important to make sure your staff is aware of the contents of each issue before it is distributed. I ask every staff member to read the newsletter and be sure he or she understands the main points of all the stories. Nothing is more embarrassing than for a patient to ask a question about a topic in the newsletter and have the staff be unable to answer it.

I also discuss the newsletter at staff meetings and encourage the staff to offer a copy to every patient and point out stories that will be especially interesting. The staff even distributes the newsletter to their family and friends.

---

*P.O. Box 11177, Lancaster, PA 17605-1177, 800-233-0196, fax 717-393-5752.

GETTING THE WORD OUT

A newsletter is only as effective as the quality of its articles and the extent of its distribution. Send your newsletter to past as well as current patients. There's no better way to inform past patients about any new areas of interest and expertise. You can target your preferred readers by renting mailing lists using various criteria, including age, sex, income, use of credit cards, and ZIP code.

When using rented mailing lists, you must be careful to match the content of the newsletter to the kind of people who will receive it. I once used a mailing list of the members of the Louisiana State Diabetes Association. I sent them a newsletter that noted the association of impotence with diabetes and described possible treatments for impotence. Since I asked for all males with diabetes, I mistakenly sent a newsletter to an 8-year-old boy! There was no apology or "I'm sorry" letter that could make up for that faux pas.

The effectiveness of newsletters, like the effectiveness of most marketing tools, is in direct proportion to the energy and effort that you put into them. A newsletter that only sits in the pamphlet holder in the reception area waiting for patients to reach out and take a copy will not generate as great a response as a carefully scripted newsletter that is mailed to a specific and potentially interested audience.

Newsletters make excellent bill stuffers. They can be included with your referral letters to referring physicians. I leave my newsletter in the hospital emergency room, and I give it to the physician referral service to be passed on to potential new patients.

You can also send your newsletter to libraries and newspapers. I routinely send mine to the local newspaper. One of the reporters read my article about "incisionless vasectomy" and not only became a patient but sent his brother-in-law as well!

I also suggest taking your newsletter with you to public speaking engagements. Give a copy to all members of the audience. This is a much "softer sell" than handing out your business card when audience members ask for your phone number. And while you cannot tactfully give out your business card to all the people who attend, you can place a copy of the newsletter on each chair in the meeting room.

Finally, if you are a primary care physician, a pediatrician, or an ob/gyn, obtain a mailing list of new residents in the community and send them your newsletter. You have to expect that only a small percentage will respond, but it will still be worthwhile, because just one new patient who uses your services for 10–15 years will pay for lots of newsletters.

NEWSLETTERS AND MANAGED CARE ORGANIZATIONS

Just as you need to let your patients know what is happening in your practice on a regular basis, you also need to inform managed care organizations of your doings. I suggest that you send them a letter on a semi-annual or annual basis telling them about events or actions that show you to have a cost-effective and high-quality practice.

Let managed care organizations know about new procedures that you do and new technology that you have incorporated into your practice that prevents hospitalization, reduces length of stay, and improves outcomes. Exhibit 40-1 is a newsletter that I sent to a managed care organization. The response from the medi-

---

Exhibit 40-1 Newsletter To Inform Managed Care Organizations of Practice Features and Activities

---

Dear [medical director],

As a physician who serves members of your managed care plan, I would like to communicate with you about the activities in my practice that have taken place this last year.

I have received 75 hours of continuing medical education credits. This includes attending the American Urologic Association's annual meeting, a seminar in urodynamics, and a postgraduate course that described a new technique for the treatment of urinary incontinence that will significantly reduce patient discomfort, length of stay, and costs.

I have published five articles in peer-reviewed journals in the past 18 months. I am including copies for your review.

Our practice has conducted a patient survey. (A copy of the survey is enclosed.) This survey demonstrated that 94 percent of patients have found our services satisfactory and would recommend our practice to others.

We have conducted a time and motion study on the time patients spend in our practice. We have demonstrated that the majority of patients spend less than 20 minutes in the reception, not "waiting," room. Nearly all established patients are seen, processed, and discharged from the office within 40 minutes of their arrival in the office. This means that your members can be seen in a timely fashion and return promptly to their jobs.

Our practice offers early morning hours two days a week and weekend hours once a month. This enables your plan members to make appointments for their urologic care and avoid conflicts related to their employment.

Our practice has a computerized callback system that notifies patients when they need to call for their next appointment. Consequently patients are contacted months later and reminded when they need to return for follow-up care.

Our practice believes in wellness and prophylactic urologic care. We encourage all men more than 50 years of age, and all men above age 40 who have a family history of prostate

---

continues

Exhibit 40-1 continued

cancer or who are African-American, to have an annual digital rectal exam and prostate-specific antigen test.

All men are given a testicular self-examination card (included) to display in their shower. This card serves as a reminder for all men to examine their testes on a monthly basis to detect early testicular cancer.

Our practice holds weekly staff meetings. We circulate an agenda prior to each staff meeting and create a to-do list after each meeting. We also have minutes for each meeting that are kept on record and made available to each staff member (sample included).

We have obtained the most common ICD-9-CM codes used in the practice and constantly monitor charges for each of these diagnoses. This exercise demonstrates our commitment to remaining cost-effective and still providing high-quality care to your plan members.

I hope this letter demonstrates our commitment to quality as well as cost containment. I would be happy to meet with you and discuss any of the enclosed data and information.

I have enjoyed working with [name of managed care organization] and look forward to a long relationship with you and your organization.

Sincerely,

Neil Baum, M.D.

---

cal director was that he had never received such a letter and that it clearly indicated that I understood the needs and wants of the managed care plan and its members.

* * *

Another way to inform your patients about valuable services you offer is to include additional material with the bill or other mailings. In the next chapter, I will look at ways you can use bill stuffers to inform and educate your patients.

41

Use Bill Stuffers To Market Your Practice

S everal years ago I received a bill from my dentist for my routine checkup. Enclosed in the envelope was an article about a new fluoride treatment that significantly reduced the number of cavities a child or an adult would get. I called my dentist, asked a few questions, and decided to have the treatment. In fact, I also sent my wife and children for the same treatment.

The informational article that dentist sent me must have generated an additional $1,500 worth of business. Later I asked him what the response from this article had been: he smiled and said, "Beyond my wildest expectations." It was at that moment that I decided to enter the world of bill stuffers.

Bill stuffers have been used successfully in other businesses for decades. However, the health care professions have only recently started to use this efficient and effective marketing technique. The technique works so well because the most receptive audience for educational information is likely to be the patients who are already part of your practice.

Let's look at the advantages of using bill stuffers. First, you have a targeted audience of receptive patients who have already used your services. If they had a good experience with you and then learn of new services you offer, they are very likely to utilize those services when they need them.

After all, very few patients are aware of the full range of your services. For example, I had a patient with benign prostatic hyperplasia (BPH) who had a transurethral resection of the prostate. When I sent him the bill, I enclosed information about an impotence support group I was sponsoring at the local hospital. This patient attended the meeting and then made an appointment with me, mentioning that he hadn't realized I took care of men with erection problems.

By including information about new or advanced methods and materials, you can let your patients know that you are staying current and keeping up to date in your field. Patients want to know that their physicians are continuing their education and staying abreast of the latest treatments and are on the cutting edge of new technology.

Sometimes I enclose my quarterly newsletter in my monthly bill statements. Each issue lists local publications and articles that I have written as well as my scheduled speaking engagements in the community.

What are the disadvantages of bill stuffers? None! I employ a high school student who comes after school to photocopy and file charts, and once a month she assists with the folding of the bills and the bill stuffers. There's no additional postage, so the cost is negligible.

Where do you find material? Once you start thinking about it, you will see that material for bill stuffers is found everywhere—newspapers, magazines, national organizations, and even your own practice. Dear Abby, Ann Landers, and Dr. Gott have syndicated newspaper columns that often provide health information. I contact the paper and ask for permission to copy the material and enclose it with my monthly statements. As long as there's no intention to profit from duplicating the material and my primary purpose is educational, the paper readily grants permission. One caveat: get permission in writing. This is easily accomplished by sending a written release form (Exhibit 41-1). You just fill in the title, name, date, and publication where the article appeared and indicate your purpose. Provide space for their signature and you have complied with the copyright laws.

I have also sent patients articles from my state medical journal that talk about the problems physicians have with insurance companies and Medicare. My purpose is to inform patients about the increasing cost of managing paperwork in a medical practice.

Frequently I enclose humorous articles that appeared in *Reader's Digest* or *Modern Maturity*. An article about the special problems of being a senior citizen was especially popular. Tasteful medical cartoons and jokes are also appropriate for bill stuffers, as well as timely announcements on national health events such as Prostate Cancer Awareness Week.

I suggest that you avoid bill stuffers associated with politics, religion, or sensitive issues such as abortion. Your goal in mailing out bill stuffers should be to educate patients about health care issues, and there is no need to risk antagonizing them.

If you have a computerized billing program, you might be able to program your computer to include a few words on the statement that will identify services or treatments that you would like to call to the attention of your patients. For

Exhibit 41-1 Letter Requesting Permission To Send Article or Cartoon to Patients

Dear [Name of Author, Columnist, or Cartoonist],

I am a physician in private practice in New Orleans, Louisiana. I would like to reproduce your [article, cartoon, column, etc.] that appeared in the [name of newspaper or publication].

I would appreciate your permission. If you would sign this letter and return it in the self-addressed, stamped envelope or fax it to my office [provide fax number], I would be very grateful.

To your good health.

Dr. Neil Baum

___ Permission granted _____ Date _____ Signature

example, when I wanted patients to know about the new collagen treatment for urinary incontinence, I mentioned this treatment on the computerized statement (see Chapter 2, Figure 2-2).

Let me conclude this chapter with a true bill stuffer story.

On April 25, 1991, *The New England Journal of Medicine* reported that prostate-specific antigen (PSA) could be used for early detection of cancer of the prostate.[1] This was briefly mentioned in *Time*'s health column as well. I photocopied the *Time* article and used it as a May bill stuffer. I sent it to both male and female patients, along with a note stating that this test was available in my practice. I received nearly 75 requests from current patients for this test. In addition, the mailing generated several new patients when women who received the bill stuffer made appointments for their husbands and partners. Those patients who had elevated PSAs also had prostate ultrasound examinations. That's not a bad return from a single bill stuffer.

If you aren't using bill stuffers (see Figure 41-1 for an example), you are missing out on a great marketing opportunity. Give this inexpensive yet effective marketing technique a try. You too will hear your patients say that they are now looking forward to opening your monthly statement.

* * *

Many physicians fail to realize how much medical manufacturing companies can help with their marketing efforts. In the next chapter, I will discuss some of the ways large companies can help, and how to form a mutually satisfying relationship with them.

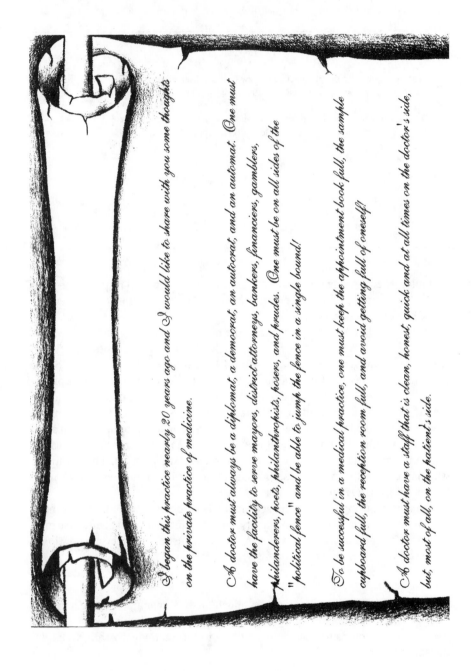

I began this practice nearly 20 years ago and I would like to share with you some thoughts on the private practice of medicine.

A doctor must always be a diplomat, a democrat, an autocrat, and an automat. One must have the facility to serve mayors, district attorneys, bankers, financiers, gamblers, philanderers, poets, philanthropists, posers, and prudes. One must be on all sides of the "political fence" and be able to jump the fence in a single bound!

To be successful in a medical practice, one must keep the appointment book full, the sample cupboard full, the reception room full, and avoid getting full of oneself!

A doctor must have a staff that is clean, honest, quick and at all times on the doctor's side, but, most of all, on the patient's side.

To sum up, one must be outside, inside, glorified, stupefied, sanctified, crucified, mesmerized, and occasionally cross-eyed. But I can truthfully and honestly say it's not a bad life – if you can stand the pace.

I have enjoyed every minute of my practice. I have enjoyed having patients like you and I give thanks everyday for the opportunity to serve you. We would like to wish you a very happy Thanksgiving and a very happy and healthy holiday season.

Dr. Neil Baum, Jackie Aucoin, Floyd Birkel, Wendy Lund, and Sandra Aytona

Figure 41-1 Sample bill stuffer I sent out at Thanksgiving.

NOTE

1. W.J. Catolona, et al., "Measurement of Prostate-Specific Antigen and Serum as a Screening Test for Prostate Cancer," *New England Journal of Medicine* 324 (1991): 1156–1161.

42

How To Get a Marketing Booster Shot from Your Medical Manufacturing and Pharmaceutical Companies

Private companies that sell medical equipment and medications can do much more for physicians than just supply them with medication samples, scratch pads, pens, and pencils. This chapter reviews creative techniques you can use to obtain thousands of dollars worth of marketing assistance from these companies.

Most of these companies have educational materials available that describe their products. You can ask them to customize educational materials for your office or practice. Customization might include printing your name and address on the materials or even printing in a rewritten version to meet your patients' specific needs.

If a company does not have appropriate educational materials, you can offer to write materials for its products. Often only a rough draft is required. The company will edit the draft and provide relevant photos, graphs, and diagrams. This process usually takes lots of time, since most medical manufacturing and pharmaceutical companies will ask their legal advisors to review any printed material with their name on it.

Many physicians have patients who are more comfortable reading educational materials in another language besides English. If a significant number of your patients are more literate in another language, these companies can translate their educational materials for you. Of course, a translation into Chinese will require more time than a Spanish translation.

Organizing a support group is an effective method of promoting your practice and serving your patients. When organizing one, consider asking medical manufacturing companies to participate in promoting and marketing the support group. They may be willing to provide promotional materials, mailing lists, or refreshments. I suggest you invite representatives from these companies to attend your support group so they can see first-hand how the group functions and how their products or medications are mentioned.

Medical manufacturing and pharmaceutical companies often have mailing lists of patients or potential patients that can be very helpful in targeting your marketing efforts. Most companies will allow you to rent their lists for a nominal fee.

Many companies will encourage you to speak to both lay and professional audiences on behalf of their products. Not only will they obtain speaking engagements for you but they also will frequently pay you an honorarium for speaking. I have represented a pharmaceutical company that makes a medication for the management of urinary incontinence and have been asked to speak to several nursing home and medical staffs on behalf of this company. As a result of these speaking engagements, I have had several patients referred to my practice.

If you are giving public talks or presenting a paper at a national meeting, ask the appropriate companies to make slides for you. Most companies have in-house audiovisual equipment that can create high-quality presentation materials. If you write articles for publication in professional journals, these companies can assist you in creating diagrams, charts or graphs, and drawings.

Most companies have contacts with other physicians who have areas of interest that are similar to yours. Ask these companies to organize a meeting of like-minded physicians where you can network with others. Networking will be the contact sport of the 1990s.

Finally, establishing a good working relationship with a company allows you to become one of its spokespersons. Frequently it will call upon you to represent it at meetings or will ask for your assistance in reviewing its products.

The first step in establishing a marketing relationship is to mention your interest to the sales representative who calls on you at your office. This is not usually enough to get the mission accomplished, since sales representatives are usually not empowered to make financial or marketing decisions.

Occasionally a sales representative will bring the district manager on a visit to your office. If you mention your interest to the district manager, you are likely to get the name of a contact person at the home office.

When you attend any national meeting, look for the company's exhibit and spend time chatting with the most senior person at the booth. Frequently the company will have one of its executives there. Ask for a brief meeting and discuss your marketing needs with him or her.

If none of these methods is successful, write to the director of marketing or public relations at the company and discuss your plans. If all else fails, write directly to the president or the CEO of the company. Usually one of these methods will get you in contact with the right decision maker.

When you present your plan or request, make sure you point out the advantages for the company. For example, if you would like it to sponsor a support group on a particular disease or treatment, make sure you point out how it will increase sales of its products. It is helpful to be able to show that yours is a win-win-win marketing idea—that you, your patients, and the company will all benefit.

After you have made your proposal to the company and it has expressed interest, you need to submit a written proposal. The proposal should include (1) the benefits to the company, (2) your resume, (3) relevant experience and expertise you possess, and (4) the estimated cost or expense to the company.

Don't be discouraged by an initial negative response or a smaller budget than you wanted. It is a good idea to accept an initial small investment by the company. Let the company get to know you and work with you on a few projects. You need to prove that your marketing efforts will be in its best interests and that you will be a worthy representative. Also be prepared for an initial delay in getting an answer from the company. Remember, you are dealing with a bureaucracy and responses take time. However, polite persistence pays.

I believe physicians are leaving "money on the table" by not developing win-win relationships with medical manufacturing and pharmaceutical companies. By asking them to participate in the marketing and promotion of our practices, we will be able to provide more education and ultimately better care for our patients. Don't miss out on this opportunity—an opportunity that's available to each and every one of us.

43

Lights, Camera, Action!
Create Videotapes To Market Your Practice

Today we are living in an age of computers and videos. Nearly 70 percent of all American households have a video cassette recorder (VCR), and more and more are using some form of video education. Just think about the increasing number of self-help and instructional tapes available at video rental stores. Videos are becoming a popular tool for educating and informing the public.

Videos also offer physicians a new way to share information with patients as well as an exciting opportunity to market their practices. This chapter, written with the assistance of Linda Morgan,* who is an expert in video technology, reviews 10 ways of using videos effectively to enhance your practice.

VIDEOTAPE TOOLS AND USES

Informing Patients about Available Services

Most patients remain in a reception area for 20 minutes before moving into an examination room. You have an opportunity to inform your patients about your services during that period by using practice-specific videos.

For example, in my reception area I use a video monitor mounted on the ceiling (Figure 43-1). I play tapes covering urologic topics such as vasectomy, inconti-

---

*Department of Marketing, Touro Infirmary, 1401 Foucher Street, New Orleans, LA 70115, 504-897-7011.

Figure 43-1 Video monitor in reception area.

nence, and prostate cancer. I obtain these tapes by videotaping lectures I have given to lay audiences, by videotaping television talk shows that have urologic topics, and by requesting videotapes from pharmaceutical and medical manufacturing companies. I also record segments of CNN's *Sunday Health* and *Science Week in Review.*

Ob/gyn and family practice physicians can obtain free videos from Milner Fenwick* that report on current trends and topics related to women's health. These videos change every 2–4 weeks and are programmed to play only during office hours.

When we want some variety, we show a video from Sea World. This video provides magnificent underwater photography accompanied by beautiful music. We call it our "low-maintenance aquarium." Remember, the public doesn't have a lot of confidence in a physician with dead plants and dead fish in his or her reception area.

Video Brochures

A four-color brochure with photographs is a time-honored tool for presenting a medical practice to new patients. But a 5–7 minute video of the physicians and the practice is like a brochure brought to life. A video brochure can offer a close-up view of you, your office, and your staff, and it gives you an opportunity to showcase the different services and procedures you provide your patients.

In addition, a video brochure can vividly demonstrate your successes by presenting patient testimonials and visuals. Taped testimonials are far more effective than praise from patients in a print brochure. With appropriate releases, real comments from real patients can boost credibility and add a personalized touch.

The video brochure can be shown in the reception area before the new patient goes to the examination room. It will serve to alleviate the patient's fears as well as project a positive image of your practice.

If you are on the medical presentation circuit, you can create a video brochure that describes your speaking experience and expertise as well as your medical services and skills. Once again, a video brochure can present a polished and professional image to interested parties.

---

*2125 Greenspring Drive, Timonium, MD 21093, 1-800-432-8433.

Direct Mail Videotape Programs

A practice-oriented brochure may also be used effectively in a direct mail videotape program. By using the latest database marketing information, you can target individuals or groups that are most likely to utilize your services. Careful selection of recipients of the tape is essential to the success of this sort of program. The use of direct mail tapes is most effective for group practices, primary care practices, and managed care programs that want to introduce medical services to a target group of potential patients.

Video Portfolios

Related to the video brochure, a video portfolio is especially useful in certain specialties, such as plastic surgery. Split-screen "before and after" video clips of reconstructive and cosmetic surgery combined with patient testimonials can create a powerful impact on a prospective patient.

A video portfolio may be used in conjunction with or as a substitute for the usual photographic portfolio. The tape could be viewed in the physician's office, although allowing the patient to take it home and watch it again with a family member would be a nice gesture.

Breaking the Ice at Support Group Meetings

I have a monthly impotence support group, and the men and their partners generally arrive 20–30 minutes before the meeting. Due to the nature of the meeting, the participants are often anxious and apprehensive. I show a video of a nationally syndicated talk show on the topic of impotence and its impact on the partner. The video provides a nice way of bringing the participants to the front of the room, relaxing them, and creating a positive atmosphere to begin the meeting. I've noted a very favorable response. In fact, several members of the audience have asked to borrow the video and review it at home.

Training Staff

Videos are now available to educate your staff about new developments in health care and office management. At a recent staff meeting we viewed a 20-minute video on office collections: *How To Increase Collections at the Front Desk*, by Karen Zupko. We discussed how to incorporate some of the suggestions into our practice. As a result of watching this video, we significantly improved our collections at the time of service.

Video News Releases

If you are pioneering an innovative procedure, announcing a new treatment or medication, or offering a new service and would like public exposure via TV, then creating a video news release is an excellent way to demonstrate your presentation to those who will make the decision whether to use you on a broadcast.

A video news release is the video version of the typed press release. It can tell your particular story to millions of people through sound, motion, and color. Sixty to 90 seconds in length, a video news release can include interviews, location shots, and footage that isn't readily available to news directors and producers. Local television stations are especially eager for medical news in these cost-conscious and health-conscious times.

Video news release production costs, like those for video brochures and direct mail videos, will vary by region and by project complexity. One caveat: because a video news release is intended for TV, its quality must meet broadcast standards. In other words, your home video camera will not work! One possibility is to use footage from medical manufacturing and pharmaceutical companies and splice that into your own personal materials. Of course, this requires their permission. But if you are promoting their technology or their medication, you shouldn't have a problem getting it.

Preparing Patients To Give Informed Consent

You can use a video to inform patients about the facts they need to know before consenting to a procedure. It is time consuming to tell patients all of the complications and side effects associated with a given procedure or operation. Asking a patient to sign a document if he or she hasn't read it places the consent in the gray zone legally. A video that explains the procedure offers sound medicolegal protection, especially if the patient signs a consent form saying he or she has seen the video. Then, if the patient declares that "the physician didn't tell me that," you can insert the video into your VCR and show it to the plaintiff's attorney, thus perhaps averting litigation.

A urologic colleague, Dr. Charles Williams, from Lafayette, Louisiana, takes the video informed consent procedure one step further. He has a video camera in his office and videos himself and the patient during his detailed explanation of the procedure and the complications. Although neither he nor I have had to bring videos into the courtroom, defense attorneys have informed me that they offer good legal evidence of a truly informed consent. Certainly a video would be significantly better than a "your word against theirs" defense or an illegible note in the chart.

TV Appearances and Sponsorships

You may also increase your visibility by developing solid media ties with your hospital's public relations personnel and local health reporters. Being prepared and poised for "lights, camera, action" can be a distinct advantage for you and your practice.

For example, if a hospital that you are affiliated with sponsors a local broadcast or cable TV show, you may ask to be one of the featured guests. Maybe an early morning news program is looking for an expert on some health care matter and you have the right background. After the program, ask for a copy of the footage and use it in your video brochure or show it to your support group.

Patient and Family Education

Videos can be used to inform patients and their families about procedures or about their coming hospital experience. Dr. David Hagen, an ear, nose, and throat physician in Thibadeaux, Louisiana, made a scrapbook and a video entitled *A Day in the Life of a TA Patient*. He photographed and videotaped a girl from the moment she entered the hospital, including her stay in the holding area and her experience in the operating room and recovery room. Finally he showed her walking out of the hospital. This was done with a minimum of equipment and on a very low budget (he used his private video camera). Dr. Hagen described the impact of the video on young patients about to have the procedure and on their families as tremendous. Because it removes all the mystique of the hospital, the result is a relaxed child and a less anxious family.

GETTING STARTED IN VIDEO PRODUCTION

Producing a video may seem time consuming and costly, but with proper planning and the appropriate resources you can create an effective, informational marketing tool that fits your budget. A typical five- to seven-minute video can range from $1,000 to $1,500 on the low end and from $5,000 to $7,000 if you opt for a first-class professional production, including background music and computer-generated effects. Factors that will affect the cost include the tape format (¾" is more costly than VHS), number of shooting days, editing time, special effects, and computer graphics. Keep in mind that costs will vary regionally.

There are several ways to creatively finance your video project. Production companies may be willing to trade production time for medical services. A urologist might consider trading a vasectomy for a video production! Hospital audiovisual departments may produce videos for physicians at a minimal charge as a perk for the hospital's frequent users. Communications students may look for topics to turn into independent study projects for class credit. A couple of referrals or speaking engagements may pay for most or all of the production and perhaps even packaging and duplication charges.

The 10 uses of video described above represent a sampling of its potential to promote your practice. Some ideas may not be suited to your particular specialty or patients. One thing is certain: video is here to stay. You may not become a medical Steven Spielberg or win an Oscar, but you can be sure you will find video an effective means of marketing your practice.

Marketing in the Era of Managed Care

In the past, medical marketing used the shotgun approach. You sent out your message far and wide—and if it hit the target, great. Little or no focused marketing was required in order to build a practice.

As a matter of fact, most of the time young physicians were able to build their practices without doing any marketing. All they had to do was be available and provide good service. Word of mouth took care of the rest.

Today, it is necessary to target markets like a laser beam—with an accurate focus on precisely the people you need to reach. You know there are several thousand people who are part of your managed care plan. You know their names, ages, and sex, and you know where they live. You can market directly to them. The advantage of laserlike marketing is that you don't waste precious marketing dollars, and your message is delivered to exactly those who are capable of using your services. This chapter reviews some methods to use in marketing to managed care organizations and for improving communications with gatekeepers.

When physicians first join a managed care plan, they often think, "Well, I've just signed up and I've got a guarantee for a given number of patients. All I have to do is list my phone number and address in the plan directory and sit and wait for the patients and my monthly check." That's probably not going to be good enough. Physicians are going to have to go out and introduce themselves to patients and demonstrate the quality and cost-effectiveness of their health care services. If they do that, they will have plenty of patients and a healthy bottom line.

In my practice, we send a "Welcome to the Plan" letter (Exhibit 44-1) to new patients when they join the plan. I write a letter saying, "I'm a urologist who

Exhibit 44-1 Introductory Letter Sent to New Plan Members

Dear [new plan member],

It is a pleasure for me to inform you of my participation in the [name of plan] health care plan. As a member of the panel of excellent urologists that you have available to you, I would like to take this opportunity to introduce myself and my staff.

I am a board-certified urologist in private practice in New Orleans since 1978. I hold an academic appointment as an assistant clinical professor of urology at Tulane Medical School. I have published two books and more than 50 articles that have appeared in medical journals and textbooks. I write the column "Man to Man" that appears monthly in *New Orleans Health and Home* magazine and I host a radio talk show every Saturday from 10 AM to 11 AM on WWL, 870 AM.

My office is located at 3525 Prytania and I have staff privileges at Touro Infirmary and Southern Baptist Hospital.

I have a wonderful staff consisting of Sandra Aytona, the office manager; Jackie Aucoin, the patient coordinator; and Ruby Haupt, the receptionist. These ladies are available to help you with all of your urologic health care needs. My staff is also available to assist you with any insurance forms or paperwork that you may have.

As a urologist, I treat diseases of the kidneys and bladder in women, and diseases of the kidneys, bladder, and genitalia, including the prostate, penis, and testes, in men. My philosophy is that curing illnesses and promoting wellness are equally important. For example, I recommend that all men over the age of 50 have an annual prostate examination and a PSA blood test to detect early prostate cancer. I suggest that all men perform a monthly testicle self-examination in order to detect early testicle cancer. I believe that both men and women can significantly reduce their risk of recurrent kidney stones by drinking plenty of water.

In an effort to control the spiraling cost of health care, I will provide you with several days of sample medication. This avoids the costly situation where you purchase a medication and develop an allergy or a side effect and then are not able to return the medication for a refund to the pharmacist. I will also give you a list that contains the price of your medication at several of the pharmacies in our community, allowing you to save 20 percent to 30 percent.

I am enclosing a copy of my office brochure, my recent newsletter, and several articles that I have written. I look forward to meeting you and serving as your urologist.

Sincerely,

Neil Baum, M.D.

practices on this plan. Let me tell you what a urologist does and mention some of the special skills and interests that I have." I offer to answer any questions that the patients may have. I also include a copy of my practice brochure with the introductory letter. Then, a month or two later, I send them a copy of my practice newsletter.

In addition to mailings to individuals and families, when a company decides to make a plan available to its employees, you can find a way to contact those employees as a group and let them know about the special features of your practice. You can often give an on-site talk during the employees' lunch hour or write an article for the company newsletter. When plan members look through the plan directory for a physician, they may see several physicians listed in the same specialty or geographic area. But if you market your practice in this fashion and target people who are members of a particular plan, you are more likely to be the one they choose.

MARKETING TO GATEKEEPERS

If you're a specialist involved in managed care, instead of marketing to hundreds of primary care doctors, you can go out and market to relatively few—the gatekeepers of plans you contract with. Let the gatekeepers know that you are user-friendly and cost-effective. For example, let them know that you have a practice that's open in the early morning and late afternoon for patients who want to see a physician before or after work. Let them know that if they send you patients, you'll respond to them promptly. (See Exhibit 44-2.)

COMMUNICATING WITH GATEKEEPERS

Once we did a survey of referring physicians to find out what they thought of our practice. Several of them said it took too long for them to receive my referral letter.

We were able to solve that problem by dictating referral letters in real time, that is, while I'm actually with the patients. This offers four advantages: it takes less time, because everything is fresh in your mind. The letter goes to the transcriptionist immediately. If you dictate the letter while you're with the patient, he or she will correct any possible mistakes. Finally, the patient perceives that you are spending more time with him or her and appreciates the extra attention.

Probably the best method we have found to solve the problem of delayed referral letters is to send referring doctors a reporting form (Exhibit 44-3). This pleases referring physicians and at the same time relieves my staff of extra work and reduces overhead. On this form we can insert diagnosis, pertinent physical findings, a list of the medications prescribed, and the treatment plan. These are the vital pieces of information that the gatekeeper or the primary care physician wants to know. If the referring physician has a fax machine, we send the completed form the same day the patient was seen in the office. Nearly all gatekeepers surveyed indicated that they would rather have this information in a timely fashion

Exhibit 44-2 Sample Letter of Introduction to Gatekeepers

Dear [Gatekeeper],

As a new provider on your health care plan, I would like to take this opportunity to introduce myself and my practice.

I have been practicing urology in this community since 1978 and am on the staff at Touro Infirmary and Southern Baptist Hospital.

In an era of cost containment I would like to mention my sensitivity to the spiraling cost of health care. I avoid the "mega" workup for common urologic problems such as recurrent urinary tract infections and prostatism. Whenever possible, I do my diagnostic studies and even surgical procedures on a one-day stay or in an ambulatory treatment center.

My approach to prostate cancer in older men with disease confined to the prostate is to offer these patients radiation therapy using radioactive iodine implants. This is a very cost-effective method of treatment compared to radical prostatectomy.

I also offer collagen implants for women with severe stress incontinence due to intrinsic sphincter deficiency. This procedure can be performed on an outpatient basis and even under local anesthesia in the office in selected cases.

One of my urologic areas of interest is the diagnosis and management of impotence. I have recently reported my results with several other colleagues and my success rate exceeds 95 percent with a two-year follow-up.

I make an effort to provide my patients with educational materials that inform them about measures they can take to prevent diseases and for early detection of urologic cancers. I provide all men with a testicular self-examination card encouraging them to perform self-examination on a regular basis. Patients are given a quarterly newsletter that discusses recent topics in health care. I also send a semiannual newsletter to referring physicians that reviews the latest developments in urology.

One of the most common complaints patients have about managed care plans is that they can't obtain appointments with the physician in a timely fashion. I would like to emphasize that my practice will not differentiate between managed care plan patients and traditional fee-for-service patients. I reserve 30 minutes every afternoon as "sacred time" that is left open for emergencies and urgencies that occur every day.

I also provide primary care doctors with fax referral forms that you can use to communicate with my office in an efficient fashion. This form will identify your patients who need to be seen immediately and patients with urgent care needs who should be seen in 24–48 hours.

I also recognize the importance of timely communications between primary care doctors and specialists. I utilize a method of notifying you in writing within 24 hours about the urologic diagnosis, the medications prescribed for your patients, and the treatment plan. If you have a fax machine and request a report immediately, it will be electronically sent to your office the same day your patient is seen.

I hope this letter gives you an overview of my practice and my office staff. I look forward to working with you and your physicians on the [insert name] plan.

Sincerely,

Neil Baum, M.D.

Exhibit 44-3 Fax Reporting Form

Dear [referring physician],

Re:

_____ was seen for a problem of
_____. The pertinent
physical findings include _____.
I am recommending _____.
I will keep in touch with you regarding his or her urologic progress.

Sincerely,

Neil Baum, M.D.

---

than wait 10–14 days to receive a lengthy dictated letter that perhaps they won't even read.

Another suggestion is to give referring physicians a pad of fax sheets outlining the purpose of the referral and the information you need from them (Exhibits 44-4 and 44-5). Now all they need to do is to fill in the blank with the working diagnosis. By checking the appropriate box saying when the patient needs to be seen, you will aid your office staff in making the appointment. For example, if a patient is referred for the evaluation and treatment of impotence, we can send the patient information and educational materials before his or her first visit to the office. If the patient has hematuria and the receptionist learns that the patient has already had an intravenous pyelogram, a urine culture, and a urine cytology, then we can send the patient information on flexible cystoscopy. Now the patient is prepared for that procedure before coming to the office. These simple techniques improve the efficiency of the practice as well as patient compliance and ultimately patient satisfaction.

This form also outlines the usual options after you have seen the patient. For example, a patient may say to you, "Dr. Gatekeeper wants you to call her after you have seen me and let her know what's going on." You will make that call—only to find out that the gatekeeper never made that request. Now all the gatekeeper has to do is check the response wanted from you, which makes it easier for both you and the gatekeeper. The gatekeeper can check a box to indicate request for action after you have seen the patient.

When we want to communicate with a managed care plan, we use a standardized fax referral sheet (Exhibit 44-6). When we need to have a patient worked up

Exhibit 44-4 Letter Introducing Fax Referral Form

Dear [doctor],

Today we are all challenged with improving the efficiency of our practices. Vital to this goal or objective of becoming more efficient is the maintenance of communication between physicians. To assist in this communication process, I would like to provide you with a fax referral form. With this form you can electronically communicate with your colleagues without interrupting your schedule or your staff's schedule. With this form you can indicate how soon you would like your patient seen and by what method you would like a response. I have been using this form for several months and have found it to be an effective way of communicating with my colleagues. The response from the doctors receiving the form has also been favorable.

I am furnishing you with the fax numbers of most of the physicians in our community. If you would like additional forms, please give me a call and I'll be happy to send them to you.

I would appreciate your comments or suggestions on the use of this faxable referral form.

Sincerely,

Neil Baum

Source: N.H. Baum, E. Osborn, and K. McIntire, *Effective Letters for the Health Care Profession* (Columbus, Ohio: Anadem Publishing, 1996).

for surgery, we don't just tell the patient to go back to the primary care physician. We send back a sheet that says, "Your patient needs this operation, which is scheduled for this date; please clear for surgery and send a copy of your report, including ECG, chest X-ray, and the specific blood tests." The physician then knows exactly what we are looking for. The major advantage of this system is that it streamlines the patient's visit to the gatekeeper, allows the gatekeeper to bill for services provided, and furnishes paper documentation for the patient's chart.

Gatekeepers may be in widely separated parts of the city, so when I operate on an enrollee of a plan, we send the gatekeeper what we call a postoperative or STAT operative note (Exhibit 44-7). If you use a form like this, all you have to do is fill in the blanks and fax it to the primary care physician. The physician receives it immediately, the same day as the surgery, so he or she knows immediately what is happening to the patient. That way if the physician receives a call from the patient or the family, he or she is aware of the patient's medical status and can answer questions.

Exhibit 44-5 Fax Referral Form

Referral from: _____

Referring doctor's telephone number: _____ Fax: _____

Referral to: _____

Patient's name: _____

Home phone: _____

Work phone: _____

Insurance info: _____

ID#: _____

Reason for referral: _____

_____

_____

Needs to be seen: _____ Immediately   _____ Within 1 week
                      _____ Within 2 days   _____ At patient's convenience

Please report findings to me by:
                      _____ mail   _____ telephone
                      _____ fax

USING A VIDEO BROCHURE TO MARKET TO MANAGED CARE PLANS

Many companies today use a video brochure to let potential customers have an "inside view," including all the latest developments. Physicians can copy from them and create video brochures to introduce patients and managed care plans to their medical practices.

A video brochure should show what the office looks like, describe the backgrounds and competence of the doctors, provide an introduction to the staff, identify the kind of patients the practice serves, and indicate where the practice is located. If possible, it should include a few patients talking about their personal experience with the practice.

A video brochure can be created inexpensively and without hiring a Hollywood producer. Often you can find a professional from a television studio that would take on a small project after hours for a reasonable fee. (Refer back to Chapter 43 for additional suggestions on video production and other uses for videotape.)

Exhibit 44-6 Standardized Referral Form

To: Dr. _____ ,
This will introduce my patient, _____
Patient's primary physician is _____
Reason for referral:
[   ] Evaluation/treatment of _____
[   ] Second opinion for _____
[   ] Clear for surgery _____ Date _____
[   ] Take over primary care
[   ] Other _____
Remarks: _____
_____
_____

Please:
   [   ] Send report to [   ] me   [   ] other _____
   [   ] Call me after seeing patient
   [   ] Other _____
Thank you for your assistance,

Neil Baum, M.D.

Exhibit 44-7 Postoperative Note

Date: _____
Dear Dr. _____ ,
Your patient, _____ , had the following procedure:
_____
The pertinent findings were: _____
_____
I recommended: _____
_____
You will be receiving the dictated operative note. Please call me if you have any questions.

Sincerely,

Neil Baum, M.D.

The best tactic is to send the video brochure to the medical director of any plan to which you are submitting an application and to the plan's nurse so that she can learn about you and your practice. You want them to feel that they know you even though they may have not met you personally. Also send it to the chief executive or to anyone else who may have a say about referrals. I suggest including a cover letter that describes the contents of the video.

I sent my video brochure to several managed care plans. Later, when I asked some of the medical directors what they thought of it, they answered, "It got our attention. We never received anything like this before." They didn't say, "The video brochure was so good we decided to select your practice." Clearly, they decided to contract with me because of my good outcomes, cost-effective care, and favorable patient satisfaction surveys. But the video brochure caught their eye and made them decide to take a closer look at my practice.

45

Ten Marketing Commandments

I n this last chapter on marketing, I sum up the basic principles that will keep working for you during the 1990s and into the 21st century—the 10 commandments of marketing.

1. Thou shalt not begin with external marketing. Don't start by producing a practice brochure, designing a logo, or publishing a newsletter. Of course, these are necessary components of any marketing program, but they should come later. Start by taking a survey of your current patients. Find out what they like most about your practice and give them more of it. Find out what they don't like and avoid it.

2. Thou shalt have written goals and objectives. Make these as realistic and specific as possible so that you don't reach too far and become discouraged early in the marketing process.

3. Thou shalt pick one marketing objective that will allow you to measure and track your results. For example, you might find it worthwhile to do a time and motion study or a patient survey. Survey your existing patients and find out what problems they perceive, address those problems, and then repeat the survey several months later after you have taken corrective action. Whichever objective you select, the process of achieving it should be enjoyable—as will be the consequences of achieving it.

4. Thou shalt work with your staff. Make sure that your staff supports your marketing program. Make sure they are motivated. Are your staff meetings a painful experience or fun and productive? Are you providing monetary as well as nonmonetary rewards for going the extra mile for patients?

5. Thou shalt have a marketing budget. How much money will you invest in your marketing plan? How much time will you devote to marketing your practice? Think about getting assistance from state and local medical societies and the national associations for your specialty.

6. Thou shalt make your practice user-friendly. Continue to bond with the patients already in your practice. Keeping patients is one of the most important goals of effective marketing. Remember, it is a lot harder to attract a new patient than to keep one you've already got.

7. Thou shalt create a positive image for your practice. Pick an area in which you have special training and become a local, state, or even national expert. Write articles, conduct seminars, and network with your colleagues on topics in this specialized area.

8. Thou shalt take direct aim. Use your marketing tools as you would a rifle, not a shotgun. If you use a "scattershot" approach, you'll get a response riddled with worthless holes. Have a clear picture of your goals and objectives. Now you'll have a stationary target, and marketing will allow you to hit the bull's eye.

9. Thou shalt go the extra mile for your patients, your staff, your referring physicians, and your hospital. Providing *lagniappe* (Cajun for "something extra") is not only good marketing, it's also an investment in your practice.

10. Thou shalt track and measure your results. How much did you invest in your marketing program? What was the return on your investment? Did your investment add to the bottom line? Did it improve the efficiency of your practice and reduce your overhead? Did it increase your positive image in the community? It is only when you track your results that you can see the benefits of marketing and can justify the time and expense of adding a marketing program to your practice.

11. (The lagniappe.) Thou shalt enjoy yourself. Medicine is still one of the most rewarding and gratifying professions in our society. By incorporating a marketing and managed care strategy, you can enjoy and feel good about your work and make a respectable and appropriate income in return for your efforts.

*   *   *

Having examined some of the marketing methods that will add to your success in the era of managed care, we will now turn to a closely related and equally important subject—how to deal with the media.

Mixing Media with Medicine

46

Are You Ready for Prime Time?

Imagine you've just returned from the meeting of a national medical society where you learned about a new treatment for a medical problem that could help not only your patients, but also many other people in your community. You'd like to get some media coverage for this exciting medical breakthrough since you feel people will be genuinely interested in your information. How do you go about getting it?

This chapter describes techniques for attracting the attention of the media and tells you how to be an effective guest when you are in front of the television camera. The advice is based on an interview with David Mobley, M.D.,* a urologist in Houston, Texas, who has a weekly television talk show that discusses medical topics.

GETTING THE MEDIA'S ATTENTION

This is the first step—and probably the hardest. Once you have some experience and understand producers' and reporters' special interests, it will become very easy.

Start out by watching local news programs and talk shows. Learn the names of the medical and science reporters and the producers of the programs. If they aren't mentioned in the credits, you can call the television station and ask for their names, formal titles, and mailing addresses.

---

*920 Frostwood, Suite 610, Houston, TX 77024, 713-932-1819.

Once you have this contact information, send potential media contacts a letter of introduction. Tell them who you are and what topics you would like to discuss on their program. Explain your special qualifications; include a resume and perhaps a photocopy of a relevant article. More important, explain why the specific topic you want to discuss is newsworthy at the present time and why it will interest viewers.

For example, if there is a new test that will make the diagnosis of a disease easier, then it will have obvious benefits for many people in the community. If there is a new treatment that avoids the need for surgery, is less expensive, or can be done on an outpatient basis, then it deserves mentioning on local television.

Mobley suggests that you describe the benefits of your topic in one or two sentences, using clear language. Most reporters and producers are deluged with dozens and sometimes hundreds of letters every day. This means it is best to summarize the benefits of your material in just a few attention-grabbing words. After all, if you can't write a short description, how will you be able to present your information in a "sound bite" on TV?

Finally, in the last paragraph of the letter, include your telephone number and the best time to contact you. Be sure to alert your staff, so if a reporter or producer calls, he or she will be put through as soon as possible. These people are as busy as physicians and they do not enjoy playing telephone tag!

PREPARING FOR A TV INTERVIEW

Once you've been contacted by a producer or talk show host, how do you prepare for your media moment? Mobley suggests that you should try to prepare the talk show host. Supply the host with background information and educational materials in layperson's language. Make sure the materials emphasize possible benefits for viewers. Depending on how well you know your host, you may even be able to suggest questions you would like to be asked. After all, the host wants the program or segment to go well. In most situations, hosts and reporters are not confrontational. Unless you are interviewed for *60 Minutes*, you will usually find your host amiable and happy to listen to any suggestions that you may have.

Try to include visuals that you can use to clarify and illuminate your message. Having something for the viewers to see as well as hear will increase the impact of your presentation.

The visuals should be large enough to be seen by the camera and small enough to fit on the table that will probably be in front of you and your host. Just to be sure they are okay, clear the visuals with the program production staff before the show. Think ahead of time about the one or two most important points that you want to get across during the few moments that you are in front of the camera. These key points should be well rehearsed and at the tip of your tongue. For example, if you are discussing a new treatment for urinary incontinence, your key points might be these:

- The procedure will allow many men and women who use sanitary napkins and diapers to avoid this expense and embarrassment.
- The procedure can be done on an outpatient basis under local anesthesia.

If you are discussing a new medical treatment for osteoporosis, you might mention that the treatment

- is nonhormonal
- decreases the risk of vertebral fractures by 50 percent
- does not increase the risk of breast and uterine cancer, unlike estrogen therapy

On most talk shows there will be a question and answer session with the studio or the home viewing audience. Prepare for this by anticipating the questions that are most likely to be asked. For example, if you are talking about the new incontinence treatment, people are likely to ask about the cost. They will want to know if insurance covers the procedure. You need to prepare for these questions and have the answers ready. If possible, have a friend or staff member ask questions in a practice question and answer session so you can get used to responding with the appropriate information.

If you don't know the answer to a question, it is perfectly acceptable to say so. Acknowledge that the question is interesting but unfortunately you are not certain of the answer right now. Even experts, if they are honest, admit that they don't know everything.

If someone asks a question that is obviously designed to put you on the spot, take the position of being an advocate for patients and you won't embarrass yourself. For example, if someone comments about the high cost of medications, you might agree that they are expensive but point out that some new medications avoid the need for surgery, decrease hospital stays, or have fewer side effects than previous medications. Your answer will demonstrate your interest in serving the public. Your goal is to be perceived as an honest, caring person who wants to help people get healthy and stay healthy.

IN THE TV STUDIO

Show Time!

Your day has arrived, and both you and the host are prepared. What next? Mobley advises his guests to be aware of how their clothing and hairstyle will look in front of the camera. He suggests that men wear a suit and women physicians wear similarly professional clothing. Avoid white and red and busy patterns, such as plaids, in your clothing and accessories. If a reporter comes to your office to shoot, then a white coat is acceptable. If a segment is being shot in the operating room, then a scrub suit is fine.

If possible, arrive at the studio early and have a look at the setup before you appear in front of the camera. This familiarizes you with the set before it is your turn and can help relax you.

Taming the Butterflies

There is nothing wrong with being nervous. Johnny Carson, with his lifetime of TV experience, said he always felt nervous before *The Tonight Show*. Don't expect to be calm. Being cool does not go with this territory. When it comes to public speaking, it's hard to get the butterflies to fly in formation.

Being well prepared is the best antidote for extreme nervousness. A famous speaker was asked his advice for preparing to make a presentation in front of an audience. His response was, "Don't forget to go to the restroom."

It's a Wrap

After the show is over, thank your host. It is also a nice gesture to send a thank-you note acknowledging your appreciation for the opportunity to appear on the program.

If you receive any compliments or, better yet, patients as a result of the program, let the producer and the host know how effective your appearance was. For example, a married couple came to my office as a result of my appearance on a TV program on male infertility. Later, after the man had a varicocelectomy, they had a baby. They sent me a wonderful note of appreciation on the success of the surgery. With the patient's permission I sent the producer of the TV program a copy of the letter as well as a note acknowledging how helpful the program was to couples whose marriage had thus far been childless.

Being a media star is not easy. Like anything else, talking in front of a camera takes practice. The more you do it, the easier it gets.

*   *   *

One important part of the process is writing news releases that catch the attention of the media and let them know you are available to discuss timely subjects. In the next chapter, we will discuss how to write these releases.

47

Write a News Release That Gets Results

Health and wellness are hot topics. The media wants to hear from physicians about new technologies, surgical procedures, and diagnostic techniques that decrease health care costs and improve the quality of life. They especially want to learn about fascinating cases with a human interest angle. Never before have physicians had so many opportunities for media exposure.

However, if you expect your hospital's public relations and marketing departments to set up media interviews for you, you may find that you have a long wait. Fortunately, you do not have to depend on help from external sources. You can publicize your availability and the subjects you would like to discuss. Getting the attention of the media is as simple as writing a creative, informative, and timely news release.

Of course, most news releases end up in the wastebasket because they don't arouse the interest of the producer or editor. Remember, most producers and editors will scan dozens and sometimes hundreds of news releases a day. You have to grab their attention immediately with one or two arresting sentences, a catchy title, or a great photo. This chapter presents guidelines for writing a news release that will get read and thus increase your chances of obtaining print or TV exposure for you and your practice.

The first key element is the headline or title. You can't judge a book by its cover but a news release will be judged by its headline. Unless the title tells a story in a few words, you are unlikely to lure the reader into the body of the news release.

Compare the title "Evaluation and Treatment of Prostate Cancer" with the title "The Prostate Gland—A Source of Pain and Pleasure." The latter is more likely to grab the attention of an editor. The reason I know this is that I tried the first one and got no response. I changed only the title, mailed out the news release again, and received a response that resulted in an interview on early detection of prostate cancer with PSA testing. Writing an effective headline takes a little effort and creativity but the payoff is worth the investment.

The next key element is the lead. This is the first paragraph, and it should contain the most important and interesting news you want to share with the public. This paragraph provides the "angle" or "hook" of your story. The editor must be able to grasp the point of your story in the first paragraph.

For example, my news release on prostate cancer started, "Do you realize the number of new cases of prostate cancer in America will more than fill the Louisiana Superdome? That's the bad news. The good news is that there is a blood test that can diagnose prostate cancer. The prostate-specific antigen, or PSA, is a $50 test that detects early prostate cancer when it is still curable."

One traditional rule of thumb is that the lead should answer the five W's: Who, What, Where, When, and Why? If it doesn't, keep writing until it does.

The body of the text amplifies the points raised in the lead paragraph and provides additional supporting material. Fill in the rest of the facts in decreasing order of importance. This is called the "inverted pyramid" structure. Don't save your best facts for last—the editor may not read to the end of the news release. Use short sentences (17 words or less), short paragraphs, and active rather than passive verbs ("The patient *led* a full and active sex life," not "An active sex life *was led* by the patient).

Be sure to use layperson's language. Don't assume previous medical knowledge on the reader's part. Write for the person who hasn't read yesterday's paper. It is better to write "To investigate blood in the urine, physicians use a kidney X-ray and look into the bladder with a lighted tube" than "Hematuria is evaluated by an intravenous pyelogram and a cystoscopy."

Generally speaking, a news release should not exceed a single page of typewritten copy, with one-inch margins. It *must* be double-spaced. Use attractive stationery with your professional letterhead for the first page. If you need additional pages, put *more* or *continued* at the bottom of all pages except the last, and use a series of three pound signs to mark the end of the release. Remember you are trying to make the news release as easy to read as possible. Otherwise it will get tossed into the wastebasket before it ever gets read. (Exhibit 47-1 is a sample news release.)

At the top of the page list the date of the release or write "For Immediate Release" if there is no holding time on the news. Under the heading "Contact" or "For Further Information," include your name (or the name of the person in your office to contact), your address and telephone number, and times when you are available. You might also include your home number or your answering service

Exhibit 47-1 Sample News Release

Release Date: Contact:

FOR IMMEDIATE RELEASE   Neil Baum, M.D.

                                                                    123-555-4444

AN INJECTION FOR TREATING IMPOTENCE

There are over 20 million American men who suffer from impotence. Now the federal Food and Drug Administration (FDA) has approved a drug that will help those who suffer from this common medical problem.

The active ingredient, alprostadil (sold under the trade name Caverject), is available as a powder that is mixed with a sterile solution and injected into the penis a few minutes before the man wishes to engage in sexual intimacy. The erection lasts 20–30 minutes.

As with any medication, there are side effects and complications. Some men complain of brief pain at the injection site (the pain typically lasts for a few minutes). About 1 percent of men experience a prolonged or sustained erection that requires emergency treatment to reverse the effects of the injected medication.

The drug requires a doctor's prescription, and most pharmacies will have the drug in stock after September 1, 1995.

#   #   #

---

number, since much of the work in the newsroom gets done after regular business hours.

If you live in a large urban area, there may be a guidebook to the local media published by the United Way, the local Chamber of Commerce, or a similar organization. However, contact names constantly change, so it makes sense to call the media and double-check names and addresses before mailing your release. Do not call the reporters—call the main number and double-check with a secretary or other support staff.

It is better to mail a newsletter instead of using a fax machine. Newspapers have so many faxes arriving that the chance of your fax being lost or misplaced is unfortunately great.

If the key to real estate is location, location, location, then the key to a good news release is editing, editing, editing. Be sure there are no misspelled words (and double-check the name of the contact person). It would be terrible to lose an interesting story just because of a simple typo. Also make sure you spell the name of the producer correctly. Probably nothing turns off a reader more than seeing his or her name misspelled.

Ask a colleague with editing skills or someone in the marketing or public relations department of your hospital to review the release before you send it to the editor. I've been able to find a retired English professor and a graduate marketing student who are willing to review my news releases and my other writings. Having your writing reviewed is inexpensive and can increase its readability.

Like any other aspect of marketing, writing an effective news release takes practice. There is no shortcut—you just have to put the pencil to the paper. Write on!

*   *   *

In addition to writing eye-catching news releases, you need to know how to deal with the media once you have scheduled an interview. In the next chapter, I will look at a few special ways of dealing with the media that will help you build long-term relationships with local and national reporters.

48

Media Manners That Make a Difference

Once you have gotten a reputation as a speaker on health care issues and have written a few articles for local magazines and newspapers, reporters from the electronic and print media will start to think of you as an "expert" and a resource and call you for comments on the issues of the day.

Building good relationships with local (and national) media can help you build your practice. Each time you are quoted in the press or appear on a TV program, it adds a little boost to your reputation. Your patients feel proud that you are their physician—they know they are going to a special doctor.

There are a few simple techniques you can employ that will have a large effect on your relationships with reporters and increase the chances that they will continue to call on you for comments. This chapter presents 10 techniques recommended by Wendy Basil, executive vice president of Halsted Communications,* which specializes in the public relations of health care. These tips are designed to make you a media darling.

1. Return calls promptly. Most of the media are on deadly deadlines. If you are unable to take a call from a reporter, have your staff arrange a specific time when you can return the call. If you are contacted by a reporter on a deadline but don't have time to do an interview, recommend a colleague who might be able to do the interview instead. Create the impression that you are media-friendly.

When you place a call to a newspaper or TV station, be sure to alert your staff that you are expecting a return call and that this call should reach you promptly.

---

*56 East Main Street, #200, Ventura, CA 93001, 805-648-9844.

I think you should tell them to consider calls from the media in the same way they view calls from a referring physician—as very important.

2. When a reporter calls, ask about the topic of the story he or she is writing before you start talking. Context alters content, and you want to be sure that your comments apply to this particular story. For example, if the writer is planning a story on sexual dysfunction, you don't want to end up talking about the sexual harassment case pending at your hospital. Or if the reporter is writing a story on the sexual harassment case, you probably should plan your comments very carefully ahead of time. When a story involves a case currently in litigation, often "I'm sorry, my lawyer has asked me not to speak on this topic" is all you can say. It is unlikely the reporter will challenge you after such a reply.

3. Dress the part if you are going to be on TV or meeting a reporter in person. Don't dress as if you were going out for a day of golf. You wouldn't dress casually to attend a business meeting or to speak at the local service club. Avoid over- or underdressing for the media as well. Even meeting a print reporter for lunch or appearing on a radio call-in program requires appropriate business dress. According to Basil, dressing casually has been shown to influence behavior—that of the interviewee and the interviewers. There is one exception: if the interview takes place in your office, you can wear a lab coat, and if it takes place at the hospital, you can wear a scrub suit. Over the phone, of course, it's dress as you please.

4. Avoid using first names. Even if you have been on the program before or have spoken several times to this reporter, use a relatively formal mode of address. First names imply a casualness that can seem jarring to observers when you are discussing a serious medical topic. At worst, the use of first names seems to suggest some sort of longstanding personal relationship, as if the reporter is doing a favor for an old friend. According to Basil, women reporters particularly dislike the unprofessionalism of a conversation scattered with first names.

5. Don't annoy reporters or besiege them with requests. For example, don't ask to review the material before it goes to press. Most writers won't let you do this. If you demand it, they will probably never call you again. Remember, they are professionals too and have no interest in misquoting you. There is seldom any significant damage that occurs when a writer fails to quote you accurately. I have never experienced nor heard of a situation where there was a negative consequence from a media interview about a clinical topic. Of course, when a reporter interviews a doctor when there is a question of fraud or abuse, that's a different situation.

Don't call reporters asking when your piece will air or appear in print. Unless you have discovered a cure for cancer or an AIDS vaccine, your material will appear when they have room for it. Local and national breaking news will frequently pre-empt your story, and it will be placed on hold for a later day.

6. Be a pal. If you are relentlessly helpful, you will become a media darling. This will ensure that reporters will think of you when they need a quick medical comment. I was once called to answer questions about President Reagan's colon polyp. Since this was not my area of expertise, I found some medical articles on the subject and had one of my office staff hand-deliver them to the reporter. I suggested the name of a surgeon who did know about colon polyps and could provide the local angle on the subject. This reporter really appreciated my assistance, and when the president had a prostate operation, I was called on to explain to the public what surgery had been done and to describe the expected recuperative process.

Be a readily available resource. Occasionally a reporter will call you for background information. This means he or she wants to gain some understanding by talking with you but will not include you in the story. Being called as a resource can be useful in the long run, however, because the reporter will probably contact you for future stories in your area of interest.

7. There may be times when you do not want to talk about a subject, but saying "No comment" is a no-no. If the question that you are asked is over your head or outside your area of expertise, politely decline to answer. Consider saying, "I'm not the right person to discuss that subject with you, but I would be happy to talk about my area of interest and expertise, which is. . . ." This polite response lets you off the hook in a classy way. If you react in this matter-of-fact fashion, you are unlikely to see "Dr. M. refused to comment" in the local paper. This technique also serves as a way to bring the interviewer back to your topic.

There's no such thing as "off the record." You may recall when President Reagan was practicing a speech and thought the microphone was turned off. He was warming up with some off-the-record jokes about women and people of Polish descent, and the whole nation heard about his jokes. Off-the-record comments are not a way to score points with an interviewer.

You don't have a lot of recourse if you are misquoted. Basil suggests that you can write or call the reporter, correct him or her gently, and ask for an opportunity to speak with him or her again, as you fear the general public will be mislead. Rarely does a misquote result in damage to you personally or to your practice.

If you really were misrepresented by the media, you can write a letter to the editor or the producer. However, this probably does diminish the chance that you will be called again for a media interview.

In medicine we don't like complications, but they go with the territory. The same applies to being misquoted. We don't like it, but it is part of the risk when dealing with the media.

8. Avoid memorized responses. Use a conversational style, as if you were speaking to a patient or family member. You may want to practice first with a colleague or family member. If you are on TV or radio, tape record your interview so you can review your performance.

In order to ensure that you get questions that you would like to answer, send the interviewer some background material on the subject and highlight key passages with a marking pen. It is even appropriate to send radio and TV interviewers a one-page sheet listing questions that you would like to answer. Remember, reporters are busy and any targeted research that you can provide them is greatly appreciated. This adds to your media-friendliness.

9. When you are in front of the camera, look at the interviewer rather than directly into the camera. If you look directly into the camera lens, you will seem to be distorted. That is the reason the interviewer always sits to one side of the camera instead of directly in front of it.

10. If you are on a program with one of your patients and the reporter directs a tough or embarrassing question to your patient, always protect the patient. After all, the patient is usually doing you a favor by being on the program and you don't want him or her to regret or be embarrassed by the experience. If a question appears to be beyond what is reasonable, you might politely interrupt the interviewer and say, "Perhaps I can answer that question for (Mr. Williams)." Occasionally you will be asked a question that is embarrassing or difficult to answer. For example, if you are asked why a new medication is so expensive, your response might be, "I know this medication is expensive. However, patients only need to take it once a day; therefore the total cost of treatment is less than the older medication, which needs to be taken four times a day." Make it clear that your overriding objective is to meet patients' needs and you will appear sensitive and compassionate.

Finally, Basil suggests that when you are being interviewed, you lighten up and relax. As long as you are not talking about death or dismemberment, it's okay to have fun on camera.

Developing comfortableness with the media requires practice. Everyone is nervous and everyone walks away wishing they would have added or subtracted something. However, after just a few media experiences you will begin to develop on-camera poise and charm.

*   *   *

It's a good idea to learn how to deal with the media as a part of your marketing campaign. Then, if you ever face the stresses of a media opportunity, you will already know how to deal with reporters, and they will already know you and your level of expertise. In the next chapter, I will look at the special techniques that will help you deal with a media crisis that may affect your practice.

49

Managing a Media Crisis

Every medical practice at one time or another is confronted with a breaking medical news story that can have a major impact on its patients. Not uncommonly patients learn from the media about a medical development that was described in a journal or at a national meeting before their doctors have had a chance to see the relevant paper. Often medical news stories will scare or even produce panic in patients. They will call for comments, suggestions, and answers—in other words, for reassurance.

There are ways to manage these all-too-common situations, reduce anxiety for your existing patients, and encourage potential patients to seek treatment. Wendy Basil, executive vice president of Halsted Communications,* which specializes in the public relations of health care, suggests several techniques that will be useful in dealing with the media when your patients are confronted with a worrisome story.

THE TYLENOL CRISIS

One example of truly skilled crisis management was the Tylenol tragedy. Johnson and Johnson, the manufacturer of Tylenol, did a wonderful job of taking a potential disaster and turning it into a marketing advantage. It was truly a textbook example of how to cope with a media crisis.

---

*56 East Main Street, #200, Ventura, CA 93001, 805-648-9844.

401

In September 1982, an unknown person contaminated Tylenol capsules with cyanide, and seven people died. Although Johnson and Johnson was blameless, it reacted without delay, recalling all Tylenol capsules and offering to exchange capsules for tablets. The public relations expenses and the recall cost the company more than $100 million. Even the hypercritical Mike Wallace said on *60 Minutes*, "J and J has been forthcoming and apparently has managed to avert disaster." Compliments from Mike Wallace are hard to come by, but Johnson and Johnson earned his praise and applause.

Johnson and Johnson didn't leave it at the recall of the medication. Two months later, Tylenol was reintroduced in triple-sealed, tamper-resistant packaging. The lesson in this story that applies to all of us is, you can overcome bad news. You can manage the crisis and turn disaster to advantage.

PROACTIVITY PAYS WHEN A CRISIS LOOMS

You may recall two recent medical/media crises: the breast implant controversy and the recent report linking vasectomy and prostate cancer. Both of these stories made the front page of newspapers and the cover of magazines. They occupied a significant portion of the evening news for months. Initially, women with breast implants wanted them removed, and men were calling their doctors to ask if they needed to have their vasectomies reversed.

The best strategy for dealing with crises like these is to be proactive. If you know such a story is going to break, then take action early. For example, when I learned from the American Urologic Association that two articles were soon to appear in the *Journal of the American Medical Association* associating vasectomy with prostate cancer, I immediately changed my consent form to notify patients of the possible relationship between the two. I also told patients who were considering a vasectomy about this soon-to-be-released information. At the same time I told them that there were other articles from reputable sources that did not find a relationship between vasectomy and prostate cancer. I had copies of those articles available for patients if they wanted to read them.

The next proactive step is to educate your staff about the impending news. Since you won't be able to talk to all patients who have questions, you must delegate this responsibility to your staff. I suggest you have a staff meeting to discuss how you want them to respond to calls and queries. In the case of the vasectomy story, I told my staff that they could expect calls from patients who had had vasectomies. Their response should be that this was preliminary data, that the risk was only slightly increased, and that the American Urologic Association did not recommend vasectomy reversal to prevent prostate cancer.

To reassure my patients, I offered them a free rectal examination and a prostate-specific antigen (PSA) test during Prostate Cancer Awareness Week. Finally, my staff told my patients that all men over 50, whether they had a vasectomy or not, needed an annual rectal examination and a PSA test. Most patients accepted this information, and I only needed to talk with a few who had concerns or questions that couldn't be answered by my staff.

During the breast implant media debacle, proactive plastic surgeons prepared a response, and when patients called in a panic about their implants, they were mailed a letter reassuring them that the likelihood of their having the maladies that were being blamed on implants was very remote. Some practices even arranged with local radiologists to provide discounted mammograms to reassure patients that they didn't have any leakage from the implants. It is likely that proactive practices had fewer complaints and possibly confronted fewer lawsuits as a result of their initiating a response instead of ignoring the issue.

When you hear about a study that is soon to be released, try to get the information before the media does. Verify the facts and have them at your fingertips when you speak to the media. Reporters will know many of the bare facts but you have the training to interpret what the facts mean. Let us never forget that we are the physicians and are especially well placed to understand the clinical implications of medical papers and reports.

For example, when the article about the relationship between vasectomy and prostate cancer appeared in *The Journal of the American Medical Association*, the authors reported a total of 183 cases of prostate cancer in 44,000 men studied. The truth is that nearly 1 in 10 American men will develop prostate cancer during their lifetime; consequently a total of 183 cases does not even approach the expected incidence of prostate cancer in a group of 44,000 men. However, these statistics were generally not publicly revealed by the media. Understandably, many reporters do not have the medical background to put a study like this into its proper perspective. You can supply the appropriate information when you speak to the media and shift the tone of follow-up stories.

In all its reporting, the media tend to focus on what is going badly. What is going well does not count as news. In the field of medicine, what gets reported is usually negative or sensational. Often the articles present information totally out of context. As physicians we owe it to our patients to help them separate the wheat from the chaff. We must be a resource to help our patients and the media interpret the data.

Of course, it is essential to be honest. Relate to the public's concerns. If you have information from a reliable source—such as the American Cancer Society or your specialty association—then offer to send that information to your patients. It is not helpful to simply offer your own opinion or say, "Don't worry" or "That's not been my experience." Unless you can back up your own experience with additional facts, your opinion is no more than that.

Make every effort to accentuate the positive. For example, in an article I wrote on vasectomy, I reassured patients that a vasectomy is still a safe and inexpensive option for permanent contraception and tried to impress upon them the need for a regular PSA blood test and rectal examination for all men over the age of 50.

You can always achieve hero status by acting as a patient advocate. If there is negative news and you show concern and compassion toward patients, give an interview that demonstrates empathy. You will appear in the eyes of the public as a champion of patient rights. Remember, bad news cannot be suppressed; it can be managed, however, by showing what the facts really entail.

I know many physicians, including myself, are out of their comfort zone when it comes to working with the media (under favorable circumstances, let alone in a crisis). The best advice is to stay calm, stick to the facts, and don't get defensive when the reporters turn up the heat and jam that weapon, the microphone, in front of your face. Stay focused on the issues and show compassion for your patients. If you follow these guidelines, you can be sure your experience with the media, even for a negative story, will be a positive one.

*   *   *

In the final section of this book, I will look at ways we can find an appropriate balance between our personal and professional lives.

VI

The Professional Life– Personal Life Balancing Act

50

Walking the Tightrope

The purpose of this chapter is to help you keep the tightrope under your feet and prevent it from forming a noose around your neck.

It's really important for those of us who work in health care to emphasize to our patients that we are compassionate human beings, that we really care about them and their health. We have to demonstrate that we aren't just thinking about the business of health care and overhead costs and how many plans we belong to. All of those business-oriented issues are important, but they are insignificant compared to the reasons that drew us into the medical profession in the first place. We wanted to be caring, compassionate human beings and dedicate our lives to helping other people.

MAKING YOUR LIFE MORE BALANCED

In order to be able to help others, it is essential to first bring balance into your life. If you get up at five o'clock in the morning to do rounds, then go to your office, then travel back to the hospital, then go home and have just enough time to read a journal or two before bedtime you'll climb the ladder of financial success but you'll probably die prematurely. You won't get to know your kids very well and your chance of a failed marriage is high.

On the other hand, if you set priorities for your personal life, just as you do in your professional life, you'll be a more well-rounded and balanced person and a better physician. You can't be a very effective physician if you are distracted by chronic personal problems.

BUDGETING TIME TO BE WITH YOUR FAMILY

Very few physicians forget to attend a quarterly staff meeting, a hospital committee meeting, or a hospital-sponsored continuing medical education event. But how many of us forget a spouse's birthday, an anniversary, or a child's Parent-Teacher Association evening? Unfortunately, probably a lot of us . . . including myself. Perhaps we need to budget time for our family and ourselves as we do for our practices.

If you know your child is coming home from college, or has a ballet recital or a Friday soccer game, make plans ahead of time so you can be with your child at the moment when it really counts. Ask your office not to book patients for an afternoon—or at least leave a gap in the schedule so you can take a child out for lunch or attend a sports event. As Stephen R. Covey said in *First Things First*, "There never was a man who said on his deathbed, 'I wish I could have spent one more day at the office'."[1]

If you don't set aside time for your spouse and your children, then the people who really make a difference to you will end up on the back burner. Of course, you probably won't need a software computer program to arrange family time, but you will need to make a commitment to your personal life of the same type that you make to your professional career.

When patients come to a doctor's office, they usually see that the doctor's family has a very high priority. They look at the doctor's desk and see pictures of the family. They see photos of vacation activities on the wall. This makes them realize that the doctor has a personal side—a life outside the office. This perception adds to their sense that the doctor is a real human being instead of just a human doing.

I usually don't allow any interruptions at all when I'm with a patient—but I make an exception if one of my children calls. Now, my children know that they shouldn't call unless they really need something or are confronting a significant problem. They all understand this, and none of them abuses this privilege. So when the receptionist tells me one of my children is on the line, I ask the patient, "Do you mind if I take this call? One of my children is trying to reach me." No patient has ever said no. The response is, "I understand. Isn't that nice that your children can call you while you're in the office."

You need to be sure to spend some high-quality personal time with your spouse. For years I tried to take an afternoon off but it never worked out. My staff always found paperwork for me to do or patients to call. I'd walk out of the hospital or my building and would often get stopped by a colleague for a consultation or to discuss a patient. My afternoon off would begin at 2:30 or 3:00 and my wife would have to pick up the children at 3:30. Some quality time! These days my wife and I always spend Thursday mornings together and have lunch as well. We find that this works best for us. We're together at the start of the day, when our energy is high.

Usually one night a week we go out for a movie and dinner or drinks. My wife is every bit as important to me as all the professional obligations that fill my life. So, I find that my life runs best if I schedule time for all the different things that are important to me. I think you too will find that your life and your practice will work best if you save enough time for the other things that are really important to you.

SETTING ASIDE TIME FOR EXERCISE AND PERSONAL NEEDS

In addition to all the things I've already mentioned, physicians need to block out some personal time for themselves. They need to pursue activities that they personally enjoy, even things as simple as taking a walk or reading a book.

Be sure to schedule time for exercise. As physicians, we're supposed to set an example by leading a healthy life. All of us are different and so are our exercise needs. Personally, I try to exercise every day, but I realize that may not be appropriate for everyone. I suggest that every physician should exercise—swim, bike ride, play tennis, golf, or walk—at least two or three times a week. Whatever we advise our patients to do we should also do ourselves.

When you can say "Do as I do," you're a better physician. Your patients will look at you and see someone who exercises often and eats a healthy diet. Would you want to go to a doctor who was overweight, was stressed out, smoked, drank too much, and didn't exercise? Would that be the sort of person you would choose as your health care counselor? Patients can tell from your face and your manner if you're living a healthy life or not.

A few months ago, I sat at a table with six or seven other middle-aged male physicians and asked them how many had had a physical examination, cholesterol test, PSA test, stool guaiac for occult blood, and stress test? I was surprised to find that I was the only one who had had the examination and tests. What message does that send to patients? It is tantamount to saying, "Do as I say and not as I do." I think it is important that we physicians do all the things we expect our patients to do. The response "I just don't have time" is hardly acceptable.

If you ask people to do things that you don't do, you will be perceived as hypocritical. That's why it is very important that you schedule an annual history and physical examination. You know, none of us is immortal.

ENJOYING THE TREND TOWARD BETTER HEALTH CARE

I believe that all of us in the health care field are living in an incredible time. There are still unbelievable opportunities for American physicians. In the last five years there has been a staggering revolution in American health care consciousness. Some doctors, however, are pretending that it didn't occur.

The reality is that Americans in large numbers are taking responsibility for the care of their bodies for the first time. Americans by the millions are exercising, jogging, swimming, Rollerblading, and riding bicycles. Some spend $8,000 to $10,000 for a home gym or a couple of hundred dollars for one pair of shoes containing a computer that tells them how fast and far they have run. Some spend $1,000 for a Jazzercise outfit. The vitamin industry is growing at a staggering pace because the American people are so committed to their health.

Yet many doctors are wringing their hands and complaining about how terrible things are and how wonderful the good old days were. I honestly doubt that many physicians would really want to go back as far as their first day in practice. I'm reminded of one senior New Orleans physician who was being nostalgic. A younger colleague suggested that he think back to what it was like to be a doctor in New Orleans before air conditioning, when the only device for fighting the sweltering summer heat was the ceiling fan.

The truth is that never before has the American public been so concerned about health care and willing to spend big bucks for quality health care. All of us in the health care industry have a golden opportunity to take advantage of this trend. We merely have to modify the way we practice medicine to fit the needs of today's patients.

Edward Gibbon, the historian of the Roman Empire, said, "The winds and waves are always on the side of the ablest navigator." The same holds true in modern health care. If we try to manage our health care ship by complaining, yearning for the good old days, and refusing to alter the way we practice medicine, then we will be tossed about by the waves of change. On the other hand, if we try to make every patient's experience a positive one, motivate our staff to exceed patients' expectations, and exploit the opportunities offered by the managed care system, we can preserve and enhance our bottom line and have successful practices.

Although wind cannot be seen, it can still be felt. Physicians who have their sails set appropriately can catch the potential benefits that still do exist.

To take full advantage of the wind, sailors must know their vessel, understand its capacities, and be skilled in exploiting them. The same holds true for physicians. We must understand our patients' mindset and recognize that today the emphasis is on wellness instead of illness. We must understand that the rapid growth of managed care means practicing more efficiently and proving that we offer quality service.

We cannot change the legislation in Washington or the choices of major employers any more than we can change the wind. Expert sailors can move in a zigzag fashion against the wind, and we physicians similarly can move forward despite the difficulties thrown at us by the government, insurance companies, and managed care plans. Remember, it isn't the gale, it's the set of the sail that determines the way you go.

I would like to conclude this book with a story of a shoe manufacturer who was interested in selling shoes to an underdeveloped country. He sent a salesman to evaluate the situation, and he returned and said, "Boss, there's no possibility of selling shoes to that country. None of the natives wear shoes." The boss was not satisfied with that response and sent another salesman. He returned and was excited and enthused about his visit. He said, "Boss, you won't believe it. We're going to be very busy because none of the people wear shoes!" Each of the salesmen had the same opportunity, the same set of circumstances, and the same products to sell. Yet, certainly the second salesman would be the more successful.

The same holds true in the health care industry today. You can see the current situation as a glass of water that is half empty or half full, the weather report as 50 percent chance of rain or 50 percent chance of sunshine, or the traffic light as a stop light or a go light. I hope that after reading this book you'll consider it a go light and that you'll take a few ideas from this book and implement them within your practice. Today, there are still excellent opportunities available in the health care profession. Just like the two shoe salesmen, we are all given the same opportunities and we all have the chance to gain access to the same number of potential patients in the community. Ultimately, however, it will be our attitude and our enthusiasm that will determine our success in today's health care arena.

NOTE

1. S.R. Covey, *First Things First* (New York: Simon & Schuster, 1994), 17.

Index